BY FRANCES PARK

Fiction

STATION WAGON IN SPAIN

VICTORINE

BLUE CAMELLIA

THE ROYAL BOX

STEAMBOAT GOTHIC

JOY STREET

DINNER AT ANTOINE'S

CAME A CAVALIER

THE RIVER ROAD

ALSO THE HILLS

CRESCENT CARNIVAL

ALL THAT GLITTERS

FIELDING'S FOLLY

THE GREAT TRADITION

PARTS UNKNOWN

HONOR BRIGHT

SENATOR MARLOWE'S DAUGHTER

THE SAFE BRIDGE

LADY BLANCHE FARM

QUEEN ANNE'S LACE

THE CAREER OF DAVID NOBLE

THE OLD GRAY HOMESTEAD

Nonfiction

THE THIRD MYSTIC OF AVILA

FRANCES PARKINSON KEYES'
CHRISTMAS GIFT

THE LAND OF STONES AND SAINTS

ST. ANNE: GRANDMOTHER OF
OUR SAVIOUR

THE FRANCES PARKINSON KEYES
COOKBOOK

BERNADETTE OF LOURDES

THE COST OF A BEST SELLER

THERESE: SAINT OF A LITTLE WAY

ALL THIS IS LOUISIANA

THE GRACE OF GUADALUPE

ALONG A LITTLE WAY

CAPITAL KALEIDOSCOPE

SILVER SEAS AND GOLDEN CITIES

LETTERS FROM A SENATOR'S WIFE

Poetry

THE HAPPY WANDERER

Juvenile

MOTHER CABRINI: MISSIONARY TO THE WORLD

ONCE ON ESPLANADE

Mollie Lee
Pryor

Roses in December

FRANCES PARKINSON KEYES

1960
DOUBLEDAY & COMPANY, INC.
GARDEN CITY, NEW YORK

*All persons mentioned in this book are real and any resemblance
to fictitious characters is wholly coincidental.*

ACKNOWLEDGMENTS

Acknowledgment is hereby gratefully made to the following
publishers and copyright holders for permission to reprint the
selections listed below:

E. P. Dutton and Company, Inc., for the poem from *Old Men
Forget* by Duff Cooper.

The New York *Times* for "Birthday Candles" by Geoffrey
Johnson; "Lightning Over a Calm Sea" by May Williams
Ward; "Roses in December" by Gertrude Robinson from
the issue of December 15, 1951; "Old Letters" by Minnie
Hite Moody from the issue of September 13, 1957. Each
has been used with the author's permission.

ROSES IN DECEMBER

God gave us memories so that we
might have roses in December.
                    —*Old English Proverb*

Part I

CHAPTER I

"In this house today a girl child was born at six in the morning."

The house was the one on Monroe Hill, at the University of Virginia, where the fifth President of the United States had lived when he practiced law there. (Ashlawn, near Monticello, the home of his friend Thomas Jefferson, was the pleasant country retreat where he spent his intervals of freedom and relaxation; it was never his regular headquarters.) Later, the house on Monroe Hill had been acquired by the University as a residence for the head of the Greek department. The incumbent at the period when the line I have quoted was written, in a hurried letter to his mother, was my father, John Henry Wheeler. The girl child was myself.

It is understandable that the day was one of great rejoicing. My parents had already been married six years. Their first child, a boy, had been born dead, and my father had been obliged to go alone with the small coffin from Brunswick, Maine, where he was then assistant professor of Latin at Bowdoin College, to Newbury, Vermont, where the family burying ground was located, leaving his sick wife and his hopes of an heir behind him. The second prospect of a baby had ended in miscarriage. The bleak period in Maine, marked by the first disaster, had been followed by a time of great fulfillment in many ways: signal recognition of scholastic achievement; means to pursue this, unharassed by financial cares, in charming and cultural surroundings; a home which was not only important, historically and architecturally, but spacious enough to permit the entertainment of old friends from Vermont, Boston, New York, and Baltimore, as well as new ones from Virginia. The dining table was never set for less than six, and it could easily and quickly be expanded to accommodate double or treble that number; the Wheelers' lavish hospitality had become a byword, even in a region where visitors were accustomed to take their welcome for granted. There was an ample household staff, including a superb cook and an accomplished butler, a gardener to care for the grounds, a groom to look after the Kentucky thoroughbreds. My mother had been a young widow at the time of her marriage to my father, and James Underhill, her son by her first husband, fitted easily and pleasantly into the family picture, dearly loving his stepfather and dearly loved in return. But long languorous summers succeeded crisp crowded winters and still there was no prospect that the professor of Greek would have a child of his own until, at last. . . .

It was a very hot night in late July. My mother had taken her usual evening stroll on my father's arm, down the garden walk bordered by yellow roses and back to the house, while Preston, the accomplished butler, was laying the table for dinner. She was eating lemon sherbet when the colored "monthly nurse," Aunt Patsy, arrived, to be gaily waved away and told to have some sherbet herself, in the quarters, before she went upstairs. But by that time, Dr. Page—a favorite physician at the University and one famous far beyond its campus— had considered it prudent to put in an appearance also. At six o'clock the following morning, he went to tell John Wheeler that a nine-pound girl had been born, that there had been no complications of any sort, and that mother and child were both doing well. An hour or so later, the proud father was admitted to look at the baby, lying in her beribboned cradle. He gazed at her with rapture and then turned to his wife.

"I hope," he said solemnly, "that she will have a good husband." (And, after all, the remark was no more premature than the first words, traditionally uttered after the birth of a girl baby in New Orleans, "I hope she will be a Carnival Queen!")

Another hour passed and the professor had retired to his study for the purpose of writing ecstatic letters to his family and friends, when Preston knocked and entered, beaming with pride, and presented his master with a silver salver on which lay a single perfect rose and a card bearing the words, "For Miss Virginia Monroe Wheeler, with congratulations and hearty greetings of Dr. James F. Harrison, Mrs. James F. Harrison and all the members of the family."[1] The name would have been both fitting and beautiful; it appealed to my parents and I should have been proud to bear it. But I am prouder still of the one that was eventually bestowed on me, after they had given the matter some thought. From the beginning, my father had ruled out Louise—my mother's name. "There can be only one Louise for me," he said firmly. In the end, the decision was left to her. "Then I shall name her for the finest woman I have ever known," she said. It is seldom that a mother-in-law receives such a tribute from her son's wife; but very early I came to understand the reasons for this. My paternal grandmother, whose story I have told before and shall tell again in due course, was undoubtedly not only the finest woman my mother had ever known but probably as fine a one as it is possible for any human creature to be.

The easy birth and the widespread welcome were followed by rapid convalescence on my mother's part and equally rapid growth on my own. "Everything goes perfectly well," John Wheeler wrote his mother. "The child was born into one of the hottest days of the year, and the thermometer has reached ninety every day of its life so far; but in spite of the heat, mother and child keep well and strong. It is more and more clear that little Frances bears a remarkable resemblance to her dad, but she has her mother's broad eyes and long fingers. You cannot imagine a prettier sight than Louise, lying on her white bed, with a pale blue cap, and the color of perfect health in her face. She has been thoroughly well for a year past, has had an enormous appetite for at least three months, and takes her food now almost as eagerly as Frances herself. The latter lies for an hour at a time quietly on the bed beside her mother, looking this way and that and tossing her arms about. She is abundantly able to move her head any way she likes. I knew Louise had some project about the name, but did not know what it was. It was settled just after I wrote my first letter to you, before the child was two hours old. Of course, the proposition was a very gratifying one to me."

[1] Dr. James F. Harrison, when he wrote this note, was the chief administrative officer of the University, then called Chairman of the Faculty. He was also Professor of Medicine, Obstetrics, and Medical Jurisprudence. He came to the University in 1867 after holding positions as surgeon in the U. S. and Confederate States navies.

All the letters my father wrote at this time were permeated with joy and those he received in return were hearty in their congratulations. One from a former Harvard classmate, who had left college somewhat precipitately for an undisclosed reason, bears the letterhead, "Massachusetts Senate, President's Room, State House, Boston." It seems worth quoting, in view of subsequent events, and reads:

"I congratulate you and Mrs. W. The old women of New Hampshire used to say—(but don't mention this to your wife):

'First a darter, then a son,
And the world is well begun.
First a son and then a darter
Trouble always follows arter.'
In haste yours truly,
A. E. PILLSBURY"

Besides the letters written to my father, there was one addressed directly to me, which came very belatedly into my possession, but which I have treasured to this day, as I have all letters from my grandmother.

N. WOBURN, MASS.
July 29, 1885

"My dear, precious, little Frances:

I hardly dare approach you, so fresh from Heaven, with my garments soiled and travel-worn by my long pilgrimage. Still I hope you have brought so much of the spirit of Heaven with you, that you will bid me welcome when I tell you that I am your grandma and that I thank God all the time that He has let you come to this world. It seems to me that, though I am getting old, and wayworn, I was never so happy as now. I am just glad, glad, glad, all the time. I am sure you have brought much of blessing to your dear papa and mama. I can distinctly hear your Father in Heaven saying to them, 'Take this child and nurse it for me and I will pay you your wages.' I have no doubt they hear the same voice and will so listen and obey, that they will rejoice with never-ending joy, over the new treasure they now possess. Your grandma wants to see you more than she can tell you in words, but will try to wait patiently. She is very happy in having your little cousin, Avis Wheeler Hill, with her. She grows every day and seems a healthy and happy child. Your Uncle Edward has just made your Aunt Carrie a visit and he says your

Cousin Helen is a very beautiful child. It will be very nice when you three little cousins, who have all come to us within one short year, can come together and play in grandma's great halls.

"Please give much love to your papa and mama and write me a letter as soon as you can. I shall be glad to hear from you every day."

The harmony and happiness of the household now seemed complete. My brother had previously been sent to the famous preparatory school at Petersburg, of which Captain William Gordon McCabe—afterward Vice Rector of the University—was then headmaster; but James was now kept home to share in the enjoyment of the new baby. Creative writing had begun to supplement teaching in my father's activities, and his first articles, published in such periodicals as *Outing* and *The New Republic,* had been so well received that there was every prospect a new source of success was opening out before him. Moreover, he had two avocations, both of which he greatly enjoyed: one of these was cabinetmaking, and the bookcases, mantel, and great library table he designed and made are among my most prized possessions; the other was horseback riding. My brother had also acquired a horse to ride with him and, before I was out of the long clothes, which babies then wore for at least the first six months of their lives, my father paused, as soon as he had mounted himself, and put me in front of him on the saddle, holding me firmly between the reins. If my mother had any qualms about this procedure, apparently she never voiced them; my colored mammy, Barbara, was more outspoken on the subject. But my father had his way about this, as he did about most things in those days. Perhaps it was because, for some reason, he did not seem to be quite as robust as formerly. He had always possessed remarkable physical, as well as remarkable mental, vigor. Now, though there was nothing to worry about, of course, there were occasional days when he did not feel like making furniture, when he did not ask to have his great bay horse, Dan—short for Daniel Boone—brought around from the stable, though he still went on with his heavy schedule of teaching and administration. Greek was, of course, his major preoccupation; but in those days the University had no president and the head of each department was responsible for its management and direction. Moreover, as he had already taught Latin, not only at Bowdoin but at the Harvard Annex—as Radcliffe was then ignominiously labeled!—his advice and help on that branch of learning were often eagerly sought and profitably followed. He also taught Hebrew and Sanskrit to the handful of students who were interested in those tongues. After all, with German, Italian, and French—which he read, wrote, and spoke with the same ease that he did English—to fall back on, one or two ancient languages, more or less, could be taken in his stride. . . .

And then, suddenly, the blow fell.

There was no longer merely a question of occasional lassitude; there was also occasional pain, and it kept becoming more and more acute. Finally, John Wheeler consented to a professional visit from his friend, Dr. Page. The physician made his examination and looked grave; then he looked grief-stricken. His patient's heart was not in good condition; well, there was no use in blinking the truth; it was in very bad condition. And there was no chance that it would get better; it would get worse—quickly, disastrously. . . .

Dr. Page did not use the word "fatally" and the faculty refused to regard such a contingency as possible. Professor Wheeler had worked very hard; he was tired. He would be given a long leave of absence; but he was too valuable to lose.

The faculty did not realize how tired he was, or why.

Sometime I hope to tell his story in detail for "my father's past comes crowding round me and I want to embrace it with words. It is an area, a region with all dimensions of space and time, as real as anything mapped with instruments, yet except it be somehow caught in this common stock of words it has no being."[2] It is revealed through the letters by, to, and about him, and through various family reminiscences, both oral and written; and it is a far greater story than mine and would undoubtedly have been much greater still, if he could have lived to make it longer. But, since this happens to be my story, I must stick to that at present, except in the cases where it has been influenced by the record of others. It seems to me that I have now come to one of those instances and that I must interrupt myself long enough to give a brief sketch of my father's career.

Both his paternal and his maternal ancestors were distinguished for their patriotism, piety, and learning. Among them were numerous officers in both the French and Indian and the Revolutionary wars; graduates of both Princeton—or Nassau Hall as it was then termed—and Harvard; the headmasters of two outstanding private schools for boys; clergymen, lawyers, and judges. But none had been rich in worldly

[2] *The Garretson Chronicle* by Gerald Warner Brace. W. W. Norton & Company, Inc.

goods. John Wheeler himself was the son of a Congregational minister, Gilbert Melancthon Wheeler, a graduate of Union College at Schenectady. Melancthon Wheeler had been twice married and had become the father of eight children, all of whom received a college education, though the ministerial salary never exceeded a thousand dollars a year. My grandmother, Frances Parkinson—herself a brilliant classical scholar—was Melancthon's second wife and the mother of his five younger children—Elizabeth, John, Caroline, Frances, and Edward. They were all good-looking and all blessed with exuberant health and spirits. But, as their mother considered wholly inadequate the educational opportunities in the various small towns where her husband's parsonages were successively located, she supplemented her children's lessons at school with the lessons she gave them herself. It was her proud boast that by the time he was seven her elder son—stocky, red-headed John—knew practically all the Latin irregular verbs and could conjugate them unaided, from memory! Be that as it may, when the boy was twelve or so, the principal of Warren Academy, in Woburn, caused to be printed in a local paper a problem in calculus which none of his own pupils had been able to solve and offered free tuition to anyone who could give the correct answer. John promptly furnished this and, with his departure from the inadequate public school and his triumphant entrance into the well-known academy, his mother's fears regarding his proper preparation for college were set at rest, as well they might have been: he was both salutatorian and valedictorian of the graduating class—a strange departure from established custom! —and entered Harvard at the age of fifteen, armed with inexhaustible energy, every conceivable scholarship, an oil lamp, a five-dollar bill, and his father's blessing.

With this equipment, he graduated four years later, having meanwhile won the Detur Prize during his sophomore year *pro insigni in studiis diligentia*. But he had no idea of letting his bachelor's degree represent the end of his scholastic attainments; he promptly went on to secure a master's degree, also at Harvard, and switched from the Harvard Law School to the Boston University Law School because tuition was cheaper at the latter; meanwhile, he taught at Noble and Greenough's Private School. This schedule must have represented an almost fantastically heavy burden and no doubt marked the beginning of the period when he had less physical and more mental exercise than was good for him, though he still chopped wood and did other chores about the place when he went home to the North Woburn parsonage

—a huge old house, still beautiful, despite its grave need for restoration, which had originally been built for Count Rumford, the most famous native of North Woburn, though this renegade never returned from England to occupy it.

Eventually, John was admitted to the Massachusetts Bar, but he never practiced; a fellowship in philosophy at Johns Hopkins having become available, he betook himself to Baltimore, where he was one of the first twenty holders, from as many states, of these coveted positions, out of one hundred and forty-five applicants. "We twenty Fellows formed a kind of academic congregation by ourselves," Ernest G. Sihler tells us in his delightful book, *From Maumee to Thames and Tiber*,[3] which he wrote many years afterward when he was Professor Emeritus at New York University. "At week-ends on Saturday evenings, we had our own meetings, a kind of junior academy of Letters and Sciences, and a social club at the same time. . . . I now come to the initial sessions of the Greek Seminar in a room in the second story of that primeval building on Howard Street, where B. L. Gildersleeve began the work so important for the development of classical scholarship in America, for which his highly dowered *ingenium* had received such enduring incentives in Berlin, Bonn, and Göttingen. I repeat the names of the five Fellows gathered around the seminar-table: Lanman, Savage, Wheeler, Page and Sihler. Only Savage had studied under Gildersleeve before, at Charlottesville. . . . Gildersleeve was clearly prepared to give us much leeway—no 'recitations' at all, but the elaboration of large tasks assigned in advance—the *seminarium* really being, as the very name implies, a *nursery* from which large and important growth (elsewhere) was to result, the more independent the better. . . . At last . . . we gathered around the academic table for the first time on December 5, 1876. In the official designation, it was called 'Philological and Pedagogical Seminary.' The work was to revolve around Thucydides. My official records of that first season contain this utterance of the Director: 'Teaching, being an art, can only be learned by long experience.' John H. Wheeler (Harvard, A.B., 1871; A.M., 1875) read his introduction to Thucydides. Gildersleeve in his critique observed that Wheeler should have included a characterization of Herodotus, and should have begun with a survey of the primitive chroniclers of Greece, the *logographers*. Stahl's introduction was highly commended."

---

[3] Published by the New York University Press.

Life in Baltimore was both fruitful and pleasant for John Wheeler. Besides the inestimable privilege of working under B. L. Gildersleeve, undoubtedly one of the greatest classical scholars of all time, the New England boy moved in a society where leisure went hand in hand with learning, and cookery was a fine art. He might well have been tempted to linger indefinitely in an atmosphere which he found both delightful and surprising; but the unexpected news that he had won the Parker Scholarship from Harvard, good for three years' study abroad, changed his plans completely and he sailed for Bremen on the steamship *Donau* of the North German Lloyd Line.

In Germany, he was to receive his doctorate at the University of Bonn, and to go from there, via various way stations, including Florence, to Rome, where he was the first American admitted to the Vatican Library for study, and found not only kindred spirits in pursuit of learning but congenial companions in various social circles, as he had in Baltimore, though this time many of them were Italian. But, meantime, something else of great importance to him had happened: on shipboard, he had met a charming young lady from New York, to whom he was immediately and irresistibly attracted—a Mrs. Underhill, who was traveling accompanied only by her five-year-old son, James, and who appeared—whether by accident or design, I do not know—on the passenger list only as "Mrs. L. P. James and child." The circumstances were so unusual, in this period, that John Wheeler very naturally assumed she was a widow, and I am afraid she did not disillusion him quite as promptly as she should have. At all events, before he knew her real name or that her husband was still living—though she had come to the (then) startling decision that a temporary separation from him would be salutary—the damage was done: John Wheeler was head over heels in love with Louise Underhill.

As an honorable man, he withdrew from her dazzling orbit until her first husband actually did die; then, along with several other suitors, he began an ardent courtship. That he was obliged to do so by letter, while his rivals could do so in person, was in itself a disadvantage; that he still had not a penny to his name, while the others were rich New Yorkers, was yet another. I have never found out how he won her in the end. But win her he did, and they started their married life together in Cambridge, while he was instructor at the "Harvard Annex." It was while he was there—before the college year was over—that he was offered the position of assistant professor at Bowdoin; and—again, before a year was over—he was nominated for the chair of Greek at the University of Virginia by no less a personage than Gildersleeve himself.

No northerner had ever been visualized by the University for such a post since the War Between the States; the nomination in itself was a triumph, the appointment a still greater one. And John Wheeler was barely thirty years old—too young, in the opinion of many authorities, to merit even consideration for such a post. But there was no question of his outstanding scholarship and his equally outstanding integrity. I do not suppose for a moment that the possession of a fascinating wife, who had just fortuitously inherited a substantial competence after the first lean years of her second marriage, had anything to do with the ultimate choice; money has never meant too much in Virginia or to Virginians. But it was this competence, which in those days represented a small fortune, that made possible the design for gracious living and lavish entertainment at the mansion on Monroe Hill. John Wheeler still had only his salary and the modest sums he was beginning to earn from his articles. The salary would cease the minute he resigned his position, and if what Dr. Page had said was true, writing would soon be impossible. John Wheeler had gradually been paying off the debts he had incurred during his long period of preparation for his profession—a period in which he had not earned enough to keep himself solvent, no matter how hard he worked; and, though economical about all other matters, he was a prodigal spender when it came to buying books. And he had worked too hard. That was why he was so tired now. That was why his heart had given out under the strain. If he left the University, he would have to live on his wife's bounty—he, who had risen from poverty and obscurity to the greatest scholastic heights in thirty years! *Live!* He knew he did not have long to live, even though he wrote to his great friend and benefactor, Gildersleeve, that he might still "cheat fate." And, before he died, he must leave the place and the post he had loved so much and make room for another man who had not worked too hard, who was not overtired, who would do justice to the proud position for which he himself no longer had the strength. *Leave the post and the place!* Presently he must also leave the little daughter, the child for whom he had yearned so long, and who was not yet two years old. . . .

He resigned from the University in June. In October, he was dead.

As far as I am concerned, I know that the loss was irreparable; my life would have been very differently ordered with his hand at the helm. As far as he is concerned, I am glad that his agony was not prolonged. Having scaled the desired heights, he had sunk to hopeless depths within six years; his pride was bruised, his spirit broken; if his life had been prolonged, he would have felt humbled past all endurance. For my mother could not have helped making him perpetually conscious of his dependence; his downfall had, inevitably, involved her. Except for the first two years of her second marriage, she had always enjoyed a life of luxury. She had been born and brought up in New York and her first husband had been a New Yorker of distinguished family, which had once owned a great farm in the Bronx and whose name—Underhill—has been perpetuated in his native city by its use in the telephone exchange! Her background was one of wealth. To be sure, her father, Edward Carleton Johnson, had come from the small village of Newbury, Vermont. But immediately after his graduation from Dartmouth, he had gone to New York to seek his fortune; and this had been so far favorable as to lead him into the prosperous family circle of a certain Mr. and Mrs. Adon Smith. The prosperity was due partly to the untimely death of a relative who had inadvertently stepped off the wharf at Charleston and disappeared forever, leaving no other heirs; and partly to a flourishing export-import trade with Cuba, Brazil, and other exotic lands, a business which necessitated, or at all events indicated, pleasurable and extensive travel. When not engaged in this, the Smiths occupied, during the summer, an enormous house in Hamilton—when Adon built it, he insisted it must be large enough, not only to accommodate his own sizable family but to ensure sufficient space for as many of his descendants as might choose to live there! And one of his sons left the table "mortified and disgusted" because a Sunday-night supper was "inadequate for the entertainment of fourteen guests whom he had invited, without any notice to the head of the house, to drop in for potluck!"

During the winter, the Smiths maintained an even more pretentious establishment at 167 Madison Avenue, then the center of fashion. This was a great corner house, made of mellow brick, with white columns in front and a spacious garden behind; it was the scene, then and later, of much lavish entertaining—indeed, it formed the setting for the farewell ball given to Colonel E. E. Ellsworth and his Zouave Regiment of volunteer firemen before they joined the first general movement of the Union forces in Virginia. This dazzling and historic function, unshadowed by the tragedy of coming events,[4] was, of course, far in the

---

[4] Colonel Ellsworth was shot at Alexandria, Virginia, by a hotelkeeper from whose building the former had torn down the Confederate flag. According to the

future when Edward Carleton Johnson came courting Delia Maria, the Smiths' daughter; but it was typical of those which the family took as a matter of course. Mr. Smith had a fine cellar and a private picture gallery. Mrs. Smith rode about in a victoria upholstered in crimson satin; her jewelry came from Tiffany, Young and Ellis, and her silks were selected for her by Mr. Lord and Mr. Taylor in person; twice a year she drove down to the Battery to choose among the dazzling materials laid out for her inspection. All these pleasant perquisites of wealth were duly appreciated by both husband and wife; but their real idol, and that of their numerous sons, was the only girl in the family—Delia Maria—who took beautiful dresses, lace shawls, fine diamonds, lavish dinners, and seats at the opera as a matter of course.

Somehow, Edward managed to marry this spoiled beauty, who was promptly given a house of her own, next door to her parents, and stocked with more silver and furniture than she could possibly use. But Edward seems to have been at least absorbed, if not actually submerged, by his in-laws. At all events, his legal career was swallowed up by the import-export business, and he became wholly urban in viewpoint and habits. Once he tried the experiment of taking his bride to see his parents, but he never repeated it; his mother, Mrs. David Johnson, after subjecting the pleasure-loving girl to both morning and afternoon "meeting" at the Congregational Church, fetched her in from the granite steps at the front of the house, where she had gone to draw breath: it was not seemly, Mistress Johnson said, to sit on the steps of a Sabbath. Delia Maria never went back to Newbury, Vermont. Her father-in-law owned not only a fertile farm, whose broad meadows swept down to the river where it formed an oxbow, but a fine library and a flourishing business which he carried on in a brick store diagonally across the street from his residence. Over a period of more than twenty years, he kept a meteorological journal of minute exactness and corresponding value; acted as Newbury's first postmaster and, later, as its town clerk—the latter a position to which his elegant handwriting gave a polished touch. He corresponded freely with friends and business associates whom he could not see personally and extended unstinted hospitality to those within easy reach. But Delia Maria was unimpressed by all this.

New International Encyclopedia, Ellsworth was regarded, in the North, as the first martyr to the cause of the Union. However, according to Webster's New International Dictionary, blood was shed in Baltimore on April 19, 1861, when a "mob attacked Union militia crossing the city en route to Washington."

She also regarded with condescension her mother-in-law's beautiful hand-woven linens and the Tuscan Rose china, which Mistress Johnson always washed herself, in a basin fetched to the dining room for that purpose. As far as her sister-in-law, Nancy, was concerned, Delia Maria was even more supercilious; for Nancy, despite a grave physical handicap and much parental opposition, had struck out for herself and become—of all things!—a society reporter and political commentator at Saratoga Springs, which Delia Maria was accustomed to visit in a far more lofty capacity. The Johnsons simply did not belong in the same category as the Smiths, and Delia Maria did not hesitate to let her husband know this.

David Johnson's father was "Colonel Thomas" of Revolutionary fame; his mother, nee Abigail Carleton, was a near relative of Sir Guy Carleton, commander in chief of the British forces in Canada and governor-general of Quebec. Abigail's background had been viewed with some suspicion when she came to the Oxbow as a bride, for Newbury was Revolutionary to the core; but gradually her devotion to her husband, combined with her great personal charm, allayed these suspicions; and even Delia Maria could not have denied that Abigail was an aristocrat to her fingertips.

Aside from resident aristocracy, there were the fashionable folk who flocked from afar to the two large hostelries, Spring Hotel and Newbury House, in the main street of the village. The Spring Hotel was considered slightly the more select of the two, though this may have been due to the advantage of certain attractions, more or less mysterious in nature, which its rival did not possess: it had a secret apartment, the location of which was known only to the proprietor, which was allegedly reached by a passage that wound its way around one of the great chimneys; and this apartment was said to be fitted with great chests for the concealment of smuggled goods. It is easy to picture the adroit efforts made by inquisitive outsiders to find out more about these intriguing features of their chosen rural retreat.

There was also a third hotel, the Newbury Sulphur Spring Bathing Establishment, located halfway between the village proper and the Oxbow settlement, in a hollow between two hills and beside a stream noted for its medicinal qualities. (The water from this brook tasted strongly of sulphur.) This hotel was later called the Montebello House, taking its name from one of the nearby hills which had a beautiful view, though the hotel itself, which still existed in my childhood, was certainly suggestive neither of a mountain nor of anything beauti-

ful. However, it was provided with a long ell, given over entirely to
a succession of bathrooms, equipped with zinc tubs in wooden casings,
to which warmed sulphur water was pumped, years before bathrooms
of any kind, much less bathrooms with running hot water, were an
integral part of private houses. Not only did the more fastidious na-
tives—among them the first Henry Keyes of railroad-building fame—
go there to bathe and, presumably, to benefit; a great many summer
people also did this, among them those who frequented the Newbury
House and the Spring Hotel, which had no bathrooms. Surely, Delia
Maria could have discovered congenial spirits in one of these three
caravansaries. Moreover, there was in Newbury at that time a very
well-known seminary, whose teaching staff was outstanding. To be
sure, she was not scholastically minded; books meant little to her;
jewels and laces, silks and silver were far more to her taste. She had
not distinguished herself in her studies at the Troy Female Academy,
where she had nominally received her education, and from which, according to rumor, she had once endeavored to elope. But among those
teachers in Newbury there must have been some who would have appealed to her in one way or another.

Be that as it may, she did not visit her parents-in-law a second time
and since she would not return to their house, Edward Carleton Johnson did not do so, either, nor did they send their only daughter,
Louise, to stay with her paternal grandparents. Later, however, during
her first widowhood—and second period of multiple courtships!—
Louise visited cousins of her grandfather Johnson's, who lived across
the street from the house which he had built and which she had sur-
prisingly inherited, owing to the death, removal, or indifference of all
more immediate heirs. But the idea of actually living in such a place
had never entered her head until she was confronted with the necessity of taking the dying professor somewhere. The New York fortune
had by then been divided so many times that it no longer represented
riches; the competence which had made life so easy and pleasant at
the University of Virginia would not go very far in the metropolis.
On the other hand, it would more than suffice to restore the long-
neglected and much misprized Vermont homestead, and to live in
comfort there until something better offered.

While her husband grew steadily weaker and sadder and her little
daughter stronger and gayer, Louise busied herself with reconstruc-
tion, ably assisted by a famous Boston architect named Bowditch.
Though the ell was more or less in ruins, the front part of the house,

built in 1806, was in excellent condition; its white paneling and the wide boards of the floors still intact, the hooks on which hunters and fishermen and farmers hung their guns and rods and whips, still securely fastened to a supporting beam in the front hall, which was papered in gold color. Without hesitation or scruple, Louise and Bowditch tore down the ell and built, in its stead, a wholly Victorian addition to the six remaining Early American rooms, bringing the total up to fourteen. If the result was something of an anachronism, it was typical of the times and it was very spacious and very homelike. It still is.

I hope that the last few months of my father's life were not as desolate as they seem, viewed after the lapse of many years. There are several letters, written to his mother, expressing a wish for a certain kind of apple which grew in the neglected orchard of the North Woburn parsonage. It seems a very humble wish, simple enough to grant, but apparently it was never fulfilled, since requests for them appear even in the latest letters. Daniel Boone had ceased—temporarily—to be a proud saddle horse; he was ignominiously hitched to a top buggy and, in this, my mother, who was a good driver, took her feeble husband for short and easy drives. She wedged these in between her building activities and her preparations for getting my beloved half brother, James, who spent most of his time riding his horse, Kaweah, off to Phillips Exeter.

I have been assured that, of course, I must remember going to the depot to bid him good-by, as I had been beautifully dressed up for the occasion in a new white bonnet, coat, and mittens; but I think this was one of those episodes which has been recalled so many times that a child is given a definite impression of it, which can be confused with actual memory. Certainly, I remember nothing about my father's death and funeral, which took place a month or so after my brother's departure for school. Perhaps this is because my mother made no effort to recall these sad events to me, though she spoke so frequently of my beautiful snowy outfit. Indeed, it was not until a few years ago, when old telegrams and letters and newspaper clippings came tardily into my possession, that I learned many things which I should think would have been sources of pride to her and which are still sources of pride to me: that Henry Cabot Lodge—a Harvard classmate—had been one of the pallbearers at the funeral, for which A. E. Pillsbury had made all the detailed arrangements, after sending a wire which read, "Give John our last message of love, if it is not too late"; that a memorial service was held in the chapel at the University of

Virginia, and that John Wheeler's former students met solemnly in
the Greek lecture room which had been his to adopt laudatory reso-
lutions; that Professor Thomas R. Price of Columbia College wrote,
calling my father "the ablest and noblest among the younger generation of scholars," and that Charles W. Eliot, then president of Harvard,
in an equally moving letter, referred to him as "the foremost classical
scholar of his age"; that the New York *Evening Post* stated, "Professor Wheeler's learning was of an encyclopedic character, and he often
astonished his most intimate friends by the extent and accuracy of his
knowledge in their chosen fields of work. He was one of the best
equipped instructors in the country"; that, indeed, the press generally,
both German and American, published long and laudatory obituaries
about him.

All this, as I have said, has come to my knowledge only within recent years, and I have had to construct my mental image of my father
from such sources and not from anything my mother told me or from
anything I recall myself. But I *do* remember the metal wreath, sent
by his former classmates and teachers at Bonn—its clinking green
leaves and its pallid flowers, shaped like closed water lilies. But that
is only because it lasted a long time and I saw it frequently on his
last resting place, beside the grave where he had buried the poor little
stillborn baby. Their two small granite headstones had on them merely
the initials, JHW, in block letters, the same in both cases; and the
family lot was—and still is—dominated by a huge stone boulder, instead of a conventional monument, inscribed merely:

JOHN HENRY WHEELER
1851–1887

For some reason I have never been able to fathom, small children
were encouraged, at least at that period and in that village, to have
their Sunday outings take the form of visits to the cemetery; and I
followed local custom, beginning at such an early age and continuing
so long that I am not certain when I first became conscious of that
dreadful metal wreath, or of the lack of any scriptural quotation or
sentimental verse inscribed on my father's tombstone, as there were
on most others in the cemetery. I do have a vague memory of sitting
in my mother's lap, before the fire in my nursery at the Oxbow, and
having my bath there, and this must have been during the next two
winters, for, after that, we were not at the Newbury house in winter
any more, for a long while. But the first really definite memory I have

is of something quite different, which took place just a few weeks before my fourth birthday.

CHAPTER II

I was all dressed up again, this time in a fluffy white dress with a broad pink sash, and I was told I must go down to the parlor, where my mother was waiting for me. By delaying, I was holding things up. Why was she waiting for me, I wanted to know? What was I holding up? Well, she wanted me to stand beside her while she was getting married. I was holding up the wedding. . . .

Someone succeeded in dragging me from my nursery as far as the first stair landing. It may have been a certain Mrs. Russell, who had been recommended to my mother by her very cosmopolitan friend, Mrs. Van Wort of New York and London, and who, with her small son, Bär, was briefly a member of our household, I imagine more or less in the capacity of a pseudo-chaperone, while the new suitor was paying court to my mother. (By birth, Mrs. Russell was a German with high court connections, who had somewhat enigmatically married an Englishman, no longer in the picture; but I would not have understood any of this, at the age of four, even if it had been explained to me then; and, as a matter of fact, when Mrs. Russell entered my life again, during the winter I spent in Berlin, at the age of eighteen, the enigma was still unexplained.) I stubbornly refused to move, except to stamp my feet and pull away from the hands holding mine. I wept aloud, shedding tears of rage. What did they mean, she was getting married? What was a wedding for? I had an inquiring mind and, though nothing was clear to me, I did not like the sound of what I heard. I did not mind mysteries, as a rule, for fairies were mysterious, and I believed in those, just as I believed in Santa Claus. But this mystery was frightening, too, and though I was hard to frighten, I was shaking now with fear, as well as rage. I wriggled about, trying to get free and run back to my nursery and slam the door after me; I rumpled my pretty dress and twisted my pink sash out of place. Meanwhile, the tension in the parlor inevitably grew greater, and repercussions of it reached the stairway.

I do not know who finally persuaded me that, whether I wanted to or not, I must go down. It was probably James, who was much gentler by nature than I was and who—though he could have been no better pleased than I—might always be trusted to do the right thing at the right time, whatever his inner conflict. He had loved his first stepfather very dearly; but he could hardly have welcomed the prospect of a second one, especially so soon; and, at eighteen, he must have been very sensitive on the subject of his mother's third marriage. Two marriages were not *mal vu*, provided, of course, that the first had been terminated by death and the second had not been considered for some time thereafter; but it was taken for granted that ladies would never marry oftener than twice, and gentlemen very, very seldom. And here was his mother, who was certainly a lady, a lady many persons found fascinating, though there were things about her that the big shy boy and a small self-willed girl could not understand very well, waiting for her children to arrive, so that a wedding could begin.

I finally reached the white-paneled parlor, propelled by someone, probably, as I have said, my brother, James; my dress had been smoothed, my sash was in place again. And besides a number of other persons who were standing about, rather ill at ease because they had been kept waiting so long, was our minister, Mr. Bates, and that handsome gentleman from Boston, Mr. Pillsbury, who had been coming to visit so often. Beside the latter was my mother, looking very beautiful in a gray satin dress brocaded in small russet-colored flowers and trimmed with rose-point lace. (Of course, I did not know then that the dress, which I still have, was made of brocade, or what sort of lace, which I also still have, was used for its trimming. I only knew that my mother looked very beautiful.) She was almost forty-two at the time, but I know now that she could easily have been taken for twenty-five, because, when I was sixteen and she was fifty-four, we were often mistaken for sisters. She had magnificent dark eyes, regular features, perfect teeth, vividly red lips, and a superb complexion—not pink and white, but a clear olive, with a dark rich glow in her cheeks. She scorned every type of cosmetic and this was not alone due to the fact that, in those days, women who used them were considered "fast"; she simply did not need them. An accident, which had resulted in a broken hip when she was a child and which, according to modern standards, had not received proper attention, had lamed her for life, and she walked awkwardly; but when she stood or sat she was the embodiment of grace. Moreover, she was vivacious, witty, and arch; I have never seen a woman to whom the word charming could be more correctly applied, when she chose to take advantage of her natural endowments.

Unfortunately, she did not always do so, but, of course, the occasion in question was one of those when she did. It is no wonder that I thought she looked beautiful, though she did not have the almost flawless loveliness that her mother had possessed. We do not need to judge this by the portraits of her; it is evident even in the crude photographs and daguerreotypes of the day.

I went and stood by my mother in the paneled parlor as I had been told to do. Mr. Bates began to speak very solemnly, and some of the other persons in the room began to cry, not angrily, as I had done, but very softly. Then Mr. Pillsbury put a plain gold ring on my mother's finger, just like the one I had always seen her wearing until that day, but which she must have taken off because her pretty left hand had been bare. The bridegroom also made a striking appearance, for he was a handsome man, judged by any standards, though nowadays he would be considered more attractive without his black mustache and well-trimmed black beard. His eyes were dark and flashing, like my mother's, and he, too, had a fine figure and infinite charm. He looked away from his bride long enough to smile at me reassuringly; and presently Mr. Bates said they were man and wife. That same evening they went away together, leaving James and me behind with Mrs. Russell and Bär.

Of course, I did not realize then that my mother had never intended to stay, for any length of time, in a quiet village like Newbury, though she enjoyed remodeling her house and driving about the countryside in her top buggy, by way of temporary diversions, and hobnobbing with the summer people who still came to the Newbury House and the Montebello House—the Spring Hotel had burned down. But it was not long after that I became aware she would never have accepted widowhood with resignation or even with philosophy, though she used stationery with black borders half an inch wide and handkerchiefs with black borders double that width. She wore a crepe veil a yard and a half long, which I found years afterward in the bottom of a trunk and destroyed; also a dress lavishly trimmed with crepe, in which she had her picture taken, and which is so attractive that I have kept it. Apparently she was still using the black-bordered stationery and the black-bordered handkerchiefs and wearing the crepe veil and the crepe-trimmed dress when her new suitor began to court her. But it has also ceased to seem strange to me, considering her general outlook on life, that she should have married one of my father's best friends, who, like Henry Cabot Lodge and William Tudor and Horace Dem-

ing, had been a classmate of his at Harvard, though he had not graduated with the others. By this time, he was a very successful Boston
lawyer and was building a big house on Beacon Street, where we
would all live together as soon as it was finished; meanwhile, we were
to live in a rented house on Marlborough Street, next door to the
Wares, who were great friends of my stepfather. Mr. Ware was a lawyer, like Mr. Pillsbury, and Richard, the Wares' son, was about my
brother's age. They would be in Harvard at the same time. But James
would always come home on Sundays—we did not speak of weekends
then—and we would all be very happy together. And rich—and gay.
It was going to be entirely different from the quiet life in Newbury.

My new stepfather was very kind to me and I grew fond of him—
not as fond as I was of my brother, but then how could I be? I was not
as fond of anyone as I was of James, not even of my mother, who did
not seem very close to me from the day I had stopped, so rebelliously,
on the stairs. She did not belong to James and me any more, but to
Mr. Pillsbury.

Years afterward, when I found the letter he wrote my father when
I was born and the telegrams he sent at the time of John Wheeler's
death, I wondered if he ever remembered these and the reasons which
first led him to make frequent visits at my mother's house. I have also
often reflected on the strange trick of fate which decreed that what
must have been the saddest month of John Wheeler's life—the one in
which he resigned from the University of Virginia because he knew
he was going to die—should have been one of great triumph for Harry
Keyes, whose life was to be closely allied with mine. Though the latter
was essentially an athlete and an aristocrat, rather than a student, he
was just then being graduated with honors from Harvard. He had
"made" the most exclusive clubs, he had been captain of the varsity
crew, and, as a crowning glory, he was chosen chief marshal of his
class. He was handsome and, what was more, he was charming; but
under certain conditions he was almost painfully shy. He declined to
dance and, as far as possible, he avoided feminine society outside of
his own family circle, where he was an adoring son, a fond brother,
and an affectionate cousin. Among girls, only his sisters' friends, who
came familiarly to the house, had a chance to enjoy much of his company, and one of these—Mabel Sanderson, who later married Theodore Vail, president of American Tel. and Tel.—was fond of relating,
years afterward, that he always "blushed deeply and sat on his hands"
when she joined a more intimate group. However, he consented to go

to Europe, immediately after his graduation, taking a younger brother with him—not to tour art galleries and cathedrals but to visit the countryside of Holland! When he returned the following autumn, he brought with him two Dutch herdsmen and some of the first Holstein-Friesian cattle imported to the United States—the nucleus of a herd that was to become noteworthy. He continued to attend football games, boat races, and club functions, directly or indirectly connected with Harvard, and to make his mother's house on Commonwealth Avenue his headquarters when he did so. At other times he was hard to drag away from Pine Grove Farm, in the town of Haverhill, New Hampshire, Newbury's twin on the other side of the Connecticut River. His father, Henry Keyes, had bought the place years earlier, but had never lived there, though he had planted many pine trees, to supplement the natural groves, and had supervised a foreman's activities with an alert eye; he had preferred to continue making his headquarters in Newbury, where he and his brothers, Horace and Freeman, had established a flourishing general store; albeit he was away from home much of the time developing manifold interests, with the expansion of railroads foremost among them. He died when his eldest son, Henry Wilder, always called Harry, was only seven; his youngest, Charles Walter, still unborn. His widow, Mrs. Henry Keyes, much younger than himself, whom he left in very comfortable circumstances, continued to live in Newbury during the summers, but joined her numerous family clan in Boston during the winters and, like the rest of the closely knit group, maintained a sumptuous establishment. It was, therefore, something of a surprise to everyone that the young Harvard graduate, who already had such a fine record and showed so much promise for the future—provided he could get over his general aversion to social life and especially his shyness with girls!—should choose to "bury himself" at Pine Grove Farm.

However, that is exactly what he did choose to do. He loved the simple spacious old house, built in 1775 by Moses Dow, another Harvard graduate. He loved the broad meadows stretching down to the Connecticut River and the still pastures reaching up to the foothills of the White Mountains. He loved his cattle, his horses, and his sheep. He loved the quietude. But—again to everyone's surprise—when he was asked to run for the office of selectman of Haverhill, he required little persuasion to do so. It developed that he was not shy, after all, when it came to something he enjoyed, and he had a natural flair for politics. By the time John Wheeler was dead, Harry Keyes had his foot on the first rung of the ladder that led, in due time, to the state capital and then to the national capital.

And, meantime, he married me. But that is getting a long way ahead of my story.

Birthday Candles

The candles lit were seven
That crowned my birthday cake;
My young heart sang to heaven
To see them shine and shake——
And then it sighed, desiring
That seventy more were spiring
From the table's polished lake.

"Why want so, why complain so?"
My mother fluted clear,
"I wish they could remain so
And keep us ever here——
You warm against my shoulder
And none a moment older
Than now, my foolish dear."

Candles tonight how many
Would match my years now fled?
I had rather not have any——
Yet burn just one, to shed
The glows of long-lost faces
From far-off childhood places,
Then light me to my bed.

                    GEOFFREY JOHNSON

Part II

"I am not really a Bostonian, just Boston-plated."
THOMAS BAILEY ALDRICH

CHAPTER III

The architectural and historical aspects characterizing most of the houses in which I have lived, even from the earliest age and for the briefest periods, have had a very distinct bearing on my thoughts, my habits, and my creative work. The rented house on Marlborough Street, where I spent the winter with my mother and stepfather when I was four years old, while our own house on Beacon Street was in the process of construction, is the one conspicuous exception to this. I cannot remember anything of importance which happened there, and the only use it has ever been to me professionally was to serve as the model for the one old Mrs. Forbes, the matriarch in *Joy Street*, always described contemptuously as the "horrible little Gloucester Street house," in which her eldest daughter and son-in-law lived. It was, indeed, typical of many houses in that neighborhood, both on the main streets of the Back Bay and on the side streets which crossed these, and which were then considered equally desirable and select for residential purposes—in fact, I lived in another just like the first one when I was seventeen; but I cannot now imagine anything less cheery and convenient. They were tall and narrow, so narrow, on the ground floor, that there was space for only a very small reception room beside the front entrance, though the dining room in the rear was somewhat more spacious because it had no exit to the street; instead, it looked down on a barren back yard, which no attempt was made to beautify, but where ash cans and garbage pails stood and washing was hung. (This back yard also served as the entrance and exit to the kitchen and laundry in the basement, to which very little daylight ever penetrated.) On the second floor were the front and back parlors, both formal, chilly, and forbidding; on the third, the front and back bedrooms— scarcely more cheerful—with a bathroom—the only one in the house —and dressing room between them. In other words, the family had to mount two flights of long steep stairs before they reached their sleeping quarters. The servants had an even longer trek, because their bedrooms were on the floor above and they also had to ascend from the basement, thus making four flights in all; and there was little or no heat, and only a service sink with running water on the top story— not even a toilet, though presumably there may have been one in the basement, and I know there *was* a little dark lavatory behind the reception room. But though ladies of leisure talked about "servant problems" in those days almost as vociferously as they do now, they had far less reason to do so; household workers were, for the most part, ill-lodged, ill-paid, overworked, and underprivileged, even in the most elegant establishments; if these slaveys sometimes rebelled, shirked, or left without notice, they were far less to blame than the employers who saw no reason why they should be given warm rooms, adequate plumbing, regular time off, and good wages.

Of all this, of course, I was not conscious at the age of four; and, as the impeccable butler, Preston, and several other dusky retainers, had remained with my mother or rejoined her when she came north, she had little of which to complain along household lines. Barbara, my colored mammy—for I was fortunate enough to have a devoted representative of this now extinct species—had married, but she had stayed long enough to establish her inimitable standards; now she had been supplanted by a governess, Miss Charlotte Jones, a maiden lady as genteel as her name; her prim dresses were always fastened with a pansy pin. I do not think she ever taught me much; her main occupation, besides caring for the linen and arranging flowers, consisted of painting little water colors. No doubt she kept me out of my mother's way, so that I would not interfere with the latter's first social activities in Boston, and took care of me, as well as she knew how, through the series of children's diseases, then considered inevitable, which began that first winter. The person and the place that really made an impression on me were my paternal grandmother, Frances Parkinson Wheeler, for whom I had been named, and the old Count Rumford house in North Woburn, where she lived with her younger daughter, my aunt Fannie—she was never called by her full baptismal name of Frances—my aunt Fannie's husband, Uncle Will, and their daughter, Avis Wheeler Hill, who was just my age.

My grandfather Wheeler had long since died; but the beautiful old house, formerly the Congregational parsonage, had again become available and, somehow, my grandmother, my aunt, and my uncle had, among them, retrieved it, rescued it from impending disintegration, after a fashion restored it, and given it the rudiments of modern conveniences. Whatever the Marlborough Street house lacked in distinction and charm was here in abundant measure. There were two rooms on either side of a wide central hall, both upstairs and downstairs; and the upstairs hall, originally designed for a ballroom, was two stories high and had a musicians' gallery at one side and an arched ceiling which reached almost to the roof. Over all was an immense attic where, according to tradition, a Revolutionary soldier had been successfully hidden for an indefinite period; and this concealment had been facilitated by a fireplace which not only provided him with warmth but enabled him to cook the food which was secretly brought to him. This attic could be reached only through a trap door, approached by a folding ladder and located in the space above my aunt's bedroom; it was impossible to carry furniture of any size up this ladder; therefore, unlike most of its New England counterparts, the attic was not used much for storage. Indeed, it was almost never that anyone went there; and my aunt shook her head and looked vague when, as soon as I heard the tale about the soldier, I eagerly asked if she had seen the fireplace.

"I'm quite sure there isn't one," she said. "It's too bad, but I'm afraid that story is just a myth."

I was not certain what constituted a myth, but I decided to find out for myself about the fireplace. Choosing a day when my elders were otherwise occupied, I persuaded my cousin, Royal Carter, who was a year younger than I and, therefore, more easy to lead astray than his elder brothers, Charles and Morris, to ascend the ladder with me and help me open the trap door. We had taken candles with us and our disappointment was great when we found that the dark and dusty space to which we had penetrated was, indeed, without a fireplace. Then I had a sudden inspiration.

"It must be on the other side of the arch, the space that can't be reached directly by a ladder and isn't used *at all*," I said. "Come on, let's go and see."

Royal was not enthusiastic. There were no footholds over the arch to facilitate ascent and descent and its top was so close to the roof that it was almost impossible to crawl over it. But, of course, Royal could not take a dare from a mere girl. Painfully, we made our way up the slope, across the top, and then down again; and when it was no longer necessary, for safety's sake, to shield our candles with our hands, and we realized that what we were seeing was no mirage, we shouted, simultaneously, in wild excitement.

"There *is* a fireplace! The story's true! Oh, isn't it wonderful!"

Of course, afterward, other members of the family had to crawl over the arch and assure themselves that the fireplace really was there, that Royal and I were not the victims of powerful imaginations. It was a dirty and difficult undertaking and I am not at all sure that most of my relatives were grateful to me for my discovery. But I triumphantly used it as the basis for my first Christmas story, which I called A *Rebel Captain's Sweetheart.*

Whether or not the expedition over the arch had really been worthwhile is not, of course, for me to say; but I can say, with emphasis, that a nobler and more striking apartment than the erstwhile ballroom I have yet to see in any American house; and, in my childhood and youth, it was the scene of many a festive, if unpretentious, gathering, to which a second group of relatives—the Carters, living a scant mile away—always came. The kitchen, where a never-ending succession of good meals was prepared, was in the ell and led conveniently out of the sunny dining room through a connecting pantry, which always smelled of "sugar and spice and all things nice"; it was as bright and pleasant as the rest of the house, and so was the room for the maid of all work, who was installed above it, also in the ell. With its two wonderful halls and eight great square rooms, in addition to the service quarters, the house was literally a dwelling place of light; and it was illumined, not only in a literal way, by sunshine and open fires, but by the lamp of learning which burned so unquenchably for my grandmother, and whose luminous rays she shared with everyone who came within her orbit.

This was not because she was charming, like my mother, or because she was beautiful and elegant, as my maternal grandmother, who died before I was born, must certainly have been. Indeed, I doubt if many persons have had two grandmothers more dissimilar. Delia Maria Johnson was the spoiled child of fortune, petted, pampered, accepting homage and adoration as her due and giving very little in return. As I have already remarked, she was the idol of her brothers and parents, and the luxury in which she was lapped more or less stifled whatever legal talents her husband, Edward Carleton Johnson, may have possessed, besides weaning him completely away from his prosperous, but homespun parents and the simple life of the village in which he had been born and brought up. After Edward died, Delia Maria, being foot-loose and fancy free, betook herself frequently to Europe, where she idled away many months in resorts on the Riviera and in Switzerland; she bought jewelry in Geneva, though no woman could have reasonably asked for more than she possessed already; and she returned, every now and then, to Paris for the purpose of replenishing her already ample wardrobe. Then, with a purpose at least allegedly more serious, she began to purchase paintings with which to supplement those already adorning the walls of the picture gallery in the Madison Avenue house. Most of those she bought were excellent copies of old masters, but one, at least, was a lovely seventeenth-century original.

Her pleasing preoccupation led her, very naturally, to Rome and there she was called upon to cope with an unexpected situation: she found a modern picture that caught her fancy. It represented a beautiful woman, charmingly if somewhat casually and revealingly clad in flowing red and white draperies, and precariously seated on a rock overlooking a moonlit sea, with mountains in the distance. The longer she looked at this picture, the more Delia Maria coveted it, and the more adamant its painter became in his refusal to sell it to her. But, at last, he bargained with her: she could not purchase the picture, but if she would allow him to paint out the profile of his original model and paint in hers, he would give it to her.

"That is all—at least all I know——
Everything happened so long ago."

However, the fact remains that she brought the moonlit picture home with her, along with numerous others, and since I inherited it, I have always had it hung in the same room as the wholly conventional —but also very charming one—painted of her in New York when she was twenty-seven. There is no possible question that the head and shoulders are those of the same woman—as a matter of fact, in her will, she identified the moonlit picture, which had been given the strange name of "Contemplation," as "a profile likeness of herself." But there is no resemblance in bearing and background between the New York belle and the Roman model. I think it also quite possible that there was a difference in the way the two—who were actually one and the same!—conducted themselves. But I have nothing to prove this, beyond the pictures, which seem to speak for themselves.

At any rate, Delia Maria eventually came home and married, *en secondes noces,* a naval surgeon who added to her stock of treasures by bringing her magnificent crepe shawls and cashmere capes, all richly embroidered, whenever he returned from his various voyages to the Far East. He survived her and passed out of the family circle the year after my father and mother were married; but Delia Maria herself was lapped in luxury until the very end and, when she died, she bequeathed all her tangible possessions to her only daughter, Louise. Since Louise also had an only daughter, namely myself, there was not much division of this type of property until the next generation, though, alas! most of the wealth invested otherwise had long since been spent somewhat extravagantly.

So much for Delia Maria. Now for my other grandmother, Frances Parkinson, the one who was such a major influence on my early years. She had been born in a log cabin, which served the community as a schoolhouse and a meetinghouse, as well as a dwelling place, until conditions in and around New Boston and Francestown, New Hampshire, became somewhat less primitive. But for generations her family had been one in which religion was a beacon light, and books came next to bread as a necessity. Her grandfather, Henry Parkinson, had been successively a student and a teacher at Princeton; John Stark's quartermaster during the Revolutionary War; and headmaster of the first private school for boys in New Hampshire. His standards set those of his descendants.

"When I went into Mr. Cochran's School at Nashua, I had read through the *Fables* in the Latin reader," Frances Parkinson wrote much later, in a brief autobiographical sketch, prepared at the request of her son Edward. "There was a large class of young men in the school, fitting for Dartmouth College, who were about to take up Sallust. After I had recited a few times to Mr. Cochran, he wanted me to go into the class in Sallust. I did so. But I had read so little Latin before that I found it pretty hard. I had to get up before light to study my Latin, as I also had geometry (Euclid) which was new to me. But I found it easy, after a few lessons in geometry, to keep the young men at a good distance behind me. I think they were some-times quite provoked that what was hard for them seemed easy to a girl. When, after beginning to teach in Nashua, I would have a few weeks' vacation, I would spend them in study in Mr. Cochran's School, keeping on with Latin until I had read Sallust, Caesar, Cicero, and Virgil, and getting, at the same time, a pretty good knowledge of French, with such other studies as were pursued in the academies of those days." (And this in New Hampshire in the 1830s!)

By alternately teaching a year and studying a year, Frances Parkin-son eventually succeeded in matriculating at Mount Holyoke College, then known as Mount Holyoke Female Seminary, where she made the acquaintance of its founder, Mary Lyon. "Most of my recitations were with the seniors," Frances Parkinson continues in the same sketch. "And, as I was a special student, Mary Lyon admitted me to some degree of familiarity with her. She was a wonderful woman in many ways and I have always been grateful for the privilege of knowing her personally."

Later, Frances Parkinson was invited to return to Mount Holyoke as a teacher; but she declined, on the ground that she did not feel worthy of such an honor. However, she continued her teaching in public schools and academies until she married a Congregational clergyman, Gilbert Melancthon Wheeler, previously mentioned, who had been active in the work of the American Colonization Society;[1] then she taught, first, her children and, afterward, her grandchildren. Her own studies she pursued until the day of her death. She was poor all her life and, fortunately, she cared nothing for clothes or amuse-ments, in the usual sense of the word; she could not have afforded them. I never saw her when she was dressed otherwise than in rusty black, but she did wear beautiful lace caps, which my mother insisted upon giving her, to hide her thin hair; these caps came from Miss Moore's select establishment on Arlington Street and were my grand-mother's only concession to vanity. Her hands were rough and gnarled, with short cracked nails. (Delia Maria's were long and slim and white; they seemed shaped expressly for showing off diamond rings and flicking a lace handkerchief and languidly waving a painted fan.) Though her cheeks glowed like small twin apples through their

[1] This was an organization founded in 1817, which settled free Negroes from the United States in a colony that, in 1847, became the Republic of Liberia.

wrinkles, the skin was rough. (Delia Maria had a rose-tinted pallor and her skin was smooth as silk.)

My grandmother Wheeler played a prominent role in family councils and gatherings—so prominent, indeed, that, on the day of her funeral, her son-in-law, my uncle Will, actually forgot the nature of the occasion and, after looking around carefully, said, "Why, we haven't provided a comfortable chair for Mother!" Her dominance was immortal; but she never expected nor wanted to have life made easy for her; to her the fear of the Lord was the beginning of wisdom. She shared her faith and her wisdom with her family, her friends, and her fellow Congregationalists, as far east as Roberts College in Constantinople. This was the be-all and the end-all of her life. Few women I have known have found it more rewarding.

She was not able to boast, in my case, that one of her eager young pupils could conjugate Latin verbs at the age of seven. But she could and did see that her namesake was taught to read at the age of four and no nonsense about it, either. She did not hold with primers, much less with alphabet blocks. She went straight to the Bible, beginning with the first chapter of Genesis, and went right along through. (I have heard since that Charles and John Wesley, the founders of Methodism, were taught to read by the same method at their mother's knee; and for all I know, many other persons, both famous and obscure, have also been taught like this, though I have never met them or heard of them.) She did not even shrink before the long chapters to which the scornful usually refer as "the begats" or the questions which these naturally provoked. "Begat means the father of," she said calmly. "Cush was the father of Nimrod, who became a mighty hunter before the Lord."

"What did he hunt?" I inquired.

"Wild animals of all kinds. Don't you remember? You learned about those when you read the story of Noah—'two of every sort.' Now go on. C—U—S—H. Cush. N—I—M—R—O—D. Nimrod. I said, go on. 'And the beginning of his kingdom was Babel.' B—A—B—E—L. We will finish the chapter and spell out all the words."

Finish it we did, that chapter and many others. Before the winter had passed, there were very few words over which I stumbled, and none of my questions went unanswered. By the time I started going to Sunday School, I had such a head start that it never took me more than a few minutes to learn my lessons. And the next generation profited by these Biblical teachings. Not that I despised alphabet blocks and primers to the same degree as my grandmother; but though my sons did not actually *learn* to read out of the Bible, and though I did not go in for the "begats" (which I had found very tiresome and not at all provocative!), I did read the most interesting Bible stories aloud to them before they could read themselves and encouraged them to do the latter, and to learn passages by heart, at a very early age. We had an abundant supply of Biblical pictures and maps to supplement the stories, and these we pored over together. Years later still, when my eldest son was at Harvard and Biblical literature was a requirement for a Bachelor of Arts degree, I asked him how he had managed to wedge in the course and pass it so creditably, considering his overcrowded curriculum. "Wedge it in?" he asked casually. "Why, I didn't need to bother with the *course*, after what you'd taught me. I just took the examination!"

I think I must have spent a good deal of time at the Count Rumford house, between measles and chicken pox and so on, because it made so much more of an impression on me than the Marlborough Street house, when I was four years old. No doubt my mother and stepfather and governess were as glad to have me out of the way as I was to go, and as my grandmother and aunt and cousin were to have me with them. My mother, as I have said, was taking her first hazardous steps toward an entree into Boston society; my stepfather was interested in keeping pace with her, especially in so far as such steps furthered his political career, for he was on the point of becoming attorney general of Massachusetts and had his eye on the governorship. He became a member of the Algonquin Club, and though this, alas! did not carry with it the same cachet, in the eyes of the true Bostonian, as the Somerset Club and the Union Club, it was not without its own prestige, and this was estimated at its full value. My parents did not neglect me and neither did Miss Jones, who was conscientious in her care of me, even though it interfered with the time she wished to devote to water colors. On the other hand, my grandmother had no preoccupations with society or politics or painting. She was concerned with me. I was all she had left to keep green the memory of her beloved son and she fostered that memory.

Less frequently than I went to North Woburn, but still often enough to make an indelible impression on me, I began to visit my step-grandparents, Josiah and Elizabeth Dinsmoor Pillsbury, in Milford, New Hampshire. They were regarded with great respect and their name is perpetuated by the Pillsbury Memorial Funds which provide a haven—in the old family homestead—for aged and indigent gentlewomen and, also, by the Pillsbury Reservation, a large tract of land comprising a game refuge and a sanctuary for migratory birds, as well as a forest reserve. I was pleased to have a grandfather and, of course, did not realize that Josiah Pillsbury was only a pseudo-grandfather; this was the first time that an elderly man had taken his place in the pattern of my life, and an elderly man makes a wonderful companion for a little girl if he is tolerant, wise, and beneficent, as this one was, and withal still able to bring a distinct masculine element into a family group. Without being fanatical on the subject, he was a strong advocate of "Temperance," as it was then called, which actually meant total abstinence; and he was a devoted and active member of the Society for the Prevention of Cruelty to Animals. He was also the superintendent of the Unitarian Sunday School and I made my initial acquaintance with this denomination when I sat in the front pew with his wife throughout the Sunday School sessions.

She was somewhat less idealistic than her husband and correspondingly less absent-minded; not infrequently, she deemed it necessary to lean forward and remind him that he had forgotten to give out such and such a notice, which he doubtless felt was of minor importance. He did not seem to resent these public admonitions; he admired her firm ways and orderly mind. She did not read with me, as my own grandmother did, but she gave me much wholesome advice; for instance, she told me that a child, like a woman, should withdraw once in a while, sit alone, fold her hands and think. I found this good advice then and I have continued to do so.

The Pillsburys' house was pleasant, architecturally less important than the one built for Count Rumford, but spacious and well proportioned and possessing one feature that was fascinating to me: it was two stories high in front, but only one story high in the back. This rear story was not on the ground floor, but on the second floor; and by stepping out of my bedroom, I walked into a small park, surrounded by clustering shrubs and grape arbors and dotted—according to season—with dandelions and daisies. Here I could play to my heart's content with Ruth French, the little girl who lived next door; it was, in a very real sense, our "secret garden." We domiciled our dolls in the arbors and wove garlands of vines with which to wreathe our heads and festoon the parlors of our relatives; we exchanged confidences, made plans, and pored over picture books with our arms around each other. There was an element of magic in that little park, its hidden entrance, its shielded enclosure; I felt nearer to fairyland there than I ever did anywhere else.

Strangely enough, there was also a powerful link with my own grandmother in Milford: that was where, as a young teacher, she had "boarded" with the Congregational minister, Humphrey Moore, and his wife when she became engaged to Gilbert Melancthon Wheeler; indeed, it was in their house that he had given her his first presents— a Bible bound in tan leather, embossed in gold and stamped with her name, and the little ring of very thin fine gold, embellished only with two tiny pearls, which bore his initials, as well as hers, and which was to serve as both engagement and wedding ring. Humphrey Moore of the first Frances Parkinson's time had long since been gathered to his fathers when I was a child; but his widow, very much his junior, was still living in the house that had been the parsonage. Moreover, the late Congregational minister was held in respectful and grateful remembrance for many reasons, among them, for his gift of a Paul Revere bell to the Milford Meeting House belfry. This bell was later moved to the Town House tower and continued to ring and remind young and old of the famous midnight ride; it is still doing so. It was and is a source of great pride to the citizens of Milford, as well it may be, for it is said to be one of only two genuine Paul Revere bells, cast during the working lifetime of the great Revolutionary patriot, which continues its useful function in the state of New Hampshire.

Mrs. Moore was a very remarkable woman, who had dearly loved my grandmother and she liked to have me remain with her for hours, while the Paul Revere bell rang them off, one after another; so when it was raining and I could not steal away to the secret garden, I spent the afternoons at her house. It is the first one I can recall in which the spacious front hall was adorned with scenic wallpaper; and that wallpaper has never been surpassed in elegance and imagination by any I have seen since. Because it so fascinated me, Mrs. Moore used to take her needlework into the hall, in order that I could sit beside her there, with my books and my dolls, instead of in the parlor. She was prettier than my grandmother, but, like her, she wore caps, though, in her case, they were made of crisp organdy and not lace. (They did not come from the same select establishment on Arlington Street; probably she made them herself.) She did the finest of fine embroidery and she was still doing this, at the age of ninety or more, when I was married; she made me a tea cloth, daintily and elaborately stitched in silk, which was one of the most exquisite items in my trousseau.

Of course, the visits at North Woburn and at Milford which I made during the winter and spring that I was five were only the first of many that were to occur in the course of the next few years, but they formed so important a part during the period which marked a great change in my existence that I feel an account of them should be given a primary place.

Late that same spring, we went back to Newbury—that is, my mother and Miss Jones and the servants and I went there to stay and my stepfather came up from Boston over Sundays. My mother was in bed a good deal of the time, and she did not like to have me bounce up and down on the springs or handle the perfume bottles on her bureau (Atkinson's Lily of the Valley, Atkinson's Heliotrope, 4711 Cologne Water). I was astonished, rather than hurt, because she spoke to me peevishly, and I was pleased, rather than otherwise, because the family physician, Dr. Carbee, came so frequently to the house. He was a very kind man whose smile was nonetheless sunny because it was obscured by a huge beard, and he had all sorts of interesting little bottles in the black bag he always carried with him; every now and then he spread out the pills that these bottles contained—red and white and golden—for me to see. Like Miss Jones, he was very conscientious; but I am afraid, by present-day standards, he was not a very expert doctor. For, when my mother was confined, she was twenty-four hours in labor; and as she told me many times, later, the baby, who was born feet first, "kept kicking until the end." But when the end came, the poor little thing strangled, and another small white coffin was carried to the Newbury cemetery. Like her half brother she was given a name—Elizabeth Dinsmoor Pillsbury; and, as in the case of her half sister, this name was in honor of her paternal grandmother. And, before the burial, the coffin was placed, open, in the white-paneled parlor and all the children in the neighborhood were invited to come in and see the beautiful dead baby.

I did not rebel against going to the parlor this time. I was awed, but I was not angry; and the baby, who looked as if she were peacefully sleeping, was indeed very beautiful. She was plump and pale, with quantities of soft black hair. It was not at all frightening to me or any of the other children to see her lying there; we stood around the little white coffin and gazed down at the baby with admiration. It was only afterward, when I went to the cemetery with my stepfather, that I began to feel fear and horror. He held the coffin, now closed, on his lap, and I sat beside him, on the back seat; the hired man, who drove, sat alone in front. If anyone else attended the burial, I have no recollection of it, though I can still see, as if it were only yesterday, that circle of wondering children who had been summoned to the white-paneled parlor for what seems to me now a very gruesome and unwholesome purpose. And I did not recover easily from the shock of the burial. I dreamed about it, and about what was happening to my poor little sister, night after night. It was quite in vain I was assured that she was an angel, happy with other small angels in heaven. I did not remember her then, in the same way I do now, as she looked when she had lain in the paneled parlor. I thought of her alone, in a little grave, which strange men had filled with earth, covering her up, while my stepfather and I stood helplessly by. I was not quite five and that is too young to make acquaintance with the grim realities of death. For months afterward, I woke screaming from nightmares. They are still vivid to me. But they took forms so dreadful that I hesitate to describe them.

The new baby was buried in the same lot with her half brother and her half brother's father, and her grave was marked in exactly the same way as theirs—only by a small granite headstone bearing the initials EDP in block letters. I was brought up to put flowers on all three graves, every year, when Decoration Day came. I do it yet or, if I am not in Newbury, I have someone do it for me and now, of course, there are more family graves which require my attention. But it is always before those three that I linger the longest, thinking how very different my life would have been if any of those who lie in them had lived.

CHAPTER IV

The fall after the new baby's birth and death the house on Beacon Street was ready for occupancy and, for the next four and a half years, our life followed a regular pattern: every autumn, we went to Boston, where we lived according to the standards of elegance then most approved for urban existence; every spring, we returned to Newbury, where we lived comfortably and pleasantly, but with only rare touches of elegance. These sojourns were sometimes interrupted by visits to my grandmother and aunt in North Woburn, to my step-grandparents in Milford, New Hampshire, and, once, by a visit to the Dunnington family at the University of Virginia, where I came down with mumps the day after my arrival, and promptly passed these on to all seven Dunnington children!

Again, the main characteristics of the houses in which I lived and visited made an impression on me that has never grown dim. The one on Beacon Street was beautifully situated at the corner of Charlesgate West and was almost as bright and sunny as the Count Rumford house. It was also, by present-day standards, enormous. (It has since been divided into apartments and I have always longed to go back and see it in its present incarnation. Like my little sister's grave, but in a much happier way, it has formed the basis for many recurrent dreams, which persisted much longer than the others—indeed, to this day, I sometimes imagine, in my sleep, that I am wandering through it, and when I see it at such times and in such a way, it is still unchanged.) Just inside the entrance was a musical instrument, rather like an xylophone, but not dependent on hammers to give forth sound —this happened when the door opened or closed, but did not take the place of a regular doorbell, as modern chimes sometimes do. Beside the front door was a small library, lined to the ceiling with books; and this, for some reason, was the place where we always had our Christmas tree, which reached to the ceiling, surmounted by a wax angel and lighted by wax candles. Preston stood watchfully close at hand, with a bucket of water at his feet, ready for any emergency. Also close at hand, throughout the holiday season, was placed a large wooden box, filled with so-called Christmas candy from S. S. Pierce. This candy was cut into short brittle strips, balls and curlicues, and its shining white sugar surface was ornamented with stripes and festoons of red. The postman and everyone else who came to the door, and who passed by the library for whatever purpose, was supposed to help himself from this box, and by New Year's it was empty. Nothing like it was provided at any other time of year.

Next to the library, at the front of the house, was the parlor. It had a bay window at the side and a smaller window, between the library wall and the grand piano, in front of which stood an onyx-topped table, always surmounted by a round glass vase, from which fresh pink roses branched out. Years afterward, when I went to Louisiana, I heard of a woman who forgave her husband all his philandering because he never failed to see that a fresh rose adorned her breakfast tray. I have sometimes wondered whether those roses on the onyx table were not intended to have somewhat the same effect, on a more lavish scale, but, as it proved, less effectively.

Out of the library and the parlor led the square reception hall, which was so large that the first dancing classes I attended were held there, and the first result of my efforts to become a writer—a pageant in twelve scenes, one for every month of the year—found fruition there in a spectacle enacted by my friends and myself, with our families as spectators. Leading from the reception hall was the dining room, where Preston was in his element, for this, too, was spacious enough to provide for large gatherings; a lavatory, a butler's pantry with dumb-waiter descending to the kitchen, and the well of an elevator, which went from the basement to the top story, completed the floor plan. This elevator, which was operated by ropes, was not designed to carry passengers, though sometimes it did; it was intended to convey trays upstairs—not only meals for the sick but my supper every night—baggage to the bedrooms, and laundry to the roof, where the washing was hung to dry on pleasant days, though the latter was not really necessary. There was a beautiful laundry room in the basement, with one whole side composed of closed compartments, which could be pulled out, revealing heated racks where any number of sheets, tablecloths, and towels could be hung. The entire basement was not only roomy but cheery—quite unlike the lower regions on Marlborough Street. At least one policeman was not infrequently found basking in the warmth of the glowing coal stove and sharing the bounty spread forth on the table covered with a red-checked cloth. Just as one whole side of the laundry had ample provision for drying clothes, so one whole side of the kitchen pantry was pre-empted by a refrigerator, which held countless one hundred-pound blocks of ice and any amount of food. Gargantuan meals were the order of the day for everyone, and these were supplemented by as many snacks as anyone in the household, either upstairs or down, felt like having.

Leaving the basement and the ground floor behind us, we went by way of an imposing staircase to the second story. Over the library was the "blue" guest room, in whose closet Christmas presents were traditionally concealed. Over the parlor was my mother's sitting room; and over the reception hall, the dining room and the pantry, my step-father's dressing room, with a walk-in closet containing shelves, cupboards, drawers, and hanging space galore; the connubial chamber with its own closet for my mother's dresses; and a bathroom. On the third floor, in the same order, were my brother's room—occupied only on weekends—the "yellow" guest room, the linen closet, the night nursery, the day nursery, and another bathroom. On the fourth floor, the pattern was again repeated. One room was for billiards, one was for Miss Jones, and the others were for the servants, who had the then unusual luxury of warm quarters and a bath of their own. The house had eight fireplaces and a powerful furnace. (Just as no one was hungry or cramped for space, no one was cold.)

It was soon decided that I was old enough to go to Miss Haskell's Kindergarten at 12 Gloucester Street where, as is usual at such institutions, children were not taught to read and write, but merely encouraged to model in clay, color with crayons, and make outline drawings with worsted. My mother had a theory that I should not go to a "real school" until I was seven. (Sunday School was different; I began to attend this at such an early age that I cannot remember when it was; and by the time I was five, I was also taken, every Sunday, to services at the New Old South Church, where the minister, Dr. Gordon, preached sermons which lasted an hour and prayed, extemporaneously, for almost as long. He was a learned and upright man and a sincere Christian; but, indirectly, he is probably responsible for the fact that I decided, before I was ten, that I was not suited to become a Congregationalist!) As I was already reading omnivorously, and somewhere along the line had learned to print and do simple sums, this program did not make much difference; but I thought, and still think, it was rather silly to devote whole mornings to types of occupation which I had long since outgrown mentally. It was a great relief to me when my mother decided I was old enough to go downstairs, from Miss Haskell's Kindergarten, which was on the third floor, to Miss Bertha Carroll's Day School, which was on the second and first floors at 12 Gloucester Street; and also to her dancing school which was in the loftier regions of the S. S. Pierce building.

Miss Bertha Carroll must have been quite a remarkable woman. The Mauve Decade did not offer many opportunities for refined ladies without visible means of support. When her father's death suddenly left her and her mother in straitened circumstances, she rented part of their home to Miss Haskell for her kindergarten and turned the rest of it into schoolrooms, except for its kitchen quarters and a bed-sitting room—forbidden territory except that once a year we trooped into the bed-sitting room to give Miss Carroll Christmas presents. The school did not take little girls further than what would now be called

the fourth grade, so it was in session only from nine to one. This left
Miss Carroll free to teach dancing school in the afternoons. As was
generally the case, the house boasted but one bathroom, and the only
complaint I ever heard our headmistress make was on an occasion
when she called the entire student body together and said that well-
trained little girls should not need to use it during the final half hour
before they left to go home, which was the only time she had to
dress. (The last classes were taught by one of her assistants.) But dress
she did, in full-length pastel-colored cashmeres, which she held up dis-
creetly, just enough to disclose her high black button shoes, as she
admonished her pupils to, "Slide, slide, slide, and step." She must
have taught, or tried to teach, other types of movement, too, though
it was not until long after this that I became anything like a credit
to her or any dancing teacher. It was different with other lessons, both
at Sunday School and day school. Thanks to my grandmother, none
of these presented any difficulties.

At day school, we were taught French from the beginning, along
with the three R's. I had a delightful book, larger than a primer, with
illustrated plates bearing French captions in the first part and little
French stories and rhymes, also illustrated, in the second part. I took
this book to show my grandmother and we read from it together. She
read French very well, and no wonder. With the first money she ever
earned, when she was teaching school for one term, in order to continue her own education in the next, she had walked twelve miles
through the snow and bought herself a copy of Racine's plays in two
volumes. She gave them to me and I have treasured them ever since.
But I did not learn French from them, the hard way, as she had. I
learned it—or rather, I began to learn it—a very easy way, with her
intermittent help, but mostly in what had once been the second-story
hall bedroom of Miss Bertha Carroll's house on Gloucester Street.

I enjoyed school days, but I enjoyed weekends still more, despite
Dr. Gordon's sermons, because it was then that my brother, James,
came home from Harvard and spent one or two nights with us on
Beacon Street. He usually arrived very late, after I was abed and asleep
in the night nursery; but I always left my box of stone blocks in the
day nursery. Then, when I got up in the morning, the neatly packed
stones would all have been removed from their box and made into
some sort of a building—a house, a school, a church, and a different
one every time. This stood for a week, just as James had built it, and
all that while I rejoiced in it; it would have broken my heart to de-

molish it, if I had not known that the next day there would be another building to take its place, probably even more beautiful than its predecessor. I do not think James ever once disappointed me. In a way, the stone buildings were even more exciting than Christmas stockings, because I found them each week, instead of only once a year.

I think James enjoyed the stone blocks, if not as much as I did, at least enough to derive some pleasure from them, for engineering, of one sort or another, was to be his lifework and this building was good practice. But he could hardly have enjoyed our Sunday walks, though he never gave the slightest sign of reluctance about them. In those days, the fashionable headgear for little girls consisted of broadbrimmed beaver hats, the crowns adorned with bows of satin ribbon; other bows were tied under the chin. The bows on the crown were fairly stationary; but the one under the chin kept loosening and, if it loosened too much, the hat would blow off, so it was necessary to stop very frequently and retie it. As I always carried a doll with me on these walks, James had to do one of two things: he could hold the doll while I retied the bow, which I had learned how to do, or, while I held the doll, he could retie the bow, which he had learned to do. For a very sensitive young man, who hated to be conspicuous, either process must have represented an ordeal. But he never said so or even gave such an impression. It was not until long afterward that I realized how he must have felt about it.

I nearly always walked wherever I went in those days, but occasionally I took the little horsecar, with seats running lengthwise on either side, that plied up and down Marlborough Street between Arlington Street and Massachusetts Avenue. This was considered a great treat, and I looked forward to those horsecar rides with anticipation and remembered them with pleasure. But one such ride proved very sad.

The car had just come to a stop for the first time, and a shabbylooking man jerked open the door at the rear and slammed it after him. Usually the behavior of the horsecar's patrons was quietly well mannered, and the other passengers, myself included, looked at this violent new arrival with surprise because he was so noisy. Then, with still greater surprise, I saw that he was shaken with sobs which he was making no effort to control.

"Phillips Brooks has died!" he gulped and slumped down in the last vacant place.

There were several shocked exclamations, a few startled questions; these were followed by a subdued murmur of grief. Afterward came dead silence. I looked up and down the long line of seats in wonderment; everyone in the car was crying.

Since then I have often wondered if any tribute paid the great bishop, who towered above his fellow citizens mentally and spiritually, as well as physically, could have been more spontaneous and more touching than that silent weeping in the little horsecar, where strangers, united only through their sorrow, sat and mourned his death. And every year, at Christmas time, when I join in singing his beautiful carol, "O Little Town of Bethlehem," it means more to me because I think of Phillips Brooks, not only as he dominated a large church from his pulpit, a large flock through his ministry, and large literary and religious groups through his writing, but also as he reached out through the power of his wisdom and the beauty of his loving kindness to all groups and bewildered humankind.

CHAPTER V

For a long while my brother continued to mean more to me than anyone else in the world. Selfishly, I preferred to have him to myself; but when he brought college friends home with him, I enjoyed those, too.

The one who came most often was his roommate, George Glessner of Chicago. He was the proud possessor of a cabin on a hillside near Bethlehem, only about thirty miles from Newbury, where the two young men enjoyed camping; so they saw almost as much of each other during the summer as they did in the winter, because it was so easy for them to visit back and forth. I became very fond of George and habitually greeted him in the same affectionate way that I did my brother. One day, after I had done so, I startled him greatly.

"I am so glad you are an old man, George," I said. "Because Mama told me the other day that I shouldn't kiss young men any more—except James, of course—and I'd be very sorry if I had to stop kissing you."

As George must have been all of twenty at this time, it is no wonder he was startled. After he and James were graduated from Harvard and went their separate ways, I did not see him again for a long time; then he re-entered my life in quite a different incarnation. His attachment for the hillside near Bethlehem had resulted in the development of a magnificent property where his parents built large houses for themselves, for him and his lovely wife Alice, and for his married sister Frances. They beautified the landscape with rose gardens and shrubbery and divided the estate itself and the outlying fields with low walls, made from the stones that were strewn about the pastures and interfered with their fertility. These walls, which will forever perpetuate and glorify the name of Glessner, are only one of the imperishable contributions made to the North Country; and they all gave of themselves as freely as they gave of their worldly goods. Glessner hospitality, like Glessner generosity, became a byword; and George and Alice both took an active interest and an active part in New Hampshire politics by the time these were an integral part of my own life. Visits between The Rocks and Pine Grove Farm became as frequent as visits between the hillside cabin and the Oxbow had been twenty-five years earlier; and every now and then George teased me by telling me he really *was* an old man now!

All this, of course, was far in the future during my early school days in Boston when I made my first friends there. The ones I had in Newbury I had known ever since my babyhood, so I cannot say, with any exactitude, when these friendships began, though I can remember sharing a trundle bed, at naptime, with my friend Jeannie Darling, whose grandfather's big brick house was the next one to ours in the direction of the village and on the same side of the street. If we slept the length of time that was considered suitable, we were then rewarded by being allowed to play with Mrs. Darling's button box, a large cylindrical receptacle lacquered in red and gold, which stood on top of her sewing table, and which contained innumerable buttons of all shapes, sizes, and colors, provided to meet almost any emergency which might require their use. These buttons we arranged in designs which we spread out on the carpet. It was a pastime that never palled.

Jeannie and her brothers and sisters came up from Cambridge to spend the summers with their grandfather and grandmother, Mr. and Mrs. Richard Doe, and we were almost inseparable—even, it would seem, at naptime; so I suppose I was not more than three or four when Jeannie and I shared a trundle bed! And I suppose I was about the same age when I began going across the street to the Haines

Johnson house for Sunday supper. (Ours was the David Johnson house, built by the same man, Colonel Thomas Johnson of Revolutionary fame, for two of his sons.) The Johnsons were not "summer people" as the Darlings were at first; they lived all the year round in the same house and, unlike my mother's branch of the family, clung closely together. The second Haines, my contemporary, was the youngest son of Sidney, who, in turn, had been the youngest son of the first Haines; and still living in the same house was the eldest son, Thomas, a cripple who had broken both legs and shuffled about on crutches; likewise his wife, Ann, who was confined to a wheelchair with what I now suppose was arthritis. We called them Uncle Thomas and Aunt Ann; but the third cripple in the household—also confined to a wheelchair—was called Cousin Maria, and her exact relationship to the rest was hazy, though no one ever questioned her right to live there, or her ready acceptance by Cousin Sidney and his young wife, Cousin Mary, when he brought the latter to live there as a bride. In those days, there were no rest homes for elderly persons and, anyway, it would have been considered a sin to separate them from their kith and kin. In season and out of season, Cousin Mary cooked and cleaned, washed and ironed, sewed and mended for her husband, her four children, and her three helpless relatives by marriage. During haying and threshing—which was called thrashing—she cooked for all the extra men who came to help; and various other persons, both related and unrelated, were in the habit of arriving unannounced for visits and remaining as long as they felt like it. Yet I never saw Cousin Mary otherwise than serene, cheerful, and unhurried. She was a capital cook, especially when it came to baking, and the memory of her pies makes my mouth water to this day. A Thanksgiving Day feast always began with chicken pie, and at least seven other kinds followed. "Why, there *aren't* that many kinds of pie!" a southern-born friend, now very much of a cosmopolitan, protested when I mentioned this to her lately. So I named them for her: apple, mince, squash, pumpkin, lemon, custard, cranberry; and that does not include the fruit and berry pies of midsummer, or the chocolate and butterscotch pies, which entered the picture later. Cousin Mary Johnson made all seven kinds of pie to perfection, and so did Cousin Ellen Bayley, who lived "down the road a piece" at the Homestead and who said the secret of being a good cook was to have a free hand and no conscience. As Cousin Ellen had three grandchildren—Norman, Richard, and Katherine

Cobb—who were contemporaries and constant companions of mine, like Haines Johnson II and Jeannie Darling, I was in the happy position of being able to compare the pies made by these two wonderful women and I must say there was little to choose between them.

But to go back to the Sunday suppers, which must have begun when I was three or four: there was nothing elaborate about those—quite the contrary. Aunt Ann sat in her wheelchair, with a big bowl of fresh milk in her lap and a loaf of bread on a bread board beside her. Haines, his elder sister Louise, and I lined up in front of her, and she fed us all from the same bowl with the same spoon, cutting off as much bread as was required to satisfy us. But I have remembered those Sunday suppers with just as much relish as I have the Thanksgiving dinners, when we had to go out and snowball each other in order to make room for more food, and which were held sometimes at one cousin's house and sometimes at another's, with rarely less than twenty persons seated at the groaning board.

The term cousin was rather freely used in Newbury, just as it is in Virginia, though not for quite the same reasons. The divisions of relationship did not lie, verbally at least, among kissing cousins, cousins, ain't cousins, and poor white trash. Instead, it included all the descendants of General Jacob Bayley and Colonel Thomas Johnson— the first two outstanding settlers of that portion of the upper Connecticut Valley embraced by the river's oxbow, both of whom later won renown in the American Revolution. To be sure, Thomas Johnson's daughter Betsy married General Bayley's son Isaac, thus forming a basis for relationship; but by the time my generation was reached, the kinship was so distant that the most rigid rules governing consanguinity would not have prevented intermarriage. This did not prevent us from calling each other cousin and acting like cousins—in all the varying degrees of the Virginia definition; and a favorite form of entertainment, besides the Thanksgiving dinners, was called a cousin party, at which half a hundred congenial spirits, young and old, met for a festive evening which generally began with oyster stew and ended with the Virginia reel. A few families, notably the Hales and the Darlings, were, by common consent, usually included in these gatherings, though they were not related to us. The Darlings were no longer "summer people," having now achieved a house of their own halfway between the Oxbow and the village, and there were four Darling children: Jeannie, aforementioned; Maida (Mary Louise), her elder sister; Lucia, her younger sister; and Richard, her brother. There were also two Hale children—Mary and Harold. All these formed a part of the group with the Cobbs (whose mother had been a Bayley), the Johnsons, and myself; and this group was so indivisibly united that, of course, we pretended their parents were cousins, too.

The cousin parties, unlike the Thanksgiving parties, were nearly always held at my mother's house; I do not know just why. The juvenile birthday parties, which were the next most important, were held, on alternate years, at her house and the Bayleys', as my birthday and that of Richard Cobb—the grandson of Cousin Henry and Cousin Ellen —came within a few days of each other, and our families agreed it was exhausting enough to have such celebrations every other year, without doing it any oftener. One of the most elaborate of these took place on my seventh birthday. The circle had been enlarged to include some Newbury children whose parents pronounced their name like our Bayleys, but who spelled it with an *i* instead of a *y*. This, according to Richard's mother, my cousin Agnes, "showed that they did not really belong to the family," and the elders did not come, like the Hales and the Darlings, to the cousin parties, though, as time went on, our generation of Bayleys and Baileys mingled freely. Our circle also included the progeny of some "summer people" from Washington: the Greelys, who boarded with Cousin Mem (short for Remembrance) and Cousin Helen Chamberlain in the village; and the Craigs, who boarded with Cousin Ezra and Cousin Lizzie Chamberlain, next door to the Bayleys', just below the Oxbow. The Greely girls were all exceptionally pretty—one of them is now a famous landscape gardener—and that caused more comment than the fact that their father, Washington Adolphus Greely, was a brigadier general and also a noted Arctic explorer. The six young Craigs were also much more interesting to us than their parents, despite the fact that their father, a small quiet man, was a colonel in the army and one of the first experts in forecasting weather; or that their mother, whom the colonel adored, was a charming and distinguished woman, on close terms with the White House—indeed, it was through her that my future sister-in-law became a great friend of the Clevelands and that this friendship remained unbroken until Mrs. Cleveland—later Mrs. Preston—died. One of the young Craigs, Robert, was just a few years older than I, and my pride knew no bounds when I was selected to appear in a Mother Goose show as his bride, to illustrate the rhyme:

"When I was a bachelor
I lived by myself
And all the bread and cheese I got,
I put on the shelf.
The rats and the mice,
They made such a strife,
I was forced to go to London
To buy me a wife.
The streets were so broad
And the lanes were so narrow,
I was forced to bring my wife
Home in a wheelbarrow.
The wheelbarrow broke
And my wife had a fall
Down came wheelbarrow,
Wife and all."

I took the tumble with very good grace because of the honor that had been shown me in choosing me as a companion of a boy from Washington, instead of a neighbor. I might well have aspired no higher than my crony Norman Cobb, who appeared alone in the same show as Little Boy Blue.

In honor of such distinguished outsiders as the Greelys and the Craigs, a special feast was provided on my seventh birthday. What was more, my brother had spent days—and infinite pains—building a miniature railroad, complete with tunnels, bridges, and hairpin curves. Of course, that was long before the days of electric toys; but the little train, which was wound up by manpower, must have had greater endurance than most of its kind. Round and round it went, over its bridges and through its tunnels, to the unbridled joy of the kissing cousins, the cousins, and the ain't cousins. It actually took persuasion to lure us away from it long enough to eat ice cream and birthday cake.

In Joy Packer's delightful book, *The High Roof*,[1] which has a South African setting, she says, in speaking of a juvenile character, "Jimmy was seven today and his party was a *braaivleis*—the sort of treat to which people under seven did not aspire. Your first *braaivleis* party was really your coming-of-age!" Of course, none of us had ever heard about a *braaivleis*—in fact, I do not think any of us knew much about

[1] Published by J. B. Lippincott Company.

South Africa! But the minute I read this passage, I knew that my seventh birthday party must have been the Newbury equivalent of a *braaivleis*.

Another red-letter day in the calendar was always that of the Church Fair, held under the auspices of the Ladies' Aid of the Congregational Church. The chief center of attraction was the fancywork table; and the same year as that made memorable by the very special birthday party, the fancywork table was in the charge of Mrs. Henry Keyes and her two daughters, Belle and Gertrude. By this time, Harry Keyes had persuaded his mother and sisters to leave Newbury and spend their summers with him in the spacious old house at Pine Grove Farm. The Keyeses did not fit into any of the categories in which the rest of us were bracketed. To be sure, Henry Keyes had come from the insignificant village of Vershire, "out back," a much less important place than Newbury, when he and his brothers established their flourishing store. However, after that, he had become not only a railroad magnate and a gubernatorial candidate but, after his death, something of a legend. My cousin Agnes did not say of the Keyeses that they did not belong to the family. It was quite true that they did not, but, instead of misprizing them on that account, she stood slightly in awe of them. So did nearly everyone else. They had a coachman instead of a hired man, and a cook, parlormaid, and laundress instead of a hired girl, and they spent their winters in Boston. (The same was true of my mother, but for some reason this did not make the same impression.)

Once settled at Pine Grove Farm, this branch of the Keyes family did not mingle much in Newbury, though two of Harry Keyes' cousins still lived there—Mr. Thomas Keyes, who owned and operated the general store, which his father and uncles had founded, and who was a pillar of the Congregational Church and a notable stamp collector; and Miss Harriet Keyes, who was even more active in good works than her brother, especially in the Foreign Missionary Society; both had large handsome houses and both were regarded as substantial citizens, though they did not come to the cousin parties. (When Newbury celebrated its Sesquicentennial, Harry Keyes remarked jestingly that he really hesitated to attend the festivities since he was neither a Johnson, a Bayley, nor a Chamberlain. He thus voiced the same sentiment which Vance Packard recently expressed in *The Status Seekers*[2] when he said, "Throughout the Midwest, many of the towns staging centennial celebrations have been manipulating the occasions

2 Published by David McKay Company, Inc.

to exalt the families still in town whose ancestors happened to get there first. Elmtown was celebrating such a centennial during Hollingshead's visit and he noticed that all the pageantry centered on old prominent families with Anglo-Saxon names. 'Eventually,' he says, 'it became clear that the backers of the centennial were primarily interested in glorifying their own ancestry.' People who had helped build the town after the pioneer era were not included." What is true of the Midwest is even truer of Newbury.)

In the "glorification" of ancestors, certain details about them were sometimes veiled in discreet silence. When my mother founded the Oxbow Chapter of the Daughters of the American Revolution, much was made of the fact that the twenty charter members all established their eligibility to that society by tracing their direct descent from either Jacob Bayley or Thomas Johnson, or both; and the ladies who traced it to both made much of the further fact that General Jacob's son, Isaac, had married Colonel Tom's daughter, Betsy. Only with the publication of Wells' *History of Newbury*, some years later, was it disclosed by the vital statistics therein that Amelia, the eldest daughter of Isaac and Betsy, was born only four months after her parents' marriage; and though there is nothing to suggest that it was a shotgun wedding, everyone concerned was obliged to admit that it was a little tardy! However, it resulted in a noteworthy architectural design: for more than a century, the "courting corner" and the "marriage arch," which form part of the paneling on either side of the parlor fireplace at the Homestead, have elicited great admiration; the room of which they are the outstanding features has been regarded as the handsomest in Newbury. But it remained for the present owner of the house— Jacob's great-great-grandson—to point out, at a family gathering, that the courting corner was located where the father of the family—namely, the once impetuous Isaac!—could easily keep his eye on it as he sat, with the door open into the adjoining living room. Amelia, in due course, had five younger sisters, Betsy, Clarissa, Abigail, Nancy, and Susan. They were all courted in the corner, under careful observation, and married under the arch at the proper time!

No tardy marriages among the Keyeses were disclosed by that candid chronicler, Mr. Frederick P. Wells, in his *History of Newbury*, and I am very sure there were none, for their code has always been one of the strictest morality. In my childhood, the branch of the family who had gone to live at Pine Grove Farm, across the Connecticut River, were by then considered "summer people," unlike their Newbury cousins, Miss Hattie and Mr. Tom. The other Keyeses were not snobbish; but they were a very large closely knit family, sufficient unto themselves; and, besides, it was natural for my future mother-in-law, who had been one of eleven children, to feel closer to her only surviving sister—one of the loveliest women I have ever known—than to her late husband's cousins. However, the Pine Grove Farm Keyeses still came to Newbury to get their mail and go to the church which my great-great grandfather had built, where they occupied the most expensive pew. (One of our richest Newbury cousins, who had married a Scot, occupied the least expensive pew with her family, a fact upon which my mother and my future mother-in-law, who did not often see eye to eye about anything, never failed to comment with an equal degree of contempt.) And every year the Keyes ladies, who were all lovely looking, helped with the Church Fair. Their table was always outstanding. The year of the gala birthday party it was especially so. What was more, the Keyes ladies had persuaded a young friend of theirs, Maude Sanderson Bullard, whose husband, a gifted musician, composed the famous *Stein Song,* to dress like a gypsy, set up a booth close to theirs, and tell fortunes. She told mine and it left me quivering with excitement.

"You must beware of fire," she told me. "Fire will be very disastrous and very dangerous to you, all your life. On the other hand, water is your most friendly element. You will spend a great deal of time on it and by it and it will be a source of joy to you." She scanned my small chubby hand more closely and laughed. "You do not believe me, do you?" she asked. "Well, I will tell you something else you will not believe, either: you will be married before you are twenty, well known before you are thirty, and famous before you are forty."

Her predictions were so overwhelming that I was very thankful when Mr. Harry Keyes came up and asked me if I wouldn't like some ice cream. This was not only because I relished ice cream on general principles; it was also because I was afraid, if I stayed where I was any longer, the gypsy would tell me something else and I did not feel I could bear any more just then. I gratefully lapped up my ice cream and then my mother came and said it was time for me to go home. I was glad rather than otherwise. I had had enough excitement for one day, and though most of it was happy excitement, that part about the fire disturbed me. I was still feeling disturbed when my mother asked me a crushing question.

"Did you thank Mr. Keyes politely for the ice cream?" she inquired, as we jogged along from the village to the Oxbow in the top buggy drawn by Dan. The question was merely a matter of form. Of course, she took it for granted that I had thanked him and that I had done it politely. She prided herself that I was a well-brought-up child. And alas! I had not thanked him at all. I had taken it for granted that the ice cream was an integral part of the Fair and, besides, my mind was full of the gypsy.

"Then you will have to write him a letter," my mother said severely.

I had never written a letter. The next day was made miserable for me until I had composed it. But, afterward, I heard something about it that lifted my drooping spirits.

As I have said, the Keyeses still came to Newbury for their mail, just as they still came to occupy the most expensive pew in church. And when Harry Keyes opened my letter in the post office, he spoke laughingly and pleasantly about it to an acquaintance who happened to be standing nearby.

"Your little cousin, Frances Wheeler, has written me a letter," he said. "I shouldn't be surprised if it were her first one. I think I shall keep it. Some day it might mean a good deal to me to have her first letter."

CHAPTER VI

But it was not only parties and fairs that made life wonderful and delightful in Newbury those days. Most of our diversions took place out of doors; but sometimes we gathered around the chair of an old lady whom we all called Aunt Nancy and listened to the fairy stories she told us: about a lovely young queen who rode through the streets of a great city in a golden coach and about an empress who lived in the palace of another great city and yawned behind her painted fan when she became bored during the long ceremonies at which she was called upon to preside. These were wonderful stories and Aunt Nancy could hold us spellbound for hours while she told them; when she died, there was no one else to do the same thing for us, because no one else in Newbury could make queens and empresses seem real to us the way she did.

It was not until many years afterward that we learned the reason they seemed real to us was because they *were* real and she had known them herself. She was the same Nancy Johnson, the sister of Edward Carleton Johnson, whom Delia Maria, as a bride, had regarded in such a supercilious manner because this sister-in-law of hers was a writer. As a matter of fact, Nancy was a very remarkable woman. When she was a young girl, one of her legs had been amputated, and she had spent a year in bed, first while waiting for the stump to heal and then while adjusting herself to some sort of a crude appliance which would enable her to walk again. During that year, to while away the time, she had written some brief essays that were sent to a Boston publishing house which specialized in religious pamphlets. The essays were accepted and published anonymously under the title of *Sketches from a Sickroom*. In order to speed her convalescence and take her mind off her writing, her father, David Johnson, who adored her, and who had bought her the first pianoforte ever seen in Newbury, sent away for bottled Saratoga water, which was considered extremely salubrious. Before she was on her feet again, Nancy had figured out that if what she wrote when she was completely disabled could find an audience, certainly what she would be able to write when she was up and around should find a wider one; also that if Saratoga water, consumed from bottles, was good for her health, water that came directly from the famous springs should be still more beneficial. It was at this juncture that Delia Maria dismissed Nancy so condescendingly; it meant nothing to the New York belle that a girl from a remote Vermont village had the initiative and the courage to strike out for herself and the intelligence to forge to the front as a writer. It did not, as a matter of fact, mean much to her parents. In order to preserve her anonymity and thus avoid bringing disgrace to her family, she took the pen name of Minnie Myrtle; and, despite this silly pseudonym, she progressed rapidly from the rank of society reporter to that of foreign correspondent, with several books to her credit along the line, one of them about the Iroquois, among whom she lived for a time, and who adopted her into their tribe. In 1857, Henry Raymond, then editor of the New York *Times*, whose warm friendship she had achieved—she dedicated a book to him—sent her to Europe; as far as I know, she was the first of the great women journalists so honored. And, unless I am very much mistaken, she achieved another friendship, even warmer, abroad, though this—like Delia Maria's Roman idyl—is shrouded in mystery. At all events, there was, acting as foreign correspondent for another newspaper in Paris, a brilliant and charming man, whose surname was also Johnson. He and Nancy quickly discovered that they were kindred spirits, for Nancy was brilliant and charming, too. She quickly became an accomplished linguist and a past master at repartee; and she had learned to dress with such tasteful elegance that this was a matter of comment, even in the French capital. To simplify their association, the two either established or invented a kinship. This was easy to do for two reasons: first, because cousins had formed such an integral part of Nancy's background that she could add another to their number, without twinges of conscience, even if this required some stretch of the imagination, and perhaps it did not; and, second, because most of her French friends would have been no more likely to guess that there were thousands upon thousands of Johnsons in the United States than untraveled Americans realized that there were thousands upon thousands of Poiriers in France. Besides, the American legation, where Nancy and the other Johnson were frequently and cordially received, tacitly accepted the kinship; there was never a breath of scandal and I am glad to feel there is no reason why there should have been. But when Nancy finally came home, broken in health and spirits, she was generally regarded as "touched." It never occurred to anyone that the stories about Queen Victoria and the Empress Eugénie and many other glamorous persons—stories she told us children on rainy days and chilly evenings, when we gathered around the wheelchair in her bedroom—were all true; and no one believed that the letters she constantly wrote and entrusted to some able-bodied member of the family for mailing were addressed to a real person. It was half a century later before I found out any of this, from the letters she had written her parents while abroad and which, like so many others that have been valuable to me, came tardily into my possession. It was later still when I found out about the letters that had never been mailed, from a real cousin who had innocently withheld them. Nancy had lived a gallant and wonderful life; it grieves me to realize that, during its twilight, she was doubted by her own people and believed herself deserted by the one man who had meant much to her. But it is a source of great pride to me that Ishbel Ross, in her excellent survey, *Ladies of the Press*,[1] pays my aunt Nancy the tribute so long overdue.

In addition to Aunt Nancy's "fairy tales," other relatives[2] told us

[1] Published by Harper & Brothers.
[2] These were sometimes told as an entity and sometimes piecemeal, one relative enlarging where another had abbreviated and vice versa; but to avoid confusion, I have thought it best to present the story as one narrative.

"true stories" of the pioneering feats and Revolutionary records of our ancestors, General Jacob Bayley and Colonel Thomas Johnson.

"Why did they come here in the first place?" we very naturally asked.

"After the surrender of Montreal, John Hazen and Jacob Bayley of Massachusetts, who had served as officers during the French and Indian Wars, returned home via the Connecticut Valley and decided, because of its beauty and fertility, it had great possibilities as a permanent settlement. At that time, there was no state of Vermont—all the land was part of the New Hampshire grants—so they applied to the governor of New Hampshire for a charter, giving them a right to property for two town sites, one on either side of the Connecticut River. Eventually, the King of England granted this charter, so this land on the Oxbow, where we now live, is part of a royal grant; and the title has come down to us direct. No one can ever dispute our right to it."

"But we thought Vermont was one of the original thirteen——?"

"No, but it was the first to enter the Union after the Revolution and Newbury was the first town where the General Assembly—or the Legislature, as we call it now—met before Montpelier was finally chosen as the capital. The meetings were held around the harvest table that is out in the front hall.

"Hazen named his settlement Haverhill, after his home town, and Bayley called his Newbury—that was the custom then. Thomas Johnson, who was a great friend of Bayley's, came with him to Newbury and they both worked hard and prospered. They built nice houses—Jacob Bayley's is the one we call the Homestead now, but Thomas Johnson built four, all grouped together. When the first one was finished, Thomas Johnson gave a big housewarming; while everyone was having a fine time at the party, a rider came galloping up through the valley, bringing the merrymakers the news of the Battle of Lexington."

"Just like Paul Revere?" we asked, showing off our knowledge of history.

"Exactly. Bayley sent word to the Provincial Congress in New York that he could raise a company of between two and three hundred men and he was appointed brigadier general of the militia in all the river-valley towns; in Newbury, a company of fifty-one, including several Indians, was formed, with Thomas Johnson as its captain.

"When General Washington realized that he must find a shorter route to Canada than the one he was using, he consulted Bayley, who told him Johnson was the man for it. Taking with him three white men and an Indian guide, Johnson plowed through the woods on snowshoes, blazing a trail that saved the troops ten marching days.

"After that, he led an independent company to Ticonderoga and also served as General Lincoln's aide. Unfortunately, however, he was captured and taken as a prisoner to Canada, where he was not mistreated, but was held for three months before he was released on parole."

We knew this was only the prelude to the story we liked best of all.

"After the war was over, all sorts of schemes were afoot to detach Vermont from the United States and sell it to Canada. Johnson knew about these schemes and that the British regarded Jacob Bayley as the chief obstacle to their fulfillment. The British commander, Captain Prichard, and seventeen scouts took up a position on the heights west of the Oxbow. When Johnson learned that the British planned to capture Bayley that same evening, he did not know what to do. He could not let Bayley—his friend and neighbor—be captured; but if Johnson warned him, the former might run the risk of having his buildings destroyed and of being returned to Canada as a prisoner. How could he warn Bayley without hazard to himself? Because Prichard's position on the heights enabled him to overlook the Oxbow, where Bayley was plowing, Johnson could not warn him in person, but, on a slip of paper, he wrote, 'The Philistines be upon thee, Samson!' and entrusted this to his brother-in-law, Dudley Carleton, telling him to go to the meadow and drop the note near Bayley, but not to stop or speak. Bayley retrieved the message, turned out his team, and headed for the riverbank. When the British came to capture him, he was miles away, so they were forced to return, thwarted, to Canada. That was the end of the attempt to sell Vermont to Canada and of Jacob Bayley's troubles, but, unfortunately, not the end of Thomas Johnson's.

"The British claimed he had broken his parole and threatened to destroy his property; his fellow townspeople accused him of Tory sympathies, very unfairly basing these charges on the fact that he had been kindly treated in Canada and that his wife, Abigail Carleton, was a relative of the governor-general of Quebec. He decided to appeal to George Washington for understanding and help."

"And he got it?"

"He did, indeed. After an exchange of letters—and don't forget those letters are among our most valuable family possessions!—Johnson was received by General Washington who 'assured him of his sympathy and acknowledged the value of his services.' Consoled, Johnson went home with a light heart."

On Sunday evenings, we generally gathered around Cousin Mary's Estey organ to sing hymns. But, aside from this and from listening to the "fairy stories" told us by Aunt Nancy, and the saga of Jacob Bayley and Thomas Johnson told us by various relatives, most of our diversions were outdoors, except for an occasional candy pull or popcorn roast. One of our favorite pastimes was walking on the teetering top rail of the cemetery fence and seeing how far we could go without a spill. I was pretty good at this, strangely enough, for I was a plump child, and it would seem as if it would have been harder for me to keep my balance than for those of more wiry build, who could move more quickly. Sunday was a special day for this sport, not only because, as I have said, children were encouraged to go to the cemetery for their Sunday outings; but also because Haines and Louise Johnson, all four Darlings, and I had to pass the cemetery on our way to Sunday School in the morning and Christian Endeavor in the afternoon. This meant we were supplied with pennies, at other times a rarity, for contribution. Alas! some of those pennies never reached the deacon's plate when he passed it. They had been spent on wagers as to who could keep on the fence the longest. I was often the winner, and had anyone ever told me to put more than one penny in the plate? Certainly not!

There were also hayrides in those days, when Cousin Sidney was getting his hay into the barn and jumping contests after it had been stowed away. There were gatherings around Cousin Henry's cider press when apples were brought in from all the surrounding farms; and every night there were the cows to bring home. It was Cousin Sidney's cows that I went to fetch, with Haines, both calling, "Co'boss! Co'boss!" as we went down the steep incline behind the big barn to the pasture beyond, where milkweed and sweet fern and bouncing Bet grew in abundance, and a little brook wound its way into the Connecticut River. It was a privilege to be allowed to go and get the cows with Haines, a privilege no other little girl shared; and much as I loved the rest, I was glad that none of them lived directly across the street from him. Not only was it less convenient for them to accompany him on those daily trips to the pasture; none of the others could stand on her front porch and by the simple process of shouting, "Come over, Haines, come over!" summon a congenial companion at a moment's notice. Haines had chores to do, morning and evening, besides going for the cows; the woodbox to fill, the chickens to feed, and so on. But aside from these tasks his time was his own in the halcyon days. He never failed to come over.

I can remember only one feature of those early days in Newbury which was painful to me, and that was the Fourth of July celebrations. There were no restrictions about the use of firecrackers in those times; indeed, the murderous type called "giant" was greatly in vogue. I was not afraid that these firecrackers would harm me; as a matter of fact, it was not until long afterward that I knew how much damage they did, though I can still remember a full-page illustration in the old *Life*, which must have come out when I was in my teens, captioned, "The Glorious Fourth," and which pictured brokenhearted parents at the bedside of a little boy who had been blinded. But the loud, sudden noise sent me into hysterics. This was regarded by all my playmates, and I think by my elders, too, as a pose; at all events, the boys in our gang, even Haines, who never failed me otherwise, delighted in setting the giants off in my proximity. I could not escape from them though I shut myself up in the house. This allergy—if such it may be called— to loud and persistent noises has lasted all my life, and I have continued to be terribly ashamed of it; but it was not until after I had gone to live in Washington that this shame was somewhat assuaged by a physician.

I had gone, in a highly official group, to a riding exhibition at Fort Meyer. In those days, the cavalry was still a major attraction, and the stunt riding, which was really remarkable, was always punctuated by a great deal of mock gunfire; cap pistols were discharged almost every time the ring was circled and, occasionally, a number of times. I was in agony and kept drawing in my breath to keep from screaming; but I could not leave, because my host and hostess were of exalted rank and so were most of my fellow guests. Somehow, I sat through it. But when I reached home, I collapsed completely and the next day I still could not lift my head; I was not only hysterical but feverish. A doctor was summoned and, when he had looked me over, spoke very gravely.

"If you were a soldier, recently back from the war, I should diagnose this as a severe case of shell shock," he said. "Have you been any place where loud sudden noises were upsetting to you?"

I told him, between sobs, about the exhibition at Fort Meyer.

"And have you ever been upset by anything of the kind before?" he inquired.

My thinking was confused, but after a few moments I remembered the Fourth of July celebrations in Newbury and told him about them. I also told him, quite honestly, that my reaction to them had been regarded as a pose.

"It was not a pose," he said, still gravely. "Almost everyone has some sort of a phobia—fear of high places, or of confinement in restricted areas, for instance. Do you mind either of those?"

"Not in the least."

"Are you afraid of anything or upset by anything except loud sudden noises?"

"Yes. I'm afraid of snakes—not of what they will do to me. It is just a kind of horror I can't explain and I have always had it—I don't even like to talk about them or see a picture of them. And elevators—when I was a little girl, I saw a woman killed in one. And dentists. Until a short time ago, I got faint as soon as I was in a dentist's chair, before he had even touched me. I had a terrible shock at a dentist's once and it always seems to come back to me."

The doctor smoothed the sheets and rose. "I am afraid you will have to go on using elevators and visiting the dentist," he said, "but there is no use in precipitating unnecessary crises. So you had better stay away from regions where you are likely to see snakes and where you will be subjected to loud sudden noises. You are entitled to that many phobias."

I agreed with him and still do. But, somehow, I have survived sixteen years in Louisiana, where there are some forty different varieties of snakes, six of them poisonous, which I have not been altogether able to avoid, and, sometimes, I have been uncomfortably close. These "represent a definite hazard to all persons who work or play out of doors."[3] I have also been through five revolutions and was caught in Europe at the beginning of World War II. None of these latter experiences was devoid of loud sudden noises.

[3] *Louisiana's Natural Resources* by John B. Robston. Silver Burdett Company.

CHAPTER VII

To the naps in the trundle bed and the Sunday-night suppers, I can fix no exact date, as I said before; neither can I do so for most of those other early pleasures—the cousin parties, the church fairs, the hayrides, the contests on the cemetery fence. But it was unquestioningly during my first year at Miss Carroll's School in Boston that I made my initial important friendships in that city. One of these was with a little girl by the name of Marion Burdett, who did not go to a private school; my mother was inclined to be a little snooty about this and, also, about the fact that the Burdetts did not live in a large private house, like the other people we knew in Boston, but in a new hotel, the Charlesgate East, which was on the other side of the small stream that flowed into the Charles River and which separated it from our enormous house on the corner of Charlesgate West. The Charlesgate East was a very superior family hotel, and the Burdetts lived there, rather than in a house, because Mrs. Burdett was very delicate and unequal to the cares of a huge establishment. Moreover, Mr. Burdett was a very successful lawyer and a great friend of my stepfather who, to a large degree, was responsible for my friendship with Marion. He had no patience with my mother's airs about this friendship, and he was perfectly right. Marion was a beautiful child, a glowing brunette, with charming ways. Living as we did, so close together, it was easy for us to see a great deal of each other and we did. We continued to do so until Marion died, many years later, and I shall have more to say about her, too.

The other two friends I made that year *were* schoolmates and, therefore, considered by my mother more socially eligible. They were Marian and Grace Edmands, who lived on Commonwealth Avenue, just about a block below Massachusetts, whereas our house, on neighboring Beacon Street, was about a block above. I walked the two blocks between our house and the Edmandses' alone, which no one seemed to consider at all strange for a small child to do in Boston then, even a small child whose mother was socially ambitious; a very friendly policeman always saw me across Massachusetts Avenue and when I reached the Edmandses', we went the rest of the way to school together—about five blocks in all. The Edmands sisters did not have a governess like Miss Jones, but an enormous nurse named Hannah.

She took excellent care of them, but she was so fat that she never could have waddled all the way to 12 Gloucester Street. It did not matter at all. We got along very well by ourselves.

The Edmandses' was not a corner house, nor was it as large as ours, but it was still large enough to meet my mother's standards of suitable urban living: that is, four stories high besides the basement. The lace curtains of their parlor window did not part to disclose fresh pink roses, as ours did, but a marble bust of Madame Récamier; such an arrangement represented the very height of elegance. I liked everything about the Edmands sisters very much—their house, their parents, their companionship, their nurse—even though she could not compare with Barbara! I was, therefore, deeply distressed when my mother came to the day nursery one evening, just before my supper was sent up on the elevator, and drew me onto her lap—a rather rare thing for her to do—saying she had something very sad to tell me about the Edmandses.

For it seemed that Mr. Edmands was not a successful lawyer, like my stepfather and Mr. Burdett; he was a partner in a business which had failed because one of the other partners had made unwise investments. At the time of their marriage, Mr. Edmands had given his bride a hundred thousand dollars—a staggering sum for those days— and had made her promise never, under any circumstances, to let it get out of her control. But she was a loving wife and when she realized her husband's difficulties, which were no fault of his, she insisted on throwing her fortune into the breach, and it was lost with all the rest of the money. So the Edmandses would have to give up their beautiful house on Commonwealth Avenue and Marian and Grace would have to stop going to Miss Carroll's School. They were going to live in a very little house, somewhere in Brookline; and Marian and Grace would go to a public school, just like Marion Burdett. But we would not let any of this make any difference. We would go on being friends just the same.

I did not see then, and I still do not see, why my mother should have thought it would make any difference. On the contrary, I admired Mrs. Edmands more than ever, and I saw almost as much of Marian and Grace after they moved to Brookline as I had before. I went alone in the new electric cars that ran up Beacon Street, which, hitherto, I had only seen from my nursery window; then I got out, about halfway to the reservoir, and walked several blocks to the side street where the Edmandses lived. Their little house—not so little, by present-day standards—is another that I remember very distinctly; but that I shall not try to describe, because it was in no way remarkable, except for the courage and cheerfulness that permeated it. And the bust of Madame Récamier still stood in the parlor window, between parted lace curtains.

There were other friends, of course, besides Marion Burdett and the Edmands sisters, though these were the closest, in Boston, and remained so for a long while. There was Gladys Olmstead, who lived diagonally across the street from Miss Carroll's School, whose father was, I think, an architect. She was an only child and was encouraged, at a very tender age, to be present when her mother had days at home; and the influence of this was so strong that she continued to have days at home herself, long after her mother was dead and practically everyone else in Boston had stopped doing so. There were the Shreve twins, Wilhemina and Carmelita, whose father was a member of the firm of Shreve, Crump and Low, the Tiffany's of Boston. They lived very far out on Beacon Street, near the reservoir; and through them I met Dorothy and Robert Jordan, the children—or, possibly, the grandchildren—of the merchant prince who established Jordan Marsh Company. The Jordans then lived in a pseudo-French château crowning a hill not far from the Shreves; but that part of Boston was not fashionable and, later, the Jordans recognized their social mistake and moved to an old, typically Bostonian house on Beacon Hill, which is now the City Club and the scene of the famous Waltz Evenings and other exclusive functions.

Then we had two different sets of distant cousins in Boston: the A. J. Gordons—Adoniram Judson had been shortened to initials, and no wonder!—who were not relatives of Dr. George Gordon, the pastor of the New Old South, though Dr. A. J. Gordon was a minister, too— the pastor of the Clarendon Street Baptist Church—and a very learned and eloquent man. However, Baptists were not considered as belonging in the same social category as Congregationalists. Besides, the A. J. Gordons lived on West Brookline Street in the South End, which was definitely not in the same social category as the Back Bay and Beacon Hill. There were six children in the family, one of them, Theodora, just about my age, and the parsonage was a big comfortable house, where I was always made very welcome and loved to go. Mrs. Gordon, nee Harriet Hale of Providence, was a wonderful woman and the sister of Mrs. Nathaniel Hill, nee Alice Hale, whose husband was among those who had "struck it rich" in Central City and had later become United States Senator from Colorado and one of the most prominent men in that state. So there was no question, in my mother's mind, about *her* social eminence and, later, we frequently visited her and her family. Apparently, it was not such a long way from Boston to Denver as from Beacon Street to West Brookline Street.

The other distant Boston cousins, the Fields, lived most of the time at a beautiful place in Weston, though, in midwinter, they moved briefly into one of those tall narrow town houses, which I have already described, so that the young people in the family could go to the parties for which they were the right age. The Fields were the kind of people who were always included in every sort of party that was worth-while and my mother was very proud of her relationship with them. "We have been to Orben-dail today and I had a nice time," I recorded in a letter written when I was seven years old. As I have frequently confessed, spelling was never my strong point. But "Orben-dail" unquestionably refers to Auburndale, the next station to Weston, where we descended from the train when we went to visit the Fields.

Another friend of whom I saw a good deal was Mary Fisher. Her parents lived in North Haverhill, New Hampshire, across the Connecticut River from Newbury, Vermont, but her aunt and uncle, Mr. and Mrs. Josiah H. Benton, Jr., lived in Boston and Mary visited them very frequently, so she really belonged to both groups of my friends—those who lived in the country and those who lived in the city. Mrs. Benton wore her beautiful white hair in puffs, coils, and ringlets; it must have taken someone hours every day to arrange it; and when she went to a resort hotel, which she did in the summer, she provided herself with a different and very handsome dress in which to appear at dinner every night. Mr. Benton, like my stepfather and Mr. Burdett, was a brilliant and successful lawyer; and, as he and his wife had no children of their own, they spared neither expense nor loving care as far as Mary was concerned.

I have called these three men brilliant and successful and that they certainly were; later, I heard references to them as "smart" in a tone I did not quite like, though nothing actually disparaging was ever said about them in my hearing. None of them came from old Boston families—my stepfather from Milford, New Hampshire; Mr. Burdett from Olive Branch, Mississippi; and Mr. Benton from Bradford, Vermont. Perhaps there was some jealousy of the "small-town boy who made good" mingled with the implied criticism when people said they were smart. Perhaps they took cases which the long-established Boston firms would not have handled, or would have handled in a different way. I do not know, though I believe that, by most present-day standards, their professional conduct would not have been considered incorrect. The only thing that troubled me, as a child, was that people did not speak in quite the same tone about old Judge Richardson, though he was another product of a small New Hampshire town—Orford—and had eventually come to live not far from the Bentons on Newbury Street—I mean Newbury Street in Boston, not Newbury, Vermont. No one said he was smart; people talked about him with respect, almost with reverence. But then he was not brilliant or successful, either, just good; and he had a very unattractive wife, not in the least like the elegant Mrs. Benton, or the exquisitely fragile Mrs. Burdett, or my charming mother; and he had no children, not even stepchildren, and no pretty little niece to make up partially for that lack. So perhaps people were sorry for him, instead of being jealous of him.

I think my mother felt that most of the associations, both hers and mine, were not quite up to the exclusive social level which she considered her birthright. She went to the meetings of the Daughters of the American Revolution, whose local regent at the time was unquestionably a blue blood. She joined the Fragment Society, an exclusive group of ladies, who met for sewing and supper at intervals throughout the winter. She interested herself in all the right charities, including this one and the Home for Little Wanderers, though she stopped taking me to the latter when I begged her to adopt a charming two-year-old orphan who ran and cuddled up to me, with an instinctive sense of sympathy. She went regularly to the New Old South, both to church and to Sunday School, and saw to it that I did the same and, also, that I went to the Sunday School parties which were periodically held in the huge church parlors and which would have been gloomy and impersonal had it not been for Dr. George Gordon's powerful personality. She also went regularly to the symphony concerts and patronized the right stores: S. S. Pierce for groceries, Hovey's for my everyday things, Hollander's for my best things, and Schwartz[1] for my toys. She gave exquisitely appointed luncheons and dinners and was entertained a good deal in return. Her visiting list, which I still have, discloses most of the "right" names of persons who lived at the "right"

---

[1] The owner of this toy emporium was Richard Schwartz, no relation to the present F. A. O. Schwartz who owns the store at 40 Newbury Street, Boston.

addresses; but I do not think she was on the terms of intimacy which she would have liked with many of these families; and, sooner or later, I sensed that she resented this, because it had not been the case, with similar families, in either New York or Virginia.

Yet I believe there were several sound reasons why this state of things existed in Boston: one was because she had married for the third time; and though, as I have said before, second marriages were regarded with tolerance and even with approval, third marriages were something else again, even though the previous spouses were dead, not divorced—perish the thought!—especially if the persons who acquired new ones so readily were women. Then there was the fact that my stepfather was smart, rather than distinguished, and that it was whispered he was something of a philanderer—whispers which, of course, I did not understand at the time, though I occasionally overheard them. A still further hindrance to her more favored existence may have lain in the fact that she not only felt superior to most of the persons she met, and who did not give her her due, but betrayed that she felt that way. She bought all her clothes in New York, going to the same dressmaker who had outfitted her ultrafashionable mother and herself when she was a young girl and a young married woman—that is, when she was Mrs. James Underhill and not Mrs. Albert E. Pillsbury. She thought nothing of spending two hundred and fifty dollars for a dress when that was a sum almost unheard of for one costume in Boston; what was worse, the styles she wore were so far in advance of any that appeared in the wardrobes of her associates—even those of Mrs. Benton—that they made her conspicuous in any gathering. She complained that the first time she went to the opera in Boston, wearing the gray and russet brocade which had been her third wedding dress and the diamond necklace which my stepfather gave her on that occasion, she was the only lady in their immediate vicinity who was properly dressed; in fact, she did not believe that most of them had been brought up on grand opera, as she had been, and probably did not know what it was to be properly dressed.

This sort of remark was not calculated to improve either her general popularity or her social prestige in a city that prided itself on culture and correctness, rather than on fashionable attire. She was also fond of saying that, at the University, everyone had told her that, except for her accent, she might have been mistaken for a Virginian, but that, in Boston, no one would ever have mistaken her for a Bostonian—and that she was equally complimented in both cases! Once a Proper

Bostonian told her, in my hearing, that, if she had been a New Englander, instead of a New Yorker, she would have had to be satisfied
with one husband, if any. "Perhaps," she retorted instantly, "but two
of my husbands have been New Englanders." This was, indubitably,
true. However, it did not endear her to the first speaker, who had never
been married at all, and who felt keenly enough that the New Yorker
had trespassed on her preserves, without having this rubbed in.

I was perfectly satisfied with my friends and not really conscious,
until much later, that my mother was not; and, though she did not
drag me into all her "at homes" and require me to remain throughout
their duration, as Gladys Olmstead was dragged and forced to remain,
I was generally supposed to put in a brief appearance on such occasions and to go with her to functions where she considered the presence of children suitable. One of these functions was the wedding of
Miss Martha Gertrude Keyes to Mr. Ezra Henry Baker, which took
place at eight o'clock in the evening at the New Old South Church
when I was seven years old. My cousin, Louise Johnson, who lived
across the street from us in Newbury—the same one who shared those
memorable Sunday suppers with her brother Haines and myself!—was
spending that winter with us on Beacon Street, going to Miss Carroll's
Day School and dancing school with me; and we both had new dresses
for the Baker-Keyes wedding. Mine was pink cashmere and Louise's
was blue cashmere. My mother was a vision of loveliness in pale yellow
brocade, in which she had her portrait painted that same winter. Harry
Keyes, then about thirty years old, gave his sister away, since their
father, as I have said, was long since dead; but the two younger Keyes
brothers, George and Charlie, were both ushers, and my first definite
memory of them is that of their amused expressions as they conducted
us to our seats. Perhaps they did not think Louise and I were old
enough to go to a formal evening wedding, even though my mother's
opinion was contrary to this. I also remember how Mrs. Keyes, the
bride's mother, who was still a very beautiful woman, looked on this
occasion, wearing black velvet and crowned with soft white hair—not
elaborately coiffed, like Mrs. Benton's, but most becomingly so; and
I remember Miss Belle Keyes, the bride's elder sister, who was the
maid of honor, and who wore cream satin with huge rose-colored
puffed sleeves, while the bridesmaids were in solid pink of a paler
shade. On her way up the aisle, Belle caught the heel of her slipper
in one of the old-fashioned registers through which hot air poured to
heat the church and, as she deftly extricated her foot, she smiled at

the trifling mishap instead of being embarrassed by it. Perhaps she thought, momentarily, of a mishap which had befallen her father's first wife, who was his second wife's much elder sister, and to whom the family always referred as Aunt Sarah: Aunt Sarah, as a young girl, was dancing with the first Henry Keyes, and her flannel petticoat fell off. Instead of showing the least confusion, she disengaged herself from her partner, picked up the fallen petticoat, retired to a secluded spot, and put it on again; she then returned to the dance floor as if nothing had happened. Her partner was so impressed with her composure that he proposed then and there.

Whether or not this was the episode Miss Belle Keyes was recalling when she caught her heel in the register, she certainly showed the same degree of smiling composure as her aunt Sarah. She righted herself so quickly that no one noticed the mishap; but everyone near the center aisle, myself included, noticed the smile and decided that she must be very pleased with her sister's choice of a husband; and I remembered the episode so distinctly that I included it in a description of a fictional wedding about which I wrote in my first best seller— *Honor Bright*—more than forty years later!

The Keyes wedding took place just before Thanksgiving. It was during our Easter vacation, the next spring, that my mother took Louise and me for our first trip to Washington. The "ride in the cars" was in itself a great adventure; the Hell Gate Bridge had not been built then, and the Colonial Express was trundled onto a ferry at one side of the river and trundled off at the other. This was very thrilling. So was the fact that some kind of a minor mishap caused the train to be very late and we did not get into Washington until about one o'clock in the morning, after having left Boston at some ungodly hour the previous morning. When we returned to school, we bragged about this nocturnal adventure for days and days. ("What do you think? We never went to bed until *two!*") We also bragged about the Shoreham Hotel, where we stayed—the "Old Shoreham" as it later came to be called; there were two sets of curtains at the windows of our suite, old-gold satin over Brussels lace, and we had a private bathroom. But of course we bragged most of all because we had been to the White House. As a matter of fact, this was not nearly as much of a personal compliment as we implied. My mother's reason—or at least her pretext—for going to Washington at that time was to attend one of the first sessions of the "Continental Congress," still held annually by the Daughters of the American Revolution. My mother was one of the earliest members of this organization and though, as far as I know, she held no office at the time, she seemed to feel her presence was imperative. (Of course, she also dwelt on the great cultural value that such a trip would have for Louise and me. One of these educational aspects was the ascent—on foot!—of the Washington Monument, with the result that I have never visited it since!) Anyway, all the delegates were invited to the White House to meet President and Mrs. Harrison, and the delegates who had brought offspring with them did not hesitate to assume that these children were included in the invitation. Louise and I were festively arrayed in our blue and pink cashmere dresses and, because my mother was proud of our curls, we wore no hats.

This omission led to a mistake which was very flattering to our vanity. The Harrisons had granddaughters of about our age, the children of their daughter, Mrs. McKee; and presently we began to hear excited whispers all around us, "Oh, just look at the President's grandchildren! Aren't they cute!" For a few minutes, we basked in unmerited glory; then the great impersonation came to an end. The real McKee children appeared on the scene and we retired in confusion. Nevertheless, we had had, if not actually "a crowded hour of glorious life," at least enough of one to make us feel it was worth a world without a name.

I was glad, later on that year, that I had something as beautiful as the Baker-Keyes wedding and as exciting as the trip to Washington to look back on. It was decided that it was high time I was vaccinated, and Dr. Gay, who was the Edmandses' uncle and the head of the Boston City Hospital at the time, came to our house to do it. He vaccinated me in three places at once, because he said it was almost never that more than one "took" and he did not want to have me go through such an ordeal a second time. Unfortunately, all three "took" and I was desperately ill for weeks and weeks. At one stage, it looked as if I might lose my life, and almost certainly my arm. I had high fever and was delirious, night after night. But, unfortunately, I was fully conscious when my arm was dressed, as it had to be, day after day. I can still see and smell the foul dressings, covered with pus and blood, that were painfully removed to allow fresh bandages to be put in their place—bandages which were in the same condition the following day. Of course, there was no more school of any kind for me that spring; nothing but pain and disgust and general misery. I wanted to die and I still think it is a miracle that I didn't, though there was

no physician in Boston more highly regarded than Dr. Gay, and none
who cared more for me personally and would have more deeply regretted injuring me instead of safeguarding me.

A few years later, one of my little cousins had exactly the same
experience. The result was that great skepticism about the wisdom of
vaccination arose in the family and I vowed I never would be vaccinated again, or permit my children to be, if I had any. I was upheld
in my stand, though I was told that another vaccination would not
"take" anyhow, because, to all intents and purposes, I had already had
smallpox. However, thirty-three years later, when I was sent around
the world by *Good Housekeeping,* I found I would have to be, in
order to get into China. So I was vaccinated again and it took again
and, though this time I was in bed for only a week and was not dangerously ill, I again had high fever and suffered very greatly. Since
then, I have been vaccinated as often as required by my travels, and
every time but one the vaccination has "taken." So I am still very unhappy on that subject and I was still deeply sympathetic when my
children and grandchildren had to be vaccinated; it was hard for me
to believe that they were not being exposed to the same risks and it
has taken a long while for me to realize that times have changed.

In the fall, when my convalescence was finally established, my
mother decided that perhaps another trip would be a good idea and
took me to the World's Fair in Chicago.

Only a few isolated experiences and impressions have remained
vivid: I thought it was great fun to be trundled around in a wheelchair, though I was perfectly able to walk; I was enchanted and not
in the least frightened by the Ferris wheel and deeply resented the
fact that my elders thought one ride in it aplenty for me; also, that I
was hurried past some of the sights on the Midway Pleasance, Little
Egypt, for instance. At night, the illuminations transformed the real
world into a fairyland for me, surpassing anything about which I had
read in Grimm or Hans Andersen; but I was not allowed to sit up
very late to enjoy the magic. As a matter of fact, my mother was on
her guard against exhaustion; before her departure, her physician had
warned her not to drink iced tea because it was too exhilarating for
her good; she must curtail her sightseeing at the first sign of natural
fatigue. I thought both the Women's Building and the Children's
Building rather dull; they looked to me as if the men who planned
them had been "talking down" to the female of the species and her

offspring. As a matter of fact, the greatest thrill of the trip came not at the Fair, but on the way home.

My mother and I occupied a lower berth together, my stepfather the upper berth in the same section. One night, we were rudely awakened by a terrific shock, followed by bloodcurdling screams; then the train jolted to a sudden stop. I was lying nearest the window and, startled by being shaken from sound slumber to frightened wakefulness, reached instinctively for the shade and pulled it up to see what was happening. Overhead, the sky was crimson and its reflection vaguely illumined the darkness of night; here and there a lantern, carried by a hurrying figure, gave an added flash of light. Men and women were rushing frantically to and fro, shouting to each other; but the shouts were drowned in the screams, which grew louder and louder. My stepfather, having hastily thrust himself into trousers, shoes, and a coat, leaped down from the upper berth and, parting the curtains, spoke to us sternly.

"Don't move, either of you, until I find out what the matter is," he said. "Nothing's happened to this car, that's certain—if we'd been derailed, we would have known it instantly and there's no smell or sign of fire. Pull down that shade, Frances."

We lay still, as we had been told to do, but I did not pull down the shade. The darkness became a glare, the noise and confusion increased. Without knowing the cause of it, the sense of tragedy grew by leaps and bounds. It was probably only a few minutes before my stepfather returned, but it seemed like hours. When he came, he forgot to scold me because I had disobeyed him. His voice was very grave.

"There's been a head-on collision with a train going west," he said. "The engineers and firemen are killed. The coaches were just tinder, anyway—there's nothing left of them. And not much, I'm afraid, of anyone who was in them, for they were the front cars, but fire engines are here now and are doing good work. So are doctors—there were some on the train and some others are on their way. The Pullman passengers are all safe, though there were a few minor injuries."

Of course, this was before the days of vestibule cars and also before standard equipment was of steel. A railroad wreck was regarded as a terrible thing, but not as a phenomenon—in fact, ladies "loosened their corsets," but did not think of undressing when they took to their berths; they were always alerted for accidents. That night, there was a delay of several hours, during which the screams and shouts gradually subsided and the sounds that reached us were mostly made by vehicles rushing to or from the scene of action. Before dawn, the red glow had disappeared and, gradually, the sky grew faintly pink. The train, comprising only the Pullman cars, drawn by a new engine and manned by a fresh engineer and fireman, started on its way again. At breakfast time, the diner, though still slightly disorganized, was open for business. My stepfather took me to it, without waiting for my mother to join us.

"I must get some food into this child," he said imperatively to the steward. "She seems to be faint."

Apparently, it did not occur to him that the faintness might be caused by anything other than hunger.

CHAPTER VIII

In June of 1894, my brother was graduated from Harvard and I experienced the thrill of commencement there for the first time. Shortly afterward, we all "went to the mountains" together, as we put it in those days. No one said which mountains. We meant Moosilauke, which is not one of the Presidential Range, but which, locally at least, ranked with it in prestige, though its name was often corrupted to Moosehillock; and, of course, we meant the White Mountains themselves, which remained uncorrupted, in name as in everything else.

I think it is a real loss that Moosilauke has ceased to be a tourist attraction. In my childhood and, in fact, until I was grown, it boasted a "tip-top house," where everyone customarily spent the night, in order to see both the sunset and the sunrise; and if accommodations were somewhat primitive, by modern standards, the rooms—icy cold even in midsummer—were clean, the food good, and the view superb. We approached the tip-top house by buckboard from Warren, over a rough and rocky road; it was a fascinating experience from beginning to end, and one which everybody we knew in Newbury enjoyed periodically as a matter of course. I do not know why its popularity waned or why the tip-top house and the buckboards ceased to exist; there are plenty of places in the West where such attractions still survive.

A trip to the Presidential Range was a more lengthy and costly undertaking and one on which we did not embark so frequently or so casually. Even so, no one went whizzing through the White Mountains in a day; you went from one highly regarded hotel to another in your own buggy, or in a hired carriage, or by stagecoach, though the latter were on the decline by the time I came along. You stopped first at the Sunset Hill House and then at the Twin Mountain House and then at the Crawford House and then at the Profile House. That was the minimum; if you had time enough and money enough, you went to several more. In all of these places, city friends were spending two or three weeks and you stayed long enough to visit with them. Of course, you experimented to see if Echo Lake really deserved its name, but you were open to easy conviction about the Old Man of the Mountain. You went up Mt. Washington on the cog railway and stoutly maintained that the view from Moosilauke was just as fine. You plodded wearily through the Flume. You bought balsam pillows and maple-sugar candy, though the latter was not *quite* as good as you had at home, and not anywhere nearly as good as the sirup on snow that you had when you went to a sugaring off. A trip like this was still considered an integral part of a child's education by the time my eldest son was eight years old and his father made a point of taking him on one. To be sure, by that time, they went in a motor car of sorts, but it was still an unhurried and comprehensive journey and my husband was conscientious about the sightseeing. I had remained at home with the baby—I usually remained at home with a baby in those days—and on the return of the travelers I eagerly questioned the younger one as to what had impressed him most. He gave his answer after careful and deliberate thought.

"You know that little pond by the Crawford House, with ducks in it?" he inquired.

I said I did.

"Well, that was the prettiest and most interesting thing I saw."

I cannot identify the prettiest and most interesting thing I saw on my first trip to the mountains; but it was certainly not a duck pond. Neither do I think it was the sunrise, as seen from Moosilauke, for sunrises—if you have to rise to see them—have never appealed to me very much, even at a tender age, when children are supposed to enjoy early rising, though since then I have enjoyed a good many, in congenial company, after dances, before I went to bed at all. I do know, however, that I began to have a strong feeling about the majesty of the mountains, and an equally strong feeling that they would never look quite the same to me when James was not there to point out their wonders to me. So it was a great blow to me when, toward the end of the summer, he went abroad to pursue his postgraduate studies, first in Madrid and later in Geneva.

Going to the World's Fair or to the mountains was supposed to be educational in character and both were family affairs. My mother and I also made a good many visits, unaccompanied by anyone else, which did not come within the educational category then, but during which I now know I learned just as much as I did during the course of the others.

Most frequently these visits took us to Concord, Massachusetts, to the home of my mother's friend, Mrs. Daniel Lothrop, the widow of the famous Boston publisher. Writing under the name of Margaret Sidney, she herself had achieved fame as the author of *The Five Little Peppers and How They Grew*[1] and other juveniles; she and her daughter, Margaret, who was just my age, lived at The Wayside, a venerable house with a notable history: it was already nearly a hundred years old at the time of the American Revolution, when it was the home of the muster master of the Concord Minutemen, Samuel Whitney, and his family; and on the very day of the battle at Old North Bridge, it was searched by British soldiers for the stores and ammunition which they suspected to be hidden in a secluded space beside the central chimney. Fortunately for the Whitneys, nothing was found, though this was unquestionably due only to the haste with which the troops were proceeding; and Samuel was able to continue his good work on the Concord Committee of Safety and as a member of the Provincial Congress, disdainful of the danger he was courting by such activities, just as he had been disdainful about the search.

The most celebrated occupants of the house, however, came later: in the spring of 1845 it was bought by Bronson Alcott, the idealistic lecturer and philosopher, who utilized the secret space by the central chimney, where Whitney had concealed stores and ammunition, as a cache for runaway slaves. His daughter Louisa was to earn far more lasting fame, as an author, than her father had achieved as a reformer; and, for seven years, this budding genius and her three sisters lived with their parents at The Hillside, as the six-room cottage had been named—appropriately, as it was situated at the foot of a wooded slope;

[1] My lifelong friend, Mary Hale, now librarian of the Tenney Memorial Library in Newbury—which stands on the site of the once famous Spring Hotel—tells me that *The Five Little Peppers and How They Grew*, generally considered Margaret Sidney's masterpiece, is just as much in demand as it was over sixty years ago.

then it was sold to a writer who had already won wide recognition as the author of *The House of Seven Gables* and *The Scarlet Letter*— namely Nathaniel Hawthorne. He changed its name to The Wayside, which was also appropriate, for it was as close to the road in front as it was to the hill behind it; and its aspect, as well as its designation, underwent a change. It was enlarged and modified in style, first to provide seclusion for Mr. Hawthorne while he worked, a parlor where Mrs. Hawthorne could receive callers, and a spare room where more leisurely visitors could be accommodated; and second, to conform to the current vogue for towers, bay windows, and other excrescences. But despite these architectural alterations, its general atmosphere underwent no change; it was again a center of cultured and harmonious family living; and when eventually the Lothrops bought it from the younger Hawthornes' daughter, Rose—who was also to achieve fame in quite a different direction[2]—this same harmony, this same culture still prevailed.

My first feeling toward Mrs. Lothrop, as I saw her when she came to our house on Beacon Street, was one of awe; she was dressed in the deepest mourning, with a close-fitting bonnet and long black veil, by which a new-made widow was then invariably identified; and these sable draperies were nearly always overwhelming to children. But when I went to visit her and Margaret at The Wayside, where the flowing draperies were not in evidence, I discovered that the essential woman, thus unveiled, was friendly and charming, as well as inspiring. She not only impressed me with her own personality and the character and quality of her work; she made the entire Alcott family, not only the four sisters, in whose bedroom she herself slept, but the impractical father and their long-suffering mother, so real to me that I began to pore over everything that I could read by or about them. To a slightly lesser degree, this was true of the Hawthornes. Margaret and I rambled at will along Nathaniel's "Larch Walk" and had our meals at the dining-room table where he had taken his with his family. Recently, his wife, Sophia, has been immortalized in one of the finest biographies of our times;[3] she and her husband were real to me before I was ten years old. Margaret and I talked about them endlessly as we sat on the platform, reached by a steep flight of steps, which

[2] She and her husband, George Parsons Lathrop, both became Catholics and she was the founder of the Servants of Relief for Incurable Cancer, a Dominican Congregation.
[3] *The Peabody Sisters of Salem* by Louise Hall Thorpe. Little, Brown & Company.

encircled one of the great trees on the hillside behind the house. They were our familiar friends.

The Wayside was not only intriguing in itself; it was an ideal center for side trips to the scenes made memorable by the "embattled farmers." American history, as well as American literature, became very much alive to me. It is not strange that Mrs. Lothrop's talent for interpreting it should have culminated in her foundation of the Children of the American Revolution, a national society of which she remained the guiding spirit until her death. Soon after I went to Washington as a senator's wife, she persuaded me to accept the position of historian general in this organization and I held it for years, resigning only when my own work as a writer precluded me from playing an active part as an officer. But my interest in its work and ideals, kindled by this gifted and generous-hearted woman, has remained alive to this day.[4]

Another place where American literature and American history came alive to me, during my childhood, was "Nipnet," the country house, near Woodstock, Connecticut, of my father's friend, Horace Deming, where he lived with his enormous family whenever he could get away from New York. Some of my father's classmates had bitterly resented my mother's third marriage and had broken with her completely as a result of it. Nothing of the sort had happened in the case of that brilliant lawyer, Horace Deming, and his cultured and tolerant wife. My mother and I were frequent guests, both at their huge apartment in New York, where there was plenty of room for company, and at "Nipnet," which was even more spacious. There were five young Demings, two boys and three girls, some a little older and some a little younger than I, but all more or less my contemporaries. The household also included three nieces, whom the Demings had raised along with their own children; all were encouraged to have as much company as they liked. The dining room could, and very frequently did, hold twenty persons at a time; but the young fry were often consigned for supper to the stillroom—the only one I ever saw in the United States, until, with happy memories of the Demings', I installed one myself in the basement of Beauregard House in New Orleans. My later experiences with them in England, together with the fact that stillroom maids also came into the range of my awed vision, may

---

[4] I am glad to say that Miss Margaret Lothrop still lives at The Wayside and that I am one of the many visitors she makes welcome there, and with whom she shares the historical and literary treasures of the past.

also have had something to do with this installation, but I do not think so. I have never achieved a stillroom maid, and my stillroom does not aspire to the elegance of the English variety in any degree, though it is a very convenient place to prepare canapés for a party, to arrange flowers, to store seldom-used china, and to wash punch cups and highball glasses when these are needed in such quantities that the butler's pantry is swamped with them. I do not know exactly what was kept in the Demings' stillroom; I suppose jams and jellies and fancy biscuits and other delicacies that were saved for great occasions. I doubt if there was any liquor, except, perhaps, a little for medicinal purposes, for the Demings, though they went in for hearty food, were one and all uninterested in strong drink. But I do remember our pleasant suppers there, the custards and blancmanges, the big mugs of milk, the generously spread slices of bread and butter; and, despite the noise we children made, there was a peculiar peacefulness about the room, so noticeable that, for a long time, I assumed it was called still because of its tranquillity![5]

Aside from the stillroom, "Nipnet" was not a source of architectural inspiration; but there were saddle horses for as many persons as chose to ride them, young and old; indeed, I believe it was Horace Deming who first interested my father in riding and to whom, therefore, I owe all those excursions on horseback while I was still in long clothes. There were also buggies and buckboards for those who did not care to ride; but daily outings, connected with horses, were an integral part of a recognized schedule. So were long walks and boating on the nearby ponds and streams; the quiet charming landscape, the pleasant towns and villages of Ashford, Fabian, and the other Woodstocks became familiar to me; so did the local flora and fauna. The young Demings knew everything I did not about wildflowers, birds, and friendly beasts. I sopped up information about these every time I stepped outdoors. But, at that, evening was the best part of the day; the children's hour was not merely a poem by Longfellow; it was the period when Horace Deming gathered us all around him and read

[5] In *Jenny* by Ada Cook Lewis, published by Rinehart & Company, Inc., there are two interesting references to stillrooms:
"I always hated needlework and tinkling on the spinet, but I liked working with Minnie in the stillroom and the linen room." . . . "I had shown Rachel the best way to make soft soap, and a new way to bleach linen, and rearranged the linen room to better advantage, and taken over the stillroom, turning out all sorts of washes and purges and waters." . . . Lady Diana Cooper has a charming description of an old stillroom maid in *The Rainbow Comes and Goes*.

aloud to us—*Robin Hood* by Howard Pyle and the *Jungle Books* by Rudyard Kipling and countless others. He was a very handsome man, handsomer, I now realize, than my stepfather, and a very different type: clean-shaven, prematurely white-haired, with finely chiseled features, erect bearing, and keen eyes that saw everything. He had a mind that could grasp a situation at a glance and deal with it in a minute; and though he looked more like a military man than a scholar, as we generally picture both, his fund of knowledge was prodigious, in an amazing variety of fields. He might easily have been sharp-spoken, but he seldom was, and he had a wonderful reading voice. He early endeared himself to me by telling me that I reminded him of my father and though I know this was only because of my wide shoulders, sturdy build, and inquiring mind, it pleased me very much; most persons said it was a pity I did not look more like my mother and a still greater pity that I did not look like her mother; I realized this was all too true and it was a comfort to know that someone did not appear to think that this mattered very much. There was great mutual devotion between Mrs. Deming and her husband, whom she did not resemble in the least, except in understanding, intelligence, and self-possession. She had a full figure and wore clothes which gave it distinction, when so easily it could have lacked this. Her sense of humor was ready, but she never paraded it; her manner was calm, but never stolid; her bearing dignified, but never forbidding. It was she who mopped up our tears when Robin Hood died and Mowgli left the jungle; but though we went weeping to bed, the next evening we were back panting for more. I think it was largely because of Horace Deming's example that I made it a practice to read aloud every evening to my children, not only stories from the Bible—those they and I owe to my grandmother —but from all the children's classics, or what we then considered as such. My sons and I are greatly indebted to him and it came as no surprise to me when Harold, the eldest of the Deming brood in my generation, was graduated from Harvard *summa cum laude,* as his father had been before him and, also following in his father's footsteps, became a leading legal light in New York.

Despite these numerous diversions and excursions I have outlined, I continued to miss my brother very much, especially in Newbury, though there life went on in very much the same way as it had before. It was at 583 Beacon Street that the real change began.

I do not know for certain whether this was merely coincidental, or whether my brother's gentle and kindly presence had really served as a balance wheel between the two very vital and inflammable personalities embodied in my mother and my stepfather; but I am inclined to think that the latter was the case. At all events, I began to be conscious, shortly after the departure of James, that strain had replaced harmony in the household and that, occasionally, this strain increased to such a degree that quarrels took place. In all fairness to my stepfather, I must say that I never saw him act unreasonably but once: that was when a cab had come to take us to the station on a terribly cold day and the driver had neglected to bring a lap robe. My stepfather angrily ordered him to give us the fur rug which he had wrapped around himself, and which was all he had to protect him from the bitter wind, on his high driver's seat, whereas we were sheltered in the closed body of the cab. "Albert, the poor man will freeze to death!" my mother remonstrated. "A good thing! It will teach him not to be so careless again," my stepfather retorted, angrily and heartlessly. So we drove on to the station with the snowflakes swirling around outside and the driver's fur robe over our knees while I, for one, took very little comfort in it. As a matter of fact, I worried a long time lest what my mother had predicted were true.

There were probably other unreasonable and angry outbursts, but I doubt if they were all my stepfather's fault, though this one unquestioningly was. Neither do I believe, in retrospect, that all other sins of omission and commission were on his side. Indubitably, he was a philanderer; but my mother could no more help flirting than she could help breathing. Probably she was adept at this before she was in her teens; certainly she did not get over her coquettish ways until she was nearly ninety; and though I do not think for a moment that this coquettishness ever took her out of bounds, it certainly could not have put her in a position to criticize her husband's more serious peccadilloes, and he may well have told her so. If she could have given him a child, I think he would have forgiven her almost anything; but a second pregnancy, after the disastrous birth and death of little Elizabeth, resulted in a miscarriage. If it had not and the baby had lived, I think she would have been equally forgiving as far as her husband was concerned and not only on account of another child. She had always found Albert Pillsbury fascinating—in fact, she freely admitted to her friend, Mrs. Ware, that, when she married him, she was more deeply in love with him than she had ever been with either James Underhill or John Wheeler; and he still had a powerful attraction for her. Moreover, by this time, the governorship seemed not only a distant hope but a well-grounded expectation; I cannot conceive anything she would have enjoyed more than the role of First Lady in Massachusetts; and she could have adorned that position. As I said before, she was, at will, the embodiment of charm; she had a flair for beautiful clothes; and she was an accomplished hostess. But she was not without a streak of vengefulness; I once heard her make an especially cutting remark and, afterward, whisper, in an aside, "I have waited twelve years to say that to Cousin So-and-So." It would have given her infinite satisfaction to snub the persons who had snubbed her or who she fancied had done so. Gradually, the vengeful streak betrayed itself chiefly in connection with her husband. He had given her cause for jealousy or, at least, she thought he had. She decided to pay him back, not in his own coin, for she would never have risked going as far as that, but in a coin which had even greater value: she would keep him from becoming governor, though this meant she would not herself be the First Lady of Massachusetts. It was an extreme measure and one which she must have hesitated some time to take. But she finally decided to do so. A man whose wife left him, especially if she attributed a certain cause to her departure, was as good as dead, politically, in those days. She killed Albert E. Pillsbury's chances for advancement to the coveted position, just as surely as she would have killed him physically if she had stuck a knife through his heart.

When she finally took action, she moved very quickly. I was sent to the Count Rumford house to spend Sunday with my grandmother—a very common occurrence. When my mother came to get me, she told me we were going to New York. To visit the Demings, I inquired eagerly, for I was very fond of the Demings. No, we were going to stay at the Murray Hill Hotel this time. When we reached there, I thought that was even more exciting. We had a beautiful suite, even more elegant than the one we had occupied at the Shoreham in Washington. But my cousin Louise was not there to keep me company this time and, after I was put to bed in the large lonely room that led from the elaborate parlor, I was vaguely troubled. I drifted off to uneasy slumber, but I did not sleep long and, when I woke, I felt so unhappy that I decided to go back to the parlor and seek comfort.

I opened the door between the two rooms slowly and cautiously because I did not want to startle my mother by making a noise; but it did not occur to me that I would not find her alone. Instead, she was talking, in an animated way, with a man whom I did not remember ever having seen before and he was talking with her in the same manner. It was some moments before either of them noticed the little girl, standing hesitantly on the threshold, clad only in her nightgown.

When they became conscious of a third presence, they glanced in my direction and came quickly toward me. This gentleman was my uncle Link, my mother explained, putting her arm around me. He was making all the arrangements for us to take a big ship, the *Champagne*. What for, I wanted to know. Because we were going abroad. I was a very lucky little girl. I was going to Europe to stay a whole year. Not many children were fortunate enough to do that. What about Papa? I asked. Was he coming, too? No, he was going to stay in the house on Beacon Street. Without us? Yes, without us. I must not be worried, it was going to work out better that way. My lips were beginning to tremble a little, but I managed to ask how we could spend the summer in Newbury if we were going to be gone a whole year. Why, we would go to Newbury when we came back. We would not return to Beacon Street, but we would return to Newbury. And, meanwhile, we would see James. Had I forgotten that James was in Europe, at the University of Geneva? Well, that was where we were going, to Geneva. . . .

Here, at last, were some crumbs of comfort. If I were surely going back to Newbury, if meanwhile I were going to see my brother, the future did not seem wholly dark. And the next day Mr. Deming came to call and complimented me on the way I pronounced the name of the ship we were going to take. "Why, you speak French already!" he said kindly. "Some, anyway, and you will learn more, very quickly!" I nodded, but the idea of learning more French very quickly was not especially appealing, if I had to do it in Europe instead of at 12 Gloucester Street and at the Count Rumford house. What about my grandmothers? My own grandmother and the kind old lady at Milford, Papa's mother, whom I called grandmother, too? Wouldn't she want us more than ever, now that Grandpa Pillsbury had died? When was I going to see her again? The great hall with the arched ceiling where we had such wonderful family parties, the secret garden where Ruth French and I wove our garlands and whispered to each other assumed new importance to me. And what about Papa, all alone on Beacon Street? Wasn't he going to be very lonely, too? Some of these questions were unvoiced, though they filled my mind; others were never answered, because there was so little time before we were stowed away in the *Champagne*. It was, indeed, a very large ship, but our cabin was minute. "There were two wide shelves, with railings, built against the wall, one above the other, made up like tiny narrow beds; and there was a tall shiny brown cabinet that unfastened in a miraculous way to disclose a washstand. Beside this was a sponge-bag made of string, and over the sponge rack were a carafe and two tumblers with towels twisted in them. Near the door were four hooks, and a small flat stitched bag with scalloped edges."[6]

We went aboard the *Champagne* late in the evening, and all night long other people kept arriving; there was a constant sound of baggage bumping down the corridors, of people talking and laughing, of hearty farewell kisses, of sad sobbing because of impending separation. I felt like crying myself. My mother complained that she had made a mistake in allowing Uncle Link to take charge of her reservations; the cabin was not at all what she wanted. To be sure, she had told him to economize, because she had spent too much money at the Murray Hill Hotel; but she had never supposed he would pinch pennies to this extent. After she had finished criticizing Uncle Link and our quarters, she went to sleep; I have no doubt she was exhausted. During the weekend I had spent at North Woburn, she had managed to empty the Beacon Street house of almost everything in it that belonged to her, and that was a considerable part of its contents. My stepfather had gone away to try a case in some distant city. He had no idea she was leaving him until he came back to a house that was practically empty. His wife had left the andirons in the parlor, because, as she told me afterward, they were the last thing she thought of, and she was too tired to bother with them then. She had also left the round glass bowl which was always filled with fresh roses and stood on the small marble-topped table in one of the parlor windows. I doubt if that were for the same reason.

I continued to worry about my stepfather's loneliness and a great many other persons and other things. I was tired, too, but I could not go to sleep. It was stuffy in the little cabin; besides, the upper berth was hard, and so narrow that there was not room for Carroll and Violet, the favorite dolls with which I always slept, to lie beside me. I was afraid they would fall out and get broken. Then I began to be

[6] The above quotation is taken from *Senator Marlowe's Daughter*, which contains a good deal of autobiography. In fact, ever since the general public decided that *Queen Anne's Lace* was autobiography, which it was not, I have written reams of it undiscovered, except by my family.

afraid of other things, too; I did not know exactly what, just that I was afraid. And I was not naturally a timid child.

At last the ship started to move. I heard someone in the corridor call out, "Come on, let's have a last look at the Statue of Liberty!" I propped Carroll up on the pillow, tucked Violet under my arm, and climbed down the little ladder attached to the upper berth. My mother was still asleep and I did not see any reason why I should wake her up. I could dress without any help, except for a few back buttons, and these would not matter, under my cape. Presently, I was out in the corridor, carried along with the rest of the chattering, laughing, sobbing crowd, headed for the deck to take a last look at the Statue of Liberty.

It was my *first* look and it was a long one. A few persons glanced at me curiously—a plump little girl, all alone, clutching her doll. But most of the crowd simply went on hurrying by. I do not think anyone heard me when I said aloud, addressing Miss Liberty, "I don't know what Mama is going to do. But I'm coming back."

Lightning Over a Calm Sea

Water is my brother
Fire my enemy.
Do not ask me whether
In each, high-handedly
I ignore another
And opposite quality.

As of now, sea is brother
Predictable and dear;
The threatening fiery other
Has lineaments of fear.
And relationship of both to me?
Too near.

MAY WILLIAMS WARD

Part III

"The Rhine is a real river."

CHAPTER IX

The desolate departure from New York, the dismal and dangerous voyage, and the first sordid experiences in France were so harrowing to a little girl that they have remained a vivid memory to this day. My mother was mildly seasick during almost the entire crossing, which was a very rough one, and remained contentedly in her berth, apparently confident that I could look out for myself. I was not in the least seasick after the first day, but I was very bored in the stuffy little cabin; so I ranged about unsupervised and would certainly have been hurled from a storm-swept deck, where one man had already broken his arm and another cracked his skull, if a steward had not caught hold of my short cape and dragged me back to safety just as I shot through the rails. After that near catastrophe, a hitherto indifferent stewardess was galvanized into some sort of action in my behalf. ("Frances almost blew overboard, but a sailor caught her," my mother wrote to my aunt Fannie, as conversationally as she had said in the same letter, "I was up very little; I just kept still and did nothing. Frances was so good all the way over that, when I did appear, lady after lady told me she was the best child on board.") My mother and I were met in Le Havre by an elderly English maid, named Annie, whom my mother had employed when she went to Europe after her previous flight from matrimony, and whom she somehow expected would be as efficient and prepossessing as seventeen years earlier. Alas! this was not the case. Annie was both grumpy and grubby, and when she was dispatched to ask for accommodations at a hotel in Paris, which we reached late at night, the inevitable answer came that none was available. This answer was repeated four or five times, as we went dragging in a shabby fiacre from one street to another. At last it occurred to my mother that the maid's manner and appearance might have something to do with the fact that there was, apparently, no place to sleep in Paris! She tardily got out of the fiacre herself and confronted a night concierge who immediately succumbed to the charm which could be so persuasive when she chose to exert it; a few minutes afterward, she and I were snugly abed under an immense red eider down in a room with dingy wallpaper, the traditional *armoire à glace*, and no adjacent plumbing. Annie slept on the floor. This, not unnaturally, failed to improve her mood.

A trip the next day to the *Nain Bleu*, where we replenished the wardrobes of Carroll and Violet, did much to revive my spirits and convinced me that there might be other places besides Schwartz, on Washington Street in Boston, where dolls could be properly outfitted; but it was not until we reached Geneva, where we found James awaiting us, and where we were promptly installed in a comfortable but unpretentious pension, that my spirits began to rise. ("We were ushered into a great room eighteen by twenty. The floor is hardwood in a pretty pattern and we have three rugs. I will make you a plan of it," my mother wrote to my aunt Fannie. The plan seems to be missing, but I do not need it to describe the room. At the rear of it, twin beds were placed end to end, each with a *table de nuit*, supplied with the inevitable crockery; and beyond my mother's was a fully equipped washstand, supplemented by a tin foot tub and a pitcher. All this was carefully screened off from the rest of the room, which contained a round center table where we often ate; a sofa where my mother often rested; a desk where we both wrote; an *armoire à glace* which must have held all our clothes—though I do not see how it could have!— as there was nowhere else to put them; several armchairs; and a fireplace which supplied all the heat we needed and in front of which I took the tub baths which periodically supplemented those in the "alcove"—the bath tub and the hot water to fill it both being brought in by a long-suffering Swiss servant.)

Annie, the sour English maid, was temporarily installed in a "pleasant room downstairs," but very shortly she was sent back to the Midlands; a comely young Swiss—the niece of our hostesses, the Mlles. Labarthe—was engaged to teach me; and I went every day by tram—at first with Annie and later unsupervised!—to the house where she lived with her parents in the suburb called Servette. There I continued the lessons in French which had so abruptly come to an end when I left Miss Bertha Carroll's School and no longer visited my grandmother at the Woburn parsonage. As a matter of fact, with the enviable ease of the young, I had added considerably to my vocabulary while I was on my own, during the trans-Atlantic trip and the short stay in Paris; and I was soon quite at ease, as far as language was concerned, in Geneva. But it was not until summer came and we went by *diligence* —for no trains penetrated there—to Chesières, high in the Alps, that I fully recovered from my sense of strangeness and bewilderment, that I began to enjoy new sights and new acquaintances, and to eat, without protest, forms of food which, at first, had been not only unfamiliar but distasteful.

Having said this much, I think it is only fair to say that, less than two decades later, I began to realize that this year I had spent in Europe, beginning shortly before I was ten and ending shortly before I was eleven, was probably the most valuable one of my entire education; and now that many decades have slipped by, this is still my considered opinion; I am always sorry when I hear parents say they will not take their children to Europe "because they would be too young to appreciate it and would not remember what they saw and did." I am very sure that my appreciation of good pictures and good music dates from that year, since, before it was over, I had been in a good many famous galleries and had heard several very fine operas, besides any number of good concerts and lilting incidental songs. Also, before the year was over, I spoke, read, and wrote French with the same facility that I did English and had made considerable progress in German as well. This achievement was invaluable to me when I began to study Latin, two years later than the other girls in the class at the Boston school into which I had suddenly been thrust. By April, I was reading Caesar with the others, having meanwhile swallowed the basic grammar hook, bait, and sinker without the slightest trouble; and by the next fall, I was reading Virgil with the same ease. Greek, which I studied while still in school, on my own initiative—for that was not required—was a source of real delight; and with this much of a background, Spanish presented no serious problem when my work as a writer began to take me into Spain and Latin America. Now, late in life, I am attacking Italian with the same confidence and enthusiasm, because future professional commitments indicate the desirability of a greater familiarity with this than the few words and phrases which constitute a tourist's stock in trade. I have seen too many writers who were dependent on an interpreter, when I was not, gullibly accepting the slant he wished to give their material, to risk the misleading impressions and statements which are all too often the result of such misplaced confidence. I will not write about any place or any people where I am dependent on an intermediary for my information; and I have been thankful, over and over again, that I have not had to sit silent, puzzled and embarrassed at some social function where no one but myself spoke English—as I have seen dozens of my compatriots do. Quite aside from these practical considerations, acquaintance with any given language enhances the appreciation of the fluency in any other; and the time to begin learning tongues that are not one's own, if this is to be done quickly and painlessly, if not actually by osmosis, is in childhood. Just as the muscles are suppler then, so, apparently, are certain mental processes. For this reason, if for no other, I would be thankful for that year spent in Europe so early in my life.

But what is true of languages is also true of geography. When, after a spring and early summer in Switzerland, my mother, my brother, and I went in the late summer to Belgium, Holland, and Germany, I turned to my elders in surprise with the remark, "Why, the Rhine is a real river!" Somehow, before that, I had not vividly associated a blue line on a map as representing actual water any more than I had associated a red line as an actual boundary between two countries. From that time on, not only the places to which I really went but the maps which represented others took on a new meaning. They have never lost it. With the same sense of enchantment that I can read a book, I can study a map; and I have a collection of old ones—including a folio of Blaev's, one of the great seventeenth-century cartographers—that is among my most prized possessions.

Such tastes, and this means of gratifying them, both directly and indirectly, I have been able to pass on to my sons, as I have my familiarity with Biblical scenes and stories; and in their generation richer and riper fruit than I could ever have foreseen has been duly borne. Two of the three—one a lawyer, the other the headmaster of a large preparatory school—have become lay readers in the Episcopal Church, as supplementary occupations. The third, in the course of his naval training, was asked by his classmates how or when he found time to study so much geography, considering the other pressing demands of the course he was taking. "I don't have to study it," he responded briefly. "I know where all those places are. I've been to most of them with my mother and the others we've found together on maps." I doubt if he would have been able to say this if I had not discovered, at an early age, not only that the Rhine is a real river but many corresponding geographical wonders, for which my appetite was then whetted.

There is still another reason why I am thankful for that particular year and perhaps this is quite as important: I have mentioned a famous toyshop—the *Nain Bleu* in Paris—as the medium for convincing me that though perhaps it was no better than the toyshop in Boston to which I was so attached, it was certainly just as good. The same sort of simile could be applied in many different directions. It is natural for a privileged child to feel that the setting and the way of life with which he is familiar is the best in the world, whether this happens to be London or Lisbon, Persia or Paraguay, or any locality in our own country. It is probably a blessing if this feeling continues through adult life, since it makes for a kind of contentment that can come only with a personal sense of belonging to a certain region, quite aside from the more impersonal, but equally strong, feeling of national patriotism. Certainly, in my case, I am never going to feel that any other cities have all that Boston and Washington can offer me, or that any countryside is as beautiful as the upper Connecticut Valley and the corresponding parts of Virginia. But when such a feeling results in the conviction that it is *only* on one's native or familiar heath that there are fine people, lovely sights, and a well-ordered and pleasant way of living, the consequences are disastrous; they breed intolerance, misunderstanding, and often downright antagonism. The sooner one learns that a lady is always a lady, the better; for this is true whether she is a Chinese or a Chilean, a New Englander or a New Orleanian. Madrid is a stately city and so is Manila. The rosy color to which we generally refer as the "Alpine glow" is just as bright on the White Mountains and on the Andean Range. I could carry on such comparisons indefinitely; and I consider that it was a great advantage for me to learn, at an early age, how sound and logical they are.

So much for the "appreciation" of what I saw and did during that first year I spent in Europe and the results of that appreciation. As to remembering what I saw and did, I must give my mother credit for making this easy, through her chosen way of sightseeing. It was her habit to travel fairly rapidly—as speed was reckoned in those days—for a month and then to remain for a month or more in one and the same place, resting physically and digesting mentally everything she had seen and done in the meantime. Our first month in Geneva was followed by a month going hither and yon in Switzerland; our month at the quiet mountain retreat of Chesières by the aforementioned trip through Belgium, Holland, and Germany and that by a month in Fontainebleau. There we visited a friend of my mother's who lived in a charming old house, once a *dépendance* of Madame de Pompadour. Then came a month in Italy before we settled down for the winter in Geneva and a month in Paris before we started home. Of course now, with swifter transportation, such a schedule of sightseeing could be considerably accelerated; nevertheless, I feel that most Americans travel too fast to retain any definite memory of their experiences, and that it is speed rather than any given age which is responsible for their confusion and forgetfulness. No trip abroad is too short to be worth-while; but if there is only a week—for instance—to spare, I believe it is much better to spend it all in one place and that two or three weeks should be similarly divided. A month in Spain—or Italy or France or England, for that matter—during which the traveler has concentrated on the sights most congenial to him, whether these be mountains and lakes or picture galleries and cathedrals, will give him "roses in December," just as such sights have given me; but the traveler who comes home to report boastfully that he has "seen" six countries in four weeks will probably not be able to tell much about them afterward, much less to cherish memories of them in his advancing years. I have actually met persons on their westbound voyage who could not describe with any accuracy where they had been!

But, after sixty-odd years, I shall have to pick and choose among the many sights and impressions and experiences indelibly instilled in my mind when I was ten years old. (If I listed them all, the number would be overpowering.) The little dogs at Le Havre who, to my surprise, were all addressed in French and seemed to understand it. . . . The shops on the Coraterie and the studio of the famous photographer Boissonais, whose rococo background for the picture he took of me was so absurd that I have kept this likeness hidden, but whose interpretation of the "Acropolis After the Rain" is still one of my choicest treasures. . . . The shop in Interlaken where nothing but beautiful ivory figurines, too expensive for me to buy, were sold, and the other shop, close by, where cuckoo clocks and wooden bears were for sale at prices I could afford. . . . The new dolls, in peasant costume, from Switzerland and Italy both, which became companions of Carroll and Violet, but never supplanted them in my affections. . . . The *meringues glacées*, which represented the rarest and most exciting item on the rather drab menus at the Pension Labarthe. . . . The introduction to and immediate enthusiasm for burr artichokes and *miel de table Suisse*, which was not really honey at all, despite its name. . . . The Thanksgiving turkey "with all the fixin's" in a private dining room at the Café du Nord, which my mother and a new-found friend of hers, Mrs. Haskell Warren, managed to secure for the benefit and to the delight of their two children and two others—Swinburne and Virginia Hale, who were in boarding school near Geneva and whose parents were in Rome. (Their father, a professor at the University of Chicago, abroad on his sabbatical year, had been a classmate and great friend of my father's.) . . . The steaming Swiss chocolate, available everywhere, a drink that soon made up for the detested boiled milk; and the chocolate bars, eaten with pears, while traveling, because the Swiss governess said this was the ideal fare on trains—you ate the chocolate because you were hungry and the pears because you were thirsty. . . .

The white statues in the Campo Santo of Genoa, representing departed gentlemen in frock coats and sainted ladies in bonnets and bustles, all pointing heavenward. . . . The marble tubs—one to a floor—the size and shape of sarcophagi, swathed in sheets, and representing such a treat in the hotels where I scrupulously bathed most of the time out of a basin in our room, from head to foot, and the puzzlement as to how to dry myself if I put on the chemise which was supplied, along with the sheets, and without which I was not supposed to be so immodest as to immerse myself. . . . The smoke pouring out of Vesuvius, making a volcano real in the same way that the Rhine had given reality to a river. . . . The Murillo Madonna in the Pitti Palace which so moved me that I spent all my allowance on a photograph of it. (I found years afterward, from one of his letters, that it had been one of my father's favorite pictures.) . . . The shadowy garden behind Madame de Pompadour's little *dépendance* in Fontainebleau, where the cool water trickled gently over the cherubic figure in the moss-grown fountain and into the overflowing pool below. . . . The full moon shining above the Venetian Church of Santa Maria della Salute the first night we glided down the Grand Canal in a gondola. . . .

The baptism of a baby in a side chapel of St. Peter's at Rome, into which, though total strangers, we were cordially beckoned both by the officiating priest and the smiling family. . . . The unexpected appearance on the stage of the Geneva Opera House, during a performance of *William Tell*, of the horse, by name Souvenir, assigned to me at riding school, and the joyous enthusiasm which caused me to jump up and down, shouting irrepressibly, "Bravo, Souvenir, bravo!" . . . The state visit of the King of the Belgians to the President of France, during the course of which I stood by the roadside in the palace garden at Fontainebleau, with a doll in one hand and a small flag in the other, waving both as the chiefs of state went by and, in return, receiving a smiling salute as they exclaimed, "*Tiens! Une petite Américaine!*" . . . The dance on my tenth birthday at the Pension de Chamossaire in Chesières for which, as a special concession, I was allowed to sit up, and the Balkan prince, allegedly incognito during his vacation, who invited me to open the ball with him. . . . The kindly bearded man who was placed next to me at the long table d'hôte in the same hotel, who asked if I were English and when I said, no, American, replied, "I have never known but one American. He was a classmate of mine at the University of Bonn and we all thought very highly of him. I wonder if you have ever heard of him? His name was John Wheeler." . . . The baby that screamed and screamed on the boat going up the Rhine, to the annoyance of its fellow passengers and the distress of its young parents, who finally supplemented its bottle with a liberal potion of beer—after which it promptly hushed. . . . The attendants who waited, sponge in hand, when the train stopped at the major stations, and ushered me into the rest rooms, of which there were none in the compartment cars—when I felt I would die if I had to wait another minute. . . . The guide going over the *Mer de Glace* who drank out of his hat and invited me to do the same. . . . The lady at the hotel in Chamonix who said she could never go to sleep without a handkerchief under her pillow and who, by the power of suggestion, imposed the same disability on me. . . . The funny little wooden-shoed children in Marken and the tiny scrubbed houses where they lived. . . . The heavy man who stepped on my foot just as I was leaving the wharf to go around the lake at Zurich and who was responsible for my angry outcry that I had been around too many lakes and didn't intend to go around any more. . . . The three American children al-

ready mentioned—Haskell Warren and Swinburne and Virginia Hale.
. . . The little English girl who was my best friend at Mlle. Dardelle's
School in Geneva, where we both went, the winter of '95 and '96, and
with whom I never spoke a word except in French. . . . The little
German girl who, with her parents, occupied the big room next to
my mother's and mine, and who was switched on the slightest provo-
cation or none at all. I had been spanked a few times, to be sure, but
that was different and I still wince at the thought of the child's pitiful
cries, not unlike those of a whipped puppy, which ceased only when
she came down with scarlet fever and was mercifully removed to a
hospital where her parents were not allowed to see her, to the great
relief of all those who had tried, in vain, to deal with this sadistic
situation. . . . The little Russian boy, who, with his titled father and
elder sister, was also among my fellow guests at the Pension Labarthe,
who was my playmate in a more exciting way than the boys I had
known in Newbury, and who was responsible for my first attendance
at a Russian church where the lavish beauty of ritual was brought
home to me. . . . The American and English tourists both singing
the same air, with different words, at the end of a concert at Lucerne—
one group caroling "My Country 'Tis of Thee" and the other, "God
Save the Queen". . . . The brief but poignant appearance of the great
Pope, Leo XIII, on the balcony of the Vatican and the reverent though
vociferous response by the multitude below.

A medley, yes. But not one that I would wish to do without. And
these memories, too, have served as the foundation for many new
experiences. It so happened that nearly thirty years elapsed between
my first visit to Rome and my second, though I had been elsewhere
in Europe during this interval. Shortly after my arrival in the Eternal
City, I started for St. Peter's with a friend who had never been in Italy
before and, at the entrance to the Basilica, we were confronted by one
of those soiled and persistent guides who importune strangers to accept their services—for a consideration. "Thanks, we don't need you,"
I said in French. (I have found, over and over again, in Italy, that it
is a good plan to speak French rather than English in the face of importunities; it startles the pests by its unexpectedness and puts them
off.) "But we need to have *someone!*" my friend objected. "You have
me," I said. "Listen—if I make a mistake, we'll go back and get the
guide. But I think I remember most of the things you'll want to see—
the *Pietà* by Michelangelo is just inside the door at the right. The
holy-water basins are on either side of the nave, near the entrance.

They're huge, they're made of blue porcelain, they're upheld by cherubs. The statue of St. Peter, whose feet people kiss, is further up, also in the center nave." And so on and so on. Rather skeptically, my friend allowed me to lead her in, otherwise unaccompanied. But, as it turned out, I had not made a single mistake.

After my return from my latest trip to Europe, I went through the photographs which I had chosen, quite unaided by adult advice, and purchased out of my modest allowance in the course of my first trip. My mother had caused these to be neatly mounted and encased in three sturdy bound folios, which are still intact. The photographs—over a hundred of them in all—are unfaded. On some the dates when they were bought have been carefully noted, but, even without these dates, it would be easy enough to follow the sequence of our wanderings and our sightseeing through these photographs. This was not particularly surprising to me. What did surprise me, briefly, was the realization that, if I had been traveling through the same countries and visiting the same galleries now and wanted a pictorial record of them, I would have chosen almost the same photographs that I did more than sixty years ago.

Recently, I have read two delightful books, passages in which confirm my conviction that my case is by no means exceptional. One of these books is *Day Before Yesterday*[1] by Mrs. Theodore Roosevelt, Jr. She was six years old, she tells us, when she first spent a winter in Rome and went to the great galleries with her mother; returning many years later, she knew her way around all of them. The other book is *The Happy Profession*[2] by Ellery Sedgwick. In this he says, "Across more than sixty years I see a face like none other. I was a child in Rome. My parents promised to take me with them to their audience with Leo XIII, the Supreme Pope of modern times. . . . Clearly as I saw him then, I see him now: that erect and stately figure dressed in purest white, the only color the immense violet stone on the middle finger. His face cut like a cameo under a skin of palest parchment, seemed to shine from within. In my childish mind there rose the picture of an alabaster lamp diffusing its shaded light, for by curious illusion the classical features seemed translucent. Such a link between earth and heaven I had not seen."

Ten too young to remember and appreciate? No one will ever make me think so!

[1] Published by Doubleday & Company, Inc.
[2] Published by Little, Brown & Company.

CHAPTER X

Nearly everyone in my family, on both sides, was a great letter writer and—fortunately for me!—a great letter saver. My mother wrote at length to my grandmother and to my aunt Fannie all the time we were abroad, and these letters were carefully preserved, along with those I wrote myself to the same persons and to my cousin Avis, who was just my age. With the help of this correspondence, extracted from a battered trunk in the attic of my house at the Oxbow, where it has lain untouched but secure for more than half a century, I have been able to supplement my own memories of that first trip to Europe.

Many sections of my mother's letters deal exclusively with sight-seeing, and while she and I obviously enjoyed what we saw and did, much of it was what any tourist sees and does. Occasionally, however, it is evident that she was "putting on side" as when some Boston friends came to spend the day with her in Fontainebleau, and she met them at the railroad station with a smart tandem and a postilion dressed in red and gold! Occasionally, too, there is a note of high adventure, as when she tried "the Empress Eugénie's saddle on a mule," preparatory to crossing the *Mer de Glace* from Chamonix; but she was "not comfortable" and changed to a chair, in which she was carried by four porters. Then, according to her, "they said I looked comfortable and I was." Bodily ease meant a great deal to her and she appreciated it, not only in the course of such expeditions as this but in her daily life throughout our stay in Switzerland. "We have yet to go to a poor hotel. The landlord is a host in all senses of the word. We pay from a dollar to three a day, according to the style.[1] In Lucerne we went to the finest there. The host was a handsome man, and though he had a thousand guests to identify, he called me by name when I left: 'Goodbye, Mrs. Pillsbury.'"

Besides the habitual enjoyment of comfort at bargain prices and the rare deeds of daring, like crossing the *Mer de Glace* in a hand-borne chair, there is one account of an experience permeated with bucolic charm. "I heard on Saturday that the midsummer fete of the shepherds was to take place the next day at Lake Chavonnes and I wanted to see it for myself. This lake is three hours higher in the

---

[1] This price, which included everything, is less than I paid for drinks for myself and my three companions during my latest trip abroad, though we drink very moderately!

mountains than we are here, making seven hours above the railroad and I knew I could not walk. So I interviewed the head porter here [the hotel at Chesières] and he did not think the road was good enough for a wagon. But James had been up the Chamossaire and had reported a fourth-class road, so I said if the means could be procured I would go. The next morning at seven I heard some others starting, so that they would not have to walk in the heat of the day— the services were to begin at twelve. At nine Frances and I were ready and so was the cart, all neat and clean from a recent washing inside and out; it was provided with only one seat and no springs, but with brakes and chains. We had a sturdy little horse whose name we soon found to be Fritz, a driver, and a guide. We took our lunch and theirs. They had red wine in a little cask from which most of the wine leaked out after their first drink because the cork was not pushed in tight enough. They politely offered Frances and me some (they drank from the bunghole), but I declined and Frances took it and smelled it, which was enough for her. The men walked and Frances and I had the springless cart to ourselves. Up, up we went, the men gathering wild strawberries and flowers for Frances on the way. Before we had gone very far, the men found out I could drive, so I drove the rest of the way. When we came to a very steep place, Fritz would gather himself together and tear upwards. By and by we reached our destination and I thought with relief how much easier it would be to come down. Just as Fritz was unharnessed, James and his friend appeared, and we sat down at a rough table to eat our lunch. We had already passed a rustic pulpit made of wood and decorated with mountain flowers, and a multitude of people, mostly shepherds and their families, were foregathered. We were up as high as the top of Mt. Washington then and had passed two smaller lakes before reaching the largest one. We had just finished lunch when the services began and I sat down in the shade of some fir trees near the pulpit. In a few minutes I found I was in the choir, so I sang the familiar tunes with French words. The Minister was a tall slender man who had stayed at our hotel the night before, and his sermon was about the Most Tender of Shepherds and how He took care of His sheep. It was beautiful and the tall mountains and the quiet lake and the attentive audience all made me think it must have been very much the same eighteen hundred years ago when Our Lord preached His wonderful sermons here on earth."

On the whole, my mother writes more about places than people, and apparently enjoys them more; in fact, she states at one point, "We have so many acquaintances here [Geneva] now that I could be entertained all the time, but I prefer to live quietly." (We must take her word for this, but it is certainly uncharacteristic.) By and large she seems to find her fellow expatriots uncongenial, but there are some exceptions, and she speaks enthusiastically about the Thanksgiving and the Christmas celebrations, which gave her an opportunity of making the holidays enjoyable for Swinburne and Virginia Hale—an undertaking on which she had resolved, out of sentiment, because, when my father died, theirs had written her the letter which she "prized most." She now records, "Only when I asked the Blessing we all choked and thought of home and I knew you were all thinking of us. But we had a great deal to be thankful for and each of us, in a small party of six, had someone with us that absolutely belonged to us. Swinburne Hale and Haskell Warren walked in from Château Lanay, where they are at boarding school, 'so as to have a good appetite for dinner.' Frances and I went to church and shortly afterward Virginia arrived. Our dinner was very good and cosy. We hired a street band which came up on the balcony outside our window and played for us. The boys cheered the turkey and they cheered the cranberry sauce and they cheered the raw celery and then when there was nothing else left, they cheered Frances and me for making the dinner a possibility. I do not believe the Café du Nord ever had a more innocent hilarious party and the children enjoyed it so much."

It is obvious that she was pleased with all this, and also that she was impressed with the German scholars and their families whom she went to Bonn on purpose to see: "Bonn is a far handsomer place than I expected and we are in the best hotel of all since we came over here. After breakfast we had a special carriage from the hotel, emblazoned with the royal arms and coronet, and the coachman wore a cockade. We first called on Professor Bucheler and also saw his wife and daughter and the daughter's bridegroom. They all knew John and we had a perfectly charming call. We saw John's photograph in their album, and when we came away Professor Bucheler gave me his arm to the carriage and they all kissed Frances very affectionately and tenderly. Then we called on Professor Usener and he was equally glad to see us. He said he had never seen a little American girl before. Both the professors were anxious to know of John's writings, as they said he was engaged in a great work, something worth much to them. I never could find anything, you know, and I, too, wonder where they can be.[2] Professor Usener kissed Frances, too, and we could see that they were all very much pleased that we came to see them."

My brother had been with us intermittently through the summer, joining us wherever we happened to be, between the walking trips he took with Swiss friends, and for our journey to the Low Countries and up the Rhine. But as early as May, my mother had written, "James thinks of returning in October. It is probably best for him, but it will be pretty sorrowful for us." As early as July, the date had been set forward to September, as the time seemed to have come for him to put an end to his wanderings. He went briefly to Newbury, but New England, especially rural New England, had lost its charm for him, and he was longing to get started on engineering in the West. Evidently there were conflicting opinions as to whether or not he should do this, but a letter, written in November, reveals that "James went to Denver, growling a good deal, and landed right on his feet. Isabel wrote that it would be of no use for him to come, as her father had no good places left, and his own nephew had a very inferior one with very hard work.[3] But James had some splendid letters from his professors at Harvard and some other men of influence, and on he went. Then he decided, while waiting for something to turn up, that he would go to see a friend at a mine forty miles north of Denver. The Superintendent employed him immediately and says that with his training he ought to know the whole workings of the mines within a year. It is the chance of a lifetime."

The parting from my brother, to whom I was devoted and whom I did not see again for more than two years, represented a very great wrench. But I was too busy and too interested in what we were doing to grieve for long. Evidently I took everything we did and saw quite seriously, for I find that my mother nicknamed me "little Miss Baedeker," and now that I am reminded of it, I do recall sitting and poring over the little red guidebooks which were the traveler's bibles in those days. On the whole, my mother was apparently pleased with my general progress. "Frances has grown taller and slighter," she wrote from Fontainebleau. "Within the next six months, if she keeps on, she will speak French as well as she does English. She dreams and thinks in French now and uses it more correctly than I do. She points out my

[2] I have found these writings still in script; their subject matter is based on Greek classical plays.

[3] This reference is to my mother's cousin, Isabel Hill, whose father, Nathaniel Hill, had been United States Senator from Colorado and was a great power in the state.

mistakes continually, a habit not to be cultivated." I can understand her irritation. She herself had been to a French school in New York and, though she either had not learned—or had forgotten—how to speak grammatically, she did speak very fluently and she understood perfectly; to be "continually" corrected by a ten-year-old must have been very irksome. However, her annoyance was soon swallowed up in satisfaction. "Frances is well at work," she writes two months later from Geneva. "If she does not know French very well by April, I shall be surprised. She goes to a French school, where she is studying Bible History, Roman History, Geography, Poetry, Grammar, Spelling, Diction, Reading—all in French. She sings in French and has a French drawing teacher and a French sewing teacher. She also studies German, translating it into French instead of English." With this schedule, it is no wonder her astonishment took a gratifying form, though she slides over the sad fact that, as I never could carry a tune in my life, I fear I sang no better in French than in any other language. "I am surprised and more than pleased at Frances' progress in French and German. She never speaks English now except to me," she writes early in the New Year with maternal pride. This achievement on my part prompted her to take a significant step. "I have asked a German governess to go home with us," she writes. "It is the Mademoiselle Riensberg of whom I have already told you. She wishes to consider the matter a little further. She is taking a course at the University here. She has already been one year in America with the Roosevelts in New York and five years in England with the Pomeroys. She would teach German, French, drawing and music. Before I write again it will probably be all settled and our passage engaged." The next letter confirms this expectation. "Mademoiselle Riensberg has decided to return with us. She will stay as long as we are both satisfied. She has an Oxford diploma and understands French as well as German. She can paint in both oils and water. Frances will have her lessons, as she does now, in French and German instead of English."

(When I found the letters which had lain safe but untouched for more than fifty years in that attic trunk, I was intrigued by the reference to Mademoiselle Riensberg's previous charges; and as Mrs. Franklin D. Roosevelt and I are about of an age, I wrote and asked her if by any chance she and I had had the same governess. Her answer came promptly. "I remember Mademoiselle Riensberg very well. She was not my governess but Franklin's. Later, when he went to Groton, he used to imitate her pronunciation of Schenectady, to the great amusement of his schoolmates." After Mademoiselle Riensberg left us in Newbury, she became the governess of Gladys Vanderbilt, whom I was to know later on—and greatly admire—as the Countess Szechenyi when her husband became Austrian Minister to the United States. I certainly have reason to be proud of my fellow pupils!)

My mother's satisfaction with me was not confined to my scholastic progress. She was also very proud of my dancing and my horsemanship—mistakenly in regard to the former, since, though I was better at that than at singing, I was not a really good dancer until I was nearly thirty! However, in the early fall of '95, she wrote, "Frances dances so well now that she has no lack of partners. She danced the quadrille with a Greek professor the last night we were at Chesières." (Ungratefully, I have forgotten the Greek professor, while remembering the Balkan prince who singled me out on my birthday.) Later, when we were settled in Geneva for the winter, after she had finished singing the praises of Mademoiselle Dardelles' Day School, where the course of instruction was so appallingly thorough, my mother continues, "Frances also goes to a French dancing school. She does not like her dancing master, but if he teaches her to make his perfect curtsey, I shall be more than glad. Frances woke me up the other night, because I was saying in my sleep, 'One-two-three-four-five-six—now again *plie*, *saute*, etc.'—a dancing lesson all over again! Miss Carroll's was nothing compared to this."

(It certainly was not. Miss Carroll did not carry, as this man did, a light cane with which to rap her pupils' offending limbs when these did not move to suit her. Whether he really injured me, or merely annoyed me, I do not know; but after dancing lessons had been going on for a little while, my mother wrote, "Frances hurt her knee last Wednesday in dancing school, so she has been keeping quiet since." I notice she does not say how my knee got hurt, but I have not forgotten; though I think the injury was really slight, except to my pride, and that if I kept quiet temporarily, it must have been through pique and not necessity.)

"Best and last, Frances goes to a French riding school and rides a dear little horse named Souvenir," my mother continues and, about this school, I am able to share her enthusiasm. "For the past two lessons she has been in the ring with four young men and the teacher. Her seat is perfect. She knows the English trot and also gallops wildly round and round and jumps beautifully. She is not in the least afraid, but quiet and self-possessed. Friday the man in front of her tumbled off his horse, and she quietly reined in and waited for him to pick himself up." All this was apparently in the ring—the manège—but I was progressing. "Last Monday she went out alone with her tutor, then Friday she went out with an escort of eight men and nine horses. She will have a *sortie* on all the pleasant days of her lessons, until she leaves Geneva." It sounds exciting, even now—particularly the reference to a ninth horse, which, so far as any explanation is concerned, could have been riderless!

Shopping occupied much of my mother's time and thought. Clothes were her main interest—the ones we merely saw, and the ones my mother joyfully bought for herself and me; and, as this was an activity which made very little impression on me, I am glad I can review the current fashions through her eyes—the only clear memory I have of the '95–'96 styles is of the enormous sleeves then in vogue! Not so my mother. Her first letter from Paris records that "hats are tremendous. Flowers as big as my fists and so many of them, with changeable bows to match or not to match. The bonnets are small and just like those at home." A letter written soon after our arrival in Switzerland observes, "Little girls are wearing large collars, as large as the yoke of a dress, with narrow embroidery. They look very fresh and pretty." She went on several shopping expeditions from Fontainebleau to Paris and tells my aunt, "I bought Frances some shoes and stockings and the shoes have heels, her first ones. There were none in Paris without them. The girls her age wear their dresses gored and we saw at Felix's a whole wardrobe going to New York for a girl of fourteen, so simple, yet so elegant. Felix made my mother's dresses." (Her mother, of course, was the incomparable Delia Maria. Evidently *my* mother thought of her often in those days, for, in the first letter written in Geneva, she says, "I found the Hotel Metropole where my mother lived so long and the shop where she bought so much beautiful jewelry.")

My first riding habit is described at length. "It is dark purple blue, trousers that button with straps under her shoes, a long skirt fitting the saddle in every part, a dear little jacket with pleats down the front and back, and under one of the pleats in front a pocket which shows a little bit of white handkerchief, above which she wears a spray of white jasmine. The jacket has a belt which also goes under the pleats and fastens with two buttons in front. With this habit she wears plain linen collars and cuffs, a little jockey cap and doeskin riding gloves.

"Frances has on her new Paris dress today for the first time," my mother writes shortly before Christmas. "It is brown, red, green and white, mixed coarse goods, and is trimmed with light brown velvet. She has on new patent leather boots with cloth tops and looks very girlish and pretty. The skirt of her dress is gored and made full in the back." (Evidently, we had caught up with the French fashions as revealed to us while in Fontainebleau!) "Her Paris hat is larger in front than a sailor hat and is trimmed with blue satin ribbon made in a bow on the side, after going around the brim, and has three quill feathers, blue and brown in each, quills pointing back, feathers coming forward. I have a new navy cloth cape that comes down to my hips, lined with gray and white fur. It has a chinchilla collar and is very comfortable and pretty." . . . "I have ordered some more dresses for Frances and myself and our underclothes are also being made."

Not content with having thus supplied herself and her daughter, my mother now persuaded my prospective governess to get a new outfit. "Mademoiselle Riensberg is having four new dresses made, also one for next winter, besides a wrapper and bed jacket." After all this, it comes as no surprise to learn that even the dolls were not overlooked. At Christmastime, the milliner had made a black velvet hat for Carroll and a blue velvet hat for Violet; now the dressmaker contributes "lovely pieces of material—all sorts of pretty chiffons and silks." These hats and these materials, the latter carefully made into dresses, still survive, which is more than can be said for any of my first European clothes and my mother's bought at the same time.

With the completion of all these wardrobes, my mother began packing well in advance of the date on which we were to sail for home and it would appear just as well that she took this precaution, for she says, "Three trunks and a big box started for Le Havre by slow freight on Friday and will not have to be examined until they are safely in New York. We take four with us to Paris, and bags and shawl straps without number." The time was drawing near for our departure from Geneva and, though I was looking forward to seeing my friends at home, I had become genuinely attached to my new playmates, both American and European, and did not face parting from them without a pang. Evidently Serge, the little Russian count, already a much better linguist than I could ever hope to be, was the one upon whom I myself had made the deepest impression or, at any rate, the one whose affection revealed itself in the most lavish forms. According to my mother, he waited for me in the salon every night after dinner and remained with me until I was dragged off to bed; she speaks over

and over again of the presents he gave me and states that, when the
time came to say good-by, "he dissolved in tears." According to her,
the young riding master was also "utterly miserable." . . . "Frances
and he had a long farewell ride together Sunday and then I packed
her habit up," she says, rather suggesting that it was high time. I am
a little skeptical about so much grief as far as the riding master was
concerned, and I am sure the dancing master—whom she does not
mention again—was as glad to be rid of me as I was to be rid of him.
The little boy's sorrow may have been genuine. Mine was at parting
from him, though no doubt this was somewhat assuaged by the fact
that I was "loaded down with presents the last few days, books, pictures, chocolate, toys." My mother and I had a royal send-off, both
at the pension and at the Geneva railroad station, and a "comfortable
compartment," which Mrs. Warren and Haskell shared with us, on the
train to Paris. They were also our fellow passengers on the westbound
voyage of the *Gascogne,* so we had a "very social time." To her further
satisfaction, my mother records that the children—this time referring
to Haskell and myself—"are very fond of each other and get on fa-
mously." I am inclined to believe this was true for, when our coachman's wife had a boy baby, shortly after our return to Newbury, I
insisted that he should be named Haskell. But, for some reason, my
mother or Mrs. Warren either did not care to continue their acquaintance or else they merely drifted apart, as persons who meet abroad
are so apt to do. At all events, we never saw the Warrens again; and,
aside from that statement about the sociability of the voyage, I have
no written record of it and no recollection of it—rather strangely, because the memory of the eastbound voyage is still so vivid, not to
mention the many other memories of the year when I learned that the
Rhine was a real river—and much besides!

God loves New England, I am sure of it——
I feel His love in all its loveliness,
As tho His hand had lingered to caress
The beauty He had fashioned, bit by bit. . . .

And He must love the villages, the neat
White cottages with hollyhocks about,
The slender spires where the bells ring out
Above the elms that shade the quiet street.

And, I am sure God listens when a bell
From such a spire rings out upon the air
To summon all the villagers to prayer—
Ah, yes, I think God loves New England well! . . .

ROSELLE MERCIER MONTGOMERY

Part IV

"In Vermont there is still space. . . ."

ELIZABETH KENT GAY

CHAPTER XI

An invitation to visit the hospitable Demings, immediately after landing, had reached us before we left Geneva; so we went straight from
New York to "Nipnet," near South Woodstock, Connecticut, and
found there not only all remembered pleasures but several new ones:
I could ride horseback with the others now, I could go for a row on
the lake accompanied by Harold, two years my senior, I could join
the drawing lessons which all the young Demings were taking with
Mrs. Rockwell.[1]

From "Nipnet," we went to Boston, where we stayed with our old
friends, the Wares. That fine old gentleman and eminent lawyer, Darwin E. Ware, had died while my mother and I were abroad, leaving a
void in the household which no one else could fill. But Richard, the
only son of the family, had now been graduated from Harvard and
had begun the practice of law himself; he was very polite to me and
had ceased—or so I imagined—to be "condescending." Evidently I regarded this as another mark of progress, like the rowboat excursions

[1] This talented woman, the widow of a prominent Brooklyn physician, was the
mother of three equally talented sons: Max, who regularly contributed drawings
to the old *Life* and who died young; Fred, an outstanding authority on roses, for
many years the editor of the Sunday *Times* garden page, who has just recently been
given a citation by the National Horticultural Society and is still active as a writer
and lecturer; and Frank, who is now a retired admiral.

and the drawing lessons; but no amount of politeness could make
Richard Ware seem like a contemporary; and while my mother was
going to dinners and receptions with Mrs. Ware, I was happy that
she left me free for overnight visits with Marion Burdett and the Edmands sisters, with whom I talked and talked and talked, after the
manner of little girls who are great friends and who have been separated a long time. Apparently, we also did some reading together, for,
in one of my letters, I said, "Today Marian and I looked over that
play I wrote when I was seven. We nearly died over the handwriting
and spelling"—this from the lofty heights of not quite eleven!

Our next and final visit before going home was at the Woburn parsonage, where my wonderful grandmother, and a brand-new cousin,
besides the one of my own age, were waiting to welcome us. It is certainly greatly to my aunt's and my grandmother's credit that, apparently, the warmth of this welcome was not affected by the amount of
baggage we had, though three of the seven trunks aforementioned
went with us—for a stay of a week! ("I am sorry to be obliged to bring
so many, but I shall need one for Frances and me and Fräulein has
her large one and our hats are altogether in the other," my mother
wrote beforehand; and in addition to the trunks there were, of course,
the usual "bags and shawl straps without number!") My grandmother
was very pleased to find how well I spoke French, and not nearly as
much pleased to learn that the "American churches" to which my
mother had been taking me in Europe used the Episcopal form of
service; she had always feared the Episcopal Church as a stepping-
stone toward Catholicism, as indeed, in my case, it proved to be; but
this was not until long after she had died and, since I was still quite
willing to follow her lead in matters of religion, her fears were laid at
rest.

Finally, my mother and I were back in Newbury, and Mem, the
hired man, was at the station to meet us, with Dan hitched to the old
carryall, and this was the beginning of a new era. For the next three
and a half years, the house which my mother had inherited from her
paternal grandfather, David Johnson, was our only home in the real
sense of the word. I do not mean that we never left it—in fact, our
trips to Boston were fairly frequent and our visits there often prolonged. I kept in touch with my greatest friends—Marion Burdett,
the Edmands sisters, the Shreve twins, and others—through the visits
I made them, as well as the visits they made me; and, as we often
stayed with the Wares, I also saw a good deal of my mother's friends

and the young men in Richard Ware's age bracket—that is, the early twenties. Less frequently than when we were in Newbury and they were in Haverhill, we saw the Keyeses. They were all in deep mourning when we returned from Europe, as Gertrude, the younger daughter of the family, had died very tragically while we were gone. The wedding which I had attended with such excitement had been the prelude to a marriage that seemed literally to have been made in heaven, it was so happy and so blessed in every sense of the word. But shortly before the birth of Gertrude's second child, her first-born, a fine little boy, had died a horrible death from diphtheria, which was then still a widespread scourge among children. She had not been able to rally from the shock; and when the little daughter, who was named for her, was only a few weeks old, an attack of pneumonia, which the mother did not have the strength to surmount, proved fatal to her. My first definite memory of the assembled Keyes family is their impressive though somber appearance in the Newbury church, where they occupied the pew behind ours, all dressed in the deepest black, to the last item of their wearing apparel. But I am glad I have happier memories of Gertrude Keyes Baker, too, not only as a beautiful bride but as the lovely young lady who had made me feel so welcome at Pine Grove Farm, when she took me to see the calves and lambs, while her mother and elder sister sat in the morning room, sorting, according to color, the masses of sweet peas which had been placed before them in milk pans, before filling innumerable clear glass vases with the fragrant blossoms. In the days when no respectable woman used make-up of any kind, young Mrs. Baker's complexion was dazzling and her hair like spun gold. Her disposition had the same radiant quality as her looks, so it is no wonder that she was the object of admiration to all those, both young and old, who came into the most casual contact with her, and of something akin to adoration to those closely connected with her.

Besides the visits we made in Boston, there continued to be many at "Nipnet" and the Count Rumford house and most of one winter was spent in Colorado, which we approached via Chicago, where my mother had several friends, and Mankato, Minnesota, where my aunt Carrie—my father's eldest surviving sister—then lived, as her husband was on the faculty of Carleton College. Having finally reached the Rocky Mountains, after this rather considerable detour, we spent part of our time with my brother, in the mining town of Idaho Springs, where he was then settled, and part of the time in Denver, where we stayed with our cousins, the Nathaniel Hills. It would be hard to find a greater contrast than the one between these two centers and equally hard to tell which gave me the greater enjoyment. Living conditions in Idaho Springs had more or less emerged from the primitive stage, but they were by no means luxurious. The hotel, a bare frame building, boasted an annex divided into so-called apartments, each consisting of two rooms, one behind the other. My brother used his front room for his office and my mother and I used ours for a sitting room; in both cases, the rear room was, naturally, the bedroom; sanitary facilities were limited. But there was no limit to the amount of riding I could do on a small sturdy horse or, occasionally, on a burro. I went joyously along with my brother, as his work took him from mine to mine or to some remote cabin, even farther up in the mountains than Idaho Springs itself. Often the rugged trails were partly obscured by snow and the cold was intense; but the atmosphere was crystal clear, the sky a vivid blue above the great jagged boulders; in the mines there were always wonders to be explored and in the cabins was always warmth and a welcome. I remember one of these shacks where a great open fire was burning and the board floor almost covered with wonderful Indian rugs. It was made of logs and had only one room beside the lean-to containing the kitchen; but the walls were lined with books and the delicious hot food and drink set before us by the cabin's solitary occupant bore no resemblance to typical mountain fare. What branch of engineering—if any—caused such a charming and cultured man to live so far removed from all his fellows, I do not know. It seemed, and still seems, to me mysterious. He never came to town, though my brother and I went more than once to see him; and though I was courteously, if intermittently, included in the conversation, on such occasions, much of it was over my head, and James never seemed to feel it necessary to give me any information about this valued friend of his. As one of our visits was drawing to a close, our host asked me if I had read *The Count of Monte Cristo*; and when I said no, he took his copy down from its place among other volumes bound in red morocco and handed it to me, saying it would be good practice for me to read it in the original French. And, over the futile protests of my mother, read it I did, very avidly, by candlelight, sitting up in bed to do so.

There were already a few rather pretentious houses in Idaho Springs and a small group of persons who considered themselves socially supe-

James Monroe's house,
Monroe Hill,
University of Virginia.
Birthplace of the
author.

John Henry Wheeler, father of the author,
at the time of his entrance to Harvard,
at the age of fifteen.

John Henry Wheeler, father of the author,
at the time of his graduation from Harvard,
at the age of nineteen.

Louise Fuller Johnson as a baby, in the lap of her mother, the beautiful Delia Maria, with her grandmother, great-grandmother and great-great-grandmother. The oldest woman in this five-generation picture was eighty at the time it was taken.

Louise Fuller Johnson, at the age of five, with her father, Edward Carleton Johnson.

Louise Johnson Underhill (Mrs. James Underhill), mother of the author, at the time of her courtship by John Henry Wheeler.

The beautiful Delia Maria at the age of twenty-six, painted in New York, allegedly by Sully.

The beautiful Delia Maria,
as interpreted by
an Italian artist in Rome,
circa 1865.

Count Rumford House, Woburn, Massachusetts (exterior). Later, the Congregational parsonage.

Gilbert Melancthon Wheeler, husband of Frances Parkinson Wheeler, the first.

Count Rumford House, Woburn, Massachusetts (interior).

Frances Parkinson Wheeler,
the first, grandmother
of the author.

"Aunt Nancy" (Anna Cummings Johnson) great-aunt of
the author and first woman journalist to be given a foreign
assignment by the New York *Times*.

The author's beloved Aunt Fannie
(Mrs. William P. Hill)

First picture of the author,
with her colored mammy, Barbara.

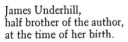

James Underhill,
half brother of the author,
at the time of her birth.

The Oxbow, Newbury, Vermont (David Johnson house).

The Newbury House, Newbury, Vermont.

Louise (Underhill) Wheeler as she appeared at the time of her marriage to Albert E. Pillsbury.

The author and her mother having tea in the reception hall at 583 Beacon Street, Boston.

Preston, the butler, in the dining room of 583 Beacon Street, Boston.

The author, at the age of five, with her mother and Dan, her father's Kentucky thoroughbred.

The author as she appeared on her Sunday walks.

The Pillsbury house, Milford, New Hampshire.

The carryall to the Tip Top House, Moosilauke.

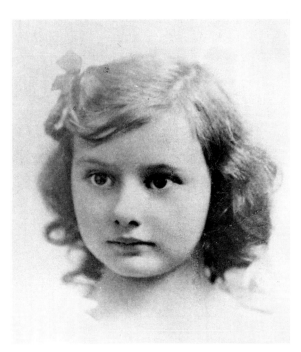

The author at the age of seven.

"OXBOW"
NEWBURY, VERMONT.

Dear Mr Keyes.
Thank you for the
nice icecream you
gave me.
Good by Frances.

First letter
written by the author.

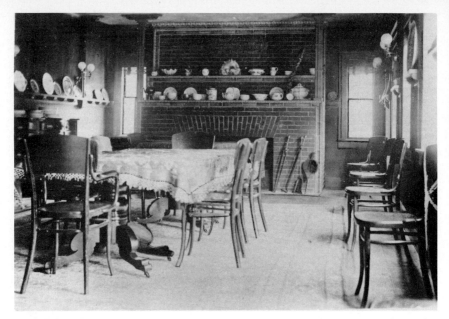

The dining room at "Nipnet," near Woodstock, Connecticut, the country residence of the Demings.

Mrs. Horace Deming

The Wayside, Concord, Massachusetts

Haying on Cow Meadow at the Oxbow.

The author with her riding master in Geneva.

Serge Kapnist,
the little Russian count,
friend of Geneva days.

The diligence to Chesières

rior to most of their fellow townspeople. My brother had never cared for society with a capital S and my mother, as I have already indicated, was alternately very much interested in it and utterly indifferent to it. That year, her indifference was centered in Idaho Springs and her interest in Denver. The latter, at least, was not surprising. The Nathaniel Hills were enormously wealthy and lived on a lavish scale. The head of the family had served in the United States Senate after making a fortune in silver mining and, more lately, he had bought the leading newspaper in Denver and had become a power in journalism, as well as politics. Besides him and his wife, my mother's cousin Alice, the household consisted of his two daughters and a granddaughter: Isabel, who was still unmarried, despite unremitting efforts on the part of countless eligible gentlemen to soften her adamant heart; Gertrude, who had been very early widowed, and whose grief at her bereavement, though sincere, was being quite effectively assuaged; and Charlotte, Gertrude's little daughter, born after her father's death, who was somewhat younger than I. In a nearby establishment, only slightly less luxurious, lived the only son of the family, Crawford, his stylish and sophisticated wife, Louise, and their two small sons. Isabel and Gertrude were great belles, in the truest sense of that outmoded word; both were fair, both were witty and charming, and both gave the illusion of beauty whether they actually possessed it or not, and I am inclined to think they did. There was seemingly no end to the amount of masculine tribute they were able to command. Every afternoon, unless they were going out on other pleasures bent, they received would-be suitors at teatime, their mother and an ex-governess hovering more or less in the background; every evening, dressed in the height of fashion, which in that era meant lustrous satins and shimmering brocades, wearing glittering ornaments in their blond hair and carrying enormous bouquets, they went to a party or were given one by their parents or their brother and sister-in-law. After all these years, the vision of those two sisters, standing side by side as they prepared to step into their carriage, their velvet cloaks thrown back to reveal their low-cut ballgowns, their violets or roses in their white-gloved hands, is still vivid and dazzling.

Charlotte was adored by her grandfather, who quoted her bright sayings in and out of season; but the Hill household did not revolve around her as the Keyes household revolved around the motherless baby, whose widowed father had generously renounced an independent life and gone to live with his in-laws, so that his little daughter might not be separated from her maternal grandmother and aunt. On the contrary, Charlotte seemed to play a rather minor part in the glowing design for living of the Hills' elaborate establishments. I played paper dolls with her, rather condescendingly, I am afraid—an attitude which underwent a very great change when we renewed our acquaintance and re-established our kinship many years later, at which time she had become not only a very brilliant and handsome woman of the world but one of the most successful literary agents in New York. However, when I was twelve and she was six, there seemed to be a considerable gap between us, which I did not make a very determined effort to bridge. Once, on Gertrude's way to a party, she stopped in the library where I sat buried in a book and inquired if I did not know how to play. Her tone was not unkind, only rather amused, but I might have been offended if she had asked her question less smilingly and if her smile had not been so enchanting. So I only said yes, I did, but just then I was reading. "Reading what?" Gertrude said, still in that lightly satirical way. "Agnes Strickland's *Lives of the Queens of England*. If I don't hurry, I won't have time to get through all twelve volumes before we go back to Idaho Springs."

Inevitably, she set me down as a hopeless little bookworm; there was no way in which she could have guessed that my zest for reading in a luxurious library was no greater than my zest for riding over rough mountain trails or for many other forms of physical activity. As a matter of fact, my capable but caustic secretary, Deanie Bullock, expressed a correlative conviction only recently, after I had remarked, in the course of a casual conversation, that I had read all Shakespeare's plays, most of the Waverley novels, and many of those by Dickens and Thackeray before I was fourteen. "Well, you didn't have much of anything else to do, did you?" Deanie inquired loftily. If either she or my cousin Gertrude had come to Newbury during that period, her viewpoint might have been very different. True, I did not have telephone, radio or television and was, therefore, free to devote much more time to literature than the teen-ager of today—in my opinion, greatly to my advantage. I read omnivorously for pleasure. "Aunt Fannie does not have *Lorna Doone*, so I cannot read that," I wrote my mother, rather indignantly, when I was visiting in Woburn while she went to Hanover for a surgical operation. "But she does have *Rob Roy*, *The Fair Maid of Perth*, and *Anne of Geierstein*, all of which have great attractions. Avis [my cousin] has a very nice child's *Life of Lincoln* and I have almost finished the Civil War." [!] Moreover, the schedule of study pursued under the direction of Mademoiselle—as we had begun to call Fräulein Riensberg for greater convenience—was amazingly comprehensive. I went on taking all my lessons in either French or German and these lessons included a staggering amount of classical literature in both languages. ("Mademoiselle isn't half as fond of Schiller as she is of Goethe, so of course I am all the time harping on him and teasing to learn his poems," I wrote my mother later in the course of the same visit. I certainly did not have to tease very hard, since it was taken for granted that I would commit to memory all the poetry included in my lessons; and I still can recite snatches of *Der Erlkönig* and the *Lied von der Glocke*, all of *Du Bist wie eine Blume* and the *Lorelei*, to mention only a few.) But English I read at odd times and seasons; and my lessons, which were confined to morning hours, never seemed burdensome.

The fact that I had a governess, while all the other youngsters in Newbury went to the public school, happily did not prevent a renewal of the delightful associations which had been interrupted by my year abroad; on the contrary, we all felt we must make up for lost time, so we rushed together the minute we were released from our desks. Every season was crowded with manifold and variegated pursuits, unrelated to book learning. In their milder forms, our amusements were represented by sugaring-off parties in the early spring and by the celebrations connected with Decoration Day, Children's Sunday, and graduation from high school in the late spring; by croquet, archery, battledore and shuttlecock and corn roasts in summer; by chicken-pie suppers, in charge of the Ladies' Aid, and Halloween parties in the autumn; and by coasting, snowshoeing, skating, and sleigh riding in winter. Birthday parties continued to mark red-letter days; but there were many other juvenile gatherings, at which decks of cards and square dances slowly but surely began to supersede parcheesi boards and candy pulls.

More exciting than these pleasurable but temperate pursuits was attendance at the county fairs, which, like the chicken-pie suppers and the Halloween parties, took place in the fall. Besides the exhibits of prize-winning jams, jellies, pickles, relishes, and other foodstuffs, and all sorts of handiwork from tatting to quilted bedspreads, which were considered not only praiseworthy but stimulating, there was a fine showing of poultry and livestock, there were harness races, and intermittent music by local bands livened the entire scene. County officials usually honored these fairs by their presence, and not infrequently state officials and candidates for important positions also put in an appearance. Indeed, it was just such an occurrence that marked my own debut as a campaigner!

The Honorable W. P. Dillingham, who was then governor of Vermont, was an old friend of the family and I was devoted to him—no wonder, for he was kindly of disposition, urbane of manner, and distinguished of appearance. His campaign to succeed the late Justice H. Morrell as United States Senator was the first to arouse my personal interest; and the county fair which I happened to attend in the course of this campaign seemed to me an excellent opportunity for voicing this enthusiasm. Teams had been left at the hitching rail provided just outside the fairgrounds and, mounting the buckboard in which we had driven over from Newbury, I proceeded to make an enthusiastic speech in the governor's favor, undeterred by the fact that my audience consisted merely of a few stragglers who were lounging on the premises, most of whom greeted my efforts at oratory with snickers or guffaws. One of them, however, took it upon himself to seek out the governor, who was attending the fair in his official capacity, and tell him what was happening; and somewhat perturbed, though vastly amused, Mr. Dillingham hastened to the scene of action, arriving just after I had reached the climax of my remarks and fallen over backward, landing on the ground! As he set me on my feet again and brushed me off, he remarked rather whimsically, "I hope, my dear Frances, that when you grow up you will marry a politician! It would certainly be a waste of promising material if you did not!"

Twenty years later, when he met me in a corridor of the Capitol in Washington, soon after my husband had entered the Senate, his eyes twinkled as he greeted me.

"Well, well," he said cordially. "I take it you have gone on making speeches from the rear of buckboards! Or, if you haven't, you must have been doing something else equally effective. I am glad to see that you and your husband have both profited by my advice!"

It was, however, not only events such as birthday parties and county fairs, or indeed events of any kind, that made those years in Newbury so joyous and so memorable; sights and sounds and scents all played an important part in my design for living. Each season had its own abundant share of these, just as each season had its own source of innocent merriment: in the spring, arbutus and lady's-slippers, wake-robin and jack-in-the-pulpit, growing in the woods; apple blossoms fluttering in the orchard, lilacs rising plumelike in the front yard. In the summer, moss roses, cinnamon pinks, mignonette, and Johnny-jump-ups perfuming the garden; black-eyed Susans, Queen Anne's lace, and tiger lilies mingling with the sweet-smelling hay in the fields. In the autumn, wild geese honking as they winged their southward flight, fallen leaves rustling as they fled before the wind and giving forth their incense as they burned; wild grapes ripening on the vines, apples pressed into a flow of cider at Cousin Henry's mill, scarlet bitter-sweet and crimson sumacs overhanging the walls, flaming maples bordering every road and sweeping over every hillside. And besides, in the autumn, came still more splendid sights: the harvest moon, huge and golden, rising on the New Hampshire side of the river and gilding the stubble of the intervening fields with its radiance; the "Alpine glow" on those same mountains, flooding their snow-covered slopes with rosy color. And in winter the merriest sounds and the most gorgeous spectacles of all: sleigh bells on the roads, snow not only on the mountains but on the fields and lawns and gardens, on the rooftops and the trees; and, at night, the northern lights dancing and darting across a cold sky and setting it ablaze with iridescent glory.

Even as a little girl, I was not dependent on either company or change to enjoy all these sources of delight; I had an infinite zest for beauty. If I could share it, that in some ways was all to the good; if I could not, solitude had its own rewards. I did not have to stir from my mother's house and grounds to see and hear and smell much of that to which I have just referred: at the south was the garden, at the east the meadows, the river, and the mountains. But when I left the premises for the woods and highways, I was always sure to find other beautiful flowers and other beautiful views. I continued to ride almost every day of my life, except in the bitterest weather and, at first, I took my rides alone, as I did my lessons. I had a pony, which I named Souvenir, in loving memory of my gentle Geneva mount; but I was both a chubby and a fast-growing little girl who liked swift movement, and the pony soon began to resent the burden and the effort which I represented. His method of retaliation was simple: when he felt he had borne enough, he simply keeled over on his side and lay still until he was rested. I was never injured by this process, for his stature was such that I did not have much of a fall and I learned to release myself quickly from entanglement; but my pride as an equestrienne suffered. Eventually, I told my mother I thought it was high time my father's horse or my brother's, both of which were eating their heads off in the stable, were put at my disposal; after all, she had a spanking new pair of carriage horses. (She had somewhat fantastically named them Amphion and Zethus, rather than Castor and Pollux, because they were friends and not brothers; she considered it quite all right to give horses names from mythology, whereas she would have thought it sacrilegious to use Biblical names like David and Jonathan!) She went driving every afternoon, accompanied by one or more guests. Why should I not have Dan and Kaweah and go riding with a friend?

She admitted that I had a point. However, none of the girls who were still my boon companions were in the least attracted at the idea of getting on a horse's back, nor were their parents enthusiastic about having them do so. Strange as it now seems, none of them went snow-shoeing, either, though they did go coasting and skating and were not debarred from "Three Old Cat" and even more pretentious forms of baseball; indeed, a mixed team flourished for some time. I might have thought my memory about this was playing me false were it not for the letters I wrote my mother while she was at the Hanover Hospital, during the same period that I lamented the absence of *Lorna Doone* from my aunt's home and commented on my preference for Schiller over Goethe. "May I get a baseball glove?" I inquired. "There are some very respectable looking ones downtown for twenty-five cents and if war comes on the price will be raised. Besides, Haines' is almost worn out and we really need one." Evidently, the desired permission was given, for a few days later I wrote, "You may let Haines know I have a baseball glove—a beauty! At least, it is not very handsome, but it is a very fine one. I found that the ones that cost twenty-five cents were hard and bad smelling, so I bought one for fifty cents. It was the only one they had left in the store and is a vivid green, but I would rather have a good soft glove in an ugly color and I have named it 'The Green Garnet.' "[2] (Incidentally, the same letter, which contains the first sug-gestion about the baseball glove, contains one for still another form of sport: "The boys around here [Woburn] have all made canoes them-selves and one boy goes paddling on the canal every night with his sister. The canoes are made of canvas covered with pitch and a little tar to make them waterproof and are strengthened with barrel hoops and one long piece of wood through the middle; the paddle is also homemade. I should think if these boys could make them, Haines and I could, and go paddling in that jolly place back in the meadows where

---

[2] This was the title of a book popular at the time.

we go skating in the winter." This suggestion was turned down. It remained for Harry Keyes to initiate me into the joys of canoeing.)

But to revert to the subject of Dan and Kaweah, from which I have been temporarily diverted by recollections of other pastimes. Though, as I have said, none of the girls on the baseball team would go riding with me, I did not have to go alone after all, for Richard Cobb promptly and enthusiastically suggested that he would like to become a horseman. He was four years younger than I and, therefore, our relationship at that time—aside from the fact that we were distant cousins—was more or less that of teacher and pupil. But he very quickly became as good a rider as I was and shortly thereafter a much better one. It is due to him, rather than to my teacher in Geneva, that I was soon almost as comfortable riding bareback as on a sidesaddle.

The riding lessons having proved such a success, dancing lessons were added to them and, again, the pupil very quickly surpassed the teacher. But I have taken a certain amount of personal pride—more I fear than is justified!—in the fact that during World War I Richard Cobb was among the comparatively few young officers in the American Expeditionary Forces selected for assignment to the famous Cavalry School at Saumur. Actually, my debt to him is much greater than his to me as far as riding is concerned: it was his letters from Saumur— which, later still, he permitted me to use, in fictionized form, in *Steamboat Gothic*—that constituted my introduction to this charming little city on the Loire and eventually resulted, not only in my many pleasant sojourns there but, to a large degree, in the setting of *Came a Cavalier*, which proved one of my most successful novels!

Richard also became one of the best ballroom dancers I have ever seen—a distinction John Gunther accords, with good reason, to Manuel Quezon, the Philippine statesman who later became the first President of its commonwealth. I myself first met this charming personage at a Christmas Eve ball, given at the famous Tiro al Blanco Club in Manila; and, as I was going back to my hotel in broad daylight on Christmas Day—for the ball did not break up until six in the morning—my escort asked me if I did not think Quezon the best dancer I had ever had the good fortune to have for a partner. "*Next* to the best," I answered without hesitation. "The very best is a cousin of mine in Newbury, Vermont."

But Saumur and Manila were still undreamed of when I first became aware that Richard Cobb rode and danced better than I did, and that our relationship would henceforth be that of companions, with the condescension, if any, on his side rather than mine. As a matter of fact, he was very generous about this, as about everything else. Sometimes, he even consented to go on long walks with me, though, for these, he showed less enthusiasm than for riding and dancing until I was given a pedometer, at which point we were equally intrigued by gauging the distances we covered. At last, we decided to go into partnership together and open a lemonade stand. For a little while, we did quite a thriving business. But Richard's mother, my cousin Agnes, who had been co-operative about the birthday parties, complained that our clientele brought undesirable elements into the yard at the Homestead. Regretfully, the enterprise was abandoned.

There is no one instance that stands out as particularly noteworthy in this early part of a lifelong friendship; but there is one as far as Haines Johnson and I are concerned and two as far as Richard Darling is concerned. In the first of these, both boys were involved. It was rumored that a great subterranean chamber, formerly used by the Indians as a council room, was located under the sandbank where we had all played as younger children; certainly there was something that might be called a tunnel on the farm belonging to Mr. Doe, Richard's grandfather. We had seen the mouth of it and, though we had not penetrated inside, we became convinced—Haines, Richard, and I— that it might well lead to a council chamber and that we would be well advised to explore it. We did not seek such advice from any of our elders, however; in fact, none of us felt it necessary to inform them of our decision.

We chose a bright midsummer afternoon when most of the men were in the hayfields and most of the women still busy with dinner dishes. Richard entered the tunnel first, I came next, and Haines followed. From the beginning, we had to go forward in a squatting position, though we could still hold our bodies erect; but very shortly we had to crouch and then continue on our hands and knees. It was rough going. Some sunlight had penetrated at the opening of the tunnel; but we had advanced only a very short distance into it when the atmosphere became unpleasantly dank and we were in total darkness. This was, of course, long before the days of flashlights, and though we had brought matches with us, it was almost impossible to use them, in view of our positions. But even when we became conscious that the top of the tunnel was coming closer and closer to our heads, we had no thought of turning back until I realized that it was impossible for me to advance another inch; a rocklike substance had dislodged itself

from the infinitesimal space still left above me and was resting firmly
on my bent back.

Richard could not possibly have turned around; but, somehow,
while he crawled a little further forward, Haines managed to get hold
of the rock and clutch it, as I wriggled from under it, going forward,
too. Then he allowed it to fall. Fortunately for us, it was both flat
and thin and did not greatly impede our ignominious progress backward. Before we emerged, humiliated but unharmed, the anguished
voice of my governess could be heard calling, "Franciska! Franciska!
wo bist du?" Somehow, she had located the approximate place where
I had last been seen—perhaps by Mrs. Doe, for the cave was not far
from her big brick farmhouse. When Haines inched his way out into
the open, feet first, Mademoiselle's anguish turned to relief. She
guessed, and rightly, that I would not be far behind. I was led home,
dirty and disgraced, but with no special sense of defeat. After all, it
was a falling rock and no lack of intrepidity that had swerved me from
my purpose![3]

I only hoped that Mrs. Doe realized this. Though I did not actually
see her, I could visualize her as standing on her kitchen porch, taking
a grim satisfaction in my discomfiture, for, inevitably, she would have
thought me much better employed in doing housework than in exploring caves. She was what was called, in Newbury, "a character."
Although her husband owned more acreage than any other farmer in
town—"Doe's land poor!" some said, but that, I am sure, was a sentiment prompted by envy!—and was himself genial and easygoing for
all his shrewdness, Mrs. Doe was very, very thrifty and worked her
fingers to the bone and, as far as she could, obliged everyone associated with her to do the same. It was said that, when she sat down to
breakfast at six on Monday morning, she habitually cast a withering
glance at her hired hands as she exclaimed, "Here it is Monday, tomorrow's Tuesday, next day's Wednesday—week half gone and nothing done!" Another tale, probably apocryphal, concerns two hired men
who shared not only a room but a bed. It was after midnight when
they were finally free to retire and the one who promptly pulled off
his boots and got under the covers was annoyed because his companion
did not immediately follow his example. "For God's sake, come and
lay down!" he exclaimed. "How can I get to sleep if you keep a-settin'

[3] Though it is no longer possible to penetrate as far inside the cave as it was
at the time of our explorations, it is still an attraction for the present generation in
Newbury.

on the edge of the bed?" . . . "What's the use of takin' off my
boots and layin' down?" the second hired man replied, "I'd no sooner
have them on the floor than Jane would call me to get up!"

It was with stories such as these in mind that I dreaded the appraisal
of Mrs. Doe who, I felt sure, did not consider me a desirable companion for her grandson! Indeed, she was fond of assuring him that "milk-
ing was just fun" and that there was no reason why he should wish to
get through earlier at night, especially since he could sit down while
he was doing it! But Richard and I continued to see a great deal of
each other and the second incident involving him that stands out so
clearly in my memory is as different as possible from the one connected
with the tunnel into which we crept on a midsummer afternoon. The
second episode had a snow scene for its setting: two hills; the brook
where they came together, one on the upgrade and the other on the
downgrade; a barbed-wire fence separating the highway from the
meadow through which the brook flowed; a new Flexible Flyer
painted bright red; and, besides Richard and myself, a boy from Boston
who was spending his Christmas vacation at the Oxbow. His name
was Alvah, his mother and mine were great friends and he was, I suppose, my first beau, in the sense that this word was generally used at
the time. At all events, there was an element in our companionship
vaguely different from that which characterized the camaraderie existing between me and the boys I knew in Newbury, though this element
found expression in neither words nor deeds.

The Flexible Flyer was Richard's. He appeared with it at the front
door the morning after Christmas and showed it to me with pardon-
able pride; then he asked me if I would not like to try it out with him
on the Montebello Road. This was considered ideal for coasting, because the momentum which a sled gathered as it shot down one hill toward the brook sent it shooting almost halfway up the other. This left
only a short distance to cover on foot before the coasters could turn
around, get back on their sled, and, in reverse, do just what they had
done before—that is, the hill they shot down now would be the opposite number of the one they had shot down previously. I accepted the
invitation with alacrity and, since Alvah was my guest, he was a little
tardily included in it.

We set off in high spirits and, as the morning progressed, these spirits
soared higher and higher. The coasting had never been better, in
fact, it had seldom been so good. The Flexible Flyer, a scarlet streak
against the white snow, more than justified its name; it was flexible

to the nth degree and it seemed to fly faster and faster each time it started down one hill and up the other. It had only one slight drawback: it required expert steering, and no city slicker could be expected to handle it as well as a boy who was country bred, in Vermont, where the climate automatically indicated coasting for almost six months out of twelve. Nevertheless, the code of courtesy indicated, unmistakably, that Alvah should be invited to steer at least once and the inevitable happened: in his inept hands, the Flexible Flyer, when it came to the bottom of the first hill, instead of shooting up the second, shot through the barbed wire and straight across a strip of meadow into the brook. The thin coating of ice covering the latter was not strong enough to stand up under the weight of two husky teen-age boys and a solid little girl. When the former succeeded in fishing out the latter, she was not only drenched to the skin; her face was badly scratched by the barbed wire and therein lay elements of real tragedy. She was not afraid of catching pneumonia; but she was to appear in a holiday fantasy that night as a Christmas fairy, and a Christmas fairy with a scratched face would convey no illusions of magic to her audience. She might be an object of pity, but it was far more likely that she would be an object of scorn.

I think my companions were as well aware of this as I was and they did not leave me to confront my mother alone. Valiantly, they accompanied me into her presence and explained that everything was their fault. (Of course, it was really all Alvah's fault, but I do not think either of the boys said this.) My mother retorted, rather sharply, that it was my fault, too; if I were not always streaking off with foolhardy boys—indeed, if I were not very foolhardy myself—such things would not happen. Then she hurried me away for a hot bath, a hot drink, and dry clothes and, long before I was fully reclad, began to apply healing lotions to my face. Almost miraculously, some of the damage done by the barbed wire was repaired before evening; the rest was concealed by stealthily applied powder and by the curls which formed a natural shield. I was a success as a fairy after all, perhaps because Richard and Alvah, seated in the front row at the hall where the fantasy was given, thoughtfully led the applause.

CHAPTER XII

I have referred to myself as a "solid little girl," which is a correct but restrained way of doing so. Shortly after I had appeared as a Christmas fairy, it began to dawn on me that scratches on my face did not constitute the only drawback to giving the desired illusion to that role. Whatever my faults—and they are many—I have never been a procrastinator. Once I had decided to get thin, I set about my preparations for doing so with a vengeance.

In those days, nobody counted calories—or, if they did, I never heard of it. Some people, through choice, ate light breakfasts, as we did, and some ate light suppers, as was the habit of a few friends and neighbors; but "three square meals a day" constituted the ideal of most, and if they did not meet this, it was usually for pecuniary reasons. Those who wished to reduce—and this was apt to be against their physician's advice, not because of it—went in for exercise and the pounds melted away. I am aware that the medical profession now tells us that you can exercise eighteen hours out of the twenty-four and practically nothing will come of it; but the fact remains that I have yet to see a fat athlete or a fat farmer! I was naturally active, physically as well as mentally, and it required no will power at all to double the length of my walks and rides. A two-mile sprint before breakfast, usually down the nearby lane leading to the river, seemed to me an ideal way of beginning the day; then came a longer walk in the afternoon, unless there were a still longer ride, and often there were both. Ideal proportions were supposed to be represented by a neck measure twice the size of a wrist measure and a waist measure twice the size of a neck measure.[1] (Nothing was said about bust and hips and, of course, at thirteen, those did not enter the picture much anyway, though, at eighteen, both were supposed to be pleasantly in evidence.) Six inches—twelve inches—twenty-four inches—those were the sizes I was after; and before long I had attained them, nor did I lose them for six years, and then only temporarily and for the best of reasons!

[1] After not hearing ideal measurements defined in this way for many years, what was my surprise and gratification to find the following on page 68 of *Folk Medicine* by Dr. DeForest Clinton Jarvis (Henry Holt & Co., Inc.): "There are different ways of estimating what your weight should be. Vermont folk medicine estimates it this way: twice around the wrist equals once around the lower part of the neck; twice around the neck at the lowest part equals once around the waist."

My mother did not like my new slimness—indeed, the subject of exercise soon became a bone of contention between us and, in as far as she could, she curtailed my rides and walks. ("Last Saturday, I rode Dan six miles over to the Keyes' farm, across the river and back; it is the longest ride I have taken this summer. Although Mama said I could not study, and could only walk two miles a day, I walked three miles yesterday and three and a half the day before, and study as usual. I am not getting a bit fatter under her treatment," I wrote Marian Edmands about this time.) But, after all, she could not keep track of me all the time, especially as she slept late and was never up and around when I started down the lane.

My preoccupation with exercise was not so great as to preclude an equal enthusiasm for bathing. I had been brought up to take a tub bath every morning—still a rather unusual practice. Tub baths, in most families I knew, were then limited to Saturday nights or, more rarely, to Wednesday and Saturday nights; more rarely still these were supplemented by daily sponge baths upon rising; and the latter, like the former, were part of my mother's regime. Why she instituted a different one for me, I do not know; but the fact remains that she did and, about the same time that I decided to get thin, I decided that one bath a day was not enough. I wanted a second one when I changed my dress in the afternoon and, in warm weather, a third one when I went to bed at night. Furthermore, I sometimes sneaked in a fourth one, before our midday meal, if I had been exercising hard all the morning. Like the long walks, these baths became a debatable point and—unlike the walks—were eventually subject to some reduction. Meanwhile, I was frequently teased about them, and my friend Marian Edmands insisted that after I became a well-known author—for she was among the first to believe that I would!—visitors would not be led to see the desk where I had worked, but the tub where I had bathed.

Frequent arguments about exercising and bathing marred the harmony of life at the Oxbow for a long while; but, as far as I can recall, the misadventure with the Flexible Flyer was the last to bring down the charge of "foolhardy" on my guilty head. The rest of that winter passed uneventfully and, the following spring, our annual major trip away from Newbury took us to Washington. My mother had become more and more active in the Daughters of the American Revolution and, for the second time, decided to attend a "Continental Congress" and to take me with her.

We went to the old Willard Hotel, which was considered fully as elegant as the Shoreham, where we had stayed before, though it was by this time in a state of shabby splendor which indicated the complete renovation that took place shortly thereafter, together with the change of its name to the New Willard. We were given a large gloomy room, without a bath and, of course, without a telephone; and the morning after our arrival, my mother, who normally did not stir until eight at the earliest, woke me before daybreak with the announcement that she was ill and that I must get help at once.

She enjoyed exceptionally good health, partly, no doubt, due to the fact that she never overexerted herself, either mentally or physically, and that if a situation was so unpleasant as to cause her the least distress, she simply turned her back on it. (The latter policy proved a poor one in the long run, but I did not find out until much later that this was almost inevitably the case, and I doubt if she were ever fully convinced of this.) I had never seen her in actual pain before and I was terrified. There was a bell in the room and, of course, I rang it, but there was no response; it was still too early for chambermaids to be stirring. I hurled on my underclothes, but was defeated when it came to my dress, which buttoned down the back; there was nothing to do but fling on a coat to cover the inescapable gap. When it came to my hair, there was absolutely nothing I could do about it. Lately, I have derived great comfort, while reading Mrs. Theodore Roosevelt, Jr.'s charming book, *Day Before Yesterday*, to learn that when she was married, she had neither dressed herself nor done her own hair; it removed some of the shame that I have hitherto always felt because I was equally incapable at the age of thirteen! That dreadful morning, I did not even try to adjust hair ribbons and side combs; I said I would find somebody and tore out of the room, without the slightest idea to whom I should appeal.

Fortune favored me. I had not gone far when I met a lady just stepping from the public bathroom. She was not fully dressed either, but she had on a neat dark wrapper and her hair was carefully braided. She looked at the little scarecrow before her, first with bewilderment and then with sympathy. I had hardly finished pouring out my tale of woe when she took action. First she went back with me to my room and told my mother she would send the elevator boy to the desk and ask to have a physician summoned immediately; afterward, she would return and stay with us until he came and, while they were waiting for him, she would button my dress and fix my hair. But wouldn't it perhaps be a good idea for me to wash my face?

That attack, undoubtedly due to some sort of food poisoning, fortunately yielded without delay to treatment, and our good Samaritan, who proved to be a Mrs. Dimick from Cambridge, became our very good friend. She was also an enthusiastic member of the Daughters of the American Revolution, and she had a daughter, Muriel, who was about my age. Muriel had not accompanied her mother to Washington, but I was to make and enjoy her acquaintance later. Meanwhile, during my mother's brief convalescence and subsequent absorption in the Continental Congress, I ranged unsupervised about Washington. The Congressional Library was fairly new then and I spent a large part of my time there, entranced by its murals, its great stairway, and its general flamboyance. But the Smithsonian Institute delighted me, too; the Corcoran Gallery occupied my somewhat critical attention for hours; and I learned to find my way fairly well around the Capitol. More than one person who saw me in the course of my rambles must have thought it was strange that a little girl should be wandering around in these great public buildings alone; but no one ever questioned my presence as I went on my contented and inquiring way; and, when I returned to the hotel in the evening, I recorded, in a ruled copybook, everything I had seen and done, not in factual, but in fictional form, as I transferred my own experiences to those of imaginary twins. It was not until I took the initiative of calling on Mrs. Craig and Mrs. Greely, whom I remembered pleasantly from the days when they spent their summers in Newbury, that I realized, from the astonished reception given me in each instance by the lady of the house, that I had been doing anything in the least out of the ordinary. But I was pleased to exchange sightseeing for contemporary companions and there were plenty of youngsters in both families to provide me with these.

An outstanding experience of this stay in Washington was the reception at the White House to which all delegates to the Continental Congress were again invited and to which they automatically took any members of their families who had accompanied them to Washington. My mother had recovered by this time and was greatly looking forward to the function; but she had not forgotten our previous visit there, when Louise Johnson and I had briefly basked in the glory of a great impersonation, because we allowed ourselves to be mistaken for President Harrison's grandchildren. She warned me that I must avoid doing, a second time, anything which would so greatly embarrass her, and I faithfully promised her that I would. However, hell is not the only place that is paved with good intentions. On this occasion, it was the White House.

As the long line of guests advanced toward the Blue Room, where the President and Mrs. McKinley were receiving against massed palms, I heard someone addressing a thick-set, white-haired, red-faced man, just in front of me, as "General Miles." Greatly excited at being so close to a celebrity, I leaned forward and spoke to him.

"Oh, General Miles!" I exclaimed. "I am so thrilled to see what you really look like. I have been reading all about you in the papers!"

My impetuous action had really been prompted by admiration, but the general did not so interpret it. The papers were full of stories about the tainted meat which had caused as many deaths as Spanish bullets among the soldiers in the recent war. Though part of the responsibility for this outrage was attributed to the Secretary of War, Russell Alger, General Miles had permitted distribution of the meat and evidence against him was also very strong. He naturally concluded from my remark that I wished to see whether or not he really did have horns and a tail, figuratively speaking. Instead of responding to my greeting, he glared at me and drew stiffly away.

Too late, I realized I had done or said something amiss and, eager to leave the scene of my *faux pas*, I rushed blindly ahead, reaching the head of the receiving line before my mother. In my agitation, I forgot that I had been told to curtsey to Mrs. McKinley, but on no account to shake hands with her, as she was a semi-invalid and had to be spared all possible fatigue. She remained seated in a comfortable chair while her husband, who was devoted to her, stood at her side and bore the burden of welcoming guests. But, in my upset state, I had seized one of the fragile hands, half hidden by fine lace frills, which lay relaxed in her lap, before I remembered the warning that had been given me. Then I was stricken with terror lest she might have a seizure, in the middle of the party, which would be all my fault; so again I plunged forward, this time into the East Room, intent on escaping impending disaster. Once lost in the crowd that was already milling around there, I felt reasonably sure that I could not be identified as a perpetrator of a rash act. Indeed, I was so successful in losing myself that my mother lost me, too, and it was some time before she found me again. She vowed she would never take me to the White House any more and she never did; but as things turned out, that did not matter very much because I went there often enough without her backing.

My first meeting with General Joseph Wheeler, which took place at the Capitol a few days later, was less disastrous than my meeting with General Miles at the White House—indeed, it was pleasant at the time and propitious for the future. An aura of grandeur surrounded the names of the men who had fought under the Stars and Bars and who, thirty years later, volunteered to serve under the Stars and Stripes; in the case of Fitzhugh Lee and "Little Joe" Wheeler this aura became a positive radiance. The pint-sized cavalry officer—"a diminutive Alabamian of terrific energy"—had had twenty-four horses killed under him during the War Between the States, but undeterred had continued to go galloping onward; the greater the danger the more he seemed to thrive. Nothing could have better suited his tastes and talents than the charge on San Juan Hill and, in my eyes, he was the outstanding hero of the Spanish-American War. Therefore, I could hardly believe my good fortune when the distinguished companion with whom I was just entering the Rotunda—for my days of wandering about alone were over!—shouted to an officer who was just entering it, "Hold on a minute, Joe! Come and meet a Yankee relative of yours!"

The general turned at once, smiling broadly and saluting swiftly. "Well, well," he said in response to the quick introductions. "So your name's Wheeler too, is it? Frances Parkinson Wheeler? John Wheeler's daughter? Well, well! But what do they mean by calling you a Yankee then, my dear child? Weren't you born in James Monroe's house, at the University of Virginia? If that doesn't make you a southerner, I don't know what would!"

Inside of a few minutes, we had hatched up a kinship which was to prove the foundation for a firm friendship when I went to Washington as a senator's wife twenty years later: General Joe's daughter, Julia, had married William J. Harris, then United States Senator from Georgia, and they lived in the same apartment house that we did—the famous 2400 Sixteenth Street, which at the time harbored no less than eleven senatorial families. Mrs. Harris kindly confirmed her father's pronouncement on our kinship and, once a year at least, we received together, besides bearing each other company as we made the then inevitable round of calls. Our husbands were colleagues, our children playmates. The cousinship may have been apocryphal; the friendship certainly was not.

Still another episode in that memorable visit to Washington, which took place in my fourteenth year, was destined to have far-reaching consequences: in the course of it, I went to Arlington for the first time. The condition of the mansion was a disgrace to the country and an insult to the memory of the original owners—so closely connected with the Father of his Country—from whom it had been requisitioned during the War Between the States. A so-called caretaker was doing his light housekeeping in the columned drawing room where Robert E. Lee and Mary Custis were married. Another noble apartment was piled high with ugly metal wreaths; so many boys had died from eating tainted meat that there had not been time to decorate all the graves in the hideous fashion which was then the vogue. The entrance hall of the mansion was cluttered with dirty rubbish. Altogether, the neglect, amounting almost to abuse of this beautiful house, nearly as important architecturally as it is historically, made a profound impression on me; I went out on the pillared portico, with eyes so blurred with tears that I could only dimly see the magnificent panorama before me; but my fists were clenched.

"When the time comes," I muttered to myself, "that I'm really an author, that I do have some influence, I'm going to make people see what a disgrace it is that General Lee's home should be left in this condition. I'm going to make them do something about it!"

I did not dare say any of this aloud, for I knew my mother would simply deride me; but I never forgot. The first public measure that I advocated, after I had become an official resident of Washington and a recorder of current events in a national magazine, was the Sheppard-Towner Maternity Bill. After that had passed, my editor asked me what I would like to advocate next and I said a bill for the restoration of Arlington. That bill passed, too.

CHAPTER XIII

From the account of my adventures in the cave and with the Flexible Flyer—which, as a matter of fact, were typical rather than isolated!—it may be gathered that my mother had some grounds for saying that I was given to streaking off with foolhardy boys; but this was not because there had been any lessening of affection between myself and the other girls who had likewise always been my boon companions; and I had begun to be conscious of their more outstanding characteristics. As small children, we had never thought much about each other's looks, temperaments, and talents; if we had a good time together, that was all that counted. Now I realized that two of the girls in our little circle were extremely pretty, much prettier than I could ever hope to be. One of these was Mary Louise—or, as she was always called, Maida—Darling, Richard's eldest sister. She had coloring like that of a ripe peach, great velvety dark eyes heavily fringed with long lashes, and quantities of dark hair that was parted in the middle above her smooth brow and hung in two great ropelike braids down her graceful back. If the word "luscious" could ever properly be applied to looks, it certainly could have been in this case. Normally, Maida's expression was demure rather than animated; but when she was interested or excited, it changed completely: the velvety eyes opened wider and wider, a dazzling sparkle suddenly illumined them, and the veiled glances from under the fringed lashes had already begun to raise havoc. Life with her and for her was never dull, for it was nearly always electrified, and while there was certainly nothing restful about her, there was much which was beguiling. But Maida was not only a beauty and a born coquette; she was what would now be called a brain. She led her classes with ease and, before any of the rest of us had even thought of such a thing, she began to talk of going to college. As a matter of fact, very few of the girls I knew talked about it even later. However, Maida early selected her goal, which was Smith, and, what was more, she inspired Mary Hale, who was younger, but who was also a brain, with the same idea. Eventually, they both carried this out with considerable distinction.

The other beauty in our midst was Katherine Cobb. Her grandparents, her parents, and both her brothers were all noticeably good-looking; but Katherine's appearance went far beyond good looks. Her type was as different as possible from Maida's. Her eyes were blue and her skin delicately rosy; her hair fell in clustering golden curls around a face always wreathed in smiles. She was not a brain like Maida and Mary; her greatest asset, aside from her looks, was as tranquil, sweet, and tractable a disposition as it is possible for any mortal to possess. Nothing angered her and nothing disturbed her, and she was always glad to do whatever anyone else wanted to do. She was the youngest among us, but no one ever felt she was in the way. She was our treasure and our pet.

When it came to the closest friendship of all, however, this was neither with Maida, who sometimes made me vaguely uneasy and, anyway, seemed much older than she actually was, nor with Katherine, who was still a plaything rather than a companion. It was with Jeannie

Darling, Richard's second sister. The tie with her was as strong as
when we had shared a trundle bed for our naps, even though she had
no taste for exploring caves, or riding bareback, or trying out Flexible
Flyers, and I did. She was perfectly willing to join in the gentler sports,
such as croquet, which we all played a great deal; and she and I did
an immense amount of sewing and embroidery together, for the ability
to turn out fine needlework was still considered a requisite part of a
girl's education. As long as we played with dolls—and we did so until
we were in our teens—we made clothes for them; I still have a miniature trunk full of these clothes, carefully cut and exquisitely stitched.
Later, we began to do featherstitching and hemstitching on our own
clothes and to help the seamstresses, who came periodically to our
houses, with hems and seams. We also embroidered all sorts of little
mats and pillows in multicolored silk floss; these were not particularly
useful in themselves, but we learned a great deal about intricate stitchery as we toiled over them. We took music lessons from the same
teacher and walked to and from her house together, a distance of
about four miles in all; also to and from church, which was about
half that distance; and once in a long while I was able to persuade
Jeannie to join me in one of my long rambles, though my predilection
for walking merely as a pastime, and not with any particular end in
view, was not shared by any of my companions of either sex.

My favorite walk consisted in going down the lane back of my mother's house on the Oxbow. It was used by the farmers whose fields lay
on either side of it, as they planted and harvested their crops, and
was bordered by shady trees. At the extreme end of it, a mile distant
from the settlement, a pleasant pasture sloped down to the river, which
was also tree-bordered. This pasture made a wonderful place in which
to break a walk and, eventually, I succeeded in coaxing Jeannie to go
there with me.

It was late July and most of the hay was already cut, but beside the
road the long grass which had escaped the mowing machine was stud-
ded with delicate white flowers, waving on slender stems. The more I
looked at them, the lovelier they seemed to me. At last, I stopped and
gathered a few.

"Do you know the name of these flowers?" I asked Jeannie.

"Yes, don't you?"

"I think so. Isn't it Queen Anne's lace?"

Jeannie nodded. "What made you stop and ask?" she inquired.

"I don't know exactly. Yes, I believe I do. I believe it was because

I suddenly thought that Queen Anne's lace would make a wonderful title for a book. I'm going to write one someday and call it that."

It was Jeannie Darling herself who recalled this incident to me, years later, upon the publication of the first of my novels which scored something like a success.

I have said—and said with great sincerity—that I thought the year I spent in Europe at the age of ten was the most valuable one in my entire education. Perhaps I should have qualified this statement by saying I believed it was the most valuable in a strictly cultural sense and as the means of enlarging what might otherwise have been rather restricted horizons. However, the three years spent largely in Vermont were very valuable, too. It is a wonderful state in which to live at any season and at any age, but especially—or so I believe—at the seasons when most outsiders do not see it, and in one's late childhood and early teens; then—as I have more recently found out—during the advancing years which are freighted with experience. "In Vermont, there is still space: physical space to move around in and psychological space to be tendentious, independent, full of personal style. Landscape and climate turn us inward on ourselves like Thoreau's crabbed wild apples. Some of us develop a concentrated winey flavor, some are just plain sour. No other area of relatively unsettled country of such dimensions exists so close to the metropolitan eastern seaboard. . . . We are trying to catch up with the rest of the country, yet at the same time hoping not to lose the qualities of smallness and independence and the beauty of scene that we enjoy as much as our visitors. Meanwhile, we cannot legally be held responsible for other people's dreams. While her everyday citizens are trying to bring her gradually forward into the twentieth century, many of Vermont's visitors see only the quaint and the old-fashioned and sentimentalize over her. The effect is sometimes to make us feel that we are living in a glass case. Summer is a fine time to visit Vermont, but it is winter that divides the museum exhibits from the human beings."

All this is profoundly true, as is much else that the same writer—Elizabeth Kent Gay—has said about Vermont in that excellent magazine, *Vermont Life*, and elsewhere. I could not, of course, have analyzed the state's characteristics and advantages at the age of fourteen, much less at the age of eleven, though I must have been conscious of them, even if I could not define them, and they have had a lasting influence on my life.

Neither was I analytically aware, at an early age, of any predominating characteristics or advantages in that particular Vermont village where I lived. It was my home and the home of most of my friends; I was very happy there. Now that, with ripening years, more capacity for analysis has come to me, I realize that in Newbury, Vermont, near the close of the nineteenth century, the standards set by two very different groups were extremely important, not only to me personally but to the community as a whole, and that their significance has increased, rather than lessened, with the years.

The first of these was the standard set by a group of women who must have been either middle-aged or elderly, none of them highly educated in a scholastic sense, or widely traveled or even moderately wealthy; but all good-looking—some with very sweet faces, some actually handsome—all intelligent and all of noble character. I have mentioned Cousin Mary—Haines' mother—and Cousin Ellen—the Cobbs' grandmother—and I might, did I not fear to confuse my readers to no especially useful purpose, mention half a dozen others who belonged to the same general category. Though, by and large, their husbands were men of great integrity, one at least was occasionally known to "have liquor on his breath," one was something of a philanderer, and more than one was irregular in attendance at Divine Service, so it was their womenfolk who determined the pattern of life in Newbury. They were industrious and frugal and, withal, hospitable, kindly, enlightened, and, in several cases, extremely devout. They were all congenial and frequently went to "pass the afternoon" with their neighbors; these visits generally took place in the kitchen and involved no ceremony beyond putting on clean aprons; refreshments were not considered obligatory, though if something were "just coming out of the oven" it was, of course, shared. Then, several times a year, these ladies foregathered at one another's houses for "tea" which, being interpreted, meant a light but delicious supper; except for these "teas" and the "cousin parties," to which I have already referred, that were always attended by men as well as women, they had almost no social diversions, nor did they seem to feel the need of any. Each had one good black silk dress which she wore without alteration—unless it needed to be let out as she grew older—as long as it lasted and this was not infrequently all her married life: such a dress had invariably been included in her modest trousseau and sometimes she was buried in it. It was the staple of her wardrobe and it sufficed. She went unfailingly to church every Sunday and to periodic missionary meetings and she could be depended upon, in the event of illness, not only to send broth, custard, jelly, and ice cream to the sufferer but to help with the actual nursing whenever such help was indicated. Malice was alien to her mind, scandal never soiled her, even by the indirect channels of gossip; discontent was unknown to her. Her life was serene.

Now that I have known many famous women in many parts of the world, I can truthfully say that I have never met any other single group which, by mere force of example and personality, exercised so great an influence on everyone within its sphere. From this group I learned that a woman does not need any of the attributes or advantages, which I have admitted its members lacked, to be an active force and a guiding star; she may achieve both ends through simple goodness and homely wisdom coupled with courage and contentment and illumined by faith.

As far as the second group, which was not that of my elders, but of my contemporaries, is concerned, those of us who belonged to it were certainly not aware of setting any standards. (Indeed, I doubt if those elder women were, either!) But I now know that, consciously or unconsciously, we had them and that they were high. A liar, a cheat, or a coward would almost automatically have been ostracized by his fellows; kindness to animals, tenderness toward younger brothers and sisters, respect for parents were all taken for granted. From earliest childhood boys and girls played together and though the nature of these games changed with dawning adolescence, the attitude of the two sexes to each other did not. As far as that goes, the word sex was never actually used; but girls knew—I think almost instinctively—that they were not welcome at the swimming hole and why; and boys recognized that they were similarly debarred from certain feminine pastimes and prerogatives. But these differences were never a subject for conversation in mixed company; and though girls were told by their elders enough for their own guidance, and sometimes confided in each other what their mothers had said to them, it was not a topic of predominant interest. (What the boys talked about, of course, I have no way of knowing.) The word guidance is hardly the right one, anyway, except in its relation to the physical changes in their own bodies which the girls must soon expect; certainly none was needed as far as their male companions were concerned. I can remember very clearly where and when I first heard what we commonly call a "dirty story"; and it was not in Newbury, Vermont, before I was fourteen. With equal clarity, I can remember when a boy first "tried to get fresh" in my presence. (I purposely use that outdated expression for two reasons: first, because it was the one most frequently used at this time and, second, because the word "tried" is especially significant; if the offender had *succeeded* in "getting fresh," he and the object of his attentions would both have immediately been labeled as "cheap.") That was not in Newbury, either, or before I was fourteen, unbelievable as it may seem in the light of prevalent teen-age standards today.

I think that too few women, when they say they can look back on their early girlhood "without a blush," put much of the credit for this where it belongs: namely, to that of the boys they knew. I am very glad to do this.

Old Letters

The hopes and dreams and trivial day-to-day
Events recounted here are lost and gone.
The persons named are dead, or moved away,
Yet I have kept the letters on and on
From year to year, for reasons now obscure,
And nebulous as youth, as one looks back;
And of this lone fact only, I am sure,
Though ink is faded that was blue or black,
And signatures cannot be reconciled
With living shape, or fingers poised above
The waiting page, when I, a lightsome child,
Knew little of the tricks of life and love
But saw the future stretch, secure and sound——
Not canceled, packeted and ribbon-bound.

MINNIE HITE MOODY

Part V

"We came from a world where we have known
incredible standards of excellence."

THORNTON WILDER

CHAPTER XIV

Some time during my fourteenth year, my mother decided it was time
I stopped studying alone and went back to school in Boston. For quite
a while my lessons in French and German with Mademoiselle had
been supplemented by lessons in English given me by Miss Fanny
Atkinson, a very fine woman who, after her graduation from the University of Vermont, had returned to Newbury, which was her native
village, become the librarian of the Tenney Memorial Library and,
in various other ways, maintained high cultural standards. She lived
with her parents and a younger sister in a fine old house on the Montebello Road, the scene of my adventure with the Flexible Flyer. I
walked down to the Atkinsons' from the Oxbow three or four times
a week and devoted most of the periods I spent with Miss Fanny to
mathematics and ancient history, though, like Mademoiselle, she set
great store by poetry and encouraged frequent recitations. I could not
possibly have had a better teacher or a finer example of high standards,
both scholastically and otherwise. But though I galloped through my
schoolbooks with ease, my mother was doubtless right in feeling it
was high time I had the association of classmates; and since she did not
approve of either public schools or coeducation, and took a very dim
view of boarding schools, Miss Winsor's Day School for Girls in Boston was a very logical choice for her.

This had started unpretentiously a decade or so earlier in two rooms on Boylston Street, with only two teachers; Miss Mary Winsor herself and Miss Harriet Paine, on the regular staff; but Fräulein von Blomberg and Mlle. Favre came in twice a week to teach German and French respectively; and later, Miss Elizabeth Winsor, who married Henry Pearson, took charge of some special courses. One of the earliest students, Katharine Sears, still recalls with enthusiasm and gratitude the great privilege of reading Greek with the latter, beside the sea, during summer vacations. Like her sister Mary and her brother Frederick, who founded the Middlesex School for Boys—which Vance Packard ranks so high in *The Status Seekers*—she was a born teacher. As for Miss Paine, who still taught mathematics when I came along, she had few equals and no peers in that branch of learning. She could unravel the knottiest problem and make the driest example intriguing; the way in which X's, Y's, and Z's became animated under her guidance was nothing short of magic. Fräulein von Blomberg and Mlle. Favre also survived in my time and each was excellent in her field.

With such a staff and with such pupils as Katharine Sears and Margaret Farlow (now Mrs. Henry Endicott and Mrs. William R. Castle), it is not surprising that two rooms were soon inadequate to accommodate the school. Moreover, Boylston Street, once lined with fine residences, was fast becoming commercialized. Miss Winsor deemed a change to larger quarters on a less crowded thoroughfare to be advisable and moved her school to nearby Newbury Street. Again, quarters soon seemed cramped and lacking in distinction; but for some reason, she passed over Commonwealth Avenue and established herself briefly on Marlborough Street before making still another move. By the time my mother made her momentous decision, Miss Winsor's was already regarded as the leading institution of its kind in Boston—a proud position which it continues to maintain—and was located in two large chilly houses, on the water side of Beacon Street, which had been thrown together and more or less adapted to their current usage.[1]

Practically next door was Noble and Greenough's Day School for Boys, which, I believe, had been there first; in any case, Miss Winsor could hardly have been unaware of its proximity. Her pupils, however, were supposed to be oblivious of this, and stern indeed were

---

[1] It has since been moved to a much more advantageous site in Brookline.

the reprimands and dire the warnings meted out to any girl who was seen walking across Arlington Street—where many a one descended from the electric car which had brought her in from the suburbs—in company with one of Mr. Noble's pupils, who were supposed to keep to the pavement nearest Commonwealth Avenue, while the Winsorites were supposed to keep to the one nearest the Public Garden. For all I know, Mr. Noble may have been equally unbending in his attitude; and since then, in reflecting at the safe distance of time and age on this situation, I have wondered if it did not bear a certain similarity to the proximity of many monasteries and convents I have seen abroad. Were the monks unaware that their neighbors were nuns and vice versa? If they were not supposed to be aware, why did not priors and abbesses see to it that the monasteries and convents were placed a little farther apart? If no such precaution were taken, is it not reasonable to suppose that there would be at least occasional communication between the two enclosures?

But perhaps this is not germane to the subject at hand, namely, that Miss Winsor's school seemed a logical choice to my mother, and I am by no means sure that the latter would have considered the proximity to Noble and Greenough's much of a drawback. But, as far as Miss Winsor herself was concerned, the choice has always seemed to me less logical, for I have never felt there was much to commend me to her. I have heard she was moved to admit me because of a letter I had written to a French friend, which more or less accidentally fell into her hands before it went on its way to its intended recipient; but this explanation has always seemed to me rather farfetched. Anyway, for whatever reason, I was accepted; my mother, who did not wish to keep house in Boston, engaged a suite at the Vendome, highly regarded as having the most conservative clientele of any hotel in Boston; and one bright and beautiful day in late September, when the autumn coloring was at its very height and the crisp weather ideal for horseback riding, I tearfully took leave of Newbury.

I think that, at the last moment, my mother's heart rather failed her, too. She had had the same people in her employ for several years, a wonderful couple by the name of Frank and Ina Danforth; but they were Vermonters born and bred and did not want to be transplanted; it is no wonder that she was unwilling to try housekeeping without them. A mournful group gathered to say good-by in the little hall back of the library; this, for some reason still not clear to me, was the place chosen as appropriate for farewells with our household. As to the other farewells which might have taken place, I think I must have avoided them as being too painful. It was early in the morning, so I could have sought out Haines in the barn, among the friendly cows which I had come to love because I so often went after them with him; but that would only have made me more homesick later on for the sound of "Co'boss, co'boss!" ringing through the pasture. And I could have mounted Dan or Kaweah and gone to the Homestead and on to the village, seeing each of my other friends in turn one time more. I knew it was better not.

I now believe that my mother was both somewhat chagrined and somewhat surprised to find that her separation and subsequent divorce from my stepfather had somewhat altered her status in Boston. The divorce, granted on statutory grounds, had taken place very quietly the previous year and she had resumed my father's name; but even though it was generally conceded that her course had been justified, impermanence in marriage was still not lightly regarded. However, once settled at the Vendome, I think she became very quickly reconciled to the move. I might have been, too, if any of the girls I already knew in Boston—the Shreve twins, the Edmands sisters, and Marion Burdett—had been going to Miss Winsor's, too, but alas! they were not. My new schoolmates, who were all strangers, looked me over with the critical appraisal of youth, which does not veil or soften its glances, and I was miserably aware of my supreme inadequacy in their eyes. Perhaps if I had not looked so much like a little girl and a little girl from the country at that, the first few weeks would not have been so hard for me and would not still linger in my mind as a painful memory. I was not very tall and I had golden brown curls which did not come much below the nape of my neck and which were tied on top of my head with a wide bright hair ribbon. I wore high-buttoned shoes. My dresses were also buttoned—down the back—and came just below my knees. The one I wore the first day I went to my new school was made of red and green checked wool; it was the triumph of a country dressmaker and was trimmed with taffeta fluting, which matched the feathers in my straw sailor. School did not begin until the first of October, but it had not occurred either to my mother or to me that I should have a new felt hat before leaving Newbury— which was probably just as well, for it doubtless would have been even more grotesque in appearance than the straw sailor.

My new schoolmates were all taller than I. They all did their hair in sleek braids which were folded back over and over until they formed thick neat buns, which were secured by small black bows. With equal uniformity and solidarity, they all wore soft dark felt hats, dark blue serge skirts which came well down toward their trim oxfords, and dark blue serge jackets; the jackets they removed, when they went indoors, to disclose starched white shirtwaists that were fresh every day.

I besought my mother to let me have a dark blue serge suit, low shoes, and a supply of muslin shirtwaists. She was adamant, for she felt sure I would catch cold if I went about so lightly clad. The next thing she knew, I would be rebelling against woolen underwear and flannel petticoats. There was nothing for me to do but to go on wearing the checked dress. I gritted my teeth and tried to think of some avenue of escape from critical appraisal.

If I had realized that an honor student is seldom one of the most popular members of a class, I might have decided that, given two evils between which to choose, it was better to be set apart by my dresses than by my marks. Fortunately, as things turned out, I did not realize this, so I set doggedly to work to excel in scholarship; and since I had no outside diversions to interrupt my studies, only a dull daily walk in which no one joined me, my progress toward my chosen goal was fairly rapid. Not that this progress was without its handicaps, for I did not fit into any established scholastic pattern, and I was shifted from one class to another before a decision was reached as to where I really belonged. I had never studied Latin, at that time a required subject; my fellow students had had at least a year of it. In mathematics, I had not progressed as far as algebra. Even my knowledge of American geography was rather sketchy, and based on travel rather than textbooks, for those Mademoiselle had used, in teaching me, were written in French and did nothing to magnify the United States, territorially or otherwise. I had assimilated a good deal of English literature on my own initiative, along with the French and German literature I had been taught; but the technical terms of grammar were wholly unknown to me. In short, I am sure that if I had been suddenly presented to the principal of the average public high school, he would have asked me a few questions, and then he would have looked at me with pity, not unmingled with scorn, and said in an aside to my sponsor, "Take this poor child back to the sixth grade. Whatever made you think she belonged here?"

Nevertheless, thanks to much good will on the part of bewildered but kind and perceptive teachers and driving ambition on my part, the chaotic conditions under which I studied at first were of comparatively short duration. Even though I knew nothing about parsing and participles, my themes came back to me week after week marked "Excellent" in large red letters; and indirectly I soon learned English grammar by learning Latin grammar. I had not been in the beginners' Latin class a week before my teacher drew me aside and told me it was obvious I did not belong there; my knowledge of French and German made the lessons child's play for me. Would I, she inquired— looking straight past the checked wool dress to my eager face—care to come to school twenty minutes early every morning? If I would, she would give me Latin lessons by myself, for she was confident that in no time I would catch up with the students of Caesar.

The kindly teacher's confidence in me was justified, for I was soon able to declare, with conviction, that all Gaul is divided into three parts. And when the first set of bi-monthly examinations was held, I passed every one of them with a mark of over ninety. I would naturally have felt very jubilant over this if, by the time the last test was held, I had not felt so dreadfully sick. My eyes ran, my throat was sore, and my head ached. My mother regarded me anxiously and said I must have caught cold after all. But I had not caught cold; I had caught scarlet fever.

I was very ill. It was weeks before I was strong enough to so much as sit up in bed again and, when I did, I still could not use my eyes. I lost all real sense of time, as one dragging, meaningless day succeeded another that was just like it. It was not until I actually started back to school that I realized I had been away from there almost two months, that examinations were about to be held again—and that I had just three days in which to make up all the work my class had done during my absence! I had set out to lead it, and unless I could achieve the apparently impossible, I would be dropped from it!

Walking alone up Beacon Street after recess, with Boston's bitter east wind blowing in my face, the tears which I could no longer keep back froze on my cold cheeks. The morning had seemed interminable. I was terribly tired, tired with that devastating weariness which accompanies weakness and discouragement. I was glad to realize that as soon as I had had my lunch, I was supposed to lie down and take a long nap—those were the terms upon which my doctor had permitted my return to school and I was only too willing to abide by them. I would be thankful to go to bed and stay there. I was ready to admit myself exhausted and helpless and beaten.

Ready, but ashamed. Ashamed to let those girls with their sleek braids and their neat shirtwaists, who had laughed at my curls and my clothes, laugh at my failure. Ashamed to let those girls who had permitted my lonely walks, while they gathered companionably at each other's houses, remark my complete withdrawal. Ashamed to let the ones I had almost beaten, at the only game I could play better than they could, gloat after all at my defeat. And permeated with the shame of all this, instead of going home to rest, I walked on and on, until I reached a small private hotel, where a retired teacher whom I had met before I was sick lived in great seclusion. I found this elderly spinster sitting in her shabby little room doing nothing and laid my case before her.

Fortunately, the flint I tried to kindle caught fire instantly: to tutor a private pupil so effectively that in three days she could do almost two months' classwork—what a challenge to any teacher! My benefactress reviewed the situation swiftly: since I was studying Latin alone, I could doubtless obtain permission to defer my examination in that, for such a postponement would inconvenience no one. At all events, we would put that question aside for the moment. French and German need not even be considered in our schedule. A synopsis of the books which had been covered in English literature could be quickly prepared by her and, no doubt, almost as quickly assimilated by me. Algebra was the real stumbling block—we must concentrate on that.

It was suppertime when I went home. Meanwhile, I had sent a scribbled note to my mother, saying that I had had my lunch and that I was being tutored, but not indicating where I could be found. I had the tradition and habit of obedience, but for almost the first time in my life I was defiant. I tumbled into bed that night unresponsive to reproaches; and when I was reasonably sure that my mother was asleep, I got up again, returned to my books, and went on studying. At midnight, I turned off the lights. At six the next morning, I turned them on again. When my mother came to my room at eight, I was apparently peacefully sleeping. But I had already been studying for nearly two hours and had snapped the switch and cuddled down again only when I heard her approaching.

It would have been possible, of course, to put me under lock and key and keep me there; to resort to either punishment or bromides or both; to reinstall a trained nurse, to burn the schoolbooks, or to stage a retreat to Vermont. As a matter of fact, all these measures were mentioned. But there was something about my grim determination that defeated even maternal solicitude. I was threatened, but I was not coerced. I went back to school in the morning, I went back to the palpitating spinster in the afternoon, and I went secretly back to my books in the evening. I did this for three days and at the end of that time I began to take my second set of bi-monthly examinations.

Again I passed every one of them with a grade of over ninety. My report card was returned with this notation from Miss Winsor at the bottom of it: "Frances' marks are just as good as if she had never been ill."

I am glad that I was still so young when I had to face a situation bigger than I was and to recognize that if I did not lick it then, it would lick me. Since then, I have never had to wonder which would happen.

History sometimes has a strange way of repeating itself, or almost repeating itself, even after a lapse of years.

In World War II, my son John was assigned, as a lieutenant (j.g.) to the Indoctrination School at Fort Schuyler for a four weeks' course. At the beginning of his second week there, it seemed advisable to determine whether or not his acute discomfort could be laid entirely to the series of shots he was getting; so he walked from the barracks to sick bay, a distance of a mile; then, as no decision was immediately forthcoming, he walked back to the barracks to get his pajamas and toilet articles and returned to sick bay, bringing the length of his constitutional up to three miles. He was next informed that he would be taken to St. Alban's Hospital in an ambulance; and, after a delay of several hours more, this arrived. By the time he reached the hospital, he could not even see to fill out the questionnaire presented to him; but there were no further delays: a diagnosis of scarlet fever was promptly rendered and he spent the next three weeks in the contagious ward.

When he was released, the final examinations were only a few days off. It does not seem to have occurred to anyone that he would have tried to take them, but taken them he had. The commanding officer admitted to some bewilderment: was it not true, he asked the young man who presented himself calmly with the statement that he did not know what to do next, as he had received no diploma and no orders, that Lieutenant Keyes had been three whole weeks in the hospital? Yes, that was true, the lieutenant admitted, still calmly; nevertheless, he had been assured that he had passed the examinations. The C.O., more and more baffled, ordered him to stand by. In a few days, the orders came through: the lieutenant was to proceed to Fredericksburg, which was the next step forward. After Fredericksburg came New York City and Baltimore, all within pleasantly easy reach of Washington, where I was still living. Then the long and eagerly waited orders for overseas duty.

Among my most cherished possessions is a letter which reads, "Everything is going well and according to plan. Do not worry about me for I am all right and expect to stay so. Love, John." This message would not seem particularly important were it not for the date: June 6, 1944.

If a siege of scarlet fever, which lasted from one set of examinations to another, had put an end to my rapid progress at Miss Winsor's School, I would not have found out, so early in life, that the only time to leave a situation is after you have licked it. If my son had not made a similar discovery, under similar circumstances, I would never have had that letter.

CHAPTER XV

The second half of the school year passed quickly, with no untoward incidents of any kind. I was no longer shuttled back and forth from one classroom to another, in an effort to find out where I really belonged, but firmly anchored in one place; this gave me a sense of stability that I had lacked before. I was still somewhat disturbed because I knew I did not have the right clothes, according to Winsor standards, but this was a minor trouble, because what I wore ceased to cause comment among my schoolmates. I had begun to make friends.

These friendships were destined to play not only an important role in my school days but, like those earlier Boston friendships and those which were such an integral part of my being in Newbury, to prove lifelong; therefore, it seems best to record some of them promptly, because, otherwise, future references to them are bound to be confusing: in the class above me, Margaret Reed and Fannie Howe; in my class, Dorothea Bigelow, Isabella Clark, Polly Cunningham, Marjorie Lawrence, Louise Lincoln, Olive Nason, Susan Sturgis, Elizabeth Sweetser, Hilda Williams, and Nanny Winsor; in the two classes below me, Helen Cutler, Helen McKissock, Barbara Niles, Theoda Bush, Hattie Jacques, and Katherine Reed; in almost every case, there was mutual affection; in some, very naturally, this was stronger than in others.[1] In one case, on my side, it quickly developed into a feeling of unmitigated admiration and utter devotion.

The object of these feelings, which never lessened or even wavered through succeeding years, was Elizabeth Sweetser. My deep and enduring love for her had no relation to the ordinary schoolgirl crush or, indeed, to any sort of transient infatuation; her presence transfigured my school days, her confidence in my character and capabilities was the foundation for much that I have been and done in the entire course of my life. From the beginning, she was a source of courage, comfort, guidance, and inspiration, transcending mere good fellowship. From the first moment that I saw her, I felt her to be a rare spirit. I still feel the same way about her.[2]

Of course, it is impossible to analyze, with complete logic, all the reasons for such intense feeling. But I can outline a few of them. In the first place, she was altogether lovely to look at—not merely pretty; nearly all the girls in the class were pretty, several of them outstandingly so. Hilda Williams' golden hair was not only sufficiently abundant for braids "long enough to sit on"—the requisite standard; it curled delightfully around her pink cheeks and was bound by a narrow black velvet ribbon, worn fillet-wise, which resulted in an effect at one and the same time demure and intriguing; Louise Lincoln was a

[1] Two still older girls, to whose friendship I could not then aspire, were Sophie Judd, of the great Hawaiian family by that name, and Margaret Farlow, who married into another great Hawaiian family—the Castles. These both became good friends of mine later on.

[2] As a result of this confidence, the Elizabeth Soule Sweetser Memorial Prize, awarded annually by the Keyes Foundation, is presented to the girl in the seventh or eighth class at the Winsor School who shows the greatest promise in creative writing. A further tribute to her memory appears in the dedication of my novel, *Joy Street*, which reads:

To
LeBaron Barker
Who kept insisting that this book must be written
Until I gave in and did it
And to the memory of
Elizabeth Soule Sweetser
Who long before LeBaron Barker was born
And also
Long before he or anyone else thought of me as an author
Was confident that some day I would write books
Which would be a credit to the Boston
Of which she was the fine flower

striking burnette, with a peachlike glow in her soft cheeks, gleaming white teeth, and a dazzling smile; Olive Nason, though less radiant, was also extremely handsome. But Elizabeth, as I have just said, was altogether lovely. In those days, when no "nice" girls ever thought of using cosmetics, naturally beautiful skin—"a good complexion," as it was called—was considered absolutely essential for anyone with the slightest claim to good looks; but very few had such perfection of coloring as this fifteen-year-old girl. It was not confined to her rosy cheeks and white brow; her eyes were deep blue; her hair, which must have been flaxen when she was a child, had turned to a golden brown; the thick braids, doubled and redoubled to form a knot at the back of her neck, were as shining as they were smooth. She was tall and beautifully built and, even at that early age, carried herself with ease and grace. Mouth, nose, and ears were all exquisitely formed. The one slight defect in her appearance very soon came to seem like an attraction because it added to her individuality; as a child, she had nicked her two front teeth while coasting, and the lower middle part of them formed a tiny V. When she laughed—and she had a laugh as merry as it was musical—this V was revealed. It was something you came to watch for.

Besides being lovely to look at, she was unusually talented, and her talents were of the type that her schoolmates could appreciate and enjoy. She had great artistic gifts and, besides leading her class in drawing and design, she made delightful little sketches of every kind and description. Some of these were kindly cartoons of both individuals and situations familiar to us; others represented her interpretation of budding beauty, as revealed in fiction, history, and our own imaginations. She could and did dash off little pictures showing the head and shoulders of girls who looked exactly as we would all have liked to look, and permanent possession of these pictures was greatly coveted. (Isabella Clark had a similar faculty, but not nearly as pronounced.) Elizabeth was also a skilled musician. She could play almost anything at sight, could memorize quickly, and could improvise well enough to meet emergency demands for her services in this direction. She did not have a remarkable voice, but it was sweet and clear and her pitch was almost infallible. Though not a student in the strict sense of the word, her marks were always well above average; she had a keen mind and could usually figure out what she did not actually know and come up with the right answer. This ability permitted her to take her lessons in the same easy stride that she took her exercise.

Had she been only lovely to look at and blessed with such attractive versatility, she would have commanded admiration, but she never would have commanded devotion, at least from me, if there had been any malice in her merriment or any vanity about her looks and accomplishments. But she was essentially kind and completely free from vainglory. I was aware of her kindness almost as soon as I was aware of her laugh, her looks, and her talents; and this, with good reason, for she was the first to befriend me. The cruelty of most schoolboys and schoolgirls to the one who is an alien among them is involuntary or unconscious; but the *enfant terrible* of our class seemed to go out of her way to tease and even torment me. She nicknamed me "Innocence"; she mimicked my earnestness by making a long face and crossing her hands devoutly on her breast; having wrung from me the admission that algebra was extremely hard for me, she twisted my book out of my hands, under cover of a raised desk, tore out the pages where the next lesson was marked, and flung the volume to the floor with a bang. Fortunately, the bell rang just then for recess and I retrieved my book before the room teacher's eagle eye could locate the cause of the commotion. Then I fled. I was afraid that if I were not the first girl out in the hall, I would burst into tears of chagrin and rage, to my everlasting shame. But I was not so far away from the scene of turmoil that I could not hear a voice, usually quiet and pleasant, raised in righteous indignation.

"Isa! I think you're horrid to that child! She's frightened to death anyway and you're making her life positively wretched. She really *wants* to study. I admit it's a strange taste, but for mercy's sake why not let her?"

A moment late I felt a comforting hand on my shoulder; the same girl was speaking again, but in an entirely different tone.

"I am sorry, Frances. I know Isa isn't kind to you. But don't take it so hard. Don't let it get under your skin. That'll only make it worse. Now hurry! Put on your hat and let's get along to the Garden."

This was the Public Garden which we had only to cross Beacon Street to reach. It was the preferred place for girls to walk, arm in arm, at recess, and the only restriction placed on such outings was that Winsorites must not leave school for them hatless, as bareheaded girls would be "conspicuous." Hitherto, after walking there several times alone, I had loitered behind in the room where, if we wanted them, we could have crackers and milk at this time; and there I had stayed until the twenty-minute interval had passed. Now, almost overcome with gratitude, I rushed to find the hideous feather-trimmed sailor hat and went with Elizabeth to the Garden. I never went there alone again. Her sponsorship had turned the tide in my favor.

Shortly thereafter, she invited me home to lunch with her. I accepted with ever-mounting gratitude; but my first experience with Sweetser hospitality, which soon became a lasting source of infinite benefit and pleasure, proved somewhat overpowering. The huge dining-room table seemed to be surrounded by rosy-cheeked, blue-eyed, flaxen-haired children who, when they did not pause to stare at me in a most disconcerting fashion, made riotous progress through an enormous meal. They clamored for more milk, for more meat, for more pudding; they banged on the table with their spoons and rushed to the window to hail every passerby with whom they were on friendly terms; and finally, replete with food, they trooped away in a state of vociferous excitement over what they were going to do next, though this appeared to be nothing out of the ordinary. It was hard for me to believe, until some time later, that there were only three younger Sweetsers—Jack, Susan, and Homer; it seemed to me there must be about a dozen. I marveled at the affectionate detachment with which Elizabeth regarded them, and the supreme calm of their beautiful mother, who presided over the family board with the imperturbability of long practice and who, from the very beginning, made me feel I was welcome at it.

This invitation was the first of many, not only to the Sweetsers' spacious and beautiful house, which was located on Warren Street in Brookline, near the reservoir, but to many others almost equally pleasant. In those days, the pupils at Miss Winsor's, though they could have lunch at school if they wished, were not required to do so, and usually they did not; they went home, often taking at least one friend with them, or they themselves went to a friend's house. It was not upsetting, either to the mother of a family or to her household staff, if a few supplementary teen-agers appeared on the scene; it took only a minute to lay extra plates and there was always plenty to eat and to spare. The youthful guests did not present a problem after lunch, either, for they did not expect to have anything planned for them. They and the girl who had invited them home with her decided what they would do next and they spent the afternoon together as they pleased. Very often their amusement took the form of nothing more remarkable than those endless conversations which never seem tedious to the young and which, at that period, inconvenienced nobody, since they took place privately in the young hostess's bedroom and not over the telephone, which occasionally someone else in the family might conceivably like to use! Elizabeth Sweetser and Olive Nason had both carriage and riding horses at their disposal and, therefore, could ask their friends to drive or ride with them; most of the others could not. This did not seem to matter in the least.

Occasionally, the girls went for walks together, though these enjoyed no general vogue and no special stress was put on the desirability of exercise; there were no organized athletics connected either directly or indirectly with school life. Moreover, homework had not begun to assume the staggering proportions it later attained. This lack of pressure, this absence of regimentation, now seems to be wholly a thing of the past and I think we have lost something because it is; the sort of program I have outlined may have been short on system, but it was ideal for fostering lasting friendships. In my case, it not only did this, as far as my classmates were concerned; it also helped me to cement those friendships I had already made, when I first lived in Boston, with girls who went elsewhere to school. The fortunes of the Edmandses had mended by this time and they had left the modest little house on Francis Street and moved to a much more attractive one, which they had built in Chestnut Hill, then, as now, one of the most delightful suburbs of Boston; their hospitality was never failing. The Burdetts, who were now very wealthy, had left Charlesgate East and taken up their residence on the water side of Bay State Road, which had come into great vogue. A beautiful oval dining room and an immense library facing the Charles River were features of their huge and elegant house, which was sufficiently commodious to provide both Marion and her brother Paul with complete suites of bedroom, sitting room, and bath. Mrs. Burdett was still in frail health and attempted very little formal entertaining; but Marion was free to have luncheon and overnight guests whenever she chose and I was fortunate enough to be her frequent choice.

In the early spring of my first year at Miss Winsor's, my mother decided to leave the Vendome and spend the rest of the school term with relatives in Jamaica Plain. Ervin Johnson, the elder brother of oftmentioned Haines and Louise, whose family lived across the street from us in Newbury, had graduated from the Tufts Dental School and now had a promising practice in Boston. He had joined forces with Frank Bayley, whose family lived at the Homestead and who had recently married and come to Boston on business, too. The young couple and the young bachelor—the latter already engaged to another Newbury cousin, Laura Chamberlain, who was a frequent visitor—had taken a pleasant house on Robinwood Avenue in which there was room for my mother and me and we were all congenial; the arrangement was both logical and agreeable. The change was especially welcome to me, because my three great cronies, Norman, Richard, and Katherine Cobb were also located nearby. Their father was connected with the firm of Chase and Sanborn and, though they were always with their maternal grandparents—Cousin Henry and Cousin Ellen Bayley—at the Homestead in the summer, their mother, Cousin Agnes, joined her husband in the winter months, wherever he happened to be stationed, and generally took their children with her for the school year. It was a source of joy to me to have these cherished Newbury friends so unexpectedly available. Moreover, Robinwood Avenue was not far from Lowders Lane, where the Nasons lived, so I saw more and more of Olive all the time and became increasingly attached to her.

With the exception of the midwinter dance at the Boston Latin School, which I attended at the invitation of my first flame, the only boy I knew who went there, I derived less pleasure from the dances, for which I was now considered old enough, than I did from other diversions which offered themselves. Most of these dances apparently took place in Cambridge, though I have no clear recollection as to why so many invitations should have come from there at this stage. I did know some boys at Browne and Nichols, but most of those I knew went either to Volkmann's or Noble and Greenough's and, in any case, invitations to dances, except in unusual instances like the one to the Boston Latin School, did not come directly from boys, though they may have had indirect influence. Perhaps some of mine were due to Mrs. Dimick, our good Samaritan of Washington, who lived on Line Street in Cambridge. At all events, these dances did not seem to me worth the bother of a long ride in the electric cars, with a transfer at Roxbury Crossing. It was a nuisance to carry my slippers in a bag, change from high-buttoned shoes when I reached my destination, and change again before I started home. Besides, though I was not exactly a wallflower, I certainly was not outstandingly popular at these parties; I still lacked ease on a dance floor and I still did not know what to say to my partners. This last lack of adroitness was particularly annoying to me, because I had no trouble at all in talking to the people I met, whether old or young, male or female, except under just these circumstances. It took me some time to learn that the best results were obtained when the dance itself—its rhythm, its stimulation, its potential magic—and not the desultory conversation which may or may not accompany it, is the main preoccupation of both partners until they leave the floor.

My lack of social success at these dances was naturally a cross to my mother, who, of course, took me to them and brought me home from them; she had hoped for better things of me and she was increasingly concerned lest I should turn out to be a bluestocking. But she was both tolerant and understanding when I reminded her she had long ago promised that if I still wished to be confirmed, when I was fourteen, she would consent to this step. Ever since our return from Europe, I had gone to Episcopal churches when the choice was left to me; and if I had had my own way, I would have become a member of this denomination long before this. Wisely, she had asked me to wait; perhaps, as time went on, I would find that I had been merely swayed by a passing enthusiasm for colorful services, but that I really belonged in a church where a simpler form of worship prevailed. She reminded me that the one in Newbury, of which she was a member, had been built by her great-grandfather, that notable patriot, Colonel Thomas Johnson; that my beloved grandmother Wheeler was the widow of a Congregational clergyman; and that she did not feel I should abandon the faith of my forebears without a great deal of thought. I assured her I had given this a great deal of thought, and this was quite true. Once I had convinced her that further argument on the subject was futile, she proved most co-operative. Dean Hodges of the Episcopal Theological School was just beginning to conduct a catechism class at St. John's Memorial Chapel on Brattle Street in Cambridge. He consented to my enrollment in this and I went faithfully to it once a week, making no complaint, as far as this was concerned, about the tedious trolley trip. On May 13th, wearing a white dress, but no veil—for St. John's belongs to the branch known as "Low" in the Episcopal Church—I was duly confirmed by Bishop Lawrence and made my First Communion early the following Sunday morning. From that day on, I went very regularly to church and almost as regularly to Communion for several years; it was a period of unquestioning faith. And another link had been formed with Cambridge.

Now that my mornings at school presented no further problems, that my afternoons with my friends were more and more satisfying and my spiritual experience especially rewarding, it is perhaps natural that intermittent episodes of a disturbing nature should still retain a vividness in my mental vision out of all proportion to their importance. One of these came very close to having a disastrous effect on my relations with my mother, despite her kindly attitude toward my Confirmation. She had previously seemed proud, rather than otherwise, of anything that might have been called a "budding talent" on my part. She had treasured my first short story, *The Rebel Captain's Sweetheart*, written as a result of exploring the attic in the Count Rumford house, and, also, the verses which I wrote annually, at Christmastime, and with a different Christmas theme each year, beginning at a very early age. Moreover, during the Spanish-American War, I had shown her, without hesitation, patriotic verses I had written, which certainly revealed more feeling than form; she had sent them to the editor of the Bradford *Opinion*, the weekly published in the village nearest Newbury; and when he printed them, she had ordered extra copies to distribute among her friends. She had also encouraged me to send little stories I had written to *St. Nicholas*, then the leading juvenile magazine, and had seemed to share my disappointment when none of these was accepted. But I was vaguely aware that, from the time I started school again, she was not as much pleased as I would have wished, either with the themes on which I was getting such good marks, or the quantities of doggerel that I was writing for the amusement of my classmates. The former she dismissed so casually that I stopped showing them to her; and without actually forbidding me to write the latter, she made it evident that she preferred not to have me. I tried to explain that Elizabeth Sweetser and Isabella Clark, who were both very clever with their pencils, constantly made little drawings as presents for their friends; my verses constituted the same kind of an offering; they represented—as they still do—my one facility in the way of a "parlor trick." Her acknowledgment of this explanation was so cool that the next time I wrote verses I did not go out of my way to tell her about them and, presently, I was writing them secretly. But I hoped and believed that if something of mine were published, not in a little newspaper like the Bradford *Opinion*, but in a really important one like the Boston *Transcript*, she might again feel that my writing was something to be proud of. I knew I was going to write whatever happened. "There was a comfortable main road leading from the brain to the pen in my hand. Whatever thoughts I have to spare have groped their way along this road ever since I began to tackle the alphabet."[3]

Presently, it seemed to me that fate was propitious and that my mother had had a hand in making it so. She enjoyed the theater and, even when she was economizing in other ways, after a periodic burst of extravagance, she went to all the best plays herself and took me with her, unless she judged their subject matter to be unsuitable for the young. That spring a drama based on A Tale of Two Cities enjoyed great vogue and we went to it. I had already been reading Dickens with her approval for some time, and I am sure that in taking me to see the play she felt she was only giving me a correlative educational opportunity. But its effect on me was nothing short of intoxicating. I returned from the matinee in a state of great excitement and—emerging only for supper—shut myself up in my room and spent most of the night writing fervid verse. When I had copied and recopied my first draft, I concealed the neatly written sheets among my books, and mailed the verses to the Transcript on my way to school.

I felt entirely safe in so doing. I had been reliably informed—for I had already begun to ask questions on this subject—that no periodical returned unsolicited manuscripts unless postage had been enclosed with it for this purpose; so I had been careful to do nothing of the sort. If my contribution were rejected, it would simply be consigned to the scrap basket beside the editor's desk and that would be the end of it; my mother would never be the wiser. On the other hand, if it were accepted, all her objections to my versifying would be overcome. The Transcript represented the very pinnacle of both respectability and culture; my plan was foolproof. Breathlessly, I awaited its outcome.

It could hardly have taken a more humiliating form. A few days later, when I returned from school, my mother called to me from her room and instructed me to shut the door after me when I came in. Her tone warned me that something was very wrong, but I had not the slightest idea what it could be. As I approached her, I saw that her expression was grim. Then I saw that she was holding my verses in her hand. The Transcript, even in the absence of enclosed postage,

---

[3] The Story of San Michele by Axel Munthe.

had returned them and she had opened the envelope addressed to Mr. Francis Wheeler.

I do not think she could have spoken to me more harshly if she had believed me guilty of cheating or theft. It was obvious, she said, that I was not getting the sort of education which would keep me from the folly of supposing that anything I wrote would be acceptable to an editor of standing; she proposed to withdraw me from Miss Winsor's and send me to a strict boarding school, where all mail, both incoming and outgoing, would be supervised. I do not think she meant this seriously, even for a minute; but I believed her and I was appalled. I visualized my hard-won happiness with my new friends wrested from me and I did not feel that anything in the world could make up for their loss. What was even worse, I realized that the one small talent with which I had been gifted was valueless in my mother's eyes. I could not draw pictures or play the piano or carry a tune like the other girls I knew; but I could write verses. And that, for some reason I could not understand, was supposed to be a source of shame.

It was my mother's scrap basket and not the editor's to which my eulogy of Sydney Carton was consigned. She tore it into tiny bits before my eyes. With it she tore something of my heart. I never again showed her my verse. Indeed, I never again showed her anything I had written, until it had first been approved by some authority which she would recognize. And even then I did so seldom and warily.

But that very afternoon, I went straight from her room to mine, opened the ruled copybook which I habitually used, and, with tears streaming down my cheeks, wrote verse far into the night.

CHAPTER XVI

The school year had ended the last of May and we returned to Newbury; on July 1st, I wrote my mother from Orr's Island, where I had gone to visit my schoolmate Margaret Reed, saying that I was having a "perfectly beautiful time." I also told her some details about my trip: I had gone from Newbury to Boston, where I had briefly visited Olive Nason in Jamaica Plain, Elizabeth Sweetser in Brookline, and the Edmandses in Chestnut Hill, before joining the Reeds at their Gloucester Street house, prior to taking the boat to Portland and then another to Orr's Island. On the face of it this would seem a wholly unremarkable program. But sandwiched in among the above-mentioned details are some regarding the first part of my trip which have a certain significance, for I made this in the watchful care of Harry Keyes.

He had become an intermittent caller at our house the summer before and, as far as I was concerned, not a wholly welcome one, for I was inclined to regard all male visitors, except those who were actually my contemporaries, with suspicion. Though in his case this was unjustified, it was not unnatural. Once my mother had established a legal residence in Vermont, obtained a divorce on statutory grounds, and resumed my father's name, rumors that she was not averse to considering a fourth marriage began to be rife. Nor were these altogether groundless. Though she was now over fifty, no one could have possibly guessed it to look at her. There was not a gray hair in her head, nor a wrinkle in her face. Her teeth were still perfect, her large dark eyes retained their sparkle, and her manner had great animation; when she chose to exert her charm, she could be almost irresistible. She enjoyed—as what normal woman does not!—rousing admiration; but unfortunately she did not seem to know how to be as selective as she should have been about the quarter whence it came and, what is more, it sometimes came from quite unexpected, not to say surprising, quarters through no fault of hers. A case in point is that of a young man who was visiting at a camp by Hall's Pond, six miles from Newbury, when my mother and I were visiting at an adjoining camp; the two groups had not yet met for the corn roast customary on such occasions when the young man in question heard my mother's merry laugh ringing across the small grove between the two places and, then and there, succumbed to the magic of her voice! This susceptible male soon became so persistent a suitor that it proved almost impossible to dampen his ardor, though I must give my mother credit for trying; he came very close to making them both ridiculous by his attentions before his infatuation finally ended; and whether this end was a natural one, or whether at last he was actually forbidden to the house, I do not know. But I do know that I was rendered so acutely miserable by it that, with the intolerance and supersensitiveness of extreme youth, I became, as I have already said, suspicious of any man who I thought might be interested in my mother, or in whom she herself might be interested; my manner to such callers was, I am afraid, extremely discourteous. Why Harry Keyes did not decide, when I was thirteen years old, that I was a brat, of whom the less he saw the better,

I cannot to this day imagine. But, undeterred by my behavior the summer before I went away to school, he reappeared the following June, not as an intermittent visitor, but as a constant one, and a visitor who, though still regarded—at least by me—warily and with some perplexity, had nevertheless assumed the status of a family friend.

Whether it was at his suggestion or my mother's that he undertook to see me safely to Boston on my way to Orr's Island, I never learned; but, in either case, the plan must have seemed a logical one to both of them or it would not have been carried out; and the first letter written in the course of my visit makes it clear that I was no longer unwilling to accept favors from Harry Keyes. From earliest childhood, I have avoided incurring obligations to persons for whom I did not have admiration and respect and I have been equally averse to bartering; but the letter also makes it clear that I feared my mother had been very close to doing what I would not have done myself. "The Champ[1] was the most agreeable person possible during the trip, but I'm not sure about the Medabrook." [sic] "He said you told him I was going to make a lot of bargains with him, which I haven't the slightest intention of doing and I wish you wouldn't make such rash statements. I was *very* provoked to find that you had given him my picture and I told him so. But he was very sweet about it, and after delivering me safe into the hands of Ervin and Alvah, withdrew most modestly and blushingly."

Spelling was obviously still not my forte, but I believe the "Medabrook" refers to a small two-wheeled carriage, known at that time as a Meadowbrook. A few years previously these had been very popular, and Gertrude Keyes had driven one before her marriage; after her tragic death, it was not used any more. Though I could ride so well, I was not a good driver—unlike my mother, who handled her pair superbly—and the process of turning a vehicle that had four wheels never ceased to baffle me. I must have confessed this to Harry Keyes; and though I am sure I would not have *asked* for the loan of the Meadowbrook, which stood neglected in his well-stocked stables, quite evidently the question of its renewed serviceability had been discussed between us; and, as a matter of fact, it was delivered at my door, directly after my return from Maine.

[1] In speaking to him, I continued to address the gentleman in question as "Mr. Keyes" for two years longer; but I did not refer to him in this way. Considering his outstanding athletic feats, not to mention the distinction he had achieved in other fields, "the Champ" seemed a logical nickname, not only to me but to others.

As I have said, I do not know whether it was at his suggestion or my mother's that Harry Keyes accompanied me to Boston; neither do I know why it was apparently decided, to their mutual satisfaction, that, once there, I should be handed over to my distant cousin, Ervin Johnson, and the seventeen-year-old Alvah, who, as I have also said before, was the first beau that I definitely recognized as such. My mother's ideas of chaperonage have always been fraught with mystery to me: if it was proper for the Champ to accompany me to Boston, why was it not proper for him to accompany me as far as "The Monument" in Jamaica Plain, where the Nasons, with whom I was to spend the night, were to meet me? It still seems to me that this would have been a far more logical arrangement. But, apparently, it was never so considered by my mother; for on all subsequent train trips between Newbury and Boston—and these were destined to be many—I was "delivered safe," as I had been this time, into someone else's hands on my arrival at the North Station.

Particulars of my visit to Orr's Island—the first I made by the sea—are duly recorded in a series of letters following the one which announced my arrival. "The Reeds' house is simply dear, without plaster, paint or paper and not very big. Besides human beings, the family consists of two dogs, two rabbits, four turtles and a cat." (As Margaret Reed had a younger sister, Katherine, and two elder brothers, Montgomery and Carlisle, both of whom had guests, the house must have been bulging at the seams, for both parent Reeds were also in residence, not to mention a faithful general maid, Hannah, who did not seem to regard the work for such a crowd as heavy.) "Montgomery, not Carlisle, who hates the water, is going to teach me to swim; he has been lovely to me all day." . . . "We have been fishing twice, but I can't abide it. Yesterday Howard [a fellow guest] and I sat and talked. He is quite a nice boy, but wasteful with his money. Neither of us caught a thing. Today I caught one fish. I assure you I am having a wonderful time, only I don't like to hurt the fish." (This was not only my first but my last experiment in angling. I never recovered from my distaste for it.) "I swam thirteen strokes yesterday and I am in hopes that today I shall be able to swim the required twenty." (Why required, I wonder?) . . . "Don't do anything about my birthday present until I get home. I want to talk it over with you." . . . "Saturday I swam twenty-five strokes and I can also dog-paddle a little, but not float, sad to say." . . . "Montgomery is going to give me one of his graduation pictures [from Harvard]; isn't that nice?"

I reached home in time to celebrate my birthday. I do not remember whether or not my mother, as I had requested, waited to consult me about a present or what she eventually gave me. But I have treasured the letter from my grandmother, in which she enclosed a dollar bill.

"My dear Frances:

"When I date this letter I am reminded that the 21st of July, a day that will always be sacred to me is nearing us, and I wish we were near enough to be together on that day.

"There are no stores here [northern Maine] where I can buy anything that would be of the least value to you, but I want to inclose my trifle, which will remind you that your birth was a joyous occasion to me, and that I still hope and trust that your life in this world may be a blessing, not only to near relatives and friends, but to many others as well, and may be the beginning of a Life Eternal. Please convert my little gift into something that will always remind you that your grandmother loves you."

My birthday party followed the usual pattern. The same boys and girls, who had already been coming year after year, were invited to it; we played the same kind of games and ate the same kind of a supper; with one exception, I received the same type of present. But that exception was a notable one.

Harry Keyes, who had not been invited, but who knew that the twenty-first of July was my birthday, sent me a dozen American Beauty roses, with stems so long that they protruded, in the most approved manner, from the pink box in which Galvin—then the most fashionable florist in Boston—habitually delivered the flowers ordered from him. A plain visiting card, with the "Mr." crossed out before the name and only the words, "Happy Birthday" written underneath, came with the roses. It was a grown-up gift, presented in a grown-up way, and I recognized it as such; but though I was pleased with it, I was also puzzled by it. After all, I was only fifteen—fifteen that day. Just what was the next move when a fifteen-year-old girl received a grown-up gift?

During the rest of the summer, Harry Keyes undertook to answer that question for me.

To begin with, a fifteen-year-old girl should be able to swim more than twenty-five strokes, and that when she was buoyed up by still salt water. She should be able to swim any number of strokes in a river with a current. He would undertake to teach her to do so.

To go on with, a fifteen-year-old girl should be able to handle a canoe, or at least to paddle in the bow of one. He would undertake to see that she would learn to do that, too; and since it was important that she should have exactly the right kind of a paddle, he would buy one for her himself. He did not trust its selection to anyone else.

A fifteen-year-old girl who was a good horsewoman was just the right person to revive interest in riding on the part of a man who had practically given it up. He was so convinced of this that he bought a new saddle horse which he named Tanglefoot, because it sometimes trotted when it was supposed to canter and sometimes galloped when it was supposed to walk. But it was a very nice horse, just the same. Kaweah was more orthodox when it came to gaits; nevertheless, he and Tanglefoot did not make a bad team, especially when it came to woodland roads, of which, at that time, there were still plenty in the vicinity of Newbury, Vermont.

The healthy appetite of a fifteen-year-old girl could not normally be satisfied by three square meals a day; she required candy to supplement these. And candy, in the vernacular of Harry Keyes, meant five-pound boxes of chocolates from Page and Shaw, just as flowers meant American Beauty roses from Galvin's; and the boxes containing the candy were usually made of satin, hand-painted, embroidered, or otherwise embellished. They were useful and ornamental long after their contents had been devoured. This seldom took more than a week. Then another five-pound box made its appearance.

Still and all, come the first of October, a fifteen-year-old girl must go back to school, because that was where girls of this age belonged. There would be another summer with more swimming and more canoeing and more horseback riding. Meanwhile, of course, she would have a very good time living in Cambridge.

I did not feel too sure of the latter.

CHAPTER XVII

The happiness of my anticipation about going back to Miss Winsor's School had been clouded ever since I learned that my mother did not intend to return to Boston with me, but to stay in Newbury all winter, if she could find just the right family for me to live with in the meantime. She made this tentative plan known in several quarters, and my

Latin teacher, Miss Katherine Cook, after consultation with *her* mother, offered to take me in. Besides Mrs. Cook, the family, which was an aristocratic one, consisted of two unmarried daughters, Katherine and Eleanor—the younger a student at Radcliffe and a great belle —and a son, Will, who was a student at Harvard. They lived in a large somber house on one of the most select streets in Cambridge and the arrangement into which we entered was not unusual among such families living in such houses so situated. In this case—and I believe in many others—it was intimated that the obligation was on the part of the paying guest rather than on that of the aristocratic family, though the price exacted for the privilege of living with the latter was high; I felt weighted down with realization of this one-sided obligation and, as time went on, it became a cross as well as a burden. I tried to accept my mother's assurance that it was necessary for us to economize, and that while it would cost a good deal for me to live with the Cooks, this would still be less expensive than any other design for living that seemed suitable to her and, having accepted it, to act upon it not only cheerfully but philosophically; but I was not altogether successful, especially as others had not failed to hint that an ulterior motive had prompted her decision to remain in the country. We agreed, before we parted, that in writing her I would try to stress the pleasant things that happened, rather than the unpleasant ones; consequently, as there was no one else in whom I could confide, many a problem went unsolved and many a heartache was suppressed, even though the agreement apparently did not preclude references to physical ailments and financial worries. As I myself go over the letters, all of which my mother kept, it is easy enough for me to read between the lines and thus to gauge the sense of isolation and insecurity underlying the surface gaiety—sometimes spontaneous and sometimes forced—the genuine pride I took in my school record and my happiness with my friends. I can understand why I said, when I left Cambridge the following spring, that I would never willingly go back there.

Allowing for the lack of proper perspective, the letters become very revealing, especially in four directions. They disclose, along with a sustained interest pertaining to my school and my schoolmates, a rapidly increasing interest in clothes and a very marked change in the degree of importance I attached to my association with boys and young men; and because the change in the social picture is so much greater than the change in the scholastic picture—though that, too, has undergone considerable revision—it is perhaps wise to attempt some clarification of the former before enlarging on the latter.

The popularity of a girl in her middle teens, at the turn of the century, was not gauged by the number of separate "dates" which she had, and the expression "going steady" would have been considered only slightly less vulgar than the practice. As for "petting parties," the very idea of such a thing had never entered the mind of anyone I knew. A well-brought-up girl, living in the Boston area, during her school year, was allowed to receive equally well-brought-up callers (whose qualifications as to character, education, and general background had all been carefully checked) on Friday and Saturday evenings and, sometimes, on Sunday evenings as well, in the case of collegians whose courses interfered with Friday and Saturday visits. These callers were admitted by a maid—one, at least, was always in attendance, even on Sundays—to whom they presented visiting cards, which the maid in turn carried on a silver tray to the waiting teen-ager; then the callers were allowed to present themselves. They could come as early as seven-thirty or eight and they must on no account remain after ten—more often nine-thirty was the limit set. No refreshments of any sort were offered them and no amusements in the form of games provided; their sole entertainment consisted in what the girl herself could provide by way of conversation; and some responsible elder always lurked in a nearby room, where at least fragments of such conversations were inevitably overheard and where any departure from strict decorum of either speech or behavior could be easily detected. Why any boy in his senses should have found such tame diversion rewarding now seems as strange to me as it does to my incredulous grandsons and granddaughters. But the fact remains that many did; and after their departure, the girl on whom they had called stuck their visiting cards in the framework of her mirror, along with the cards inviting her to teas and dances. Then, on Monday mornings, when classes were resumed after the weekend, almost the sole topic of conversation in teen-age feminine circles centered on this subject. The girl who had had eight or ten callers could lord it over the girl who had had only two or three; and it was rare indeed that it was not possible to boast of at least that number and often of many more. It was reliably reported that one rather desperate father in our circle patiently inquired of his daughter every Friday noon how large a proportion of Harvard College he might expect at the house over Sunday!

As the parlor at the Cooks' house was reserved for Eleanor's callers

and Mrs. Cook had to sit in the library, in order to chaperone both her
daughter and her paying guest at the same time, only the reception
hall was available for my use, and, though spacious, it was chilly,
gloomy, and generally forbidding of aspect. Nevertheless, it does not
seem to have been altogether discouraging, either to me or to my
visitors. "Guy came to see me Sunday just after you left," I reported
early in the school year. "The Cooks think he is beautiful. He stayed
quite a long time. Alvah did not come and I was awfully disappointed."
Apparently, this was a rather lean weekend! . . . "Will had an awfully
nice lad to supper and I have been having considerable sport. Queer,
boys about eighteen are not uninteresting, as a rule. Will made an
awful break at supper about 'girls who are only fifteen and wear their
hair down.' I shall never let him hear the last of it." . . . "Of course,
I told Mrs. Cook that I met John the other morning and that he
walked to the Square with me. She wasn't a bit shocked; just laughed.
She really isn't half bad. John said as we went to school at the same
time, and I walked to the Square every morning, we might *happen*—
just *happen* to meet again. And I said yes."

By this time, the football season was in full swing and there are
numerous references to this. "Miss Cook says it is all right for *any*
girl to go alone with *any* nice boy to any football game; that it is
entirely proper; she says of course you would never have any objections, so I am going to the Carlisle Indian football game. I wish I
could go to the Pennsylvania game, the best of all.

"Dudley and Guy came to call while I was at Chestnut Hill spending Sunday with Marian Edmands. I am so provoked for now I'm almost sure I shan't get to the Pennsylvania football game. John came
to call last night and was awfully nice. I was terribly afraid he wouldn't
go home on time, so when the clock struck nine I counted on my
fingers, nodded my head, laughed, and said, 'Exactly.' Then he
laughed, too, and said, 'Yes, exactly. I must go home.' And then we
both laughed and in a minute he went. . . .

"The freshmen in Alvah's and Kerr's course have recitations both
Friday and Saturday night, so I fear I'll never see them; I'm terribly
disappointed. You see the college boys have to work weekdays just
like me, and that is why I hoped they could come Sundays."

As I have freely admitted, the letters reveal a very marked change in
the degree of importance I attached to my associations with boys and
young men; nevertheless, my greatest and most sustained interest was
still centered in my school. "I took a Radcliffe exam in preliminary

French on Monday and had only two mistakes," I reported in mid-October. "Miss Winsor was much pleased and surprised. I got an A in a Latin sight translation. I've had no mistakes in algebra so far. My theme was read on Friday and as it was one of only two out of eighteen, I felt quite complimented. They are working us like machines. The girls sit up and study until eleven, get up at unearthly hours and Polly even does her geometry in her tub so that no time may be lost. Miss Kinsman, the new teacher is a fiend."

That we were encouraged to take an interest in the current political situation, the letters written in early November make very clear. "I'll tell you about our voting at school, and themes on the presidential campaign on Wednesday, when I shall know for certain which way the school goes. It's rather close. We go around: 'Are you for McKinley?' . . . 'Yes.' . . . 'Good work! For Imperialism?' . . . 'Yes, are you?' . . . 'Good work! Indeed I am!' I have been overburdened with questions: 'Frances, I love you; please explain trusts.' . . . 'Frances, you're looking extra sweet today—would you mind making the Philippine problem clear?' . . . 'Frances, what does sixteen to one mean anyhow? Why is foreign trade to be impaired?' and so many questions that I nearly went frantic. Of course, I am for McKinley and Expansion." . . . "I rejoice to say that I belong to a good Republican school," I wrote four days afterward. "The votes stood 89 to 1 in favor of McKinley, and the rest were blanks. My theme on the campaign was announced by Miss Winsor to be one of the two best in our room, and is to be read on Friday."

The new girls in my class, as well as the new room teacher, received their share of comment. "Frances Goodwin, who lives in Cambridge, is only two days older than I, but she wears long dresses and has her hair up part of the time; we are all positive that she laces, she has such a suspiciously small waist for a girl of fifteen, and at Miss Winsor's the girls highly disapprove of tight clothes." My next report on her, made after we had both attended the same dance, is no more favorable. "Frances Goodwin was the belle of the ball; she sat with her legs crossed and swung her feet between all the dances. Her hair looked like a rat's nest, and she was laced so tight that she couldn't really dance—just sort of stalk—but it doesn't seem to make a particle of difference with youths. There is no accounting for tastes."

I hope this severe criticism was based mostly on the youthful intolerance which I find is still prevalent in teen-age circles toward looks and behavior that do not conform strictly to an established local pattern; but I am afraid it was also tinged with jealousy, conscious or unconscious. It was some time before I was anything like the belle of a ball myself; however, I already knew what it was like to be one; and I agree with Billie Burke when she says it is sad that, in these days of dating and going steady, "a girl can't enjoy an experience like that." . . . "I suppose the basis for going steady is that a good man is still hard to find. There are not enough 'real neat' guys to go around. So a girl achieves social security by tieing up a boy. What she misses is the rush, the thrill of being sought after, competed for. The young males of my day liked competition. They brought a girl to a dance to show her off, like a prize. They introduced her to their friends, and looked on with pride. After all, she would leave with the boy that fetched her. A girl can't enjoy an experience like that now." . . . "Just the other day a story appeared in all the papers here which said that in many Midwestern colleges the 'proms' and 'hops'—they have various names—were being abandoned. These big delightful events which used to be so gay and charming, creating so many gay memories, are being called off because—well, what's the use of spending all that money for a huge ball, a name band, corsages, and food when you're going to dance with the same girl all night? The same girl you have a date with every night? It seems to me that in losing their proms the kids are losing something that's fun and romantic, but at the same time perhaps the young men are coming to their senses."[1]

This, happily, was all in the future when Frances Goodwin was the belle of the ball at a Browne and Nichols dance in Cambridge and I must have quickly revised my first estimate of her, for I became very fond of her and saw a great deal of her—indeed, as far as I can recall, the first formal luncheon I ever attended was at her house, and I described it enthusiastically: "The lunch table was beautifully set, bare with lace doilies, heavy silver and flowered china, with flowers in the middle and little silver trays of salted almonds, chocolates and dried prunes set around. We had clam broth with whipped cream on top, with bread sticks; scalloped halibut (spelled right? I got 98 in my spelling exam anyhow) with graham sandwiches; potted pigeons, green peas, tiny fancy potatoes, hot rolls and chocolate with whipped cream on top; strawberry parfait, macaroons, lady cakes, candy, etc." As I have previously remarked, no one was calorie conscious in those days, and no one was overweight, either!

[1] *With Powder on My Nose* by Billie Burke, with Cameron Shipp. Coward-McCann, Inc.

Four days after my first report on Frances Goodwin, a further item appears which seemed no more important at the time, but which very shortly thereafter began to assume a good deal of significance. "There is another new girl at school, small and unusually bright, who is staying at the Reeds' until her mother gets settled. Her name is Theresa Helburn." The comment that Theresa Helburn was "very bright" was certainly what would now be called the understatement of the year. The talents which were eventually to make her so outstanding in theatrical circles were manifest by the discouraging ease with which she did all her lessons.

"It was a common saying among us," I wrote in *The Atlantic*[2] many years later, "that our teachers did not assign history and English lessons by the page, but by the number of inches that multitudinous pages would cover when pressed closely together. This was really not much of an exaggeration. Our algebra lessons did not cover quite so many pages, but our teacher of mathematics considered ten intricate problems a very reasonable number for daily solution. Some higher power decreed that not all of these should be classified as homework, but that we might spend the final period at school in solving, or attempting to solve, the first one or two. We were all extremely grateful for this concession.

"The period lasted forty minutes, from ten minutes before one to one-thirty. On her first day at school, Terry raised her hand at ten minutes past one and, having attracted the room teacher's impersonal attention, inquired whether she might go home. Patiently the teacher explained that Theresa would be much freer that afternoon if she had made a good start on her problems.

" 'I've finished them,' Terry announced tersely.

"Involuntarily, the teacher glanced at the clock. There was a moment of electrified silence. It did not seem probable that this small cheerful child . . . could solve ten difficult problems at the rate of two minutes apiece. 'Bring me your notebook, please,' the teacher requested.

"With complete self-possession, Terry rose, slid from her seat, and approached the teacher's desk. The silence was now not only electric but breathless. It was broken by the crisp sound that the pages of the notebook made as the teacher turned them. Then she closed the book with a snap.

[2] *The Theatre Guild's Terry Helburn.* April, 1953.

" 'The answers are all correct,' she said levelly. 'You may be excused. The rest of the class will please proceed with the problems.'

"Terry nodded and departed, her pleasant rosy face wreathed in smiles. But she left no smiles in her wake."

In no time at all and with the greatest possible nonchalance, Terry had edged me out of my place at the head of the class, though she was two years younger than I and, up to then, I had been the youngest girl in it. I liked and admired her too much to resent this; with my admiration and affection was mingled a certain amount of sympathy, for she did not fit into her strange surroundings any better than I had the year before. "I was very sorry for Terry—she had no gang," the much maligned Miss Kinsman, by that time Mrs. Fred Munroe, greatly beloved by us all, said of her some years later. It is true that she had no gang, but Miss Kinsman's sympathy, like mine, was entirely wasted. Unlike me, she did not want to belong to a gang at Miss Winsor's School on Beacon Street in Boston. She had come from the Horace Mann School in New York and was headed for Bryn Mawr College; to her, the Back Bay represented only an unfortunate interlude necessitated by her father's temporary professional commitments in Boston. Her stay at the Reeds' was brief, for the Helburns were very soon established in a pleasant apartment on Commonwealth Avenue, where I was frequently invited; and our first association was the beginning of a lasting friendship, terminated only by her recent death, and one of the most important and rewarding in my life. But I seldom, if ever, met any of my classmates at her home. They had not welcomed her when she came to Boston as a stranger; very well, why should she welcome them later on? Nothing I could say or do would move her from this stand. However, a few years ago, she began offering a prize to the girl in the senior class at Winsor who showed the greatest promise of dramatic talent. This prize has now been perpetuated in her memory.

Still another new girl at school that year caused quite a sensation, not, like Terry Helburn, because of her remarkable scholarship, but because of the wealth revealed by her exquisite clothes and divined by what we knew or guessed about her mode of life. This girl was Dorothy Jordan, the only daughter of the great merchant prince, Eben D. Jordan. As I have already mentioned, I had known her slightly in a previous incarnation, through my friends the Shreve twins, when she lived in a pseudo-French château on an elevated part of Beacon Street beyond Coolidge Corner. The Jordans had eventually decided that this location was not sufficiently aristocratic and had moved to Beacon Hill. Though I had been numerous times to the French château, I was never invited to the house on Beacon Hill, and I think Elizabeth Sweetser was the only, or almost the only, girl in our class who was; it was from her that we listened, with bated breath, to the stories of the Jordans' magnificence. To do her justice, Dorothy herself never dwelt on this; but somehow it set her apart, just as the delusive simplicity of her custom-made clothes set these apart from blue serge skirts and flannel shirtwaists. Her coloring—dark eyes, golden hair, and a fair skin delicately tanned, long before the last was generally considered an asset—was also sufficiently striking to attract attention, and she was uniformly amiable and approachable; but she made almost no overtures in response to those proffered her. Years later, when I served on a committee headed by Ella Lyman—now Mrs. Roger Lee, the wife of a very distinguished physician—to raise money for a portrait of Miss Winsor, Dorothy Jordan was the only one of my former schoolmates, solicited by me, who declined to contribute, though she certainly had been one of the richest girls who ever attended the school. Her letter of refusal was perfectly courteous; but she had never felt, so she explained, "as if she belonged at Miss Winsor's." Though she later reconsidered and sent a small contribution to Ella Lyman, who approached a second time all those who failed to contribute when first requested to do so, I think Dorothy Jordan, now Mrs. Elbridge Gerry Chadwick of New York, was probably right in her estimate.

Through my letters, my awakened interest in clothes is as evident as my interest in my callers and my schoolmates.

"The flares on the sleeves of my pale blue shirtwaist are all worn out," I reported during October, "and I wish you would send me a little lace to put there in their stead, for otherwise the shirtwaist is all right, and besides it is the only one I can wear with my brown suit; so please send some at once. I cannot find my black velvet hat; please ship it along, for everyone is wearing them and mine is perfectly good. I've never worn it more than a dozen times."

Later the same month comes a more extended entry: "Saturday morning I met Elizabeth at Stevens, where I had my jacket altered and left directions for my rainy day skirt to be shortened." [Probably as much as four inches off the ground.] "Elizabeth had a lot of shopping to do, and the way she knew her way around dazzled me. The idea of having nerve enough to tell anyone right to their face you didn't like this or that and must have something different. She was in a state of smothered laughter over my ignorance. When I told the girls last Monday that I had never been down town alone before, they thought I was fibbing! Elizabeth had on a very pretty new hat, which she had bought the day before; it was dark blue felt, trimmed with rich blue velvet and feathers, and was about five times as pretty as mine is. It cost *five dollars and a half!* Then, as her Sunday suit is to cost forty dollars, she said she must get a cheap coat for school. She bought a dark blue one, lined with black satin at Stearns, which was very becoming, and that cost twelve dollars. She thinks I have far too many clothes and so does Marion Burdett, who you think is always so beautifully dressed. So does Polly; so does Helen, the best dressed girl at school now that Isabella has gone away.

"Yesterday morning I went in to try on my party dresses and they are simply dear. My white dimity is all fixed over with Harvard ribbons and becoming is no word for it. The other two dresses are awfully pretty, but being fancy and very full, they look too short so I had them made a little longer. All the other girls except Marion are going to wear dresses that touch, and hers are to be very long. I had to use my own judgment and I hope I did all right. Mine are not quite to my ankles—about three inches from the ground. All the girls are getting their hair pushed in one direction and their skirts in another. Little Sally Bliss, only fourteen, wears her dresses to her ankles, and Helen, of the same tender age, has her hair demi-up." (Sally was the girl whose father patiently awaited a large section of Harvard College as callers over the weekend.)

My greatest problem at this period was obviously one of finances. "You told me that you had arranged with Mrs. Cook about the washing, but she says you haven't, and I haven't enough allowance to pay for it every week. The woman charges sixty cents a dozen for plain things, fifteen cents apiece for shirtwaists. Now you see washrags and handkerchiefs and all that cost just as much as nice underclothes, so colds and things will be abnormally expensive. Don't you think it would be cheaper to go and arrange for a certain regular sum per month? Be sure and tell me, for I am in despair. I don't even dare to get myself a few hairpins, for fear my money won't last to the end of the month, and I need them very much, as my hair gets wet every morning. You said I needn't pay for my washing and, even though I'm just as careful as I can be, I couldn't help having seven handkerchiefs as a result of that cold, and one shirtwaist." . . . "I have just been to see the washerwoman," I wrote a few days later, "she has six little children, the eldest certainly not eight years, the youngest *two weeks* old! I saw them all, so I know this is a fact. How has she ever done my washing these last two weeks? She will do it for seventy-five cents a week, but shirtwaists and white skirts extra; and will press my party dresses. She has always had more, and that will be much cheaper than it would have been otherwise, for handkerchiefs, stocks, washrags and the like would have counted up terribly. I hope this is all right."

The item of "stocks" will doubtless be unintelligible to the present generation. Webster's dictionary defines them as "large wide soft cravats, worn formerly." At the turn of the century, the term was applied to a stiff piqué collar, to which strips of hemmed muslin were attached. These strips crossed in the back and were brought forward to tie in a bow. Stocks were the prevalent form of neckwear among schoolgirls and, of course, a clean one had to be worn every day. The present generation will also of course wonder why I did not wash "undies" myself and use Kleenex. The answer is primarily that bathrooms, in that era, had not yet been turned into makeshift laundries, and Mrs. Cook would have swooned with mingled surprise and anger if I had attempted any such conversion in her house. Secondarily, it may be noted that "undies" consisted of a muslin chemise, usually ruffled, muslin drawers with ruffles, a muslin corset cover with ribbon threaded through the beading that trimmed it and which had to be removed between each laundering, an embroidered flannel petticoat, and anywhere from three to four muslin petticoats, all with ruffles. If I had attempted to wash and iron these garments, I would not have had much time left for homework. As for Kleenex, that had not yet been invented, any more than nylon and "drip dry."

Laundry continued to be a vexatious problem; before the month was over, I had written about it a third time. Even more of a handicap to both work and play were chilblains and dentistry. "My chilblains have come back and I can scarcely walk," I wrote—and this was *still* October!

"Ervin did not hurt me much Monday, but he made me very nervous. I am to have a gold crown on the back tooth each side and a big gold band fastened on to that crown with screws, which will be tightened and loosened. He says the straightening will take at least six months. Though I never flinched or fussed, I was almost wild when he finished."

Perhaps I neither "flinched nor fussed" on that occasion, but I am afraid there were many others when I did, though at the moment I continued in somewhat happier vein. "As my brown low shoes are the only ones I can wear without suffering terribly, and as it is getting rather cool to wear low shoes[!] I bought a pair of little brown gaiters for seventy-five cents. I hope that wasn't extravagant. It takes time to find cheap things.

"Last night I went to a dance in Boston, so I spent the night with the Wares. I started off in a very happy frame of mind. Maggie dressed me and took the utmost care that every fold of my frock was perfect, that nothing showed which shouldn't, did up my arctics and everything. Haskell took me across the floor and in a second Alvah and Kerr were both at my side. I danced the first dance with Alvah. He looked unusually handsome and danced to perfection. But after that I didn't have a bit of a good time. I suppose I had more attention than at any party last year and much better than a good many girls—those Dodd things, for instance. Will took me for supper and danced with me a lot besides. Kerr danced with me twice. He was much nicer than ever before even, and smiled his darling little smile, and used his adorable expressions and remembered how the first time he saw me I was puzzling over the gerund and gerundive and how he troubled me with that awful Virgil quotation and how quickly we got to know each other and so forth, so forth, so forth. But he made two remarks that hurt my feelings. I will tell you what they were when I see you.

"I went to church with Mrs. Ware this morning to hear Dr. Ames and I enjoyed the sermon very much. On our way home we stopped at the Lenox and it is beautiful. After lunch, I talked with Mrs. Ware until after three. You say I say horrid things about you, but I think you say horrid things about me. Mrs. Ware says you told her I wasn't at all affectionate; that made me feel terribly, for I was at least never accused of that before. She thinks you are in love with the Champ. She asked me if there wasn't a man, that you were so contented in Newbury. I told her no, of course not. Then she asked me if I was going to marry him some time. I said no, I wasn't thinking of it then. She asked how old he was, and said, 'Oh, well, he's too young for your mother. But she thinks he'll do very well for you.' I said she was all off, or something to that effect, only more politely. I guess she thought she was going to pump a lot of things out of me, but that's where she got fooled."

Quite evidently, Mrs. Ware's question had flicked me on the raw; marriage was certainly not in my mind; I was still far too immature for any such serious consideration. The number of callers I had over a weekend; the immediacy with which I was on the floor at a dance; the invitations to football games; the suggestion that I might "happen" to walk in a certain direction on my way to school—these were the criteria by which I judged my standing with my collegiate friends and theirs with me. But the memory of the previous summer's swimming, canoeing, and horseback riding in more mature company, the most congenial I had ever enjoyed, had not been obscured by any of the winter's pastimes and associates, and I did not want it marred, either. It had been an idyllic interlude. I had rejected, when I first left for school, the suggestion that my mother might have had some motive, other than economy, for remaining in the country; and here it was, raising its ugly head again in a different place. I do not think I would have said any "horrid things" about my mother; but I certainly began to harbor some troubled thoughts. With grim resolution, I dropped the unwelcome subject that had been broached and ended my letter on a triumphant note that had no connection with affairs of the heart:

"Friday I got my report, with which I am sending this letter. Well! that 'Very Good' in German is something disgraceful! I feel like hiding my head in shame. (Very good is about ninety per cent.) *German* of all things! But that Excellent in Latin staggered me so that I nearly tumbled over, for I believe Miss Griswold only gave something like three Excellents in Latin all last year, and is considered the hardest marker in the school. Then four Excellents from Miss Kinsman alone, who declared that she would only give Excellent when the work would seem extraordinary. *Oh,* that Excellent in Latin!"

CHAPTER XVIII

For the next month or so, the letters indicate more or less conformity with a recognized pattern:

"I went to Dr. Garland's to see about my chilblains yesterday, but he is very ill himself and cannot attend to anyone," I wrote in mid-December. "The skating is superb now, and the Cooks are wild because I do not go. The skates, the ticket to the rink, the dress-suitcase and the piano would altogether cost only two dollars more than those beautiful furs. Please, Mama, don't have any more party dresses made for me now. I have as many as I can possibly wear out, and they can't be used after the end of the summer because, next winter, I shall wear my hair up to parties and will have to have my dresses touch. It isn't going to make any difference to people whether I have lots of fancy dresses or not. But it's going to make lots of difference whether I skate well, and whether I know more about music."

The furs to which I refer were a gorgeous red fox muff and tippet— as a stole was then called—so showy that I would have felt conspicuous whenever and wherever I wore them. I had dissuaded my mother from buying them on this account, quite as much because I knew she could not really afford them. Like most teen-agers, the height of my sartorial ambition was to be dressed as much like my companions as possible— the desire to set, rather than to follow, a fashion generally comes much later and I was no exception to this rule. The reference to the piano, and to music generally, reveals an even greater cause for concern. I was, as I still am, only too conscious of my lack of musical ability; but I have always loved music, and I longed for a piano on which I could practice, less with the hope that I would ever be able to perform on it acceptably than with the longing for a more intelligent appreciation of what others accomplished. My failure to make my mother understand this was a source of never-ending disappointment to me.

"There were so many things I had to do this morning that I didn't get to church," the same letter which refers to the furs and the piano continues in happier vein. "I meant to stay in this afternoon, too, but Will wanted me to go to walk and I was afraid if I refused a second time he'd get discouraged. He has decided that fifteen is the right age after all, and that it's really nicer for a girl to be small. We walked about four miles into the country, and there we found a delightful little path into the woods and up a hill, so went on and came to the Insane Asylum. I proposed leaving him there, but he said it wouldn't be safe for me to go home alone. He was just bound to go about five miles further, but as it was getting dark I made him come home. We took the car at Waverly and rode the rest of the way. Will kept peering out of the car windows and saying it really wasn't late, and wanted to get out and walk around the Reservoir; but I wouldn't, so he had to content himself with making plans for the future walks in the spring when it won't get dark so early. He 'souped' in a play last night, and is so set up over it that he doesn't know what to do. We are wishing it was the fashion for girls to 'soup,' so we could go together."

Obviously, the chilblains must have been better by this time, despite lack of treatment, or I could hardly have walked four miles for pleasure, and parties, both present and prospective, were occupying more and more of my attention. "Mrs. Dimick and Muriel came to see me last night and there are twenty-six girls and only twenty-four boys for the series of dances Mrs. Dimick is organizing herself," I say with some concern, "and fifteen boys are going to a dance at Brattle Hall the first night. Won't that be *highly* interesting! I am sure John will go there, for he is invited to everything nice." Alas! this was not the case, for "poor John broke his collarbone about three weeks ago, which accounts for my not having 'happened' to meet him on Brattle Street. I am awfully sorry for him. Elizabeth and I started a note together to him, but didn't finish it. I know you say it isn't proper to write to boys, but I was sure this was different. Anyhow, it didn't get sent."

Visits with school friends continued to play an important part in my schedule. "I'm at Elizabeth's having an awfully good time. Yesterday, as I was coming out of school, Helen asked me to come to lunch, and I very gladly accepted." Not all my visits were as uncomplicated as these. "At the end is a very ambiguous sentence," I complained in answering a letter from my mother. " 'Do not talk to Marion about the Sewing Circle and do not stay to lunch there.' Do you mean the thing girls join when they come out if they are anybody? What made you think I'd talk about that to Marion? I never talk about it to anybody, for it's too uninteresting a subject. As for staying to lunch, when I telephoned to see if she would make her party call on Gladys Olmstead and Mrs. Carleton with me on Saturday afternoon, she asked me to come to lunch, and I accepted without the slightest scruple."

It is, perhaps, needless to say that the reason I did not talk about the Sewing Circle to anybody was not because the subject was "uninteresting," but because it was taboo, like discussion of possible admission to private clubs, though its origin was primarily humanitarian, rather than social: during the Civil War, two groups of young ladies, whose relatives and sweethearts had joined the Union forces, banded together under the names of the Chestnut Charity Club—some of the leading members lived on Chestnut Street—and the Maiden Aunts and sewed for the Sanitary Commission, which preceded the Red

Cross in similar activities. The girls met at each other's homes and the sewing was sent from house to house in big crates or laundry baskets. After the war, these congenial friends continued to meet and though, as the need for it became less urgent, they did not do as much work, the members of the Chestnut Charity Club and the Maiden Aunts merged under the name of the Sewing Circle. From the time of its foundation in the eighteen sixties to the time of its absorption by the Junior League in 1905, membership in the Sewing Circle was part of the recognized program for all Boston debutantes; and, in due course, Marion Burdett was one of its most attractive members. My mother's premature reference to it is still "ambiguous"; but the rest of the sentence is now easier to understand: she herself had recently been a house guest at the Burdetts' and the visit had not been altogether a success. I am afraid she realized that she was not likely to be invited there again and was slightly piqued to find that I was still made welcome. But she soon realized the injustice of this attitude and nothing further was said on the subject of my visits.

The letter I have just quoted is one of many which refer to the urgent duty of making party calls. An invitation, whether or not accepted, even to the simplest sort of a function, obligated its recipient to make a formal visit within ten days on the lady who had issued it. Armed with card cases and dressed in our best, we went doggedly from Corey Hill to Beacon Hill and from Cambridge to Brookline; failure to do so, for any cause less cogent than grave illness, would have been frowned upon with the same severity that was meted out to the girl who, having accepted an invitation to a seated dinner, reneged at the last moment. "The only valid excuse that can be given for this," my mother was fond of saying, "is death. And, in that case, the bereaved family should provide a satisfactory substitute for the girl who was invited in the first place." Like many other exaggerations, this warning had a salutary effect!

I went to spend the midwinter holidays that year with my grandmother and her family at the Count Rumford house and reported, "Christmas presents have been arriving galore all the week until I now have thirty-five and I know of two more I am going to have." A glowing account of these follows. With less enthusiasm, I continue, "I had a very proper note from the Champ, saying he was going to send me —and hoped I would accept or permit or something like that—a book

which he had enjoyed greatly." This proved to be Miss Hersey's[1] *To
Girls*, full of good advice about wearing overshoes and flannel petticoats and not staying up too late at night or going to many parties.
I am, therefore, not surprised that the reference to it is not ecstatic.
My greatest thrill came from the first sonnet ever addressed to me,
which I received at the same time as the admonitory tome, and which
represented a very clever *tour de force*.

It was composed by Bär Russell, whom I had never seen since he
and his titled German mother had spent some months as our house
guests at the time of my mother's third marriage—that is to say, for
more than ten years. But lately the two families had been in touch
with each other again through correspondence, and in one of my letters
to Bär I had confessed to difficulty in using the sonnet form for verse
—a difficulty which certainly has been shared by many a more experienced writer than the members of Miss Kinsman's English class! (As
far as I can find out, girls in their middle teens are no longer expected
to reel off sonnets, any more than in my day they were expected to
be proficient in *all* the Latin classics, as they were in my grandmother
Wheeler's day!) Bär's reply, from Berlin, revealed not only his mastery
of the sonnet form but his even more astonishing ability to use the
fourteen letters in the name Frances Wheeler for the arrangement of
an acrostic. "I send you a copy of this sonnet," I wrote my mother,
"observe the first letter of the first line, the second of the second, and
so on till you reach the fourteenth." Bär entitled his poem, *A More
Than Usually Difficult Sonnet*, and I confess I still swell with pride
as I review the following lines:

> "Fate has not cut me out for sonnets, I
> Err little if I only make a few,
> If any other form of verse would do,
> Then I would rhyme in that—at least I'd try.
> Well can I fancy sonnets make you sigh,
> They're stubbornest of all their self-willed kind—
> Practise the art, and presently you'll find
> Your pen winged quite and sonnets far from shy.
> Wrestled have I with this, I must admit,
> Acrostics ever have been rather hard
> I don't yet see however I got through;

[1] Miss Hersey was the headmistress of a girls' school which antedated Miss
Winsor's and had enjoyed the same prestige in Boston. Her book was highly
regarded.

But if this paltry verse have any wit,
Surely 'tis so because the struggling bard
Knew even as he wrote 'twas all for you!"

CHAPTER XIX

The New Year started off on a cheerful note, heightened by the after-glow from the sonnet. "I came back [from my grandmother's] to the Cooks' on Tuesday morning and they seemed glad to see me. I found waiting for me a beautiful box of candied fruit—three pounds—from the Champ, with best wishes for a happy New Year." Obviously, this gift made a more favorable impression than the book sent at Christmastime, or a note, which I had not kept because it was "stiff" and therefore could not show my mother, as she requested. "Tuesday afternoon Will wanted me to go skating with him, but as I didn't feel well, I couldn't. He stayed in and read aloud to me. Alvah rang me up in the evening. He wants to arrange to go skating with me and so do John and Guy.

"School is fine. Miss Kinsman has come around, just as I knew she would if I only didn't try too hard to please her. I have, with Miss Cook's advice and Miss Winsor's highest approval, adopted a plan at school which is going to make my work both now and in college very much easier. I am to have Greek, which, as I have it alone, I am only to work on as long as I well can, but never more than an hour. Miss Griswold is going to teach me and seems quite pleased." School continued to be a source of satisfaction, but friendships meant even more. "Friday I went to Susan Sturgis's to lunch and then to the Symphony with her afterward. It was a perfectly beautiful concert and I never in my life saw such wonderful execution as Adele aus der Ohe's, who was the day's soloist. Susan was to lead the German with Kerr that night and we talked about it a good deal.[1] I have been spending Sunday with the Edmandses and went to church with them, but came home directly afterward, because I had agreed to go and call on Elizabeth with John this afternoon. We walked over, a distance of about four miles. The whole Sweetser family were there and everyone was very nice, including Elizabeth's college brother, Frank, who brought me tea and crackers and talked with me about Greek and sonnets—we being

[1] Let us hope during the intermission!

mutually interested in those things. I did not like him very well when
I saw him before, but it is different now."

Even if everything about that whole winter did not suggest a period
piece, as I review it, this entry would certainly do so: that a girl of
fifteen and a boy of nineteen would discover they were kindred spirits
through their mutual enjoyment in studying Greek and their appreciation in the sonnets of Shakespeare and Keats seems utterly fantastic to
my granddaughters. Nothing but their confidence in my essential
truthfulness saves me from their outspoken conviction that I have
strayed from the field of fact to the field of fiction in describing this
scene. Nevertheless, I can still see the pleasant living room at the
Sweetsers', with its friendly fire, its comfortable well-worn furniture,
and, at the rear, its big windows overlooking the lakelike reservoir;
I can still see the simply spread little table, with Frank sitting on one
side of it and me on the other, while we sipped our tea and munched
our crackers. I can still hear my exclamations of envy as he began to
talk easily about certain passages in the *Iliad* and my humble confes-
sion that I was advancing, so far, no faster than Xenophon's parasangs.
And I can re-create the awed silence in which I listened to the rapt
reading of "Shall I compare thee to a summer's day" and "Bright star,
would I were steadfast as thou art." I went home feeling that my day
had been touched with magic—of course, to pore over volumes in
which were imprisoned beauties I had only half recognized before. The
next time I met my mentor I was ready with a suggestion myself: "Let
me not to the marriage of true minds admit impediments." Frank
wasn't so familiar with that? Well, might I read it to *him?*

"I'd like very much to have you," he answered.

I opened the little volume I had brought with me, hoping for this
reply, and read slowly:

> "Let me not to the marriage of true minds
> Admit impediments. Love is not love
> Which alters when it alteration finds,
> Or bends with the remover to remove:
> O, no! it is an ever-fixèd mark,
> That looks on tempests and is never shaken;
> It is the star to every wand'ring bark,
> Whose worth's unknown, although his height be taken.
> Love's not Time's fool, though rosy lips and cheeks
> Within his bending sickle's compass come;

Love alters not with his brief hours and weeks,
But bears it out even to the edge of doom:——
If this be error and upon me proved,
I never writ, nor no man ever loved."

I closed the volume and we looked at each other solemnly. " 'Ever-fixèd mark,' " I repeated. "That's the way I think of it—of love, I mean," I added, blushing slightly.

"So do I," Frank told me.

Within a few years, we were both to bear witness to the truth of Shakespeare's definition. Meanwhile, after that first afternoon, we continued to read aloud to each other, not frequently, for we did not see each other frequently, but almost every time we did meet, and not only that winter but long afterward. And whatever my granddaughters may say, I think we were much better employed, both for the time being and as far as future enjoyment was concerned, than if we had been listening to the radio or watching television or going to the movies or talking to each other endlessly over the telephone.

As I have said, my path did not cross often with that of Elizabeth's elder brother. He called on me twice during the spring, but I was out both times, for of course the calls, as was then the custom, were made without previous arrangement. It was evidently John whom I saw most frequently of all my male friends in those days, for there are constant references to him. "I walked to the Square with John on Monday. He was awfully nice, and said he wished I would do so every morning, but of course I said I wouldn't. I don't see why I shouldn't though, for we just talk about Elizabeth and lessons and his troubles and pleasures—never mine—and the like. Would twice a week be too often? Don't you see that I shall 'happen' to meet him every morning that I walk to the Square?[2] I thought I explained that carefully before. Of course, I shall not state what mornings I shall do so, if you think that isn't best. He asked me this morning if I would walk to the Square Friday, and I, mindful of your letter, said that perhaps I would and perhaps I wouldn't. Still, it is great fun and, as you say, if I happen to meet him what ever is the harm?"

This argument and others similar to it continued off and on all winter, together with numerous complaints about other aspects of my mother's attitude. "I wish you wouldn't speak of my 'being taken care of' at a dance, as if no one wanted to dance with me and I took along

[2] This is, of course, Harvard Square.

a few youths who would be obliged to. I have six dances engaged
for the next time, so that sounds as if I'd get along fairly well,
doesn't it?" . . . Evidently I did, for the next entry is enthusiastic.
"Miss Hinkley [the director] said I could bring Elizabeth to the
Browne and Nichols dance and Mrs. Cook asked me if I wouldn't like
to have her spend the night with me. So Mrs. Sweetser sent a maid
over with her and we went together and had the time of our lives.
Alvah and I danced together six times and Guy and I nearly as many.
The party didn't end until I don't know when.

"You know Alvah wished on a bracelet of mine last summer, and
then when the time was up, he was going to wish on another; of course
he didn't then. But last night when Guy and Dudley and he put us
in our carriage, he felt my glove, and said, 'Is the bracelet there?' I
nodded, so he found it and put his fingers on it for a minute, and
then said, 'Until next summer!' and laughed and tucked us in and
shut the door."

The fact that our various swains saw us to our carriage and "tucked
us in," but then left us, will doubtless strike present-day teen-agers as
one more quaint custom which has, happily, been discarded. As a
matter of fact, there were rebels against it even at the turn of the
century; and one of my vivid memories of the charming and aristocratic Kerr Rainsford centers in an argument he had with my mother,
during the course of which he asked her, rather sarcastically, if she
preferred to trust her daughter to a cabman rather than a gentleman!
His viewpoint then seemed and still seems to me logical; but he did
not succeed in overpersuading her. The drivers for the famous firm
of Kenney and Clarke were considered, with reason, extremely reliable;
but one of my former classmates has lurid recollections of a driver,
employed by another well-known livery stable, who was nearly always
drunk when the cab in which she was riding after a dance went lurch-
ing up the hill toward her home in Brookline.

Her mother apparently remained unconscious of this hazard and
mine was equally content with livery-stable arrangements in Cambridge; moreover, she must have viewed the practice of "wishing on a
bracelet" with both understanding and complaisance or there would
have been some reference to it in her next letter. (The complaisance
rather surprises me, considering all the other rigid rules by which we
were governed; and the understanding puzzles me still more, for I
myself have entirely forgotten the significance of this sentimental gesture and none of my contemporaries whom I have consulted can ex-

plain it either.) But, as I might have expected, the reference to the
number of dances I had had with the same partner brought about an
immediate maternal rebuke. Unlike most of its kind, it did not depress
me. Instead, I answered it with spirit: "As for dancing more than four
times with anyone, it is perfectly proper. Will went to a party this
winter and danced twelve times with the same girl. Don't be afraid
that I shall make myself conspicuous; I hope I have a little sense."

Probably an outlook as bright and independent as all this indicates
was bound to become cloudy sooner or later and I must have realized
this, even at the age of fifteen. But I hardly could have expected the
variety of complications I was called upon to face while the year was
still young. At first, I was rather apologetic when writing about these.
"Today I haven't been out," I began by admitting. "I woke up with
a backache and sick headache, and only got up long enough to write
for my lessons." She must have written me that she *was* worried and
that Harry Keyes, whom she had obviously seen since I had, was also
concerned, for I replied, rather tartly, "Worried indeed! I must say he
acts like it! He hasn't been near me in nearly six months!" There was
injured pride, of course, rather than sad conviction in this outburst,
and probably some homesickness as well. I could not have doubted
that, if I had been at the friendly Oxbow, instead of at the formal
house on Appleton Street, I would have enjoyed the same companionship which had made the previous summer so pleasant. But in
Cambridge I was and in Cambridge I had to stay and a week later
the report on my health was no better and financial problems were
crowding close on physical troubles. "*Where* is my allowance? It was
due on Friday and I am bankrupt," the next Sunday's letter states
desperately. "Ervin has been obliged to tide me over. I had to pay
for all my medicine and it was quite expensive. I have economized
in every possible way and not bought a thing or taken a car to the
dentist's,[3] except when it's poured, or anything, but I shall have to
borrow again." The atmosphere of the house on Appleton Street was
also becoming increasingly hard to bear. "Oh, Mother, whatever we
do, let's not live in anyone else's house, *ever* again! Perhaps you think
we'd be just as happy at someone *else's* house, but whatever we do,
don't let's try that! Please save your money. Then next winter we can
have a cunning little house, rented all furnished, on Cypress Street—
there are packs of them. Aunt Fannie, without my inquiring at all,

___
[3] This means a *street*car, of course. The fare at that time was five cents.

said she thought that was the ideal thing for us to do. I have reckoned out the cost and it is small. Then I can take music lessons again and practice, instead of embroidering, and we can have a maid like Ina. Oh, it would be perfectly ideal! Only fifteen minutes from Marian and ten from Helen and Polly and five from Elizabeth and twenty from school! And you with me!"

Aside from its proximity to my friends, there was nothing remarkable about Cypress Street, but it had become a symbol to me for a different design for living and I mentioned it over and over again. Even without my unsatisfied longing to take music lessons, it is not surprising that I was tired of embroidery. I had always done a good deal of it and, of late, I had been following the current vogue of embroidering "Harvard pillows" for the most favored friends who went there, and had completed three in rapid succession. But my malaise was by no means only a matter of occupation. The strain between my hostesses and myself continued to increase, and it seems possible that my mother's refusal to take their advice in regard to medical treatment was not the only reason for this, as I wrote, "Don't think of asking Will to the next dance. I shan't ask him to any more or have anything to do with him for the present. Don't think he's been fresh or anything, for he's as nice as he can be and I like him ever so much. But I know his family don't like it because he likes me or because I like to have him like me. So I will just show them I don't consider it such a wondrous favor on his part."

As Will had been one of the recipients of a Harvard pillow, this declaration constitutes something of an about-face. But, thanks to my distant cousin Guy, my horizon was no longer limited to freshmen, as far as callers were concerned, and I was, perhaps, feeling my oats a little. "I didn't tell you about my nice invitation for Thursday, did I?" I asked in the next letter, rather smugly. "Well, at half-past three Guy appeared and we walked down to the Square, where we met Mrs. Carleton, Mrs. Swan, Guy's sister Ruth, Dudley, an old maid friend of Mrs. Carleton's and that nice Mr. Whitney. Then we went to that nice Mr. Jones's room in the Dana Chambers—the prettiest college room about I ever saw—and that nice Mr. Minot and his mother joined us. I felt quite complimented to be the only girl invited. We had grapefruit and sherry, delicious chocolate, fudge, and fancy crackers. Mr. Minot played exquisitely on the piano; after staying a little over an hour, we went through the Yard, past the demolished pump, all over the Phillips Brooks House, to the gym, where the afternoon class was taking place, and then to Memorial 'to see the wild animals eat.' It was great sport. Then we went to Mr. Minot's room where Mr. Hoyt had everything prepared, and partook of Russian tea, chocolate cake, Page and Shaw candy, olives, etc. At last, I said I really must come away. Guy brought me home. I was a little late to dinner, but Mrs. Cook was so impressed because I had been to two college teas at the age of fifteen, and invited for the amusement of *six juniors* that she didn't care at all!"

Of course, I was very much impressed myself; but the "six juniors" and the ever-increasing number of visitors on Friday, Saturday, and Sunday evenings did not altogether make up for the one who did not come, for I wrote of my own accord, "I guess the reason that the Champ doesn't come to see me is because he doesn't want to. You may tell him that if he doesn't appear with speed—that is, the very next time he comes to Boston—*I shall cut him dead* the next time I do see him." This warning, if given, was without the desired result. For the next reference to Harry Keyes was meant to be scathing, but failed of the desired effect because I was still not strong in spelling and weaker still in Egyptology. "Have you seen the Champ lately? He might be an Egyptian scarabee for all I know of him."

After this outburst, I did not refer to the Champ again, and perhaps I did not give his apparent indifference much thought at the time, for, during the intervals when I was well enough to enjoy such diversions— though these intervals were getting fewer and shorter—I was reveling in a series of small social triumphs, which at that age of course seemed very important to me. "Miss Winsor had a tea yesterday, to which I was invited and went. It was a slow thing, I thought. But Miss Hopkinson[4] was there and we came home together. The girl Frances Goodwin gave the luncheon for is visiting at the Hopkinsons' and Frances is Miss Hopkinson's cousin. Well, Miss Hopkinson said this girl—I can't remember her name—came home and reported that there was a Frances Wheeler at the luncheon who was simply the life of the party. Miss Hopkinson said yes, she knew me, and then the girl went on to observe that I was so gay, so amusing, so full of delicious little anecdotes. Wasn't that nice? I was afraid afterward that I had behaved terribly." . . . "The party last night was G L O R I O U S!!! We danced until after eleven. After a good night's sleep, I got up Sunday morning and went to church with Margaret, to a little bit of a High Church

[4] A niece of President Eliot's and one of the room teachers at Miss Winsor's.

off Bowdoin Street.[5] I never went to such a High Church in all the days of my life, the Advent cannot compare with it. The services lasted almost two hours. Of course, Margaret and I walked both ways. Well, when we got almost back to her house, I discovered that I did not have my purse. I was frightened to death, for it had quite a little money and lots of stamps in it. We hurried back with palpitations of the heart, and there it was, safe and sound! I dined at the Reeds'; Mrs. Reed makes me positively tired. She talks of nothing except the impossibility of having Margaret go to college. She says only the exceptional girl can do that. Hump! There must be a good many exceptional girls at Miss Winsor's."[6]

A few days later I wrote happily about a new project. "We are going to act Sardou's *Mademoiselle de la Seglière* in French the last day of school. Elizabeth is to be the hero and I the heroine. The time is 1830 and I am a darling little French marquise and Elizabeth my plebeian lover. Of course, I've got to wear 1830 clothes; so please bring down for my part *your* white Leghorn hat, open-work white silk stockings, little white lace parasol, and white silk-crepe embroidered shawl. All the silk stockings of striking colors you can collect will be handy. (I am to manage the thing, helped by Mlle. Favre and Miss Arnold, the two French teachers, and so must begin early to search for supplies.) Two pretty old fans will be needed. (It strikes me you have some.) Have you any old-fashioned slippers my size, three and a half? The dresses they wore then had short waists and rather narrow skirts reaching not quite to their ankles. If that pink crepe thing of yours is not cut up, I could wear the skirt of that pulled up high, and then just a little fichu and short lace sleeves for one of my dresses—the prettiest one. I think you possess more things that would be nice, but this is all I can remember at the present instant. There are two females only in the play, and lots of men. Oh! that heavy silver necklace, fichus, etc. We are very much in earnest over our play, and Miss Arnold and Mlle. Favre are delighted about it. Just think what an honor for me to

---

[5] This was the Church of St. John the Evangelist, run by the Cowley Fathers. There had previously been numerous references to the Advent. My preference for High Church ritual was developing fast.

[6] As a matter of fact, it *was* only the exceptional girl in our circle who went to college in those days. Ninety per cent of them made their debut after finishing school, at which time their education was considered complete. It is interesting to note that now the ratio in similar circles is exactly reversed—ninety per cent go to college.

be the heroine! It is to be the principal thing of the last day, without doubt."

Mademoiselle de la Seglière was never produced with Elizabeth as the hero and me as the heroine on graduation day. In fact, the play was not produced at all, and I gathered—though I was not present—that the occasion was a rather quiet and subdued one all around. The complaint that we were "being worked like machines," which I had made early in the school year, was not without basis; indeed, as I look back on the matter, I do not see how any girl in her mid-teens could have been expected to carry so heavy a schedule. We studied French, German, and Latin and our lessons in all these languages included both literature and composition and, in French and German, conversation as well. We wrote short daily themes and long weekly themes and studied both English and American literature. The course in these included several Shakespearean plays, and we took sample college-board examinations, left over from former years, to gauge the amount of progress we were making. Though I had given up English history—the course in which we insisted our lessons were not reckoned by the page, but by the number of inches covered by pages—in order to study Greek, the others had all gone plodding along in their monumental task. In mathematics, we were rapidly advancing toward calculus. Science was represented only by physiology, but considerable time was devoted to this. Drawing lessons were no longer obligatory, but the first period of school was inexorably set aside for singing, spelling, and geography, and from these exercises we were never excused.

Before the year was over, it had dawned on the school authorities that this *was* too heavy a schedule; but unfortunately the realization did not come in time to prevent several breakdowns, some not very serious, others more so. Mine was one of the more serious ones. I do not think it fair to lay this wholly to the school schedule; when my teachers realized that I was studying too hard, an effort was made to lighten my labors—in fact, I was induced, not without difficulty, to give up Greek, which I did with the utmost reluctance, and nothing was substituted in its place. But I still could not regard a mark lower than an A with any degree of resignation, and I either went on studying until I was sure of getting this or fretted and fumed if I were not. Moreover, as I look back on it, I do not feel that my physical activities were any better regulated than my mental activities; on almost every school day, I walked a mile down Brattle Street from Appleton to Harvard Square; then took a streetcar to the corner of Massachusetts

Avenue and Beacon Street; and then walked another mile before reaching school. Going home, I reversed this process, which meant that I generally walked four miles, in all kinds of weather, before I had my lunch—the first hearty meal of the day—and very often I walked some more in the afternoon; and this with the intermittent but extremely painful handicap of chilblains, the more constant and still more painful experience of teeth straightening, and the tardy discovery that I had curvature of the spine! Added to all this was the nervous tension of living apart from my own relatives, with a family whose attitude toward me, while not voluntarily unkind, was for the most part aloof and superior and occasionally crushing. One night, for example, when I had one of my frequent bad colds, I asked the Cooks' housemaid to bring me a hot lemonade at bedtime. It did not occur to me that this was an unreasonable request; hot lemonade was a standard remedy for colds in those days and someone had always brought me one at home whenever I wanted it. At ten o'clock, Mrs. Cook herself appeared at my bedside with a steaming glass in hand and an unmistakable expression of rebuke on her face. "You should remember, Frances, that this is not a hotel," she said sternly. "Never make such a request of my maid again." I never did—as long as the maid in question worked for Mrs. Cook. That summer she came to the Oxbow and willingly brought me hot lemonade or anything else I wanted at any hour. But I had no way of knowing she would be glad to do this that night when I cowered shivering under the blankets. I only knew that Mrs. Cook herself had not been glad to minister to me and that I must try harder than ever to keep my colds and other ailments to myself.

There were also nervous tensions at school, quite unconnected with the amount of studying I was doing there. I have mentioned that several Shakespearean plays were included in our literature course; we were expected to memorize large portions of these and to analyze them in our weekly themes. One of these plays was *Romeo and Juliet*. The day after my theme analyzing this had been handed in, Miss Kinsman called me to her and spoke to me more severely than she had in some time. Pointing to a paragraph which had offended her, she said I had put "a very unpleasant interpretation" on Romeo's conduct. Completely bewildered, I reread what I had written: that Romeo's imagined love for Rosalind was based only on her attraction to him as a charming woman, but that when he met Juliet, he realized the difference between infatuation and real love. What I had written, Miss Kinsman assured me, was "indelicate"; I should have said merely that he was "in love with the idea of love." When I told her that was not the way I had interpreted the play, she sent me to Miss Winsor, who had likewise read the offending theme.

I was more and more bewildered, more and more unhappy. I had a great respect for Miss Winsor, whom I considered eminently just. She always allowed a girl to state her own case and, if the case were not convincing, that was almost without exception the girl's fault and not hers. I felt that this time was the exception; I still could not see that what I had written was indelicate and Miss Winsor did not succeed in changing my viewpoint or breaking through my self-defense. Eventually she said, regretfully, that I should not read love stories until I was more mature.

"Then why am I required to read them?" I asked desperately.

One of my former classmates, with whom I recently compared recollections of our school days, confessed that Miss Winsor's hands, which were strong, capable, and rather red, had made a deeper impression on her than our director's firm and noble face; and when I expressed surprise at this, my informant went on to say that she was always so terrified, when summoned into Miss Winsor's presence, that she never dared look any higher than her teacher's hands! I was hurt and angry on the occasion I have just outlined, but I was not terrified; and I looked Miss Winsor full in the face as I asked my question, to which there was no logical answer; for *Romeo and Juliet* was, indeed, only one of many love stories which I had been required, not only to read but to analyze. Miss Winsor realized this; she dismissed me kindly and from that day on I was treated with the utmost thoughtfulness and consideration by my teachers, who recognized signs of strain, without knowing all the causes for this: that I felt more and more in the way at the Cooks'; that I was kept so perpetually short of money that I often hesitated to spend a nickel for carfare; that the backaches were growing worse and worse and other unfavorable symptoms were developing fast; and that the dentistry had become an endurance test. "Today has been pretty hard," I wrote my mother. "I had two exams (also had two yesterday) and I was at the dentist's nearly two hours. I never was hurt so in my life. The skin is so torn where his sharp little instruments have slipped that there are long hanging pieces of limp white flesh which I must cut out. When he finished I couldn't stand alone. Thank fortune, I shan't have to stay more than ten minutes at a time now for the next month or so. Then he is going to put on another band, so I will have one in front of my teeth and one behind. I hope he can fix my upper jaw this spring; he is waiting for it to form more, but I don't want to go through this all over again next year."

I have been much interested in learning from another schoolmate, whom I consulted lately and who for a time was on the school staff, that not long after this Miss Winsor began to recognize certain adverse symptoms among her pupils as being directly connected with the processes of teeth straightening, which was then done much more rapidly and with much less regard for a patient's nerves than it is now. When these symptoms appeared, she made due allowances for them; but that alas! was too late for me. Shortly after writing the letter I have just quoted, I collapsed completely. Before the end of May, my schoolbooks had all been put away and my pleasant engagements broken. I was back at the Oxbow and a practical nurse had been temporarily added to our household staff.

At Majority

When you are old and beautiful,
And things most difficult are done,
There will be few who can recall
Your face as it is ravaged now
By youth and its oppressive choice.

Your look will hold their wondering looks,
Grave as Cordelia's at the last,
Neither with rancor at the past
Nor to upbraid the coming time,
For you will be at peace with time.

But now, a daily warfare takes
Its toll of tenderness in you,
And you must live like captains who
Wait out the hour before the charge——
Fearful, and yet impatient too.

Yet someday this will have an end,
All choices made or choice resigned,
And in your face the literal eye
Trace little of your history,
Nor ever piece the tale entire

Of villages that had to burn
And playthings of the will destroyed
Before you could be safe from time
And gather in your brow and air
The stillness of antiquity.

ADRIENNE RICH

Part VI

"Romance was now in our midst."

CHAPTER XX

This practical nurse was especially good at massage, toward which I have always felt a deadly hatred; instead of finding it soothing, it has the invariable effect of setting my teeth on edge. I tried hard to submit to the conscientious and no doubt skilled ministrations of my nurse, but before long we both knew it was a losing battle. She told my mother I would have to get along without her and took her unregretted departure.

For a time my principal distractions—besides surreptitious writing! —were in trying new styles of hairdressing and making myself new clothes. I was now considered old enough to do up my hair and this solved a troublesome problem for me: the short curls of which I was so ashamed would never make into adequate braids; but gathered into a knot on top of my head, they were not unbecoming. The lengthening of dresses was, as we have already seen, a subject of vital interest to the teen-age girls of that period, and I was no longer satisfied to have mine merely "touch," as I had reported everyone's except Marion Burdett's were doing the previous winter. I wanted trains! And incredible as it now seems, the dress in which I was photographed on my sixteenth birthday—a lace-trimmed flowered muslin which I had made myself!—swept the ground by several inches unless I lifted it carefully as I walked.

Though I slowly regained my health, at first I was not particularly happy to be back in Newbury. I had a dreadful sense of failure: surely I should have managed somehow to finish out the school year, no matter how ill anyone thought I was or how ill I myself felt! Moreover, I was very lonely. I missed the classmates I had lost, and my friends in Newbury did not immediately compensate for the severance of ties in Boston; the two years away at school had had the effect—an effect, I am glad to say, which was only temporary—of alienating me from my closest companions in the country. But the opportune arrival of a new girl in town soon worked wonders.

Of course, almost any newcomer in a village of that size, especially a village where nearly all the families had lived for several generations, would have caused ripples of interest. This one roused actual excitement. She was almost exactly my age, she was as pleasant as she was pretty, and that was saying a good deal, for she was as pretty as a picture. She had rosy cheeks, gray eyes, and soft dark hair, which she permitted to fall in loose waves over her shoulders, indifferent to the current craze for "putting up." Her name was Betty Chamberlain, and her father was the celebrated journalist who wrote the feature called "The Listener" in the Boston *Transcript*. Now he and her mother had separated, though there was no divorce nor any talk of one, and Mrs. Chamberlain had brought Betty and her younger brother and sister, Raymond and Dolly, to live in Newbury for the present. An elder sister, Helen, after being graduated with high honors from the Massachusetts Institute of Technology, had married a fellow student, Walter Dodd, and moved to an abandoned farm near West Newbury, which they were bent on reclaiming. We all knew about "The Listener" and the Dodds and were greatly impressed with their achievements; we were all more impressed by what we soon learned of Betty's: young as she was, she had mastered deaf-and-dumb language and had been the great Helen Keller's interpreter and companion. But this connection, though an honor, had also been a strain and it had been decided that Betty must have a rest from it. Mabel and Maude Sanderson and their mother, who had made so many friends in Newbury during their intermittent sojourns there, had written numerous letters bespeaking a welcome for the Chamberlains, whom they had known in Boston, and of whom they were very fond. It was a cordial gesture, but in Betty's case, at least, it was hardly a necessary one; she would have commanded a welcome anywhere. The first time Richard Darling laid eyes on her, he asked her if he might see her home from church. He was not quite eighteen then, just getting ready to leave for the University of Vermont and, as far as I know, he never looked at another girl with any real interest from the time of that first walk.

Romance was now in our midst: not only romance in the case of Louise Johnson, Haines' elder sister, who was graduating from high school that year, and who had already long held the undivided attention of her classmate, Frank Brock; not only romance in the case of Ervin Johnson, Haines' elder brother, who was actually to marry Laura Chamberlain that coming autumn;[1] but romance in our very own age bracket. And why not? Juliet, I recalled—and did so without a pang for the first time since the writing of that "indelicate" theme!—was only fourteen! I wondered why I had never thought of that before, why it had taken Betty to put it into my head.

With the aura of romance around her, she not only penetrated quickly to our tight little circle, she became a favorite member of it. And, as far as I was concerned, there was a special reason for a bond of sympathy between us: like myself, she had been taken away from the work she loved and in which she was doing well, because it involved too much strain. As I saw how cheerfully and successfully she was adapting herself to a way of life entirely alien to her, I ceased to be ashamed of my breakdown and began to realize that, if I were to be ashamed of anything, it should be of my failure to feel contentment. I was not among strangers, like Betty; as a matter of fact, I was back where I really belonged. I never had been, and never could be, more than a semi-Bostonian. Once I had accepted this, my summer was an extremely pleasant one.

Betty Chamberlain was not the only newcomer that year: the household at the Filley Farm, which lay just north of Pine Grove Farm on the New Hampshire side of the river, had three delightful additions from Rochester, New York. These were Joseph, Frances, and Mary Kittredge, the nephew and nieces of Miss Anne Filley, who, since her sister's marriage, had been a year-round resident of Haverhill, though the family had previously divided its time between St. Louis and New England. Joe was already a junior at Cornell and, as so advanced a collegian, might have very well considered me too young to bother with—despite my happy teas in the Harvard Yard!—if he had not shared my enthusiasm for horseback riding and had a mount at

---

[1] Laura's parents, the "Mem" Chamberlains, and Betty's parents, the Edgar Chamberlains, were related, but only distantly.

his disposal. Moreover, his sisters, though both a little older than I, also found me congenial, happily for me; so first and last, I saw a good deal of all three and frequently visited the Filley Farm.

One day when I was heading in that direction, I stopped in the village and asked Betty if she would not like to go with me. She readily agreed and we set off in the "medabrook," which had again been loaned to me. This, of course, was long before the days of hard-surface roads and, except when snow was on the ground, we usually alternated between thick dust and deep mud when we went driving. After a heavy rain, the hill between the Keyes farm and the Filley farm was as slippery as if it had been greased; and the welcome sunshine which brightened the little jaunt Betty and I were taking had only just broken through the clouds after a prolonged spell of bad weather. Suddenly, Kaweah, normally sure-footed, stumbled and slid forward; the "medabrook," with Betty and me in it, inevitably slid after him; and in a minute we were all upside down at the bottom of the hill!

None was the worse for the tumble; the little cart righted itself almost without help. Kaweah struggled up, regaining his foothold, and stood still, breathing hard but patiently awaiting developments; Betty and I made our call, unshaken by our mishap and unabashed at the condition of our clothes. But the next time I saw Harry Keyes, I painted a lurid picture of what I jestingly termed a very grave accident, for which the shocking conditions of the Haverhill roads were responsible. It would serve the selectmen right, I said, if Betty and I brought suit; in fact, we were seriously thinking of doing so. . . .

He took my teasing in good part and, in due course, replied to it in a way which was to have far-reaching consequences. He had several times asked me if I had never considered keeping a scrapbook—he had done so for many years and had found it far more satisfactory than a diary. I had received the repeated suggestion without much enthusiasm and had dismissed it from my mind as soon as the subject was changed. Now my morning mail brought me a letter which re-opened it.

TOWN OF HAVERHILL,
New Hampshire.

Henry W. Keyes,   Albert F. Kimball,
  Charles J. Pike,   *Town Clerk.*
Dexter L. Hawkins,   Herbert W. Allen,
  Selectmen.   *Treasurer.*

#1002.   6. A. M.

No. Haverhill, N. H., Oct. 22nd., 1901.

Miss Frances P. Wheeler,
    Newbury, Vt.

Dear Madam:—

Some time ago information reached the Chairman of the Board of Selectmen of the town of Haverhill to the effect that you had met with a painful injury while driving on the highways of said town, and that said injury was directly due to the falling of your horse while descending the hill north of the Keyes Farm so-called, and that it was your intention to bring a suit against said town to recover damages.

Section 7, Chapter 76 of the Public Statutes of New Hampshire distinctly states that every person making a claim against a town by virtue of accidents happening on highways shall, within ten days from the date of receiving injury, file with one of the Selectmen and the Clerk of such town a written statement, under oath, setting forth the exact place where and the time when the injury was received, a full description thereof, the extent of the same, and the amount of damages claimed therefor.

This accident, it is understood, occurred in the early part of the summer of 1901, and consequently the time has long since passed in which a claim for damages could be legally entertained.

I would say, however, that there is no disposition to take advantage of any technicality, and that it is felt that some recognition should be taken of a matter of such importance, and one so deeply to be regretted. It is hardly necessary for me to say that a money award commensurate with any injury you might have received would of course be something entirely beyond the ability of the town to meet.

At a meeting recently held in Haverhill, at which the writer was present, it was voted *unanimously* to leave the adjustment of this regrettable case to the Chairman of the Board.

Acting upon the decision of this meeting I have taken the liberty to have forwarded to you at Newbury by today's express a small package, a *scrap* as it were, which I hope you will see fit to accept as an earnest of the writer's good will.

Trusting that you have fully recovered and that your unfortunate experience was not such as to forever keep you on the Vermont side of the Connecticut River, I beg to remain,

Most Respectfully Yours,
Henry W. Keyes.

Dictated.

H/W

The "scrap" proved to be two beautiful large volumes bound in red morocco and stamped in gold with my initials. Their big blank pages invited filling; and, presently, I was pasting into them, not without nostalgia, invitations, programs, school reports, score pads, visiting cards, and ticket stubs saved from the previous winter, but still scattered helter-skelter in my desk and bureau drawers. Such pasting was the beginning of a fixed habit. Those two beautiful red morocco books have been followed by a series of others, less elegant as to binding, but enriched with delightful and authentic reminders of what I have been seeing and doing in all parts of the world for more than half a century. I have only to turn to them to visualize again a court at Buckingham Palace—a Royal Polo Match at Santander—a tea party given at Shanghai by Mei-ling Soong[2]—State dinners at the White House, at Malacañan Palace in Manila, at Government House in Singapore—a special audience with the pope—the canonization of Mother Cabrini at St. Peter's—a carnival celebration in Lima as seen from the Presidential Pavilion—luncheon with Mrs. Roosevelt at Hyde Park, with the Duke and Duchess of Windsor in Paris, with the ex-Kaiser and Princess Hermine at Doorn—tea with Lady Isabel Howard at Hampton Court, with the Earl of Iddesleigh "on the terrace"—two National Democratic and two National Republican Conventions—the inaugurations of a President in Cuba and in Mexico and of five American Presidents—the dedication of the Lincoln Memorial and the Tomb of the Unknown Soldier—a command performance given in honor of the King and Queen of England during a state visit to Italy

[2] Now Madame Chiang Kai-shek.

—the opening of Parliament in Ottawa and London and Cairo. . . .

Harry Keyes never told me why, for seven months, he had not once tried to get in direct touch with me and I never asked him. I think now he felt that, as long as he had reason to believe I was well and happy in Cambridge, it would be better not to attempt any further suggestions as to what a fifteen-year-old girl might be expected to do in a grown-up way; that even when he began to doubt whether or not the winter's arrangements had been wholly satisfactory, he hesitated to interfere; but that when she came home, neither well nor happy, it was time for him to resume his visits, with the hope that they then might be beneficial as well as pleasurable. At all events, though my other friends in Newbury and its vicinity vied with each other in giving my many house guests a good time, none of them did as much to ensure their enjoyment of the region as Harry Keyes.

A tragic loss, which had taken place the autumn before, had altered his way of life very materially. Fortunately, the loss was not one of life this time, though it was of something very near and dear to him: the fine old house in which he lived, and in which his mother, sister, and little niece, to all of whom he was devoted, spent the summers with him, had burned to the ground. Historically and architecturally this was a great calamity; from the viewpoint of sentiment it was an even greater one. In earliest manhood, Pine Grove Farm had become his chosen home, and year by year he had labored to make everything about the place more beautiful. His extraordinary aptitude as a forester and landscape gardener had transformed the grounds; his predilection for interior decorating was marked by almost unerring taste. He had just finished a major undertaking of modernizing the old house, adding more bathrooms, better service quarters, and a new ell, while bringing out still further the best characteristics in the eight main rooms, four upstairs and four downstairs; now all were devoured by the flames. In those days, there were very few telephones, and no automobiles, and there was no organized fire department within twenty-five miles, while the water supply at Pine Grove Farm depended, as it still does, on a privately owned spring. As soon as the emergency was known, help came hurrying from far and wide; but in most cases this was not until the blaze could actually be seen or made known by word of mouth. I myself had jumped on Kaweah and galloped at top speed up and down the valley, spreading the alarm. My mother had at once put the three other horses at the disposal of anyone who would use them and had gone herself to the farm in one of the laden vehicles. As she entered the south driveway, she met one of the Keyes wagonettes coming out at furious speed; beside the coachman sat Harry, enveloped in a blood-stained sheet. He had cut an artery in his hand and was being rushed to a doctor; his very life was in danger. When he returned to the farm, nothing but a pile of ashes remained of the house he loved so deeply and had done so much to beautify.

This disaster had, of course, been a tremendous blow to him and his family. As it was almost time for his mother, sister, and little niece Gertrude to return to Boston for the winter in any case, they had done so after staying a few days in the vicinity with relatives. Harry had spent the winter at the foreman's cottage, which had fortunately escaped the general holocaust, and had supplemented his quarters there by a small one-roomed building, hastily run up, to which he referred only as "the Shack." This he used for an office and living room and, with characteristic good taste, made it seem homelike and attractive. With the return of warm weather, he also began to spend some time at the camp he had built on Lake Tarleton, which was about ten miles from Haverhill, with a situation a thousand feet higher than the Connecticut Valley. To ensure complete privacy, he had bought all one side of the lake and had declined to permit the building of a road leading to this property; it could be approached only by a trail he had blazed through the woods and by a rowboat which he kept tied to the wharf of a small primitive lodge on the opposite shore. With his talent along such lines, he had made this woodland and lakeside retreat extremely attractive; and the previous summer he had given a housewarming there which my mother and I had attended, along with about twenty other privileged guests. Now he generously put it at my disposal for the entertainment of all my visitors and proved an ideal host, both to them and to me.

Elizabeth Sweetser and Helen Cutler both spent the latter part of July and the first part of August with me at the Oxbow and when they left Newbury I went with them, first to visit Elizabeth at the Sweetsers' summer home in Marion on Buzzard's Bay and then to visit Helen at the Cutlers' summer home in Hull on Boston Harbor. The letters I wrote my mother in the course of these two visits were full of understandable enthusiasm. "Mr. Sweetser met us at the North Station and took us to the Union Club, where he gave us the best lunch I ever had in my life—fancy consommé, soft-shell crabs, chicken croquettes with soft delicious white sauce and an enormous omelette soufflé. Then Elizabeth and I said good-by to Helen and got to the

South Station nice and early to take the 'Dude,' which is a special train, all parlor car, and does the fifty miles from Boston to Marion in sixty-eight minutes. Mrs. Sweetser and Homer had come to meet us and we had a beautiful three mile drive over to the house. The place is lovely, just exactly as I expected it would be. F. E. S., Jr. and Francis Colby were waiting in the door for us, wreathed in smiles. Francis Colby is a nice clean looking boy about nineteen and I don't believe he and I are going to get on as badly as Elizabeth seemed to fear. Frank is terribly gone on a girl from Philadelphia and is cross because Elizabeth wouldn't have her over to lunch today." . . . "Yesterday afternoon it poured; I read *Lamia* (a work of Mr. Keats) aloud to Elizabeth and embroidered; late in the afternoon she went driving with Francis Colby and I didn't do anything special. Frank lay on the sofa, long, dumb, lanky and cranky, deep in a novel of Meredith's, with huge black-rimmed spectacles on his nose and a Gibson-in-distress frown on his forehead. Oh! I do like him so much and I was beginning to be afraid he doesn't like me a bit, then in the evening I had a lovely long talk with him.[3]

"Saturday morning after I had written you, I composed myself in a chair to read. I'm not quite sure how it all happened, but suddenly F. E. S., Jr. with his finger in his book was opposite me and we were arguing as to which were the more sensitive, women or men. We talked for almost two hours, and it finally got so interesting that Francis Colby and Elizabeth chimed in. Then we four went out sailing in the 'Marion Squizzle.' It was awfully rough, so the little boat tipped terribly. We all got soaked, caught on our mooring, went aground, etc., etc. I tell you it was fun; we all laughed ourselves sick, except F. E. S., Jr., who kept his accustomed dignity. We had to hurry in and dress in all our best to go to a big stand-up lunch at a certain Mrs. Rice's, who owns all Bird Island and has a stunning place as you might expect. Mine consisted of creamed lobster, cold ham, gallons of coffee ice cream with white parfait inside and whipped cream

---

[3] A photograph taken in the Sweetsers' Marion living room, carefully preserved in my first scrapbook, is labeled, "Keats, Meredith and Philosophy," so I gather these were the subjects we were at this time discussing. Recently, J. Donald Adams devoted the major part of his feature, "Speaking of Books," in the New York *Times* to a discussion of Meredith, which was very far from complimentary, and further quoted excerpts from *The Ordeal of Richard Feverel* in the "Treasure Chest" to prove his point. But I still think *Richard Feverel* one of the most beautiful novels ever written and am glad to acknowledge my indebtedness to Frank E. Sweetser, Jr., for my introduction to this and my subsequent wide acquaintance with many other novels by George Meredith.

all around it, and two pieces of rich chocolate cake and one of some other kind. Besides all this, there was some drink called claret punch which F. E. S., Jr. said was the 'real stuff.' He drank seven glasses of it. Francis Colby assured me it would be proper for me to drink it, so I had a glass and a half, besides a glass of iced tea."[4]

Shortly after my return to Newbury, the long engagement between Ervin Johnson and Laura Chamberlain came to a happy end in their marriage. They had a home wedding, like most young country couples in those days; and, as Laura's parents had moved from their pleasant little house back of the Newbury Common to a large stone house in South Newbury, which was surrounded by spreading lawns, there was ample space for all the cousins who flocked from near and far for the occasion. And not only cousins, by any means; the bride and groom were both immensely liked by everyone who knew them and countless friends came to wish them well. It was a beautiful day, warm enough at midafternoon to permit the guests to wander freely over the wide verandas and pleasant grounds; and it was glorified by the vivid coloring of the "fall of the year," which has now come to be so common and curtailed an expression that we have almost forgotten that it really refers to falling foliage which in few places, if any, is as gorgeous as in northern New England, where the scarlet of maple outshines the golden of other trees and the quiet roads are bordered with blazing banners and every hillside seems aflame.

But it is not only because the occasion was one of such general rejoicing and because everything about the setting seemed so propitious and harmonious that this wedding stands out in my mind. As I have said before, the visits of Harry Keyes to the Oxbow and his hospitality to my house guests had now become recognized and established; but he had never singled me out for special attention at any social gather-

[4] Francis Colby, to whom I referred thus briefly and nonchalantly, was destined to have a very remarkable career. Before the entry of the United States into World War I, he served with distinction as an officer in the Belgian, French, and Italian armies and received almost every possible military decoration. At the end of the war, he was commissioned major in the American Army and sent, as military attaché, to Belgrade. His exploits as a hunter and explorer were even more remarkable; his scenes of activity ranged from Alaska to Africa, and his game included bear, moose, caribou, lion, buffalo, elephant, rhinoceros, and many kinds of antelope. His skill at polo, his success as a banker and lawyer, and his role as a country gentleman, resident—intermittently!—in Hamilton, all of which were likewise noteworthy, were inevitably somewhat overshadowed by his more spectacular occupations.

ing—indeed, to the best of my knowledge, he had not attended any
social gathering in the vicinity for many years, except on the rare occasions when he went as a member of the little local band he had
organized, and then he kept as much in the background as possible.
(At one such gathering, all the members of the band had filed un-
obtrusively up the back stairs to the little balcony off my room, where
they performed, and never left it at all until they filed, equally un-
obtrusively, off again!) But he came to the Johnson-Chamberlain
wedding all alone; hitched his smart rubber-tired runabout among
the less pretentious buggies and carryalls; and made his way to the parlor where the wedding party was getting ready to receive. Then he
turned and, after courteously acknowledging the welcome with which
he was greeted, came to the corner where I was standing and suggested that perhaps I would like to have some refreshment.

"That would be nice. And this time I won't forget to thank you
for it."

"Well, if you did, perhaps you would write me and that would be
nice, too."

It was nine years since I had written that first little note, and he
had not forgotten, any more than I had. We moved away together
toward the dining room, from there to the veranda and from there to
the lawn. His arrival had caused a subdued stir of excitement, partly
because his very presence was remarkable on account of his retiring
habits; and partly because that presence, for all his characteristic diffi-
dence, was charming and distinguished. Moreover, he was extremely
good-looking and extremely well built and he wore his clothes with
the accustomed ease of a man who has always taken a good tailor
for granted and is therefore quite unconscious of the effect they pro-
duce. Inevitably, he would have been conspicuous that day and, for
once, he did not seem to mind. Inevitably, anyone he singled out
would have been conspicuous, too.

I did not mind, either, though I knew that, as far as Newbury and
Haverhill were concerned, I was "Harry Keyes's girl" from that day on.

CHAPTER XXI

I was only mildly disappointed when my mother informed me, shortly
after the Johnson-Chamberlain wedding, that she did not consider me

well enough to go back to school that autumn. She had corresponded with Miss Winsor, who had promised to save a place for me, and I could return the following year and graduate. Meanwhile, my mother would consent to a moderate amount of studying—enough so that I could keep up with my class and take my first set of examinations for Bryn Mawr. (College examinations at that time were always taken in two parts, on successive years, and were known as "preliminaries" and "finals.") I had not yet wrung her consent to the college course on which I had set my heart; even so, I realized she was making a concession which might lead to it and with this I tried to be content.

Most of the "moderate amount of studying" I was supposed to do by myself, and it was a relief not to be obliged to do it surreptitiously, the way I had read Cicero the summer between my first and second years at Winsor. Now I continued my study of Virgil and read some Ovid and some Nepos besides, partly alone and partly with a certain Mrs. Taggart, who had attended Smith College and whose husband, Charles Ross Taggart, was a professional entertainer. His act was entitled "The Man from Vermont" and he was on the road most of the time, but he made his headquarters in Newbury and his wife and children were settled there. I walked to the village three times a week to read Latin with this lady and five times a week to recite with the geometry class at the Newbury High School. I was supposed to stay only long enough for this recitation; though my mother had accepted the arrangement as the most feasible under the circumstances, she did not view it with enthusiasm. However, I was able to join Jeannie Darling, who was in the same class, when I reached her house, and we went the rest of the way to and from school together. Afterward, we often also worked out our geometry problems together, before we took up the needlework which continued to occupy our interest and attention, as it had ever since we were little girls. The only difference was that now we made clothes for ourselves instead of our dolls.

The winter was a very quiet one, except for the midwinter holidays, when I had several visitors from Boston and celebrated New Year's Eve with a really hilarious party. The first part of the evening, before we had supper and danced the Virginia reel, was spent in a treasure hunt, during the course of which teen-agers darted from attic to cellar and from the kitchen pantry to bedroom closets, untangling the threads which my house guests and I had spent hours stringing around; then finally, with shouts of joy and triumph, the trifling gifts at the ends of these threads were unearthed and brought to light. This was the first party of its kind that anyone had given in Newbury and was the occasion of great enthusiasm; so was the game that someone thought up to play as the clock struck midnight: we were all provided with scraps of paper and tiny pencils; the trick we were given to perform was to write a wish on the paper and burn the scrap while the clock was still striking; if we could do this, and show the ashes to prove it, the wish was supposed to come true. The timepiece we chose to go by was the grandfather's clock which stood in the dining room, made by Richard Carleton of Haverhill, and treasured in the family. Its selection, however, was not due to its important status as an heirloom; though it still kept good time, its striking was erratic—in fact, it had once come close to disrupting a parlor prayer meeting, because, just as the officiating clergyman had begun a long extemporaneous prayer, it went on and on, loudly striking over a hundred times! Most of us were secretly hoping that on New Year's Eve it would do something of the kind again; then we would have plenty of time to write our wishes, and there would be no reason why they should not all come true, for no one had said that the clock must not strike more than twelve, only that the wish must be written and burned while it *was* striking! Unfortunately, from our point of view, it did not repeat its most fantastic performance; nevertheless, a good many wishes were recorded and burned and, to my certain knowledge, several of them came true!

I think the state of my health had really been better, in the fall, than my mother had chosen to admit, for I was not only equal to party giving and partygoing, on top of my studying, but did a tremendous amount of snowshoeing—mostly down the lane alone—and an even greater amount of sleigh riding—mostly with Harry Keyes, who, after his one memorable appearance at the Johnson-Chamberlain wedding, attended no more local social functions, but who was, nevertheless, much in evidence at the Oxbow. He had a beautiful little red sleigh, equipped with huge bearskins and buffalo robes; and it never occurred to him or anyone else that zero weather was unsuitable for prolonged outings in the fresh air.

Whether or not I pushed my luck in this direction too far, I do not know. At all events, late in the winter I came down with a very bad cold, which quickly developed into acute bronchitis, and my convalescence was slow and unsatisfactory. By then the quietude of Newbury had begun to pall on my mother, as it always did after a certain length of time, and she decided the moment had come to pay my brother another visit.

He was still living in Colorado and, since our stay there four years earlier, had married a very lovely girl by the name of Lucy Stoller. We had never met her, for the wedding had taken place while I was dangerously ill with scarlet fever and my brother was engaged in a special engineering project in California; to avoid a long separation, Lucy and James had been quietly married there. Now they were back in Idaho Springs, where they lived with the great simplicity which they both preferred; and, as there was no guest room in the apartment where they did light housekeeping, my mother and I again stayed at the hotel, which provided more amenities than had previously been available, but which was still very far from luxurious. This troubled me no more than it had before; I loved everything about life in Idaho Springs: the rugged scenery, the mysterious mines, the bracing air, the hospitable people. However, once in a while, I became vaguely aware of some undercurrent in family relationships that was a little disturbing. Gradually, I gathered that my mother had not acted with the generosity that her only son and his bride thought they had a right to expect, either at the time of their marriage or afterward; she, in her turn, was disappointed because they did not have a baby, or any prospect of one, and voiced this disappointment more frankly than was customary at that time in speaking of such things. Somehow the visit was not as much of a success as I had expected, and this distressed me very much, as I was still deeply devoted to my brother and delighted with my new sister-in-law; and my disquietude must have had some foundation for my mother never visited them again. After my marriage, I did so on two occasions, several years apart, taking my eldest son with me the first time and my youngest son the second; and both visits were extremely pleasant, as far as the boys and I were concerned. But though I was not aware of it, there must again have been some undercurrent of disharmony; for not long afterward it became all too evident that James and Lucy would not welcome us again. My affection for them never lessened; I was puzzled, as well as hurt, when I found this affection was no longer reciprocal. Lacking a father, the importance of the role which a dearly loved brother could have played in my life had great potentialities of helpfulness. It will always be a matter of grief to me that I was deprived of this without ever knowing the reason for it, though I tried over and over again to find out what it could be.

During the course of that visit, when I first began to feel uneasiness from the family angle, I was also troubled about my studies. My brother had found a friend who was willing to tutor me in geometry and I went regularly to him for lessons in this subject. Otherwise, I was not keeping up with schoolwork at all, and "preliminaries" were coming closer and closer. But when I reminded my mother of this, and said I thought we had better go home, she announced that she had decided to prolong our trip: we would first proceed to Denver, where we would visit our beautiful cousin, Isabel Hill, who had at last succumbed to importunities so urgent she could not dismiss them, and was now Mrs. Franklin Knott, with a fine establishment of her own; afterward, we would go on to California. The American Federation of Women's Clubs, in which my mother's interest was new but intense, was meeting in Los Angeles, and the Santa Fe Railroad was offering special rates to members of this organization who wished to go there; as usual, the families of such members were included in the rates.

I did not view this plan with favor, but that, of course, made no difference and, once I had succeeded in dismissing the impending examinations from my mind and was on my way, I am bound to admit that I had a very good time. As on the occasion of my earlier visit, I was dazzled by the luxurious and sophisticated atmosphere of our cousins' establishments in Denver and, since this time, I was considered old enough to hover more closely than before on the outskirts of grown-up parties, I had an even clearer vision of their fascination. Then the trip from Denver to California opened still wider vistas. I am sure there breathes no man—nor girl—with soul so dead that the first sight of the Painted Desert, the Indians at Albuquerque, the flowering orange groves, the Californian Missions, the Seventeen Mile Drive, and the Golden Gate does not deeply stir. I saw all these and much besides and did not worry because we failed to come East until my examinations were actually upon me. Then I went to stay with the Edmandses while I took them and my mother went on to Newbury to reopen the house.

The examinations were then held in one of the classrooms of the Massachusetts Institute of Technology, which was still housed in rather grim old buildings on Boylston Street. Between tests, I managed to send reports on my progress.

"The original exercises in geometry were very hard; I guess I managed to skim through though. The French was mere baby play. I do not think I got honors because of a careless mistake I made, but I am sure I passed all right. . . . The Latin Poets and Latin Prose Authors were enough to overwhelm a strong man. You know I've always considered Latin my forte, but heavens! I never 'saw the loikes' of these papers. Latin Composition was not as awful as it might have been. Yesterday I had lunch at Mrs. Ware's, which consisted of eight glasses of lemonade and six sardines, then I went over to Tech for German. Just before the exam began a girl came running in and said, 'They've changed this paper at the last moment and put in a lot of things which have never been required before!' Well, if it wasn't so! I never was so mad in my life, for I think it was a terribly mean thing to do. . . . The Tech boys were perfectly awful; although there was a big sign outside stating that the Bryn Mawr exams were held in that room, they kept poking their heads in, taking a general survey of the girls, grinning, and then departing. When we came out at twelve, about twenty-five were stationed in the hall to see our exit. . . . Safely through at last, alive, well and happy! . . . Don't forget that I'm coming home a week from Friday on the one o'clock train to Haverhill and be sure to inform Mr. Keyes[1] of that same; Helen has just informed me that he is much smitten on some Boston girl."

Certainly none of this bespeaks much concern. Despite the vague anxiety I had felt earlier in the year, I had been getting A's in examinations for so long that apparently I felt, when it came to a showdown, I was reasonably sure of doing the same thing again. Therefore the report from Bryn Mawr, when it came in, was a terrible shock: I had passed French, Latin prose, and even geometry with flying colors and had squeaked through German and Latin verse; but I had failed in Latin composition. This was a terrible blow to my pride, and the hurt went deeper than that: Latin, as a language, represented a branch of learning that I loved more than anything else, except stringing words together to form a theme; and I had failed, both as a linguist and as a writer. It was almost like failing a beloved fellow creature.

Fortunately, any kind of a setback has represented a challenge to do better, rather than an acceptance of inferiority on my part. As soon as I had my second wind, I wrote my Latin teacher at Winsor, saying

---

[1] This is my first written reference to "Mr. Keyes," instead of "the Champ," though—incredible as it may now seem!—I still addressed him in the former way—and that when we were actually hovering on the brink of an "understanding!"

The author at the age of eleven,
with her kitten.

The author at the age of eleven,
with her pony.

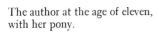

The parlor at the Homestead, showing the Courting Corner and the Marriage Arch.

The author at the age
of thirteen, with bow
and arrow.

The author at the age of thirteen with her first beau.

The author at the age of fifteen.

Henry Wilder Keyes

Elizabeth Sweetser,
at the age of fifteen,
in riding clothes.

Marion Burdett,
as a budding belle
at the age of fifteen.

The author at the age
of fifteen, canoeing.

Typical invitation for an outing.

Dear Frances.

It occurred to me as
I drove home yesterday from Woodsville
that Marion had not been out on
the river, and I am writing to ask
if you would not like to take
a short ~ Thursday, afternoon

about half past three. in the
green

The author
on her sixteenth
birthday.

The author ready for a "grown-up" horseback ride.

The Sweetsers' house in Marion, Massachusetts. Left to right, the author, Susan Sweetser, Francis Colby, Frank E. Sweetser, Jr., and Elizabeth Sweetser.

Living room of the Sweetser house in Marion. Scene of discussion of Keats, Meredith, and philosophy.

Mrs. Frank E. Sweetser

The author's cousin,
Isabel Hill,
daughter of Mr. and
Mrs. Nathaniel Hill
of Denver.

Dr. Rhallys

Boothby Bazely

Edel von Witzleben

The house at Pine Grove Farm, North Haverhill, New Hampshire.

One of the groves
at Pine Grove Farm.

The Congregational Church,
Newbury, Vermont.

Brougham in which the author went to her wedding.

The Misses Grace Edmands, Marion Burdett, and Marian Edmands, three of the author's bridesmaids, on the lawn at the Oxbow.

The Keyes' camp at Lake Tarleton, New Hampshire (interior).

The Keyes' camp at Lake Tarleton, New Hampshire (exterior).

The author as she looked at the time of her wedding.

I hoped she would not feel I had disqualified myself for my "finals" and adding that, if she did not, I would deeply appreciate suggestions for a course of study which I might pursue myself during the remainder of the summer. Nothing could have been kinder than her answer. "I like immensely the spirit in which you have taken your defeat," she told me; then she outlined a program for me to follow alone until I was back in school. After that, she assured me, she would make my problems and my needs her special concern; there was not the slightest reason to doubt that I would be well prepared for my "finals."

During July and early August, I had numerous house guests, among them my cousin Avis Hill, Marian Edmands, and Harold Deming, and, as in the case of my visitors the summer before, no one did as much as Harry Keyes to make their stay pleasant. My birthday, besides the usual celebration, brought a typical letter from my grandmother:

"I am very glad that the cousin, who preceded you in entering upon her earthly life by only a few short weeks, can be with you today.

"I hope you will have a very happy birthday and that the future will prove that each birthday has found you a year's march nearer your heavenly home. You have been often impressed, doubtless, with the thought that there is no going backward for any of us. We must press forward to the end. May this find us reunited with the dear ones who have gone before us, where there will be no more separations."

I am afraid I did not give as much thought just then to my heavenly home as this saintly woman might have wished, though I *had* begun to grasp the important fact that there is no going backward for any of us and that we must always press forward. Moreover, my days were not devoted wholly to having a good time; I worked hard on the course of study my Latin teacher had sent me and by early August I had covered nearly all the ground that had been suggested. Then—as September would still lie clear before me—I felt justified in spending two weeks in Marion, this time with the Burdetts.

These weeks were a whirl of gaiety, a joyous medley of swimming and sailing, presents and dancing, as my letters plainly show. The ruling which limited callers to Friday, Saturday, and Sunday evenings did not apply to summer vacations and Marion and I had the equivalent of what would now be called "a ball."

"This is a great place. I'm glad I came.

"I had a nice time coming down with Mr. Keyes. I went immediately to the South Station, where Marion's grandmother, Mrs. Warner, was waiting for me on the cunning little 'Dude.' The Burdetts' house is awfully attractive. I have a room of my own, which is great, but Marion and I are going to sleep together in her room. As soon as I was unpacked and washed and dressed in my white muslin, we had dinner and, immediately after dinner, two youths, Mr. Young and Mr. Weeks appeared. We walked down to the casino with my bathing suit, and over to the post office and then came back for Mrs. Warner to chaperone us to a concert. This was an informal affair. The boys bought seven bags of peanuts and flung them (as did everybody) at all their friends, usually making excellent shots. They talked through the whole thing; it seemed awfully queer not to pay any attention to the music, but no one did. When the concert was over, they moved away the chairs, swept up the peanut shells, with which the floor was completely covered, and danced. It was quite good fun."

"We are going sailing in Paul Burdett's boat with him this morning, and driving and swimming this afternoon, and horseback riding tomorrow morning. Mr. Young and Mr. Weeks are getting up a sailing party for next Monday night (the night before full moon) and a canoe trip the next night (full moon). Mrs. Young will chaperone the sailing party."

"After supper, when we had got the mail, we went to the casino for the midweek dance, and had a simply glorious time. It was another perfect night, and sitting on the piazza between dances was beautiful. I had plenty—more than plenty-of partners. Marion is so popular that I reap full benefit.

"Mr. Keyes—the lamb!—sent me down seven boxes of Page & Shaw the other day, and all the boys are regaling themselves on it. Paul, who goes off on a three day cruise after the race this afternoon, takes two pounds with him. Eight pounds goes a long way, even among boys. Mr. Keyes has also sent the August number of *Country Life in America*, and an English *Country Life*, and a note to say he could not get the Cambridge edition of Matthew Arnold.

"Just starting for the Race!"

"I wrote you Friday just before the race. Well, we hurried down to Long Wharf where Weeks was waiting for me, and in a minute Stone appeared for Marion, and off we went to the starting point. Soon the preliminary gun went off and all the pretty little sailboats, which looked like white birds, began to assemble in their classes, and came up to the starting point. We were in the fifth class, so we had the fun of watching all the others begin, before our gun went off. Edward Stone with Marion in the 'Teddy,' Don Nolton in the 'Raffle,' and Allen Weeks and myself in the 'Albatross' comprised the class. It was the most exciting thing I ever did in my life. It was awfully rough— the boat shipped water four times. I had to sit up on the back of the stern and cling on the little iron rail by which the sail slides, for dear life, except once when Weeks had to fix the sail and I had to manage the boat. Of course, we were drenched to the skin. Don Nolton was about three minutes behind us all the time, but Stone and we were very close all the time. It kept getting more and more exciting every minute, and finally when we crossed the line at last, we had just enough energy left to howl, 'Who won?' And then the answer came back to us, 'You, by two seconds!' Wasn't that great?"

"If our digestions are not spoiled it will not be our or the boys' fault, for besides all the candy Mr. Keyes sent, the boys—every one— bring it every time they appear, besides insisting on our having all kinds of drinks,[2] whenever we are the least bit hot or thirsty. One day I had two ice cream sodas, two huge lemonades and two pounds of candy between four and ten P.M.

"While I was eating my breakfast, Don Nolton came tearing in to inform us that Allen Weeks and Howard Smith were already waiting for us down at the wharf, whence we had agreed to go with them to the Beverly Yacht Club for lunch and to see the races. So we tore down and started out in Don's big, beautiful sailboat, the 'Hector.' There was a fine breeze, and we went like the wind. We got to the Club just in time for lunch. Paul with Edward Stone and Foster Kellogg, who were off on their cruise, met us there. I never saw such beautiful boats in my life. We had a magnificent sail home, reaching Marion at quarter of four. Then I—Marion wouldn't—went in swimming; my arms are so tender that the salt water scraping against the bathing suit has hurt them terribly; they are raw from shoulder to elbow, and I'm not going in today, to see if they won't heal a little, for they're awful now.[3]

[2] Needless to say, soft drinks!

[3] The bathing suit was, of course, made of alpaca and liberally trimmed with braid. It consisted of a waist, which came almost up to the neck, and had elbow sleeves. This waist was attached to bloomers and these were covered by a skirt, which came well below the knees. With this costume, long thick black stockings

"There was a hop last night, but there was a perfectly glorious moon and a nice little breeze as well; so when Weeks and Nolton turned up, as they did immediately after supper, we decided that, as we were all tired, a good moonlight sail would be infinitely preferable to a hot dance. Mrs. Warner was easily persuaded to come, for we were all minded to stay out a long while, and thought we better have a chaperone. Well! Mother dear, we left home at twenty minutes past eight and returned at half-past twelve! I never saw anything half so divine in my life. We were all tired, and we just sailed quietly on and on without talking, but all just reveling in the glorious beauty. We did not intend to be quite so late, but the wind went down and we couldn't help it. Don Nolton, I grieve to say, starts on a long cruise today, so I shan't see him again; but plenty of others remain!

"Last night I got Matthew Arnold from Mr. Keyes. It is perfectly beautiful, in five volumes; I asked for the Essays, you know, for my wager, but for some reason he sent the entire works."

"Another absolutely perfect day! I never saw such weather. About half-past three we heard a great rumpus at the front door and, presently, the maid came up to inform us that there were five youths downstairs —Foster Kellogg, whom I had met before here, as he stays here summers, and Bobby Jordan—Dorothy's brother—Kenneth Moller, Will Branhall and Stillman Dexter, all of whom you've heard me mention as they are great friends of Elizabeth and Helen. The last four are cruising together. They stayed until half-past five, when they departed to the Cutlers' for dinner, all except Foster who remained here. He is the nicest thing you ever saw, the third boy I might have lost my heart to since I got here; but the others have paled in comparison to him. Well, he stayed to dinner, as I said, and then Allen Weeks appeared, and we decided to go moonlight sailing; so we did. I'll tell you about that sail when I get home. Oh!"

I am not sure that I did tell her, for, according to the standards of the times, Marion and I had been guilty of a grave indiscretion: we had gone on an evening sail without a chaperone! Mr. and Mrs. Burdett were out of town and Mrs. Warner was not feeling well. With some difficulty, we persuaded this saintly old lady that "just this once" we might go without her. It was a beautiful calm night, we would be home early. Beautiful it certainly was and calm—indeed, so calm

---

were worn. Why we did not all drown before we ever learned to swim at all still seems to me a minor mystery.

that soon there was not a breath of wind to swell the sails! For hours
we remained as motionless as "a painted ship upon a painted ocean."
In one sense, we did get home early—about two o'clock in the morning—to find Mrs. Warner on her knees, praying for our safety. When
she rose from them, it was plain that her relief was mingled with the
terror of scandal; if what we had done were ever noised abroad, our
reputations would be ruined. The boys would never be trusted to take
out nice girls again; the girls would be lucky if nice boys paid them
any further attentions. Finally she collapsed in a medley of tears and
recriminations.

Foster and Allen apologized profusely and took their cowed and
repentant departure; Marion and I slipped away to bed, appalled at
the desolate future ahead of us. But before breakfast time, I had
recovered sufficiently to sit up in bed and scribble a parody on Ham-
let's immortal soliloquy:

> "To sail or not to sail—that is the question?
> Whether 'tis wiser for a girl to settle
> Well chaperoned upon a screened piazza
> Or to fare forth upon a sea of chances
> And by a failing wind to stay there.
> Two boys, two girls, one boat——
> Aye there's the rub. . . ."

Everyone, including Mrs. Warner, felt better when I had read this
masterpiece aloud. The boys, hoping to find the old lady's ultimatum
softened, had, of course, appeared bright and early; Marion and I soon
discovered that we were not social outcasts, after all. Nothing could
have been more glowing than my final report from Marion.

"It seems impossible that this is the last letter I am going to write
to you; this visit has been so crowded full of pleasant things that it
has fairly flown. Thursday evening, Rosamond Weeks, Allen's very
attractive sister, gave a party, so Marion and I arrayed ourselves in our
pink dresses, and Allen paddled us down. Marion was, as usual, surrounded and, as usual, when the boys could not get her, they took me.
I led the German—which was the first thing—with Allen. Then the
next dance, a Portland Fancy, I had with Harry Stone, Edward's elder
brother, and the next thing, a two-step and supper with Foster. Foster
hates to dance, so we parted from the maddening throng, and had a
great time. We found a simply wonderful place. Then, by-and-by, we
were joined by Marion and Allen! Oh! it was delicious. Then Marion

walked home with Edward and Ralph Flint and I with Foster; he is awfully slow—as slow as Frank, that kind seems to attract me—and would *not* walk fast! When we got home, Marion sent Edward and Mr. Flint away, but Foster came in for a few minutes."

I was still under the spell of this visit when I took the train for home, making the trip, as usual, with Harry Keyes. I described my experiences in glowing colors, but did not get as enthusiastic a response as I had expected. He said he was glad I had enjoyed myself so much and then conversation, for some reason, languished.

After that, several days passed during the course of which he did not appear at the Oxbow; but this did not strike me as strange. He had gradually recovered from the shock of the great fire at Pine Grove Farm and, though at first he had been too discouraged to consider rebuilding, he had finally decided to go ahead with it. His great friend, Herbert Hale, the famous architect and the son of Edward Everett Hale, had drawn plans for an enormous brick house and Harry had been acting as his own contractor. The project had become of the greatest interest to him. Now the house was just finished and his family was getting installed there. After the separation of the previous summer, which his mother, sister, and little niece had spent at Gray Gables on Buzzard's Bay—the home of their friends, ex-President and Mrs. Cleveland, who were spending the summer elsewhere—because no suitable accommodations were available at Pine Grove Farm, it was natural that he would wish to see as much of them as possible, and he was needed to help with the settling. Besides, the drives and rides and paddles that he and I took together were more often than not without prearrangement: there was a telephone at Pine Grove Farm, but there was none at the Oxbow and both the expression and the actuality of dating were still nonexistent: if a girl received an invitation for some future outing, she accepted or declined it, as the case might be, in writing or in person, also as indicated; but more often these outings took place more or less on the spur of the moment and she regarded them in the same light that she did impromptu callers; if she was not invited out and no one came to see her, she did not worry; there was always something else to do.

So, in this case, I did not resent the fact that Harry Keyes had not come on Tanglefoot to go riding with me and saw no reason why I should not ride by myself. I got on Kaweah and started rather aimlessly toward the village. I had not even thought where I would go after that and I took, also rather aimlessly, the Montebello Road, instead of the longer one, by the Darlings' house, which was much more my usual route. I had just reached the hollow between the two hills—the scene of my great adventure on the Flexible Flyer!—when I saw Harry Keyes coming toward me on Tanglefoot. His expression displayed slight surprise.

"I thought you didn't usually take this road," he said, as he reined in beside me.

"I don't. I don't know how I happened to this time. As far as that goes, you don't either."

"No, I don't. I don't know how I happened to this time."

"Well, anyway, we've met. Shall we go back to the house? Or do you want to go for a ride?"

"I think I'd rather go back to the house. I've come for a rather special reason." He paused and then he said the last thing I expected: "I've decided to go away for an indefinite period. I've come to say good-by."

There seemed to be no immediate answer I could fittingly make to this, even if I had not been speechless with amazement. We rode in silence to the Oxbow. Then, as we dismounted, I said, "If you've come to say good-by and aren't in the mood for riding, what would you think of walking down the lane? It's nice and quiet by the river. Whatever you want to say, you wouldn't be interrupted there. My mother's at home and you know how she is. She might walk in on us any minute."

"I think you have a very good idea."

"All right, just wait a minute while I change my clothes. I'll tell her where we're going and why."

She looked at me rather strangely, I thought, when I ran into the library, and told me she would like to kiss me, which was a very unusual thing for her to say. But I said I didn't feel like it, which was quite true, and ran straight out again, not stopping to think that I might have hurt her feelings until I was halfway down the lane; then I stopped thinking about her altogether. And by the time we reached the pasture at the river's edge, Harry had evidently forgotten that he had come to say good-by. Anyhow, when we went back to the house, several hours later, it was to tell my mother we were engaged to be married.

CHAPTER XXII

She did not seem to be as much surprised as we had expected. Indeed, while we were at the riverside, she had apparently been planning just what she would say to us for, hardly pausing to wish us well, she announced that of course I would not go back to school; that I would stay at the Oxbow and hem sheets; that the engagement would be announced immediately; and that the wedding would take place in the spring. This did not coincide at all with Harry's views or, for that matter, with mine, though he was the spokesman: of course, I must finish school and, of course, the announcement of the engagement should not be made while I was still there; this should be done after I had been graduated and we would be married the following fall.

With some reluctance, which my mother made no effort to conceal, she agreed to this plan, but with the proviso that Harry's immediate family, my brother, and my mother's financial adviser—who was also an old friend—should be told of the engagement in confidence, at once. Harry in turn accepted her conditions; then, in a very practical way, he began to outline the source and amount of his income past, present, and (potential) future, to explain that he was not as well off as was generally supposed, but that he thought he could support me suitably, though we would have to live quietly and economically, making Pine Grove Farm our year-round home. Again my mother's disappointment was obvious—but not too obvious. The interview ended on a courteous, if not overcordial note and, after a few minutes, Harry took his departure.

During the next few weeks he came to see me frequently, in a way that was satisfactory to us both. We did not talk much about the future and I, at least, felt no compulsion to do so; the present, with its unhurried adjustment to a new aspect of a relationship which had long been happy and harmonious, seemed sufficient. Eventually, prompted by my mother, I hesitatingly mentioned the fact that my fiancé's mother and sister had not been to see me, or asked me to come and see them, though they were still at Pine Grove Farm—indeed, one day my mother had met them driving in the direction of the Oxbow when she was driving in the direction of South Newbury and had immediately turned and come home to await a call that did not take place. There had been no letter, either. Visibly embarrassed, Harry said that of course he had kept his promise to tell his family, but that the members of it were taken so completely by surprise that I must give them time to get used to the idea of the engagement. They had felt sure that he did not ever intend to get married. This answer satisfied me, though it obviously failed to satisfy my mother when I reported it to her, until I reminded her that the letter we had received from my brother, in answer to the one telling him the great news, had been one of only qualified approval; he thought she must have used undue influence, for certainly I was too young to know my own mind; it also seemed to him that the difference of ages was a great disadvantage; he admitted that he had nothing against Harry, but there was a suggestion that he did not think so highly of another member of the family whom he had known at Harvard. Were we sure that it was the right one for me to consider entering? The reminder of this letter, which she had been trying to dismiss from her thoughts, temporarily silenced my mother, and no more was said on the subject of the indicated call that had not been made. Evidently she derived a certain amount of satisfaction from feeling that if I had not been welcomed with open arms, the hesitation was not all on one side. However, she did ask me to tell Harry that "she would like to have another little talk with him." Whether or not this little talk ever took place, I do not know, though I am inclined to think that it did not.

We remained at the Oxbow until the end of September and then returned to Boston to spend the winter with our friends the Wares at their Marlborough Street house. This was, to be sure, a much more satisfactory arrangement than sending me alone to spend the winter with the Cooks, for I was fond of both Mrs. Ware and her son, Richard; but I was bitterly disappointed because my mother had still not seen her way clear to renting a small furnished house or apartment, where we could have had more privacy, and where I would have been free to have my friends drop in, casually and frequently, as all my schoolmates did. As a matter of fact, I was less comfortably quartered and more hampered about having visitors than I had been at the Cooks'. My bedroom at the Wares' was a tiny one at the rear of the fourth story, where there was neither heat nor plumbing. This house was a twin to the one where we had spent our first winter in Boston, after my mother's marriage to Albert E. Pillsbury, while our Beacon Street house was being built: the one bathroom was on the floor below my cubbyhole, between my mother's room and Mrs. Ware's; and the tiny reception room, which was the only place where I could receive callers, was directly beside the front door. This never seemed to stop opening and shutting, to admit the visitors for my mother or Mrs. Ware, who received in the front and back parlors directly above; or Richard and his friends, who had to climb still higher; or the postman; or the tradesmen and errand boys who refused to go through the alley to the back door of the basement kitchen. Many of these persons more or less automatically entered the reception room, which was not shielded from the front door by so much as a portiere; all of them inevitably let in terrible drafts of icy air. I still had a good many callers, for my fiancé had decided that I should continue to receive them, as before, until my engagement was announced, in order to avoid rousing suspicions of this; and my mother had been equally emphatic on the subject, though not, I imagine, for quite the same reason. So collegians continued to come, in ever-increasing numbers, all that winter. There was less emphasis on the presentation of cards now, for a maid was not always on duty; and my chaperone—either my mother or Mrs. Ware—did not sit in the next room, as Mrs. Cook had done, but either in the front or the back parlor on the floor above— the latter sometimes designated as the library, though it did not contain many books. The lady on duty never went to bed until the last caller had departed and sometimes, if the visit seemed to her overlong, she paced up and down through the narrow upper hall from one room to another; but calling hours were permissibly longer without rebuke and the whole atmosphere was one of less restraint and formality. "The lads who like Marion so much go to see her all dressed up and sit in the parlor and—I suppose—say adoring things to her," I wrote. "But they come here in their oldest clothes, on perfectly awful nights, and smoke and talk about dogs or books, or their troubles, as if I were their sister. Last night Foster came to see me and stayed so late that I began to think that I should have to send him home. He remarked that everybody turned to me in trouble, and very nicely added that he didn't wonder."

Unquestionably, one or two of these boys did regard me in a brotherly way, and with these I had no difficulty in dealing. One or two others—and this admits of no question either—regarded me "differently," as we put it in those days, and with these I tried to deal warily, without feeling any more certain what an engaged girl should do, under the circumstances, than I had been two years earlier about what a fifteen-year-old should do when she received a grown-up present. (And this time with less help in solving the problem! It is not strange that once I wrote, "I can't help wishing sometimes that I need never see another boy until my engagement is announced!") The majority, however, impressed me chiefly in giving convincing evidence of New England perseverance in the face of the adverse conditions under which I was obliged to see them: they were simply proving that frequent intrusions and icy drafts would not deter them, once they had made up their minds to call on a certain girl! And one—Foster Kellogg—left me everlastingly his debtor by initiating me into the treasure trove of Kipling's poetry, novels, and short stories, not to mention almost the complete works of Bret Harte, which he loaned me, one by one, bringing a new volume every time he came to see me. Indeed, through his selections, he revealed much the same taste and discrimination that Frank Sweetser had shown when he led me into discussion of "Keats, Meredith and Philosophy."

At school everything went smoothly: the maladjustment of the first year and the tension of the second were now happily both things of the past. I continued to see a good deal of the first friends I had made and I also found congenial spirits in two who were new that winter—Bertha Russell of Winchester and Ruth Farley of Auburndale, the latter a cousin of Sophie Judd, from Honolulu, who had now been graduated and with whom I had had only the slight acquaintance which a younger girl is able to achieve with one who had reached the lofty heights of the higher classes. Ruth and I were immediately kindred spirits and were to remain so as long as she lived. I also found Terry Helburn as congenial as ever; and Mary Tudor, who had entered Miss Winsor's the year I was absent, quickly became another close friend. "I met Polly Cunningham and Elizabeth Sweetser on the steps, and I had hardly got inside 95 Beacon Street when a girl by the name of Mary Tudor came running downstairs," I wrote my fiancé. "She shook hands with great effusion and exclaimed in accents of joy, 'Oh Frances, you are beside me in the new room!' I was very much surprised, for I have only met her once or twice, but I immediately hurried upstairs to discover what the new 'room' might be. And what do you think? Miss Winsor has had two tremendous rooms, about fifty feet square, I should say, added! The lower one is to be used for recreation on rainy days, with a piano, a fine floor and the like. A little private staircase leads to the upper room and there, with the most popular teacher in the school, are ten girls of the graduating class—ten who know each other and have for a long time and who get on well together and who are likely to wish to be with each other outside of school—and I am one of them! I feel so happy about it! Elizabeth and Polly and Louise Lincoln are all there and the rest I know, though not so well. The rooms are beautifully finished in black walnut and are just fine. By the way, Miss Winsor embraced me most cordially, as did all my teachers, with whom I have got on pretty well. I am going to have Latin alone with Miss Cook which will be great. Then I'm going to have College Algebra, College English, German and American History—all easy but the Algebra. As I wish to do a little extra English work, I'm also going to take a course in daily themes."

If my place in the class had not already been snatched away from me by Terry Helburn, I would have lost it, perhaps not quite so swiftly, but none the less surely, to Mary Tudor, who was proving herself almost a match for Terry. I was conscientious and hard working, with a good memory and a certain facility for learning languages and expressing myself on paper; but my good marks were the result of unremitting labor. I was never a naturally brilliant student, and both Terry and Mary belonged unquestionably in that category. Aside from this, no two girls could possibly have been more different, and it is not surprising that, though they both became such great friends of mine, they never became great friends of each other. Their one similarity, besides their brilliance, was their inability to "fit in" and this for reasons as different as possible, except for the fact that any outstanding student in a girls' school—and probably in a boys' as well—needs to use extreme care not to "fling her good marks in the face" of those who do not get them. Neither Terry nor Mary used such care—or at any rate their classmates felt they did not. Moreover, if Terry was too much of an outsider—which is entirely possible—Mary Tudor was too much of an insider—if this be possible. Most of the other girls in the class lived in the suburbs—the most select suburbs, to be sure, but still the suburbs—and came of well-established, but not strictly Brahmin families. Mary Tudor lived on the water side of Beacon Street, and it was impossible to imagine her living anywhere else, with the possible exception of Louisburg Square; she was a Bostonian of Bostonians. Her family, on both sides, was as noteworthy as the name she bore, and her appearance, and that of her two older sisters—Elsa, who became the Countess of Pierrefeu, and Delia, who married Louis Thatcher—was as noteworthy as her name. To be sure, one of her classmates uncharitably remarked, "All those Tudor girls look as if they have been cut out with a pair of scissors," and there was indeed a certain sharpness in their profiles; but it was a sharpness of extreme distinction, not unlike that in the profiles of the Adamses; and it was mitigated by their fine eyes, beautiful coloring, and really magnificent hair. They were as much at home in continental society as Boston society, for they had spent a good deal of time in Europe and moved in the same circles there. But they were not snobs in any sense of that objectionable word—indeed, I have never known anyone who was completely secure in an exalted social position to speak of this with intent to impress; it is taken so much as a matter of course that it does not require emphasis. Socially secure the Tudors unquestionably were and consequently could afford to be casual about it; they were also casual, at least outwardly, about the things which they could not afford. They were very far from being wealthy and it must have required the most careful budgeting to maintain the huge Beacon Street house. But maintain it they did, with a lofty acceptance of the rigid economies, beneath the surface, which made that surface seem smooth, and fine disregard for any discomfort thereby entailed. Their hospitality was characterized by the ease of the accomplished in that art, and theirs was still another table where my welcome was assured, well before the tardy discovery that I was John Wheeler's daughter, that my father and Mary's had been classmates at Harvard, and that great mutual admiration had existed between the two. Now another lifetime friendship was established and was destined to be carried on to still a third generation. "I've had such a pleasant afternoon with Mary Tudor," I wrote, early in the new year. "I've decided that the reason so few people seem to like her is because there is too much about her to appreciate right away. To be sure, she is nervous and high strung and quick tempered, but I think, if you can get used to that, there is a lot behind it—intellect, breeding, frankness, even charm, but none of it sufficiently on the surface to attract. Do you know what I mean? I can't seem to express myself well. Anyway, I went to her house immediately after lunch and stayed until it was dark. It is one of those huge forbidding Beacon Street houses, which might seem cold and gloomy and stiff to some people, but which is really full of beautiful things. We sat on the floor in front of the big fireplace in the dining room, with a little black kitten and numerous books and viands within reach and talked about books, music, pictures, school, housekeeping, etc.—quite a pleasant change from the usual topics of boys and clothes. When much against Mary's will, I left, she said something very nice to me and I know you will not think me conceited if I tell you what it was: 'I love to be with you, Frances, and hope we shall see a lot of each other in the future. You know so much and talk so well and think so clearly that it is a great pleasure to me.'"

Though I had lost my place at the head of the class, I had no trouble swinging along easily in my studies, despite the added burden of extra work in Latin composition. The redoubtable Miss Kinsman, who had begun by seeming such an ogress among teachers, now seemed almost like a contemporary and, increasingly, was treated like one. Several of my friends invited her home to lunch with them, in the same casual way that they did their classmates, and I would have done the same if the little house on Cypress Street had only become a reality. Even without this, however, we established a certain amount of camaraderie, untinged by the critical and slightly suspicious attitude on my teacher's part and the apprehensive one on mine, which had formerly marred our relations. My former classmates tell me I was the only girl who dared "talk back" to her and that, far from lowering me in her estimation, this caused her to admire my independent spirit; but this is only hearsay. She still had the habit of springing the unexpected upon us, and one day she surprised us by asking us to read aloud the short daily theme which presumably we had written the day before. Not a line of mine was on paper; but without hesitation I rose, copybook in hand, and, with my eyes fixed on the pages covered with the text of some previous composition, reeled off a little story which I made up as I went along. This in itself was not too much of a trick; it was more of one to get the story on paper soon enough afterward to be sure that the written and the spoken word bore enough resemblance to each other to preclude detection. But somehow this was accomplished and, after the theme came back to me with a good mark on it, I confessed what I had done. Instead of a sarcastic reprimand, I received a laughing caution not to push my luck by doing the same thing twice. I promised and the incident was closed—or rather, it led to better understanding and co-operation between teacher and pupil.

"Examinations are over and I have drawn two A–'s. So on every one of the Bryn Mawr papers I have taken during the mid-years I have got High Credit, the highest possible honor—two clear A's and two A–'s. Considering how little work I have done I feel quite proud of myself—much more so than if I had tired myself out 'working for marks.' Now there are two months of peace ahead of me before we have any more examinations." . . . "We are studying *The Merchant of Venice* for College English and have had to learn twenty lines by heart, choosing any we wanted. So I chose Portia's speech to Bassanio. Can you guess why? In case you don't remember it, I'll quote it.

> " 'You see me, Lord Bassanio, where I stand,
> Such as I am: though for myself alone
> I would not be ambitious in my wish,
> To wish myself much better; yet, for you
> I would be trebled twenty times myself;
> A thousand times more fair, ten thousand times
> More rich;
> That only to stand high in your account,
> I might in virtues, beauties, livings, friends,
> Exceed account; but the full sum of me
> Is sum of something, which, to term in gross,
> Is an unlesson'd girl, unschool'd, unpractised;
> Happy in this, she is not yet so old
> But she may learn; happier than this,
> She is not bred so dull but she can learn;
> Happiest of all is that her gentle spirit
> Commits itself to yours to be directed,
> As from her lord, her governor, her king.' "

After all these years, I have no difficulty in "guessing why." I did think of the man I had promised to marry as a "lord and a governor and a king." It was very different from the way I thought about my collegiate callers. (Incidentally, it is interesting to me to note that apparently the twenty lines I selected to memorize were not considered unsuitable; so by this time I must have been regarded as mature enough to evaluate love stories better than when I wrote the unfortunate theme on *Romeo and Juliet!*)

Evidently, I thought my fiancé would be interested in my shopping expeditions as well as my marks at school: "I have already written you about my dinner dress, white silk embroidered in tiny pink rosebuds. Now we have ordered another dress for me. It will be a dear, I think, pale blue crepe de chine, lined with a paler shade of silk. It is to be very simple, accordion pleated, high necked and with long huge sleeves, with just a little lace at the throat and wrists. Do you like the way that sounds?"[1] . . . "I have taken the three beautiful old linen sheets that were my great-grandmother's to have big initials stamped on them. Mother will embroider them and they will make beautiful bedspreads. But I cannot have many new linen ones, as they cost ten dollars and fifty cents a pair, so that a dozen pair with their pillow slips come to about a hundred and fifty dollars. Mother says I will have to have more cotton sheets and fewer linen ones and I guess I shall, unless we go without some other necessities. The house at Pine Grove Farm is tremendous for a small girl like me to provide for. I will go over my list and the altered list with you the next time you come to see me."

My trousseau was already very much on my mind, and I was horrified to find how little in the way of household equipment five hundred dollars—the first estimate of what I should spend on essentials— would buy. I was also hard put to it in trying to allay suspicions about my engagement. Though I continued to have callers, I did not accept invitations for football games, and though I went to a few dances which were held in the spacious homes of my various friends, I attended no general subscription dances. Moreover, I never "happened" to meet a youth while walking to school and I did not even consent to accept the escort of one to church. All this was so contrary to my previous schedule that it inevitably caused comment, but once, at least, I seem to have been fairly successful. "Marian Edmands came to see me this afternoon and we had a very nice visit together, though she asked some leading questions which were hard to evade. However, I did my best and you may guess that I thoroughly misled her, when I tell you that, as she was leaving, she said, 'How absolutely indifferent you are to men! Even that angelic Mr. Keyes! Why don't you reward him as he deserves? You're a stony-hearted wretch!'"

I lied, I think not very convincingly, about the gold bracelet which was my first engagement present and which I began to wear about the middle of December. I said my mother had given it to me and Elizabeth valiantly seconded this statement, though she did not believe it herself. I would much rather have told the truth about it, but had to content myself by doing this only in a letter, in which I said, "The bracelet is beautiful, and I shall never take it off, at least until we are married. I think it is the prettiest one of the kind that I have ever seen. Just the same, I did not want it for an ornament, but

---

[1] This is the dress I wore for my "engagement picture," taken in Berlin.

simply so that I could possess something which you had given me and which I could wear all the time as I couldn't have a ring." It is too bad that I did not know then that a bracelet is always the official engagement present in Spain; the ring comes later and is merely incidental! Familiarity with this good old Spanish custom would have afforded me much satisfaction, even if I could not talk about it.

With my school life so satisfactory, my circle of friends so enlarged, with hospitable houses at which I was welcome dotted all over the Back Bay, Beacon Hill, and the suburbs, there is a great deal about the winter which is pleasant to remember and I should not be giving a well-proportioned account of it if I failed to record this. For the first time, I had both the leisure and the opportunity to satisfy the predeliction for gazing at fine pictures, which had been roused during the year I spent in Europe. Now I went to the public library, not only to read books but to linger before the murals by Abbey, Sargent, and Puvis de Chavannes; I stood spellbound before Turner's gorgeous paintings in the Museum of Fine Arts; I visited innumerable exhibitions, mostly of water colors, at the St. Botolph Club and various private and public galleries. Frequently, Mary Tudor was my companion on these jaunts, and her father, an artist of no mean talent himself, encouraged us to undertake them and often made helpful suggestions as to what he thought we would most enjoy. But if Mary were not free to go with me, or were not in the mood for doing so, I did not in the least mind going alone. The pictures themselves were good companions.

In addition to the afternoons spent intermittently in this way, two other afternoons a week automatically provided cultural enjoyment of another kind: I had a season ticket to the symphony and went to the public rehearsal every Friday, where my seat was directly behind that of my friend Bertha Russell, so that during the intermission we went out to the lobby together and met our friends who sat in different parts of the hall; these little rendezvous were always very gay. Almost as regularly, I went to a Saturday matinee, usually with my mother, who, as I have said before, loved the theater and encouraged my taste for it. I remember that she was bitterly criticized because one of the plays to which she took me was D'Annunzio's *Francesca da Rimini*, with Eleonora Duse in the title role; very definitely it was not considered proper theatrical fare for a seventeen-year-old girl. But now that I have seen thousands of actors and actresses in hundreds of plays,

I still feel this was my supreme experience in the theater and am very grateful to my mother for so superb a memory.

The outstanding concert of the year, as far as I was concerned, was evidently one in which Marcella Sembrich was the soloist. "I had never heard her before—indeed I have never heard such music," I confessed to my music-loving fiancé, "and I enjoyed it tremendously. I did not know any of the songs which made me feel very much ashamed. The ones I liked were an aria from Handel's *Joshua*, an aria from *Der Streit zwischen Phöbus und Pan* by Bach, *Nussbaum* by Schumann, and *Zickeltanz* by Grieg. I suppose you know them all. She was beautifully dressed in a black net thing that sparkled, and a big black hat. The audience was very enthusiastic. She was encored and encored, and at last she sat down and played her own accompaniment which simply brought down the house. She had three bunches of beautiful flowers. I thought her manner was charming indeed."

As a matter of fact, thanks to my year in Europe, I had already heard more music than most of my friends, and that year I was to hear a good deal more. Fanny Bloomfield-Zeisler, Timothée Adamowski, and Horatio Parker were among the soloists who performed with the symphony and many of their selections became familiar to me. I also went to hear the chorus of the Thursday Morning Club and the women's chorus of the Choral Art Society of Boston and *The Messiah* as rendered by the Handel and Haydn Society. Best of all, I went to hear Nordica, Schumann-Heink, and Édouard de Reszké in *Lohengrin*, which roused my unbounded enthusiasm. "I never conceived anything so divine in my life. I almost wish I could hear it again next week, instead of *The Magic Flute. Lohengrin* is so much better than any opera I have ever heard before that I don't want to go to something I'll enjoy less. Oh! That 'Swan Song' and that 'Wedding March!' They made me feel all queer inside. Do you know the feeling?"

As to plays, besides *Francesca da Rimini*, I find *The Rivals* with Joseph Jefferson, *The Comedy of Errors* with Stuart Robson, *The Greatest Thing in the World* with Jane Irving, and *Julius Caesar* with Richard Mansfield high on my list. I also saw Ethel Barrymore in *Carrots* and *A Country Mouse* and thoroughly disapproved of the latter play, which shocked me deeply. I went, as I have already said, with my mother to most of the plays I saw that winter; but as one of my former schoolmates has recently reminded me, our class went almost en masse to *Julius Caesar* with Miss Kinsman as our chaperone. According to her, it was a good performance, except that Brutus was pronounced throughout as if it were written Brutoos, with the accent on the second syllable; and of this she did not approve. My own report was that Mansfield was "very stiff—all the other actors better." In the spring, as a great concession, I was allowed to attend a matinee of A *Country Girl* with my fiancé—and without a chaperone.

My mother was recapturing, to a certain extent, some of her social contacts, among which she had always given the Fragment Society very high rating, and Mrs. Ware readily fell in with her suggestion that a meeting should be held at the Marlborough Street house. I do not seem to have been very much impressed with this aristocratic and philanthropic group, for I wrote, "Yesterday, as you know, was the meeting of Mother's Fragment Society, at which about sixty ladies came together in gorgeous clothes, nominally to sew for the poor, but really to talk and eat, from five to nine. Avis, Marian, Elizabeth, Helen and the Shreve twins were invited to help me thread the ladies' needles, supply them with work, and—which was infinitely more difficult —with food. I never in my life saw people eat so. To be sure, the food was delicious, but they simply *gorged*. Helen couldn't come because she has tonsillitis, but the rest of us worked like slaves. Elizabeth looked perfectly stunning and everyone enthused about her because she really *was* lovely in every way. I guess society rather than school is her element. The twins, too, looked awfully pretty."

This account of the meeting, written with the intolerance of youth, does scant justice, alas! to one of the most venerable, effective, and worthy charitable organizations in Boston. It was founded in 1805 and the garments on which its members sewed were carried from house to house in hampers, in very much the same way that the Maiden Aunts had their sewing transported when they began their work for the soldiers half a century later; therefore, fragments were literally gathered up. With dues of only three dollars a year—which have never been increased—augmented from time to time with legacies and other gifts, and wisely invested, the capital of the Fragment Society eventually became so substantial that any member could draw on it, almost at a moment's notice, to meet an emergency need. These ample financial means and the absence of red tape have meant that an inestimable amount of good has been done in the century and a half of the Fragment Society's existence; and never has it been as active and as efficient as it is today. Its meetings are no longer held from the hours of five to nine, once so logical and now so unfitted to a modern design for living; nor do the members attend in "gorgeous clothes," as un-

deniably they did in my mother's time, though there was an unwritten
law that their dresses, while elegant, should not be décolleté for these
occasions. I am glad that, with more sense of proportion and value
than I possessed at the age of seventeen, I can now set the record
straight.

The Shreve twins, who were among my helpers at my mother's
party, came out shortly thereafter and I attended the gala tea which
celebrated their debut. This impressed me no more favorably than the
meeting of the Fragment Society. "If that is the sort of thing I'd be
doing if I stayed here next year, I don't see what you think I'd miss
living in North Haverhill with you," I wrote scornfully to my fiancé.
But I continued to chafe because it was not often that I could have
guests, other than formal callers, at Mrs. Ware's house. Richard Ware
did what he could to relieve this situation: as a member of the Algonquin Club, he could arrange to let my mother and me give occasional
dinners and luncheons there and this he very kindly did; it was a
privilege that meant a great deal to me. "Mother's dinner is to be at
the Algonquin Club on the night of the 13th," I wrote my fiancé.
"Richard offered her that and the Puritan. I shall be there in my pink
dress and shall hope to see you then—and before." He came to that
dinner, as did my old friend Harold Deming, but as far as I can recall
it was the only time we formally entertained either one during the
winter. Luncheons were more frequent than dinners and were usually
limited to schoolgirls and their mothers. "My lunch party came off
today and was a great success," I wrote. "We all came up to the
club from school—eighteen of us—and we had the same little suite
that Mother had for her dinner. The table was scattered all over with
pink carnations and lighted with pink candles under pink shades. For
lunch we had pink grapefruit with pink sherbet in the middle; chicken
soup in cups; fish done up in little rolls with cucumbers; breasts of
chicken with mushrooms and fancy potatoes; Waldorf salad; ices in
the shape of pink roses; chocolates, olives, nuts, etc. After we had
finished our lunch, the pinks were brought out on a big silver waiter
and distributed around."

Lest a six-course luncheon seem prodigious, according to present-
day standards, it is perhaps worth recording that another letter de-
scribes one of *nine* courses which took place at the Burdetts' house
during the Christmas holidays. I had spent the previous night with
Marion and we were cautioned to finish our breakfast by seven-thirty,
since all the rest of the morning would be required to get the dining

room ready! Elizabeth was hostess at still another festive occasion during the holidays, in the course of which I was also adding to my trousseau. "Wednesday morning I went shopping with Mother and got some things I needed very much. We were quite late and I simply had to tear home to dress for Elizabeth's lunch and finally got there by the skin of my teeth. It was a very pretty one in the smaller dining room of the Union Club. The table was covered with pinks and we each had a bunch at our place besides. After lunch, we went to the theater. The only thing in town that had a Wednesday matinee and was proper for us to see was *Foxy Grandpa*. It was a silly little light thing with a lot of stale jokes and some flat tunes in it. But we had a good time for we talked and laughed through the entire thing and then we were driven home. In the evening I went to bed very early as I was quite tired."

I wish it were possible to describe my last year at school wholly in terms of good marks and my lessons, pleasant visits with my friends, trousseau shopping, symphony concerts, Saturday matinees, and pink luncheons. But, unfortunately, it had several other aspects. Though my health was very much better than it had been the winter I spent with the Cooks, I was frequently handicapped by the terrible backaches from which I had always suffered intermittently. (One of these I laid to my labors the night that the Fragment Society met with my mother, but this is hardly fair, for I had many others just as bad.) Less frequently, I was prostrated by severe headaches, which had never troubled me much before. But I missed little or no school on account of these ailments and I was singularly free from colds. Indeed, I felt I had every reason to congratulate myself that *this* year there would be no inconvenient "time out" on account of illness, when I began to be conscious of pain in my right side. I did not pay much attention to it at first—after all, it was just a series of little twinges! Then suddenly the twinges came closer together and grew sharper. Dr. Foster L. Bush, the father of one of my schoolmates and the cousin of my friend Foster Kellogg, who had been named for him, had succeeded Dr. Garland as our family physician; and when he looked me over, less complacently than usual, he said he would like to have his friend, Dr. Warren, look me over, too. I did not like the sound of this, for I knew that Dr. Warren was not a diagnostician, but a very famous surgeon. I liked what Dr. Warren himself told me much less: he said that I had appendicitis and that an operation must be performed immediately.

In those days and in fact for some time thereafter, a hospital was regarded as the last resort of those for whom no better provision could be made; there was no talk of sending me to one. On the other hand, it was obviously impossible for me to stay at Mrs. Ware's. Again, the Hotel Vendome seemed to my mother the best solution and I was hastily bundled up and taken over there. Two nurses were immediately installed—shifts were then for twelve, not eight, hours each!—a suite was transformed into a hospital and the next day the operation took place.

There were no complications, but any abdominal surgery—even when the patient was young, slender, and basically healthy—was then still regarded as critical and hazardous. It was two weeks before I moved from a bed to a sofa, several more before I was allowed to walk around. But after the first few painful days, my convalescence was far from unpleasant: the suite, with all traces of hospitalization removed, was sunny and spacious; all my friends of both sexes and all ages came faithfully to see me and showered me with flowers and gifts. Allen Weeks, who was one of my most frequent visitors, taught me to play poker and endless hours were whiled away at that game, which, incidentally, I have never played since! Foster Kellogg, running true to form, supplied me with unlimited reading material. All in all, I might have felt there were great compensations to invalidism, had it not been that my school year was, after all, badly broken up. My marks had been so good that there was no question as to whether or not I could graduate with my class; but, meanwhile, as soon as I was up and around, I was ordered off to the country and told to stay there until my strength was fully restored. Moreover, there could be no question of allowing me to undergo the strain of final examinations for college.

I was bitterly disappointed and my disappointment was not assuaged by the comfort for which I sought from another quarter. Since midwinter, all had not been going smoothly with my engagement. My mother had certainly done nothing to prevent this, though, in all fairness to her, it should be said that she had done nothing to precipitate it, either. But that she was not altogether satisfied with the course it was now taking had gradually become more and more clear to me; I worried about it a great deal and occasionally my concern showed in my letters. "You will have to talk things over with Mother, but for heaven's sake talk them over with me first." . . . "I think you can guess what my trouble is, though I cannot tell you—yet." . . . "Mother has been ill and is not well yet, so she is a little morbid and gloomy and says queer things, but I am sure everything will soon be all right." Like most very young girls, I was convinced that marriage would put an end to all my problems. "It will be a great relief to me to be married and have only one person to please." . . . "I shall just have to make the best of certain things until we are married. It doesn't do any good to think or talk about them much, but sometimes it's awfully hard not to because I do try with all my might and main to do right and I get so discouraged." . . . "I am so glad that three months of the twelve, before the time fixed for our marriage, are already more than gone, it seems too good to be true. Don't forget you are *promised* to me for Christmas Eve and that you are going to dine with us that night. There will be no other guests and we will open all my presents together and have a lovely time in the library."

So ran the letters earlier in the winter. The promise, to which I referred, was not kept, on the ground that my fiancé felt he must spend Christmas with his family, as he had also spent Thanksgiving. I do not think he realized what a shattering blow this was to me, and the only direct allusion I made to it was to say, "I feel terribly that you will not come on Christmas Eve and don't think I will have the courage to invite you any more." But later, there was an indirect allusion to it. "I don't believe you realize what it means to any girl to promise a man to marry him; and when a girl as young as I am promises, of her own free will, as unconditionally and unreservedly as I did, it means a great deal more than you will ever know; you cannot realize because you are a man."

There was no conscious reproach in this, or in anything else that I said or wrote, and I continued to dwell happily on the future. "*Next winter* we will have a nice open fire in your den, and a big easy chair and Tennyson's *Idylls of the King* and Matthew Arnold's *Tristram and Iseult* for me to read to you. Don't you love to think about the time to come when we will be married? I do! I dream about it every night. All the bright future makes the present seem less cold and lonely." I knew that for some time previous to our engagement my fiancé had been planning a hunting trip with his brothers and, evidently, the subject was brought up again and I interpreted this as meaning that the expedition in question was to take place during our honeymoon. "Do you really and truly wish to go to New Brunswick— or Newfoundland, or whatever place it is that you talk so much about?" I asked. "Because if you do, it does not make the least particle

of difference to me where I go, and if you would be happier off shooting caribou than doing anything else, I am perfectly willing to go
there. I suppose I could see you in the evenings. I do not wish to
stand in the least in the way of anything of this kind which you may
wish to do *ever*. You have planned so much about this hunting trip,
that I feel somehow as if you felt I was going to spoil a long-cherished
plan, and I don't want you to think of letting me stand in the way of
what you wish to do."

Very reluctantly, I had ceased to demur against a brief trip abroad,
though even the promise of a more elaborate trousseau than we could
have afforded to buy in Boston had not reconciled me to the idea.
"Mother went to see Mr. Hart [her business manager] the other day
and he thinks, with her, that I must go to Europe for two months,"
I wrote my fiancé. Instead of strengthening my opposition, as I had
counted on having him do, he replied that he had no right to interfere, as I did not belong to him, and that I must trust him to decide
what was best. He coupled this with the statement that he had been
"troubled about something for two years." Afterward I learned that
the trouble was occasioned because he had wanted, for two years, to
ask me to marry him before he finally did so; obviously, even if he
were trying to teach me how a grown-up girl should behave, when I
was fifteen, that was not an age at which it was proper for me to
receive a formal proposal! At the time I received his disappointing
letter, he did not explain the trouble and I did not venture to refer
to it in answering. My reply was unhappy, but resigned. "I do belong
to you, whatever you say, and I am willing to trust you absolutely in
everything. But oh! I don't want to go to Europe!" Then I added,
"How I wish I had been born a year earlier!"

If I had been born a year earlier—in other words, if I had been
eighteen instead of seventeen—I could have married without my
mother's consent; and, as I sensed her growing opposition, I was more
and more eager to evade it. If Harry and I had consented to the arrangement she originally favored, we would have been married in June
and that would have been the end of it; it was at our insistence, not
hers, that the engagement had remained unannounced and the wedding postponed until October. But autumn was still firmly fixed in my
mind as the time when I would be married. Nothing had been said to
make me feel that the arrangement to which my mother had consented
was to be altered, except for the change in her attitude toward my
fiancé. When she told me, shortly after my operation for appendicitis,

that I must ask whether this plan was still the one he wanted to follow, I declined at first to do so. It was only when she said that if I
did not, she would, that I wrote him hesitantly and apologetically,
asking what seemed to me a wholly superfluous question. His answer
came like a bolt from the blue.

He did not feel it would be wise to announce the engagement in
June. In fact, he could not tell me when he thought it would be wise
to do so. As for an October wedding, that was quite out of the question.

CHAPTER XXIII

"You think you know your own mind, Frances; but you're very young
and very inexperienced and very much in love. You make mistakes."

"I suppose I do. But I'm not making one this time."

"Harry Keyes was infatuated with you—briefly. There's nothing surprising about that. Older men are often infatuated with young girls.
But it's seldom a feeling that lasts. It hasn't in this case. He doesn't
really want to marry you."

"Yes, he does. He waited for two years to ask me, because he
thought I was too young before that. But he's wanted to marry me
ever since I was fifteen years old."

"Do you think it looks like that now?"

"No, I don't think it looks like that now. But that's the way it is,
just the same."

With much the same expression as when she had called me foolhardy because I explored caves and coasted on Flexible Flyers, my
mother said I was hopelessly self-willed and that there was no use in
trying to argue with me. I hastened to agree with her. The less the
subject of my engagement was discussed, the easier the situation was
to endure.

Of course, I had not forgotten Harry had said, eight months earlier,
that his family had been taken entirely by surprise when he told them
he was engaged. Now, as kindly and as courteously as he could, he
admitted, for the first time in words, that the news had been unwelcome, as well as amazing, and that they were still not reconciled to
the idea of his marriage, that we would have to give them a little more
time. More than this he would not say, except to add that they had
nothing against me personally.

"Mother thinks I don't know my own mind. Is that what your family thinks?"

"Well, you are very young, you know."

"How old do I have to be to know my own mind?"

It was, of course, impossible to give a definite answer to this and Harry did not try to give an indefinite one. I pressed him no further. Naturally, I had long realized that something was wrong, because no one in the Keyes family, which had hitherto always been so friendly, had made the customary call after being informed of the engagement and because not even a note or a personal message had taken the place of a visit. But I had not attached too much importance to the matter—sooner or later I felt confident there would be some satisfactory explanation of it and when that time came, Harry would give me this explanation. The fact that he could not do so, even now, and that this obviously troubled him, troubled me, too; but not to the same extent and in the same way that it troubled my mother.

By the first of May, we were back in Newbury and it appeared that we were going to stay there all summer after all. The plan of a two months' trip to Europe had been given up. What was the use of taking it, my mother asked, since there was no immediate prospect that I would need a trousseau? I did not quite follow her line of reasoning, but I certainly did not want to be the one to start further arguments and, anyway, at that stage, Europe held no attractions for me. As a prospect, Newbury had seemed very inviting; but as an actuality, it was disappointing. This time, I did really seem to have grown away from my old friends; besides, most of them were away, either at school or at college, and Betty Chamberlain, who was fortunately still at home, became my only close companion for the time being. I had hoped and expected that when I was back in the country, I would see more of Harry again, but in this respect also I was disappointed, for he was busier than ever.

At his instigation, I had begun to read newspapers regularly, which my mother had never encouraged me to do; and throughout the winter, when the Legislature was in session—or, as it is called in New Hampshire, the General Court—I had tried to follow its proceedings, since Harry was a state senator. After Governor Dillingham had passed out of my orbit, by leaving for Washington, I had ceased to feel much personal interest in politics; now such an interest was revived, but it was an unenlightened one, and my fiancé did not always have time to keep me abreast of developments and explain these to me. "I hear—

at least I read—that you have been appointed to some nice lucrative position," I wrote him that spring, "I am so glad! Why didn't you tell me, you bad man?"

"The nice lucrative position"—which paid, as I recall it, as much as $2500 or $3000 a year!—was on the newly formed State Excise Commission, of which he had been appointed treasurer and was afterward to become chairman. New Hampshire had lately voted in favor of local option, with every town and city deciding for itself whether or not liquor might legally be sold within its borders. The headquarters of the commission were in Concord; but the process of setting up machinery for the innovation it represented, and the business of supervising its enforcement, required endless traveling, with frequent meetings and conferences from one end of the state to the other. Harry wrote me briefly from Portsmouth, from Nashua, from Lancaster, saying he did not know when he could get back to Haverhill. When he did get back, he still had his duties as selectman of the town, and as president of the little local bank, clamoring for attention. Moreover, it was not only the responsibilities of the State Excise Commission which called him away; he was co-owner, with his brother George and his brother Charlie, of paper mills in Pepperell, Massachusetts, where they both lived; he spent a good deal of time with them. All in all, he was at Pine Grove Farm very little.

During one of his brief stays there, however, he asked me to go through the new house with him. My mother had been there to call, before the tidings of my engagement had brought about a breach between my fiancé's family and mine; but I had never seen it except from the road, and I was happy at the mere prospect of riding again through the pine groves between the gateposts and the lawns, for I had loved these from childhood. With the interior of the house itself, I was entranced. "I have spent hours already trying to decide which of the downstairs rooms I like the best," I wrote shortly after the visit took place, "and every one is so lovely that as I think of them in turn, the last one I think about always seems most beautiful, no matter which one that is. Upstairs, I like your room and the little pink room best. Oh, that is sweet! And the huge linen closet and the bathrooms and the nice big windows—well, I just keep seeing everything over and over again in my mind."

My enthusiasm is understandable, quite aside from the rosy picture of the future which it evoked. The mammoth house, made of mellow brick and adorned with white columns, was (and still is!) shaped like a gigantic H with the entrance at the center of the long hall which constitutes the cross section. In the arm at the left were situated the living room and the "morning room." (The latter became the library when I went there to live, partly because to me no house is complete without one; and partly because, until I became a professional writer, at which time I sought a more secluded spot, I never had time to sit down in the morning, according to the pleasant habit of my mother-in-law and sister-in-law—I was too busy doing housework and taking care of children.) The arm at the right contained the dining room and Harry's office, the latter, according to the custom of the times, being called the den; this had a separate side entrance, so that employees on the farm and business visitors could get to him direct and without coming through the front door. Beyond the gigantic H stretched out an ell, containing a butler's pantry, a kitchen pantry, a kitchen, and a servants' dining room; the laundry was in the basement; on the second story were ten bedrooms, three baths, a very large linen closet, a store-room, and innumerable closets; on the third, four more bedrooms, a playroom, and two spacious attics. There were eight fireplaces, two large piazzas, one smaller piazza, two porches, and a porte-cochere. The windows, as I had observed, were very large and were supple-mented with several doors, also equipped with glass panes, leading to the piazzas, so that as much sunshine and fresh air as possible could be admitted.

As a summer home for my future mother-in-law, sister-in-law, and little niece—whose widowed father always came to spend Sundays with her—it would be impossible to imagine a more elegant and de-lightful residence. Moreover, they had an experienced cook, waitress, and chambermaid-laundress in their employ, besides a German govern-ess for little Gertrude; and one of the hired men kept the woodboxes well filled for the open fires, emptied trash and garbage, and took the great oriental rugs outdoors to beat them. Therefore, the family had few, if any, domestic problems. Fortunately, on that ecstatic day when I first visited the premises, I did not realize what it would mean for an inexperienced girl to try to run such a house with only one or two household helpers, or what a strain on the limited budget the problem of heating it in zero weather could become. It was beautiful; that was enough for me then.

This visit to the house at Pine Grove Farm, which I visualized hap-pily and without concern as my future home, marked a red-letter day in an otherwise monotonous month. I was feeling more and more at loose ends. Previously, I had become somewhat reconciled to the decision that I was not to go to college; my fiancé had been no more enthusiastic than my mother about this project, which was so dear to my heart; and, with the understanding that I was to be married in October, I had been forced to agree that, of course, I must abandon the idea. Now that I knew I was not to be married then, the argument lost its force; so the state of my health was next advanced as the reason why a collegiate course would be unwise: did not the infallible Miss Hersey say, in the course of her wise counsels, that no girl whose physician pronounced her health to be uncertain should attempt the strain of one? Well, that had undeniably been the pronouncement of Dr. Foster L. Bush! He had even forbidden me to take my final examinations on the same grounds. The seal of unqualified approval by the College Board would have meant a great deal to me, especially as I had failed to secure it the previous year, and I yearned for it so greatly that I did not give up the struggle to get it without a fight. I finally consented to do so in a rather startling manner: I would agree to drop the subject, provided Harry would promise that if we ever had a daughter and she wanted to go to college, no impediment should be put in her way! The conversation is memorable for two reasons: first, because it was, I believe, the only prenuptial promise which I exacted; and second, because the possibility of future offspring was not then recognized as a suitable topic between courting couples and I was usually reticent when it came to departing from established custom.

The promise was given and I said no more about my disappointment; but the prospect of the following winter became more and more bleak. Marian Edmands, Mary Tudor, and Terry Helburn—whose physicians had not pronounced their health uncertain!—were going to college; all my other Boston friends were coming out. I had been more than willing to give up plans for a debut in favor of a wedding and, even now, a ceaseless round of luncheons, teas, dinners, and balls held no great attractions for me. But I began to realize that when I heard all about the festivities in which I was taking no part, I should feel left out again, just as I had when I first went to school. I was glad that I was at least to share in the graduation exercises and to make a brief round of visits, beginning with the Edmandses, in late May and early June. For the first time in my life, I wanted to get away from Newbury, because my departure would put an end to drifting, even if only temporarily.

In this experience, at least, there were no disappointments. "Mrs. Edmands is exceedingly nice to me, as she always has been. She says she hopes I will not feel next year, simply because Marian will be away at college, that I can't come whenever I want and stay as long as I like, for she and Grace will always be delighted to have me, which is very kind of them, I think. I am having a wonderful time as usual. But I wish when I'm visiting, you wouldn't use the sort of paper that has all that about the Commission printed on the outside, so that everybody knows who the letters are from. I get teased all the time about the 'advertisements' I receive, particularly when they come by special delivery, and it's deeply embarrassing to me.

"Well, yesterday I went to school, as I had learned that I was wanted there for lunch and a dress rehearsal. I was a little late for lunch, but Elizabeth had saved a place beside her, so I was all right. We had a very hurried meal and then rushed upstairs, where I made myself generally useful, tying strings, lacing bodices, running for pins and paste and finally, when the others had started their act, criticizing and suggesting and pretending I was the audience. The ten girls in my class—excluding myself—are giving a charade. Each girl is dressed to represent some country, and they come in separately and sing or dance or something; then they all stand in a row, and the first letter of the country they represent spell Miss Winsor—Mexico, Ireland, Spain, Switzerland, etc. At the end, they sing the song, the words for which I wrote. The whole thing is really very pretty, the song goes off finely, everyone likes it mighty well and I'm so pleased! Well, at last the girls realized that there was nothing to inform the audience what they were doing. Then they all clamored for a Prologue, and though Elizabeth tried to hush them up and informed them that 'she didn't want poor Frances kept awake all night,' I knew she wanted it as much as the others; so I said I would write it and learn it and telephone it to her tonight to see if she liked it. All of this has now been done and she thinks it is perfect. It is written in a sort of old English, plank [sic] verse, and I am to come in and recite it, dressed in a cap and gown. I am really pleased to have something to do and, as I can't sing or do regional dances, but *could* do this all right, I am glad it has happened that way."

Two days later, I wrote still more happily: "I was so weary last night that I simply couldn't write to you, but before I start out on my

daily round, I will tell you about the great day. The festivities began
soon after nine, the whole school, arranged by classes, being grouped
in the music room. The prizes given Classes IV and V for reading and
writing were awarded, the best book lists read[1]—Elizabeth and I
had the best book lists for summer reading—together with the ex-
tracts from the girls' comments on the books. Two of mine were read.
About twenty minutes of eleven, the first part of the program ended
by having the members of the graduating class called one by one, and
then clapping them in a most violent manner. The younger girls next
brought up viands to the girls and their mothers and then the second
part began, our room—which is huge—being used for the stage and
the mathematics room for the audience. First came a scene from *The
Tempest* done by the Shakespeare class. Then an awfully cunning
German play by the fifth class (girls fourteen and fifteen); then a darling French play, ending with ballet, by the fourth class (girls thirteen
and fourteen);[2] then a charade by the seventh class (the one next to
ours) given in honor of the graduating class—the word was Diplomas.
After it had been acted and guessed, one of the seventh class girls
came out with a huge clothesbasket filled with great rolls of parchment, tied with red ribbon; each diploma had big black initials on it.
Instead of calling out the girls' names this time, two words beginning
with their initials were called out and each girl had to go forward and
take a bow as she received her diploma. For instance, Polly Cunningham was Perfect Corker, Mary Tudor's, Marvelous Toiler, Bertha Russell's, Belated Rustic, etc., all of which were very true and caused
shrieks of laughter. But those that brought forth regular howls were
two of sarcastic nature: one of the most popular girls in Brookline, Hilda Williams, was Hopeless Wallflower and the very last one
given was Elizabeth Sweetser, Estimable Spinster. That simply
brought down the house. Mine was Famous Wit.[3] Last of all came
our own Prologue, charade and song and they went off splendidly.
By the time we had finished singing the song however, half of us were
in tears and as for Miss Winsor, the tears were running down her

[1] Every girl was required to do a certain amount of summer reading. A list was
given her, from which she was free to make her own selections, but she was supposed to read not fewer than ten books.

[2] I cannot recall this without a great sense of pride. How many schools are
there, I wonder, where girls under sixteen can give, in the same program, a scene
from a Shakespearean play, a German play, and a French play?

[3] We did not learn, until long afterward, that it was Miss Winsor herself who
had characterized us so cleverly and thus revealed a side of her which we did not
often see—or appreciate.

cheeks, and she came and caught hold of me and said it was the sweetest thing she had ever heard and that she would never forget it. She said a lot more nice things when she was telling me good-by, but as they were about me and not my song, I won't repeat them, for that would sound conceited.

"The farewells were simply dreadful—going and embracing a long line of weeping teachers, all telling you how much they loved you and how they would miss you, meanwhile feeling yourself as if you would like to sit down and *wail aloud*. I was thankful when it was over. But I couldn't have had a nicer last day, for all the teachers seemed sorry to have me go, and several of the mothers paid me so many compliments that I had to flee and all the girls kept giving me invitations, most of which I had to refuse.

"Bertha and I went and had lunch with Theoda Bush. I was dead tired and the lunch was awfully long and rich, so I didn't enjoy myself as much as I might have. I was glad to get back to the Edmandses' and rest. Tomorrow I am going to Elizabeth's, then to Mary's, then to Marion Burdett's. Monday, I begin my visit at Ruth Farley's."

After this visit I was back in Newbury, again with the feeling that I was merely drifting, but looking forward to a break in the monotony of life at the Oxbow when I made the visit to Marion which had now become an annual event. Meanwhile, Mary Tudor came to stay with me, admittedly tired after the strain of her college examinations, in which she had won an important scholarship, ranking second among all those who had taken finals for Bryn Mawr from New England. I could not help envying her and wishing I were tired for a similar reason, instead of from doing unaccustomed housework. For the first time in my limited experience we were having "servant troubles." The invaluable Ina of my preschool days had been succeeded by an equally invaluable Sadie, who cooked, washed, ironed, and cleaned, all with an equal degree of dispatch and skill, and was perfectly satisfied with her wages, which were five dollars a week. But some family crisis had arisen in Nova Scotia, where she and most of the best maids in New England then came from, and she had hurriedly left with a vague promise of returning "as soon as she could." Her temporary replacement, Annie, could not cook and would not clean; my mother liked to do chamberwork, but she had never made so much as a piece of toast in her life; a French omelette represented the sum total of her accomplishments in the kitchen, though she could—and did— make the best salad I have ever tasted, always mixing this at table in a deep green dish shaped like a lettuce leaf. She went on doing this with her usual skill, but she calmly stated that she could not and would not do anything more in the way of providing us with nourishment. The task of coercing the reluctant Annie or myself getting some sort of a meal together was left in my inexpert hands.

Even my birthday failed to provide the usual thrill. I had made no plans for the customary party, because there had been a prospect that I might go to Harry's camp instead. Then he found that he would have to be at the other end of the state on the date that seemed so important to me. At first, I took this unwelcome news philosophically. "It *is* too bad that you cannot be here on the twenty-first," I wrote, "and I am particularly disappointed because I have been looking forward to it for so long. But do not worry about it, for I know you cannot help it." Later I showed myself less sensibly composed; both my fiancé and my mother annoyed me, instead of comforting me, when they tried to assuage my disappointment. "Please don't trouble about my birthday," I said in my next letter. "You and Mother made me quite *angry* last night, trying to console me, as if I were a small child. I've had some much worse disappointments this summer and no one has thought of being sorry. The fates are against me this year."

Of course, the very tone of this letter betrays the fact that I was much less mature than I liked to imagine, though, in justice to myself, I must say it is the only one I have found in which I did not seem to accept my fiancé's inevitable changes of plan with unprotesting composure. But perhaps I can be forgiven this one outburst: I really did feel "the fates were against me," not because of this minor frustration, but because I was not going to college, nor was I going to be married, and I had, up to then, failed to find the satisfactory answer as to what I should do instead. As far as my birthday was concerned, I ended by having a small luncheon to which only Louise Johnson, Jeannie Darling, Betty Chamberlain, and Patsy Slemmons—Betty's house guest from Florida, where the Chamberlains now spent their winters—were invited, and in the evening going to a dance at Betty's house where, unexpectedly, I had a very good time.

For the rest of the month, between intervals in the kitchen, I apparently buried myself in books. I read Green's *History of England*, which I pronounced "very dull"; Emerson's *Essay on Nature*, which inspired me to read more of the great philosopher's essays and two novels by Charles Reade, one of which, *Love Me Little, Love Me Long*, I enjoyed very much, while the other—*The Cloister and the*

Hearth—I dismissed as "a needlessly unpleasant story." These works I had selected at random from my father's large and variegated collection; I also kept dipping, no less haphazardly, into what I called my "personal library," which I meant to take with me to Pine Grove Farm when I went there myself to live and which my fiancé was constantly enlarging for me. He had asked me whether I would rather have trinkets or books for a birthday present and I had suggested books: "Shelley or Wordsworth or Bryant or Lowell in the Cambridge Edition"—though, if he preferred, "I should very much like two little pins like the one you gave me when I had appendicitis—a gold safety pin about an inch and a half long, with a baroque pearl in the middle, like this— —do you remember? I want the additional ones to wear for cuff pins."

Characteristically, Harry had given me both the poetry and the trinkets, but the former had been delayed. Now I wrote enthusiastically, "The books came last night and I can't thank you enough for them. I wonder if you realize how many nice ones you have given me? Jane Austen, Meredith, Matthew Arnold, Keats, the Brownings, Whittier, Shelley and several novels, and I already had Hawthorne, Scott, Tennyson, Longfellow, Mrs. Jamieson's Art Books and a good many novels and histories. Every addition is a treasure to me." The ending of the letter is not as much of a non sequitur as would appear on the surface. "I do not care in the least what those disagreeable people in the Manchester *Union* said about you. They probably do not know you very well, for I have never seen anyone who did really know you that did not like you *very, very, very* much. Anyway, as I have told you, I am a young person with a mind of my own and even if the whole world should say disagreeable things about you, I should not change my mind a single bit. P. S. Yes, I think I know what 'the long way off present' is, but I suppose that is impossible at present."

I went on with my browsing, more or less contentedly, and at last the domestic situation cleared; Sadie made good her promise of returning and I was free to pack my trunk and leave for Marion. When I next wrote to Harry, I said, rather whimsically, that I had to find time for letters "between boys." My hostess, Marion Burdett, was as popular as ever—certainly *she* did not miss the experience of being a belle, in that delightful, if outmoded, sense of the word! And I was quickly caught up in a whirl of gaiety which she always created.

"Robert, who is Marion's best beau at present, was on the train, and Foster and Marion were waiting at the station to meet us with open arms—at least Marion was there to meet me and Foster was there to meet Robert. Then we all drove up from the station together, and after Marion and I had left the boys at the Kelloggs', we came home and found Allen waiting for us. The other boys reappeared in a minute and then I unpacked my bathing suit and we all went swimming. The water was great and I had a perfectly fine swim. Robert and Marion swam way off out of sight and then Foster and I swam to a float a long way from the Casino. Before we'd finished dinner, the boys were back again and we went for a moonlight sail. Foster says I'm not as much fun as I was last year, but it was a great night, not a cloud in the sky and we stayed out until after ten. Now we have just finished breakfast and here are Foster and Robert again, so I must stop." . . . "Yesterday afternoon came the water sports, which were perfectly great as we knew nearly everyone who took part. Marion and I followed the swimming races in a canoe. It was awfully exciting. Foster and Paul each got a first prize and Allen got two first prizes. After the races we all decorated Marion's boat for the evening illuminations and had a short sail, then came home to a seven o'clock dinner. Afterward, Mrs. Warner, Allen, Marion and I went out in Allen's canoe to see the illumination. I never shall forget it as long as I live. There was not a cloud in the sky or a breath of wind and the moon was full; every boat was illuminated with as many Japanese lanterns as it could carry, and all the houses along the shore were outlined with lights and had long festoons of lights going out to their stables. Besides that, there were great red lights going out at intervals of about six feet all along the shore; these were kept going by men in boats. Finally there were the most gorgeous fireworks I ever beheld. It was just like fairyland."

Again I was swimming, sailing, driving, dancing, with countless congenial companions of my own age. Again, evening after evening, callers appeared bringing boxes of candy, urging us to come to the Casino, to go with them to a clambake, to join them in the races. Caught up in the whirl of it, I forgot that I had been drifting, that I was disappointed about college, that the first glory had faded from my engagement. . . .

We still made something of a ritual about going for the mail, as we had the previous summer. A merry group of young people always went together and usually we combined a trip to the post office with a swimming party or a sailing party. The letters I received from Harry were brief and hurried, dashed off, as he himself dashed about the state of New Hampshire; this did not seem to matter as much as when I had nothing to do but wait for them, in Newbury, and keep wondering what had happened when no letter came. My mother did not write at all and this mattered still less. She could present a better case on paper, when I could not answer back, than when I could argue with her. I did not want to have her case presented any more cogently than it had been already.

Then the letter came—not *a* letter, but *the* letter—the one that was to change, for better or worse, the entire course of events, and certainly those sounded to me as if they were to be for the worse.

My mother issued an ultimatum: either my engagement was to be announced immediately or she would take me to Europe after all—not for two months, as she had originally planned, but for an indefinite stay. In short, she would keep me there until the date for such an announcement had been set, and this time so irrevocably that there could be no further equivocation about it. At the same time the date for the wedding would also have to be set and this must be for one not more than two months later than the announcement of the engagement. Meanwhile, I was to meet her a week from then—August 21st— in Mr. Hart's office. If Harry wished to be present at the meeting, she would have no objections. In fact, it might be a good thing. But her passage and mine were already engaged on the *Saxonia* of the Cunard Line, sailing from Boston August 25th.

Doubt not, brave heart, oh never dare to doubt,
  Lest care and calumny should breed distrust,
  Lest the fine steel of faith should gather rust,
And we should lose what we were lost without.
Our castle of delight is girt about
  By envious allies, Jealousy, Disgust,
  Weariness, Separation, Age and Lust,
And still the traitor at the gate is Doubt.

Mount guard with me, beloved; you and I
  Will baffle our besiegers with disdain.
The royal standard of our troth flies high
  As e'er it flew, and shall not dip again;
So all assaults shall only serve to prove
Our faith impregnable, our changeless love.

DUFF COOPER

Part VII

"The Ever Fixèd Mark"

CHAPTER XXIV

My first sensation was one of such profound shock that I could neither speak nor move. I stopped short in the street where we had been happily walking and stared, unbelieving, at the letter I was holding in my hand.

"What's the matter? Are you sick?" someone asked me.

I shook my head.

"Have you had bad news?"

I nodded.

"Is someone else sick?"

Again I shook my head.

"Well, for the love of Mike! Tell us what's wrong!"

At last I found my voice. "I can't. But I want to see Elizabeth."

If any feelings were hurt by my sudden and complete withdrawal, no one showed it. Elizabeth, we happened to know, was spending the day with Helen. Unquestioningly, the friends I was with took me to the Cutlers'[1] house and left me there. Elizabeth was with her "crowd" and Helen's—a different one from Marion's; they were all seated together on the veranda, drinking lemonade, and sprang up to welcome me.

"I want to see Elizabeth alone."

[1] The Cutlers now spent their summers in Marion, not Hull.

Again, no one showed resentment or surprise. Elizabeth took one look at my stricken face, drew me into the house, and closed the study door after us. I burst into tears.

"Tell me about it," she said, when the storm at last subsided.

I had promised not to tell her or anyone else that I was engaged and I kept my promise. All that I said was that my mother was going to take me to Europe, almost immediately, and keep me there indefinitely, against my will, unless something could be done to prevent it. Elizabeth asked what could be done and I said I did not know. Then I began to cry again. She did not ask any more questions and I did not try to tell her anything more. But when I left her, I had recovered my self-control and I was, to a certain degree, comforted; she had given me not only a feeling of sympathy but of support. I went back to the Burdetts' and wrote to Harry, telling him about my mother's letter.

"You have always said," I reminded him, "that it is harder to go than to be left behind. Now our positions are reversed; I am going and you are the one to be left behind. So if you are right, this is harder for me than it is for you." Beyond making this statement and outlining my mother's plans and position, I said only, "I will try to be cheerful and learn all I can, not only in books, but in other things, so that in the end I may become more worthy to be the wife of a man like you."

After writing and mailing this letter, I felt exhausted and hoped that by some miracle I could have a quiet evening. The miracle did not happen. Joe White, the former captain of the freshman crew at Harvard, had come cruising in to spend the night with his great friend, Foster Kellogg, and, joining forces with Robert and Allen, they came to take Marion and me to the dance at the Casino. We had agreed to go before *the* letter came and I now had no logical way of backing out, without telling the truth, which my pledge of secrecy prevented. Marion was, as usual, "overwhelmed with partners," and I had nearly as many; but when she and I reached home, I pleaded a headache, which I did not have to pretend, and went straight to my own room. Usually, I shared hers at night, and we lay side by side, whispering about sweet nothings, after the immemorial fashion of schoolgirls, until Mrs. Warner, Marion's grandmother, sternly ordered us to stop talking and go to sleep. This time, I did not want to whisper about anything; I wanted to be alone, with a chance to think my problems through; and as, for once, our escorts had left us at the gate, I believed I had a fair chance of doing so. I might have known, by the unprecedented speed with which they had departed, that something else was afoot. I was hardly settled in bed when I heard the tinkling of a guitar, accompanied by strains of song. Marion and I were being serenaded, and one sentimental ditty, occasionally interrupted by smothered laughter, followed another. This time I was only too glad when Mrs. Warner intervened. At last everything was quiet and I could try again to collect my confused and troubled thoughts.

I knew that much would depend on Harry's answer to my letter. Of course, it was not impossible that he would agree to do what my mother asked: consent to the immediate announcement of our engagement and set a date for our marriage. Even so, the sojourn in Europe could probably not be averted this late in the day; but at least it would not then need to be one of indefinite duration; in fact, I had ventured to suggest that perhaps we could be married in December, in which case I would not be abroad much longer than if the original plan of a two months' trip to Europe had been carried through. However, at the same time that I considered the glad *possibility* of this, I dismissed it as a *probability*. Whatever Harry's reasons might be for feeling that the engagement must be kept a secret and that no date could be set for the wedding, it was doubtful that he could find a way to override these in a week, and that was all the time there was. I had better make up my mind, then and there, to a long separation. . . .

Perhaps he would like to be released. If that were the case, of course he had only to say so. I would never try to hold him, or any man, against his will. I hoped and believed that I had made that abundantly clear. And he had not asked to be released; I felt reasonably sure he never would. Then should I be the one to break the engagement?

I could see several reasons why I should. The most urgent of these was, of course, that his family did not want him to marry me. I was puzzled and hurt because of this, and I could see that my bewilderment and my unhappiness were likely to increase; besides, my self-respect was involved. Did I have so little pride that I was willing to force myself into a tight little group where I would be unwelcome? My mother had rallied me, more than once, because of my "desperate desire to feel loved." I still had the desire to be loved, and though it had not been desperate, when she began her bantering, it was now. Not to be loved by just one person, either, but to feel myself surrounded with affection in a family circle, as I did among my friends in Newbury—as I did in Boston—as I did here in Marion. . . .

Inevitably, this thought led to another. Perhaps I really had *not* known my own mind. Only a year before, from this same place, I had written my mother that I had met three persons to whom I "could have lost my heart." I did not add, "if I had not already lost it to someone else," but that was what I meant. Well, perhaps I really had not lost it then, perhaps I still could. I was having plenty of encouragement in that direction. And I could be sure of a welcome in other family circles, I could indeed be surrounded with affection. . . .

Besides, I was tired of evading answers to logical questions by telling fibs. Why should I pretend and call them that? They were downright lies; and lying had never been among my many faults; on the contrary, in my determination to tell the truth, I was inclined to be too outspoken, with not enough regard for other people's feelings. It was fitting that I should try to smooth the rough edges off this bluntness; but it was not fitting that, in the process, I should let a lack of sincerity creep in. At first I had been merely embarrassed when I was questioned about my engagement; now the situation had become more serious; it distressed me to keep on lying about it. What was more, I had learned, to my still greater distress, that there were quarters in which I should have confided, long before, if not to whom I was engaged— that might have been avoided—but at least the fact that an engagement existed. All too fresh in my mind was the memory of a dreadful walk in the course of which my companion had asked with righteous anger, when I was driven to confessing this much, "Why didn't you tell me long ago? Do you think you've played fair with me?" I knew I had not played fair with him and I could not explain. I also knew I had forfeited a great deal of his respect, and his respect was something I valued highly; I had hurt him badly and I would not have hurt him for the world. If the engagement was to stand, I must not have any more experiences like this one.

So much for one side of the question. What was the other side?

I knew that when he was a very young man my fiancé, like most young men, had fallen deeply in love. Without, of course, telling me who the girl was, he had told me this and had also told me that she had given him every reason to believe she returned his affection. Then suddenly she threw him over. It had taken him years to recover from the blow, longer still to believe that any woman would be true to him. That was the main reason he had remained so long unmarried.

Then, at last, he had come to feel he knew a girl on whose steadfast-ness he could depend; afterward, he had never once doubted it. That girl was myself. I knew it had not entered his head that I would not keep my pledged word. If he lost his faith in me, then that would be the end; he would never again trust any woman as long as he lived. Did I have a right to destroy his faith?

What faith, moreover, could any other man put in my word? If I accepted someone else, who did not know I had been engaged before, I should have to tell him this; it would be against my code not to do so. An engagement, even one as hemmed in by both convention and natu-ral reserve as mine had been, presupposed certain prerogatives to a fiancé which no modest and well-brought-up girl then permitted any man except the one she had promised to marry; and every man—at least every man of my acquaintance—felt he had a right to receive her first hesitant kiss and gradually to awaken in her the same ardor he had felt when he asked her to marry him. I had been engaged for a year now and had long since passed from the stage of hesitancy to one of response; that of course was as it should be, if courtship were to provide the gradual and beautiful preparation for marriage. In a second engagement, this lovely awakening would perforce be lacking; even if another man said—and thought he meant—it did not matter to him that the girl he loved had been engaged before—could he *really* mean it? Perhaps he could, if he were thinking only of those guarded caresses; but might he wonder, if a girl would once break her word, whether or not she might do it again? How could he be sure in the face of such instability? I thought such confidence was too much to ask of any man. . . .

And, in the last analysis, wasn't there something else? Was I ready to admit that I didn't know my own mind? No, of course not. Was I ready to accept, as well as to offer, something that was second best? No, of course not. Hadn't I learned, several years before, that the only time that you could put an unpleasant situation behind you was after you had licked it? Yes, of course. Had I licked this one? No, not yet. Very well then. . . .

When at last I went to sleep, I knew that I would never be the one to break the engagement.

When Harry's answer to my letter came, I knew that he would not either. "Your letter just received. I am so shocked, so disappointed (with myself) so unhappy and so sorry I don't know what to do. I will try to write you more at length later. I suppose there is but one thing that could change your mother's plans, and God knows that would take place at once if I honestly thought it would be for your happiness and best welfare. To me the blow is a harder one than you can imagine. It seems to me almost cruel to force a parting between us at just this time. Your mother, I feel sure, is displeased with me and this is evidently one of her ways of showing it. Perhaps, dearest, it is all a mistake and I should never have told you of my true feeling for you. I certainly would not have done so if I had not expected to make you my wife before now. I have delayed our marriage simply because I have feared that, under the existing circumstances, I could not make you happy. My thoughts have been solely for your happiness. God knows I love you with all my heart and soul and to have you leave me seems more than I can bear. You are to go far away from me and all because I, in plain language, am a failure."

I succeeded in convincing him that in my eyes, at least, he was not a failure; but that he was terribly unhappy was clear; that he felt powerless to improve matters was clear, too, though later he wrote, "No ocean is wide enough to keep us long apart, that is as long as you love me as much as I believe you do now. How I wish I could stop this whole journey! Reckless thoughts are now occurring to me and perhaps I had better say no more." Of course, he said a good deal more and so did I. But however "reckless" the thoughts on both sides, nothing could be done to stop the journey, despite a dream, about which Harry wrote me at length and which was, in part, prophetic: "I dreamed that your mother had thought it best I should not see you any more before you went away and had told me not to meet you in Boston. So I tried to keep away from you, but finally ventured to call at your aunt's in Woburn. She informed me that you were ill in bed and that, of course, I could not see you. I was about to depart when I heard a faint little 'Come' and bounded upstairs, much to the horror of your aunt. (Where your mother was at the moment, I don't know.) I found you pale and sick, but very glad to see me. I remained with you until your mother came and I told her you were in no condition to go to Europe and that I proposed to take you off myself just as soon as you were able to travel—at which you gave me such an affectionate kiss that, hang it, I awoke! I don't often write about my dreams, but I thought I must tell you this one."

As a matter of fact, no impediments were put in the way of meetings in Boston. We rode about unchaperoned in hired cabs; we lunched and shopped together every day—at the Touraine and the Parker House, at Collins and Fairbanks and Bigelow Kennard's. I went with Harry to choose my ring, which I was to have at last, and he also insisted on giving me some money to use in case of emergency. But on sailing day I *was* very ill, so ill that Harry told me afterward that he would indeed have insisted on "taking me off himself" if by that time I could possibly have gone. I had to be carried aboard ship and, until we weighed anchor, I lay on the hard little sofa in the tiny cabin I was to share with my mother, biting my lips so that I would not cry out with pain as well as with grief. My left hand, allegedly injured—one last lie!—was wrapped in a handkerchief to conceal the band of sapphires and diamonds that glittered there; and pinned securely to my chemise was a little chamois bag containing five twenty-dollar gold pieces. When Harry bent over me to say good-by and I could feel his tears mingling with mine, it was very hard to keep from breaking down. But once we were under way, I sat up on the sofa and scribbled this line, which I sent back by the pilot: "I will prove to your family that I love you! And I will have you in the end."

Obviously, this was the note on which we had parted: that his family, like my mother, were clamoring that I did not know my own mind and were counting on me to change it. In itself, this was quite enough to strengthen my resolution; admittedly, I was a self-willed girl. I did not learn until much later the real reasons why his family had so bitterly opposed the match or what steps Harry took to break down their hostility.

This was based on the fact that they so thoroughly disapproved of my mother that they could not countenance the idea of any connection with her. A story had reached them in a roundabout way that she had told one of our neighbors Harry had asked her to marry him and they were appalled; she was much older than he, she had been married three times already, and one of these marriages had ended in divorce; moreover, at best, her type was not the kind they admired. I am afraid she may have said something of the sort to a neighbor, for I had once heard her do so myself, in a small family gathering; but I had not paid much attention; it was the sort of thing she was apt to say, jestingly and not always accurately. She was still a very charming woman, accustomed to masculine attention, radiant when she had it, astonished and aggrieved when she did not. It is quite possible that when Harry first began coming to the Oxbow, she honestly thought he came to see her and jumped more rapidly than she should have to another conclusion; it is also possible that when she realized her mistake she was piqued and in her resentment made statements that were both unwise and baseless. To this day, I do not pretend to know the whole truth; I am inclined to believe there was some right and some wrong on both sides. I have always been willing to make allowances for a viewpoint which I cannot share, even when it affects me adversely. I know it is not uncommon, outside of the United States, to find marriage regarded as a family, rather than as an individual, affair; and my future mother-in-law was a Canadian by birth and I could well understand that was her viewpoint. When I learned that one love affair had failed of fruition because of family opposition, some years earlier, I ceased to feel that I had been singled out for exclusion; and this feeling was intensified when, a few years later, still another engagement was similarly opposed, for no reason that I could see. In this case, the relative rebelled, as Harry had done, the marriage took place, and, later, the unwelcome bride became a cherished and respected member of the clan and the mother of two charming children. These two cases have helped me to better understanding of the situation. But my own feeling is still that it was tragic that an innocent young girl and an upright man, who were genuinely in love, should have suffered for intolerance on the one hand and indiscretion on the other and to reflect that, if my father had only been living, the first hope he expressed for me, when I was only an hour old—that I would have a good husband!—would have been fulfilled without sacrifice on the part of anybody.

So much for the cause of opposition. The means taken to break it down were desperate: Henry Keyes, the great railroad man, had left no will; consequently, in accordance with the laws of Vermont, his widow received a third of the estate and the other two thirds were divided among five children. This meant that Harry actually owned merely a fraction of the property at Pine Grove Farm; and though the family had once been very wealthy, the failure of the Santa Fe Railroad, after death had removed its guiding genius—the first Henry Keyes had been the second president—had greatly reduced the rest of their inheritance. By concerted action, it was quite possible for the family to prevent Harry from having enough to support his wife at Pine Grove Farm and establishing it as their home. The only other place available for him to take her was a small shabby house, entirely devoid of modern improvements, situated on a nearby farm which he had acquired independently; and he finally issued an ultimatum in his turn: either the objection to the marriage would be withdrawn or he would move to that place; he was sure Frances would not refuse to live there. The famous herd of Holstein cattle, which he had imported from Holland, was at least his and he would take that with him, together with the rest of his personal property; if necessary, some of the beautiful cows could be sold; in any case, they would provide some income. For the time being, he and his wife could live on that and his salaries from the Woodsville Bank—$1000 a year!—and from the State Excise Commission; he would withdraw his shares of stock in the Pepperell mills; the future would have to take care of itself. But, if he left, that would be the end of the family circle which the others had been determined to maintain unbroken and to which they had not been willing to admit the girl he had chosen for his wife.

All this, as I have said, I did not know on that desolate day when I sailed on the *Saxonia*, as bewildered and uncertain of the future as I had been the first time I embarked for Europe—indeed, I did not know it until many months later. If I had believed that anything more damaging than my extreme youth and the fear that I did not know my own mind were postponing the marriage, I probably would have broken the engagement after all. I, too, had a sense of family loyalty, and I might well have thought that I must stand by my mother. Moreover, I would not have wanted the man I loved to give up the home he had deliberately chosen, many years before, for his own, and to which he was attached by one of those strong ties which bind a human being to his land and his hearthstone—ties which can sometimes be the strongest in his life:

> "From primal sources, scarcely understood
> Springs love of land—potent as ties of blood."[2]

I would have doubted, not without reason, whether or not I could ever make up to him for a loss such as that of Pine Grove Farm would have represented. Moreover, Harry worshiped his mother, the memory of the sister that had died, and her little daughter, and he was deeply devoted to his surviving sister and his two brothers—indeed, the attachment existing among the Keyes brothers—three in each generation[3] for as far back as anyone could remember—had become proverbial. A breach between him and his family would have meant rup-

[2] Christina Rainsford. New York *Times*. December 13, 1959.
[3] I am glad to say that a strong bond among three brothers has continued from generation to generation: I had three sons and my youngest son also has three!

ture of his very being. Later, he went so far as to show me a letter from one of his brothers in which the latter said, "My wife understands and yours should, too, that no woman will ever mean as much to us as our mother." Possibly my sister-in-law did not find this hard to understand; having been taught to read out of the Bible and to memorize large portions of it, I did. I had not forgotten the words of Our Lord: "Have ye not read, 'that he which made *them* at the beginning made them male and female,' and said, 'For this cause shall a man leave father and mother, and shall cleave to his wife: and they twain shall be one flesh?' Wherefore they are no more twain, but one flesh. What therefore God hath joined together, let not man put asunder." Nevertheless I knew that while Harry would say he respected this order, in his heart of hearts he would have yearned for his mother if he had left her.

Since I lacked knowledge of the great risk he had taken, the engagement stood as firmly as a marriage.

CHAPTER XXV

The prediction which Maude Sanderson, in her capacity as a fortuneteller, had made so many years before was to prove true now and many times in the future: the sea is my friend. After I had dried my tears, so that I could write a note to send back by the pilot, I shed others only at intervals; and though from time to time, despite my mother's protests, I shut myself up briefly in my cabin, because my mood was more atune to solitude than companionship, I had not been aboard the *Saxonia* twenty-four hours when my sufferings, both mental and physical, were somewhat assuaged. Within another day or so, I enjoyed sitting in my deck chair between meals and eating those at the captain's table. Moreover, the chief engineer, Mr. MacFarlane, was a great friend of my uncle Will, my aunt Fannie's husband, and went out of his way to make the voyage both pleasant and interesting for me. I wrote Harry every day, more or less in diary form, saving the letter, which ran to forty pages, to post when we reached Queenstown. So I have a very complete record of what took place and some parts of it are, perhaps, worth quoting:

"Wednesday: There are lots of people on board we know—Doctor and Mrs. Washburn of Roberts College in Constantinople, great

friends of Morris Carter's; Mrs. Kellogg and her son, friends of Richard
Ware (this is not my family of Kelloggs, though I believe they are
cousins); and a Mr. Fiske of Boston, who knows both Richard Ware
and Mr. Hart. So Mother is having a very good time indeed. She
thinks I'm horribly unsociable to all these people and instructed me
that I ought to speak to the young man beside me at the table, though
I don't see why I should. I got up about half-past ten this morning and
found my way to my steamer chair where I made myself comfortable
and read Kipling's *Many Inventions* while Mother went off walking
with Mr. Fiske. The young man in the steamer chair beside me had on
a green sweater with a big yellow V and Mother decided he must be
from the University of Vermont, so she asked him and he said yes, he
was; then she talked with him a few minutes and finally told him I was
her daughter; so the young man began to talk to me.

"Friday: When I went up to the library late this afternoon, several
elderly males came and talked to me while I sat embroidering. There
is one quite nice one, Mr. Adams by name, and in age about sixty-
five of whom I think I have made a conquest. He is a great traveler
and is going to plan out trips for me. I do so hope that now we are
going—which is bad enough—Mother will go to one or two places
that I want to see—Italy again more thoroughly and France. Mother
wants to stay in Germany and the British Isles, and as far as I can
make out that is what we are going to do.

"Sunday, August 30th:[1] I wonder if you are thinking about me as
much as I am about you today, dearest. I have got up to breakfast
for the first time and have come directly from the table to the library
to write to you. It is a perfectly beautiful day, clear and sunny and
calm—very much the same kind of a day that it was a year ago—as
far as weather goes. Oh! I wish we could have been together today—
just today! It really seems like our right, doesn't it? I amused Mother
very much last night, about half-past eleven when we were both in
bed, by asking her if she took it into her head to go to Europe again
before I was twenty-one, and I was married, could she take me? She
burst out laughing and said, 'No.' Thank heaven for that much! I'm
afraid she thinks I'm terribly ungrateful, and I truly try not to be, but
I do want you so!

"Monday: After Divine Service in the Grand Salon yesterday, Mr.
MacFarlane invited us to take tea with him and said he would take

---

[1] The anniversary of our engagement.

us up and show us the Marconi system at the same time. Mother with her usual loquacity, informed the entire table of this at luncheon, and was promptly forbidden by the Captain to do anything of the sort. It was very dangerous getting up there, he said, and besides, Marconi wanted it kept secret—no one was allowed. The Captain glared at Mother and left. He is a big placid man, but he looks as if his anger, once stirred, would be dreadful. So I was frightened half out of my wits, and terribly mad with Mother as well. However, when Mr. Mac-Farlane appeared, and I told him what had happened, he said it was a shame, but that at least it would do no harm to wander down to that end of the ship. No sooner had we got there than a young fellow came leaning over the little Marconi deck, and Mr. MacFarlane introduced us, and told him about Mother's break. Then Mr. Ashley, that's the young fellow, came down the little ladder and shook hands with us, and said, 'Ah! But won't you come anyway?' Mother gave a look at the ladder, and said no, but I recollected the Captain had said nothing to me, and in a minute I was up there. Mr. Ashley wasn't in the least reticent about explaining the whole thing to me, and made himself awfully agreeable. It seems he is a full-fledged civil engineer and he told about the work he has done before this, and about the position in Germany he will have when he is a little more experienced. It had somehow never occurred to me that a Marconi operator would have such a superior and extensive education. Besides, he looks so awfully young. At last, we went down the ladder and found Mother and Mr. MacFarlane were still patiently waiting at the bottom. Then Mr. MacFarlane invited Mr. Ashley to tea, and when we got to the cabin, the table was set for four people, so he must have intended to all the time. Both men made themselves *very* pleasant. Before we left, Mr. Ashley said that we would be in communication with the *Etruria* this morning about eleven, and would I come and see exactly how it was done? I said I would. Then, as we were going out, he asked me if I would be walking about the decks that evening, to which I said, 'No,' because he might have known better than to ask me to do so many things, when he'd just met me. After dinner, however, I went quietly out to settle myself in my steamer chair and look at the moon and think about you. Then, without any invitation—in fact, after I told him that I wanted to be alone—Mr. Parker, the young Vermonter I mentioned before, came and planted himself down beside me. Some people are *so* tactless! I didn't talk to him much though. It was altogether too beautiful a night to waste on a mere man, unless that mere man be a certain person whom you may have heard me say I rather like.

"Tuesday: We shall get to Queenstown at twelve o'clock tonight and to Liverpool before dinner tomorrow, so it looks very much as if this would be the last installment of this perfect journal of a letter. Yesterday, when I had finished writing to you, I went up on deck to take my constitutional, in which I was immediately joined by Mr. Parker. Mr. Kellogg started to join us, but began tactlessly by saying, 'I'm coming to chaperone you, baby,' and that made me so mad that I told him in glacial tones that I didn't need any chaperone and that I was legally of age by the laws of Vermont and, after such a chilly reception, he could not well do otherwise than take himself off. Mr. Parker left me at quarter past six, as he had to shave as well as dress, and then Mr. Adams joined me and walked with me the remaining twenty minutes. He is the pleasantest man on board, to my mind, and awfully nice to me; he keeps paying me the most extravagant compliments, and then telling me that he does it in a purely paternal way—as if anyone would expect anything else from a man about seventy.

"I hope you are enjoying your hunting trip and that it is doing you lots and lots of good. You certainly needed rest and change."

The landing in Liverpool took place in weather which the English passengers described as "nasty," a term I had never used before in connection with weather, but which I was inclined to regard as accurate, for it was a "perfectly horrid day, cold and damp and drizzly." After a considerable delay at the customs, "despite the good offices of Mr. Adams and his valet," we went to the North Western Hotel, where we "waited for some time before being casually informed there was no room." So we went to the St. George, which seemed to me "a very nice sort of place." But I added, "I hate to get anywhere, however, at eight o'clock in the evening—too early to go to bed and too late to do anything else; and as our trunks hadn't come, all we could do was to sit in our room and twirl our thumbs."

The messages we sent to our various new-found friends, telling them of our change in hotels, failed to reach them, as we later learned; so after a dull morning in Liverpool, spent in "waiting around, which I hate," we took an early afternoon train to Chester, with which I was immediately charmed. "We came at once to this fascinating hotel, the Grosvenor (pronounced Grovner—what a way they have over here of spelling a word with about a dozen letters, and only pronouncing half of them!). We were going to leave for Malvern tomorrow, but this place is so delightful that we have decided to stay here until Saturday."

The next letter was written from Malvern, but before beginning to describe my experiences there, I covered several more pages with further comments on Chester and its surroundings. "As soon as we had finished breakfast, we went to the Cathedral, which is perfectly beautiful. First we walked all around the outside, then to the interior and finally through the cloisters, where I felt as if I were back hundreds of years—a little nun ancestress of myself! But she couldn't have been an ancestress of mine if she had been a nun, could she? Well, probably she was just a novice, and before she took the veil she stole into the cloisters on a moonlight night and met a nice man with blue eyes and eloped with him.

"We got to Malvern at half-past four and came straight to the Imperial Hotel. This is a fashionable English watering place, scarcely known to Americans, I think, which Mr. Adams told us we would enjoy, and which I think we shall very much indeed. We are going to stay a week. It is a lovely little town, beautifully situated among the mountains near the Welsh borderland. The air is superb. Besides being so charming itself, it is a good center for several interesting places we wish to see—Worcester, Tewkesbury, Gloucester, etc."

The next few letters contained enthusiastic descriptions of all these places, interspersed with comments and questions of a more personal character.

"How do you think I would look in a black dress? There are some beauties here and I am seriously considering having one in my trousseau. I should think it might be rather becoming—you know black hats are. Do you think I am *altogether* too young to have one?" (The answer to this was that if I were not too young to be married, I was not too young to have a black dress and velvet was the fabric suggested. My mother, however, was adamant in her refusal to let me have my way.)

"Did I tell you that when we got to Liverpool I made Mother buy me a nice little rubber tub, which folds up into no space at all and can be carried all about? It is a blessing over here where it is either difficult or very expensive to get a nice bath unless you have a tub of your own. This tub will also be great to take to camp."

There are also some comments that are less cheerful. "You can't conceive my joy, upon returning after a tiring but delightful outing, to find three letters from you awaiting me. They were simply dear, all of them, and arrived at a very opportune moment, for I was feeling weary and homesick and rather blue. You don't know—you never can! —how glad I was to get those letters, especially the one written the 30th of August. I do want you so terribly! I send you all my 'heart and soul and life, dear' and say again and always, 'God bless and keep you until we meet again.' I pray for you every night."

In Malvern, I made my first English friend and my spirits rose, though it is obvious that her conduct as an engaged girl baffled me. "This morning I took a long and delightful walk with a young English lady who is staying here—a Miss Forsythe. We kept getting caught in the showers, and finally landed at the lodge of Madresfield Court and stayed there nearly an hour before it cleared.

"Miss Forsythe, who is engaged, had noticed my ring, and therefore seemed to consider that there is a bond of sympathy between us. She is awfully pretty and very young and confided all her love affairs to me—which is more than I did in return.

"This afternoon we drove to Eastner Park and Ledbury and Mother invited Miss Forsythe to go with us. Although she was expecting her fiancé 'Jack' to arrive in the middle of the afternoon, she accepted with alacrity. I wondered what *you* would think if I went off driving when you had taken pains to come to see me! Well, I am always so crazy to see you that nothing would drag me from the house. We had a delightful drive, and when we got back we immediately ordered tea. Presently Miss Forsythe's 'Jack' turned up, and she greeted him with a quiet handshake, not even rising. I again wondered what you would think of such a cool reception. 'Jack' didn't seem to mind, however, but sat down calmly and took tea with us. He is very attractive. By-and-by she suggested going to walk, which was the first sign of kindness she had bestowed on him."

The letters from Oxford revealed better spirits, and indeed it is hard to imagine an eighteen-year-old girl who would not have found it pleasant under the same circumstances that I enjoyed during my six weeks' stay there. Through the good offices of Mrs. Deming, my mother and I were admitted to the more or less congenial circle of paying guests at St. Rognvaldo, the home of Dr. Whitmarch, a don at St. John's College, and his agreeable wife. Besides several elderly spinsters, who were only shadowy figures then and who, of course, are still more shadowy now, this circle consisted of three foreign students, one East Indian, one French, and one Greek, and two widows very different in type. Of the East Indian student, I remember nothing except the way he identified himself—Kumar Shree Agitsinghji of Morvi

—and the fact that "Harrow School" was also engraved on his card—
a version of the old school tie which was new to me. Of the French
student, I do not remember even the name, but I do recall that he
always looked rather rumpled, and that he once said sotto voce to the
Greek, "*Est-ce que vous êtes amoureux de la dame qui est quelque
fois assise à côté de vous?*" The Greek, who was small, neat, and
bearded, and who had twinkling eyes and a merry manner, vehemently
denied that he was in love with this lady or anyone else. He seemed
to feel very strongly on the subject, for once he slid under my door a
small photograph of himself, bearing the legend, "The stage owes
much to love, life nothing," and signed with a flourish "G. Rhallys."
However, he accepted responsively, if not enthusiastically, the overtures toward friendship which one of the widows, Mrs. Francis, made
toward him. She was plain, middle-aged, dowdy, rather dull, and completely proper; but she was genuinely kindly and her kindliness embraced Dr. Rhallys as well as the rest of us. The other widow—the one
about whom the Frenchman badgered the Greek—had bright red hair,
eyebrows arched like a crescent moon, and a skin that looked as if it
had been calcimined; she wore very deep and very expensive mourning, fashioned in the latest Paris mode. After a few days, she disappeared from our midst and I overheard whispered comments about
her, which I did not in the least understand. It was not until long
afterward that I learned widow's weeds are sometimes worn by light
ladies who are on the lookout for diversion and consider fashionable
black the best means of attracting attention, instead of grief-stricken
relicts who are fleeing from it. I now suppose, however, that the individual in question was suspected of belonging to the former group
and asked to leave the scholarly and chaste enclosure of St. Rognvaldo.

I was neither interested nor curious about her sudden departure, as
many other things were claiming my attention. "There wasn't any
guide on duty at the Porter's Lodge when we first went to St. John's,"
I wrote, "but just then an attractive looking young fellow came down a
flight of stairs and Mother went up and spoke to him. I knew the
minute he answered her that he was no more a guide than I am; but
he looked at me and I smiled sweetly upon him and he said that if
we'd wait a minute he'd go and find some keys, which he proceeded
to do. Then he took us to the library and the Great Hall and the
Chapel and everywhere; he was so nice and I was so certain by that
time he was a student having a lark that I asked him if we couldn't
see some of the rooms. He said, 'Yes,' with the greatest alacrity and

conducted us to some awfully nice ones, which I presume were his own, as he picked up some laundry that was lying on the bed and shoved it into the closet. He told us loads and loads of things (Mother had caught on, too, by that time) about the college, not only about Archbishop Laud, who is supposed to absorb all one's interest, but also about more modern things 'cuts and sconches' (that's fines) and how the boys get in when they're out too late, etc. I guess they act much the same way as they do at Harvard."

Subsequent visits to other historic places proved less intriguing than the first, but there were compensations in the form of different outings. "This afternoon we went out on the river and Dr. Rhallys went too. It was so peaceful and beautiful and restful after our tiring morning. We hired a lovely boat, and a nice boatman, and he rowed us slowly up the calm stream. Oh! it was lovely. Miles up the river we came to a little place called Sandford, and there we got out and had our tea—the most *delicious* tea! Now I have just come up to bed after an exciting evening at bridge. Do you know how to play it? I didn't like it very well at first, but it certainly has a great fascination as you begin to see into it a little."

Bridge soon became a regular pastime, outings on the river a scarcely less frequent diversion. I consented to one more sightseeing trip—to the Ashmolian Museum—though I spent all my time in the art gallery. "There is nothing I enjoy more than fine pictures and there are some wonderful ones there, not only paintings, but valuable sketches by Raphael and Rembrandt, woodcuts by Albert Dürer, water colors by Turner, etc. Then there are several charming Rossettis, some good Van Dycks and Gainsboroughs, so I enjoyed my morning very much. Just the same, I shall be glad to leave for London."

Shopping constituted another welcome diversion from sightseeing. I purchased nothing of great value, from the monetary viewpoint. But a tile, inscribed with a motto, made a great and lasting impression on me. I still feel that the motto is one that might very well be more generally adopted:

> "In men whom men condemn as ill
> I find so much of goodness still;
> In men whom men pronounce divine,
> I find so much of sin and blot,
> I hesitate to draw a line
> Between the two—since God has not."

A day or two after my last outing, I had what was apparently a psychic experience, and I still do not believe it was wholly a figment of my imagination, especially as it was the second of much the same kind. The Sunday before leaving Oxford I wrote, "I have not written you since Thursday, not because I haven't been thinking of you constantly, but because I've been sick in bed—nothing but the same old thing, you know, and I'm nearly all right again today. I did *so* want you, dearest. It seemed all the time—don't you have queer fancies sometimes when you're sick?—as if you weren't very far off, and yet I couldn't quite get at you, although I did want you so terribly. And do you know, all the time that I was sickest, my ring burnt me like a circle of fire, and though it hurt, it was heavenly. Do you remember that some violets you gave me last winter burnt me? You said it couldn't be so when I told you, but now it has happened again, and I'm sure of it. What a silly superstitious little thing you must think me, do you?

"We couldn't go to London yesterday because I wasn't well, but we are going tomorrow without fail."

Homesick and lovesick I unquestionably was; but the peace of the English countryside, the mingled grandeur and quaintness of the cathedral towns, the lore and majesty of Oxford were all acting as antidotes to my depression. So were the outings on the river, the games of bridge and ping-pong, the leisurely hours spent at the tea table. I had always hated teas of the type with which I had hitherto been familiar—noisy, crowded affairs, where no one had room to sit down and where everyone seemed to be trying to outshout someone else, without ever saying anything worth listening to. But these English teas were different: here was quiet friendliness, here was interesting conversation, and—not the least important in my opinion—here was delicious food and plenty of time to enjoy it—bread set on a wooden board, buttered while still on the loaf and then sliced very thin; fruit cake, also sliced very thin; piping hot scones and muffins; orange marmalade, strawberry jam. Indeed, I find many references in my letters, which would supplement my recollections, if this were necessary, as far as that particular item were concerned, to the "delicious English food"—and not a single critical comment about it. My English secretary, who has heard numerous such comments in recent years, assures me it was because I was not as discriminating then as I have later become. I do not agree with her. Both at the Oxbow and in

Boston meals were excellent, as well as enormous, and I was used to feasting every day. Moreover, the letters written from Germany, just after leaving London, are full of complaints about food and I lost so much weight in Berlin that all my clothes had to be altered. But England nourished me, not only adequately but royally, and this is true in the figurative as well as the literal sense of the word. I started on the next lap of my journey in a state of improved health and improved spirits and, from the beginning, everything about London delighted me.

My first letter from there begins with an enthusiastic description of our quarters at 11 Half Moon Street. "This is a small private hotel,[2] on a quiet little street leading off Piccadilly, the most beautiful and fashionable district in London. We have a parlor and two bedrooms, all very good sized and completely furnished, and a bathroom. Our parlor doubles as a private dining room and a very good-looking and immaculate butler serves us with delicious meals—at least, the two we've had so far have been delicious, so we hope and believe the following ones will be, too."

(The word bathroom is sheer euphony. A cold little cubbyhole contained only what the English call a W. C.—one of the many terms new to me. But this did not matter in the least, for there were "commodes" in both bedrooms, and twice a day—following early morning tea and again following afternoon tea—tin tubs and a plentiful supply of towels were placed in front of the glowing coal fires and the tubs were filled with steaming hot water poured from a tall tin pitcher. All this was done smilingly, expertly, and as a matter of course in the same manner as our meals. English service at that time was certainly the last word in perfection.)

"Immediately after lunch, we started out on a shopping tour," the first letter continues, "and went first to Nichols, the Royal Tailor,

[2] I have recently come across a small card, issued by the private hotel at 11 Half Moon Street, on which the rates are given. The hotel contained nine "suites of apartments" for which the charges ran from two pounds, two shillings a week to five pounds, five shillings. As the pound was worth five dollars at that time, this means that the most expensive suite in the hotel cost only a little over twenty-five dollars a week. The usual charges for meals were two shillings for breakfast, two shillings sixpence for luncheon and four shillings sixpence for dinner and "to each suite of apartments a charge of four shillings per day is made for lights, linen, bath and service and includes all extras for the whole party taking the Rooms." Tips were entirely optional and very modest ones were received with grateful enthusiasm. Although this schedule indicates somewhat greater expenses than those incurred eight years earlier in Switzerland, where three dollars a day was the maximum per person, it certainly leaves one almost breathless with envy for the good old days.

where I was measured for a riding habit and bought a covert coat. We got home just in time for tea and scarcely had we finished when Mr. Adams's card was brought up. You remember, that nice old gentleman who was on the steamer. Mother had written him when we were coming, as he requested, and I'm sure he appeared very promptly. He has invited us to do several nice things with him and evidently intends to make himself quite agreeable to us."

This expectation was amply fulfilled. The next letter says that "He came and took us to tea at his club, a great big handsome building, but of heavy style. I did not think it as pretty as the clubs I have seen at home. I was, however, very glad to see a London club and I think it was awfully nice of him to ask us to go." (The pleasure I felt in visiting a London club for the first time is, I am glad to say, one that has been repeated over and over again with a number of delightful hosts.)

Two days later, the schedule appears to have been both crowded and varied. "Early in the morning, we went out on another shopping tour. First Mother went to the bank and got the wherewithal to buy things, and then we went to Peter Robinson's and I got gloves, corsets, etc., and next we went to Nichols and I had the first fitting for my habit. It fits like a glove—short skirt coming just below my feet [!], long coat, very tight fitting to the waist, and then flares to the knees. Before we went home, we went to Scot's—the English Phipps and Atchison—and I got a hat—a big black beaver, very much the shape of the summer one you liked so much, trimmed very simply with black satin bows.

"Dr. Rhallys drove up just as we ourselves got home. He had invited us to go to the Tower with him, to meet a friend of his, Lord Dillon, there at half-past two, so Mother asked him to lunch here first. Directly afterward, we started off and had a long and very interesting drive to the Tower. Lord Dillon met us promptly; he is one of the chief officials and could take us everywhere in places where most people are not admitted.

"We didn't get home until five and I was so tired I went straight to bed and had my tea there. After a good rest, I got up and took a bath and dressed in my best clothes before going to dinner and the theater with Mr. Adams. The dinner was delicious. The performance was all music and ballet—no drama at all, but the most beautiful dancing, costumes and scenic effects that I *ever* saw!"

And I have never seen anything more beautiful since! The spectacle was "Vineland," captioned as "A Fantastic Ballet in Four Tableaux." These represented "Old England, the Alderman's Wine Cellar; The Rhine with the Lorelei Rock; Oporto—on the Quay; and France—the Vintage of Champagne." The Spirit of Port Wine, the Spirit of Rhine Wine, the Spirit of White Grapes, the Spirit of Black Grapes, and the Spirit of Champagne were all embodied in the persons of beautiful ballerinas; and one of these—Adeline Genée—was to the dance what Eleonora Duse was to the drama—the greatest of her time, not even excepting the divine Pavlova! I saw Adeline Genée many times after this, for Boston was one of the many places where she achieved her countless triumphs; and a slipper of hers became a treasured souvenir of Father Van Allen, rector of the Church of the Advent in Boston, who was one of her greatest friends.

"Vineland" was only the first of the many spectacles which convinced me that London was without a peer when it came to theatrical performances—a conviction which is as strong today as it was more than half a century ago. Before my mother and I left for Berlin, we saw, by ourselves, Beerbohm Tree in *Richard II*, E. S. Willard in *The Cardinal*, and J. M. Barrie's *Quality Street*, with an all-star cast; also Edna May in *The School Girl*, again as the guests of Mr. Adams. We also went to hear young Kubelik, the Bohemian violinist, at Queen's Hall, "And oh, it was perfectly divine! Such beautiful music! It is the first time, too, that I have seen an English audience really waked up and thoroughly enthusiastic."

Neither drama nor music, however, could dislodge painting from its primary position in my absorbed attention. Statuary, as a rule, intrigued me less, but the Elgin marbles were an exception to this rule and, besides, at the British Museum, "I fell in love with the beautiful Venus. She is one of the most charming women I ever beheld. The fact that she is made of stone doesn't in the least alter the fact that she seems quite alive and very fascinating. She is much younger than the Venus de Milo—not a day over twenty—and she is in love. I can tell by her expression."

Both Mr. Adams and Dr. Rhallys continued their courtesies. "Today I donned my best bib and tucker and drove with Mother to the Oriental Club where I had been invited by Mr. Adams to a small luncheon. Mother dropped me there and I had a very good time. It was different from any American luncheon I have ever been to. One of the ladies had on a pink suit—she was very young and pretty—and the other, the chaperone—I had her husband to talk to—also young, had a very handsome blue cloth suit, trimmed with fur and *cut out at the neck!* There was no water *at all* to drink, nothing but sauterne and champagne and I knew it wasn't proper at home to drink champagne—for young girls, I mean—and so I wouldn't here, although Mother has assured me since it would have been all right. The food was delicious and everyone was very nice. At half-past three Mr. Adams took me to the Book Lovers' Library where I met Mother. This was an anticlimax. . . .

"This afternoon, Dr. Rhallys gave a small tea to which he kindly invited me and again I had a very good time indeed. I am getting more and more thankful that I can talk French, for one of his other guests, a Mr. Rothschild, could hardly speak a word of English, and Dr. Rhallys talks nothing but French to me—except occasionally a little German—though as a matter of fact he can now talk English very well. He has some cousins by the name of Valerie and they have been very kind to us, too. We drove out to Kensington, where they live, in *sheets* of rain. Their house is one of the largest and handsomest I ever saw, the tea was delicious, the people charming, so altogether, I had a very good time and was glad I went."

There was a darker side to the days when I had these good times, as other paragraphs in the same letters betray. "Mother never kisses me and I do miss it terribly." . . . "I have been trying to write you for an hour and all that I have written I have torn up. It doesn't do to complain on paper, does it, when we're so far apart?" . . . "The English climate doesn't seem to agree with me very well, for I've had another bad cold and been housed again for two days. Besides, everything seems to be at sixes and sevens and I'm rather unhappy. This is the last letter I am going to write you from England and I will be lonelier than ever in that desolate Germany. I do hate German and Mother has just broken the news to me that we are not going to Italy and the South of France at all—the only places in all Europe that I wanted to see! But Mother didn't want to go there and there isn't enough money to do everything, of course, so we're just going to skip *all* the places I wanted to visit and stay in that horrid Berlin all winter! I can't help feeling that it is a little unfair, though I don't mean to be selfish, especially as she's been promising me right along that I should go to Italy. Perhaps she'll dislike Berlin herself—she can't speak a word of German, you know, and I only hope she will hate it. We leave London tomorrow, cross the Channel and get to Brussels tomorrow night; stay there till Wednesday, go to Cologne and stay there till Friday, then go straight through to Berlin."

In the absence of any encouraging news about the possibility of setting a date for my marriage, my relations with my mother had inevitably become more and more strained. I continued to insist that the news would come any day; she continued to say that it did not look that way to her. Again I retorted, as I had in Newbury: it might not *look* that way, but just the same it *was* that way. Before we left London, I was able to say, "I told you so." December was not feasible, I learned, for several reasons; but if my mother and I could plan to be back in April, the engagement could be announced immediately and the wedding could be in June. I had better start getting my trousseau and selecting my bridesmaids; the friends I wanted in my wedding party and any relatives whom I especially wanted to take into my confidence must of course be "told," before there was any formal announcement.

Armed with this letter, even the prospect of a "horrid" city like Berlin began to seem less desolate.

CHAPTER XXVI

Just why my mother decided on Berlin for our winter headquarters never was explained, though I had not been able to stifle completely a suspicion that she thought romance might enter the picture again, in the form of Bär Russell, farfetched as it seems to imagine she could have based such a notion on the strength of a single sonnet, addressed to me when I was only fifteen years old! I had, to be sure, been thrilled when I received it and had pasted it in the famous scrapbook; after that, however, I had forgotten about it until my mother reminded me of it. Her generation and her mother's had set more store by sonnets than mine, as two beautiful books, bound in red morocco and filled with page after page of verse, penned in fine Spencerian letters, still fully attest. (Each sonnet is written by a different admirer, but the delicate handwriting varies very little!) Bär did not write any more sonnets, to me at least, and it was twenty years before I received a second one, from quite a different quarter. I also think it is possible that Bär's mother, as well as mine, might have entertained hopes that the renewal of friendship between the two families might have some happy results; but these hopes, if they existed, were soon dispelled.

The first letter written to my fiancé after leaving London was mailed from Brussels and bore the address of the Hotel de la Poste. (Though we generally went to a pension if we were to be in a city for any length of time—London and Paris were the happy exceptions to this rule!—my mother believed in patronizing first-class hotels if we were moving rapidly from place to place.) "At last we have got to a place where there is some sun! You may be surprised to have me begin a letter with such enthusiasm over a mere matter of sunshine, but it is much more welcome and much more unusual than anything I have seen in ever and ever so long. It has been a perfectly beautiful day, bright and calm and warm, and coming after the dampness and cold of London it seems like a godsend. We have had a carriage all day and seen loads and loads of wonderful things. I was here eight years ago, but I don't remember caring much about Brussels then. However, the first time I was dragged about to places, whether I wanted to go or not, and now I do the managing. In the afternoon we went to the Cathedral, which is beautiful, but I wish the Catholics of the present day didn't think it necessary to put so many hideous and ghastly images, all dressed up in tinsel and cheap lace, in their magnificent old Gothic churches. We got out of the carriage to walk through one of the splendid 'Arcades,' or 'Galleries,' as they're called here—they were 'Rows' in Chester and 'Arcades' in London, and what they will be next I have yet to learn."

We reached Berlin late at night, "after a long tedious day, but not nearly as uncomfortable as the one we had going from Brussels to Cologne. There was an Italian in the car who talked to Mother and tried to talk to me, but I hate this custom people have over here of talking on the train to strangers, so I read or looked out of the window very haughtily and only answered with yeses or noes. Bär Russell met us at the station; I have not seen him since I was a little girl, though occasionally we have written to each other. He seems to be very nice, but he is not big and strong and athletic, the type I like, as you know, and his eyes are not blue. He knows a great deal—too much, I think—and is quiet. I don't believe he'll prove troublesome in the least.

"Mrs. Russell was waiting for us at the pension. She is a dear—a German countess that married an Englishman, who spent all her money and died when Bär was a baby. So she's very poor now, as her family hated this man and disowned her, I believe. Anyhow, she is sweet and has a lovely voice, a thing I do so love and admire, though

I know—and even you tell me—I can never hope to have. Mother asked the Russells to stay and take late supper with us, for which I was rather sorry, as I wanted to get at my pile of mail and rest."

Mrs. Russell, at my mother's request, had selected the pension where we were to stay and our first impressions of it were far from favorable. The rooms into which we were shown after that long and tiring journey were small, cold, and dingy and had no outlook but a dark and dreary court. Mother had written that she wanted to economize and these quarters were the natural result of her instructions; but, as usual, she changed her mind when she found that economy and discomfort were synonymous, and the next morning we were moved. "We have two perfectly enormous rooms," I wrote cheerfully, "so big we are nearly lost. We are just now sleeping separately, because I do hate sharing a room with Mother. But I think we shall turn her room into a parlor after all. Because, do you know, I think she is going to let me have music lessons! If she does, I shall be beside myself with joy for your sake, because I feel that might give you some pleasure and that nothing else I know—I mean in the book line—ever will. I can practice a lot because I shan't have much else to do, except mend and embroider. Mother sits and knits washcloths, one after the other, and at the end of a day, she unravels what she has done and starts over again the next morning. She seems to think she is like Penelope waiting for Ulysses."

Irritated comments on my mother's sacrificial washcloths are repeated more than once. There are also frequent references to mending and embroidery through the winter and my stitchery had more purpose. The black stockings worn in those days, though durable in appearance, were by no means holeproof; long hours were spent in darning them and it was dull work. The embroidery seemed more rewarding; although I could hardly hope to achieve "a dozen dozen of everything"—then every well-to-do girl's ideal for her trousseau—I meant to come as close to it as I possibly could, as many a towel, tablecloth, and napkin still bears witness. However, I did find plenty of other things to do, for music lessons, as well as German lessons and riding lessons, soon became a reality and not a plan. I enjoyed them all. Bär Russell and I found very little to say to each other. He did, as I had observed from the beginning, "know a lot" and he made a conscientious effort to share his knowledge with me, especially of literature. But his attitude was that of a pedant and mentor to a degree surprising in one so young; he did not have the faculty of clarifying and animating both verse and prose and thereby kindling a responsive enthusiasm for everything we read together, as my contemporaries, Frank Sweetser and Foster Kellogg, and my father's friend, Horace Deming, had done so superbly. Bär and I went to a few museums and libraries and took a few walks together, but these expeditions became more and more infrequent. He found me no more stimulating than I did him; indeed, it was difficult for him to conceal the fact that he regarded me as a hopeless ingénue, though laboriously and politely he tried to do so. My mother was disappointed in this and in other aspects of the acquaintance so hopefully renewed after many years of separation. She was shocked by the straitened circumstances of the Russells —circumstances which were made all too apparent by the cold little flat in which they received us and which was painfully clean and pitifully bare. Mrs. Russell was equally shocked because my mother did not see her way clear to relieving these conditions; and gradually old rumors, long silenced, about the unfortunate German countess's girlhood and the potential reasons for her marriage to an untitled and obscure Englishman and her family's desertion of her were again bandied about. Whether there was a word of truth in these sad stories I do not know; but the Russells passed out of our lives, not with the same suddenness that they had re-entered it, but with a strange sad slowness.

By the time the inevitable break was evident, it was too late for us to leave Berlin and, though my first impressions of it were as unpleasant as I expected, meanwhile I had found congenial spirits at 123a Potsdammer Strasse, just as I had at St. Rognvaldo's. The pension in Berlin was run by Frau von Witzleben, a very beautiful woman of exalted birth, who had separated from her husband, apparently for good cause, and had chosen this way of earning her living. In the management of the pension, she was assisted by her elder daughter, Edel, who was about my age, and a young and pretty woman, formerly a governess in the family, who was known only as Schulzchen. My fellow guests included the usual number of foreign students and unattached widows and spinsters, most of them very pleasant; and Frau von Witzleben and her younger daughter and two sons—who were away at school and college—as well as numerous nephews, nieces, and cousins who were frequent visitors. She was closely related to the von Moltke family, and among the visiting nephews were two who were also the nephews of the great field marshal. Thirty-five years later, when I was staying in East Prussia with another noble German family

—as a real, not a paying, guest this time!—an elderly officer, still erect and elegant, who took me into dinner, somehow looked vaguely familiar to me and, presently, I realized that the impression was reciprocal. After glancing at me in a questioning way several times, he said, "Am I dreaming, or were we friends long ago? Did you by any chance once spend part of a winter with my aunt, Frau von Witzleben? If so, you will be sorry to hear that my brother Ludwig was killed in the war.

His brother, whose full name was Helmuth Johannes Ludwig von Moltke, had become a general almost as renowned as the field marshal, and my dinner partner had his full share of distinction; they were all men of "The Great Tradition," about whom I wrote in the book to which I gave that title and for which I was gathering material when this strange encounter took place in East Prussia. Great names had meant little to me when I was eighteen; but friendliness, then as ever, meant a great deal, and of friendliness I was soon abundantly conscious at the pension in Berlin. After dinner, the paying guests generally foregathered in the large salon for coffee, chamber music, and conversation—all excellent; and upon invitation they went, two or three at a time, to Frau von Witzleben's private parlor for slightly more elaborate refreshments, even better music, and animated small talk. To a large degree, these evening diversions made up for the abominable food and the horrible weather; and—in the sense that a compensation is something which does not quite compensate—it assuaged my homesickness. Besides, I was studying hard, sightseeing eagerly, and hearing marvelous opera and concerts night after night.

"My lessons are in full swing now," I wrote. "Mondays and Thursdays, music from twelve to one; Tuesdays and Fridays, German from twelve to one; Wednesdays and Saturdays, riding from three to four. I practice from two to three hours a day, study, embroider, mend and sleep. Some of the time I have been shut up with a sore throat, but I'm much better and had an unusually good ride yesterday afternoon. You can't really feel too badly with a good horse underneath you and I went like the wind. There was a Princess von Hohenzollern with her father and fiancé in the ring, two grooms, six horses, and innumerable beautiful rugs and coats, all with huge coronets embroidered on them. One gets used to nobility (of title, I mean!) over here because you scarcely meet anybody without one. In conduct, however, I think many of the Germans are the rudest, most disagreeable people I ever saw. The men call you 'Gracious Lady' and kiss your hand (no one has kissed mine, don't worry, but it's the custom here) and bow all the time, but they're more likely to bang the door in your face than to hold it open for you and the way they knock into you on the street, without even saying, 'I beg your pardon,' and sometimes really seeming to do it on purpose, is dreadful. I have been obliged to cultivate such a cold and haughty demeanor since I got here that you may find me hard to thaw out when I get home." These comments did not apply, of course, to any of the von Witzlebens or von Moltkes, who were punctiliously courteous, as well as very kind. But I was terribly shocked—indeed, terribly shaken—by the conduct of many German officers whom I saw on the streets. In appearance, they were quite the most gorgeous-looking creatures I had ever beheld: beautifully built blond giants, with the glow of perfect health on their arrogant faces. Their helmets glittered above their proud heads, their swords at their slender sides; their great cloaks fell in long graceful folds over their splendid uniforms. Had their manner matched their magnificence, it would have been easy for me to visualize them as the reincarnations of their own legendary heroes. But would Siegfried or Parsifal have shoved a gently bred young girl off a sidewalk to make room for his own splendid progress? Would he have deliberately affronted her? Of course not! I had not been in Berlin a week before its military aspects had lost all their glamour and become a matter of abhorrence. "I want you to promise me the next time you write that you will never, as long as I live, let me go away from you again," I wrote. And later, I added to this, "You can go if you like—it isn't half so heart-rending to be left behind as it is to feel yourself going—going—going away from the person you love. Every time I am in a train or on a ship I nearly go crazy with that feeling. . . .

"I forgot to tell you that Mr. Alfred Rothschild, that nice man we met at Dr. Rhallys' tea, was in Berlin this week. He knew we were going to be here, so he wrote to us in care of Baring Brothers, asking if he might come and see us, and it was forwarded. He made a very long call Thursday night. He is now gone, so I suppose we will not see him any more. . . .

"Yesterday, though the weather looked rather dubious (as it nearly always does here) Mother decided that we'd better go to Potsdam, the celebrated suburb of Berlin. We had quite an exciting time when we started out, for the Crown Prince and two of his younger brothers went out on our train, as a matter of fact, in the next compartment to ours, and there were carpets and policemen and guards and gorgeous officers. This is the second time I have seen the Crown Prince, for he was at the Vecsey concert we attended Sunday, and he looks very much like you."[1]

The letters written between Thanksgiving and Christmas contain many passages of a wholly personal nature and the affectionate tone of these should certainly have dispelled any doubts as to whether or not I had experienced a change of heart. "I was very glad indeed to get a letter from you today, though it was evidently written when you were feeling tired and discouraged. Darling, I wish you never had to economize and that I were bringing you a fortune instead of just myself. I know it is dreadfully hard for you to be poor, especially as you were brought up with so much money. But I can't help feeling that there are many greater things than wealth in the world and that we possess a good many of them—or will by this time next year! To think of living in the same house with you, and having everything you want to do perfectly proper and no one able to take me away from you! It all seems too heavenly to be true, yet, thank God, it is true and that is the blessedness of it."

Now that the date for my marriage had been definitely set, I had begun to make purchases for my trousseau. The weather was not conducive to much window-shopping. ("Yesterday when I was out I felt as if a sponge which had been dipped in cold water were being applied to me all over. I never knew such penetrating dampness! The pleasantest and warmest time of day—strange!—is about four o'clock in the afternoon. It is by that time totally dark, but the streets are brilliantly lighted and the daily rain has usually ceased.") But fortunately a beautiful linen shop, Mosse's, was situated next door to the bank where, once a week, my mother went to draw on her letter of credit; and this location proved almost too convenient. More than one long paragraph lists the various items of beautifully embroidered table covers, bureau scarves, centerpieces, and doilies I had purchased; and half a page is devoted to a picture of handkerchiefs, "some perfectly plain, hemstitched, with just the initials 'F.P.W.,' others much finer, exquisitely embroidered with elaborate monograms," not only for me but for my bridesmaids. "Mother wanted to give the bridesmaids extravagant presents, but I wouldn't let her, since I feel that this once in my life I have the right to have the money spent mostly on me—on us, rather.

[1] I think I confused the looks of the Crown Prince's with those of his next younger brother, Eitel Fritz, who, as a young man, was strikingly handsome and in coloring, carriage, etc. actually did not look unlike my fiancé, who had a good deal more chin than the Crown Prince.

When the things come home I just sit and gaze at them and feel them and think how lovely they will be in our house and try to decide where we will put them and so on. It seems as if I thought of nothing except the time after I get home and particularly after the middle of June."

My own engagement was not the only one over which I was re-joicing that month. "I have just received the most exciting letter, and the best of it is that Helen says I may tell you though it is a *profound* secret. She has been engaged since the 1st of October to a man by the name of Russell Mott, whom she and all her family adore, and whom all her friends seem to like quite well. It is not to be announced until the 20th of March, her eighteenth birthday; but she has told her best friends, Elizabeth, Polly, myself, etc., and said I might tell you, too. It is not a great surprise to me, for he was visiting at her house most of the summer. He is eight years older than Helen and Frank Sweetser says he is a very fine man. She seems to be very happy and in love with all his family, some of whom have been on from Chicago, where they live, to see her. I can't help feeling that Helen and Russell can't be half as deeply and half as devotedly and passionately in love as you and I are, but I suppose everyone feels that way. Helen says she real-izes now, a great deal better than she did at first, what a dreadfully hard time I must be having away from you."

Of course, I could not help mentally comparing the welcome Helen was receiving from her fiancé's family with the continued withdrawal on the part of the Keyeses; but I was careful not to put this comparison into words and, as a matter of fact, my friend's letter had done so much to raise my morale that it gave me greatly needed self-assurance, rather than rousing the green-eyed monster: Helen was a whole year younger than I and obviously no one had suggested that *she* did not know her own mind! As for background, I knew that my family could match the Cutlers' any day when it came to so-called social position; and as far as culture, measured in terms of select schools, college ed-ucations, pleasant homes, abundant reading material, extensive travel, and so on—all of which had been taken for granted through genera-tions—my family had the advantage! I could afford to stop crying and apologizing and, if necessary, stand up for myself. This, however, was such a new idea that I was not immediately successful in putting it into practice. "Last evening we went to see *Othello*—the play, not the opera. I had heard that Shakespeare's plays were very finely given here, so I wanted to see one, but I was rather disappointed in it. The Iago was excellent, but neither Othello nor Desdemona was any good at all. Mother, to whom Shakespeare does not seem to appeal any more than statuary, observed that she thought it was a lot of fuss just about a handkerchief and that, as I lost mine almost every day, she thought the outlook for me was rather gloomy. I laughed at the time, but just the same I can't help wishing that you would not seem quite so *determined* to misunderstand so many things that I do and say. I write you that I haven't thought or said anything disloyal to you for at least two years and that I don't think I ever shall. What more I could say, I don't see, and yet you interpret my words to indicate doubt on my part. What doubt? I am absolutely positive that faith-lessness of any sort is not among my numerous faults. Then, when I further tell you that I am hungry for love, you twist that around and say your efforts to appease my hunger must have been unsuccessful. *Of course*, what I meant was that I am hungry for love when I am away from you and you can't show me how much you care, as you do at home. I think I must have told you more than once that Mother never kisses me and I do not think she has said one single word of encouragement or comfort since I left home. I see very little of anyone except her and never can get off by myself—we sleep in the same room and sit in the same room. She doesn't talk to me very much, but when she does it is usually to find fault: I have driven her wild by my prac-ticing, I have tired her out making her go to picture galleries, I have led her into extravagance by teasing her to go to the opera—and ten to one she had told me only a short time before she was so used to my practicing that she scarcely heard it, had herself suggested going to a gallery or asked me what opera I would prefer to hear next. I don't like to tell you these things because I know they will make you un-happy without doing me any good, but you almost force me to ex-plain. I *know* that when I get home I shall have all the love I want from you and from my family and friends, and that the period of hun-ger is more than half over now, all of which is a great consolation."

Very shortly after writing in this unhappy vein, my drooping morale was raised again, partly by another letter from Helen and partly by decisive action on my part. "Helen and Russell have found that they simply could not wait until March, so they have already formally an-nounced their engagement! Half of Helen's letter was filled with an account of Russell's various perfections and the other half was devoted to sympathizing with me. 'You poor dear, I feel so selfish begrudging the time away from my man when I see him so often, while you are over there in Germany all alone! I just ache for you to come home every time I think of you.' This is really very nice of Helen, because she seemed to think, when I left, that I was making a good deal of unnecessary fuss and now that she understands, she is willing to own up that she was wrong." . . . "Well, Saturday, after I wrote you that awfully blue letter, I really thought I couldn't stand things as they were any longer; so, when I had sent it, I sat down and had a good talk with Mother and I think things will be better from now on."

The outlook did seem to be brighter, not only because of some softening on the part of my mother's attitude but because I saw more of other people whom I found congenial and who made new opportunities and pleasures possible for me.

"A little after four, a young Englishman, who is here studying German to go into the Diplomatic Corps, came up to see me. I haven't mentioned him before because the only times I've seen much of him were once when he came and talked nonsense to Mother for about an hour and occasionally in the salon downstairs. His name is Boothby Bazely and he is very highly recommended—that's all I know about him, except that on his card he has Brasenose College, Oxford University, and the Isthmian Club; but from what you said about Mr. Adams, I gathered that you wanted me to tell you all I could about the men who are nice to me. This Mr. Bazely is a good-looking, healthy, wholesome boy, much nicer than Bär with his everlasting talk about books and disagreeable subjects about which I know little and want to know less, not more. Well, Bär came in, too, and they stayed and talked until half-past six, at which time Bär left and, as I hadn't had any dinner, because I had gone to an early afternoon concert, Mother suggested that she and Bazely and I should all go down to the Rudesheimer Restaurant and have a square meal. So my hunger was appeased and Mother and I were both greatly cheered by the nice boy's nonsense."

News that another romance was happily blossoming in Brookline occupies first place in my next letter, which continues with equally cheerful accounts of my own occupations. "It never rains but it pours! I have just received a lovely long letter from Elizabeth today, dealing chiefly with her great happiness in her engagement. The lucky fellow is Kenneth Moller, a very handsome and perfectly splendid man. All the fellows I know that know him, too, have told me that he had one of the finest characters possible in a man. He is very young and very poor, so the engagement isn't coming out for quite a while yet, but Elizabeth said I might tell you. I have met Kenneth three or four times and like him very much. But if I think Elizabeth is fortunate, perhaps you may imagine what I think Kenneth is! For I believe he has won the love of one of the truest, purest, sweetest, strongest girls God ever made. He's been in love with her ever and ever so long and she's been very fond of him for about a year; but because he was so young and so poor they didn't get engaged until they couldn't stand it any longer, they were so in love, and now they are as happy as they can be. Everyone that knows is delighted and I think it all the better that Kenneth is poor and that Elizabeth loves him just as much and is willing to wait for him. I wish I had everything to bring you that she has to give him—beauty and wealth and talent. But I know that in one way we are alike—neither of us has frittered away our affection along the way and all our youth and love and freshness are stored up for one man.

"This afternoon Mr. Bazely came to the *Reitbahn* and rode with me. This evening I amused myself telling people's palms and have created roars of laughter. Mother seems in much better spirits and I'm so glad! But oh, I do dread Christmas!"

A box of candy, together with Bazely's card inscribed, "To a palmist from one of her victims," was delivered to me the following morning and bore witness to the fact that my enjoyment of the ride and the fortunetelling had been shared. Moreover, though I was quite sincere in saying I dreaded Christmas, I found much to enjoy about that, too, not only in the day itself but in the preparations for it and the attendant festivities. "Late this afternoon, Mother and I went for a little walk," I wrote on December 20th. "Here, for the last two weeks before Christmas, the shops are all open, and now the streets are full of Christmas trees and men selling all sorts of funny toys; and all the people are going about with their arms full of packages and such happy expressions on their faces. Mother and I have bought a little tree and some ornaments to put on it. This evening Frau von Witzleben has asked me to help her make paper flowers for the big Christmas tree in the salon." On Christmas Day, I continued this theme. "As I wrote you last Tuesday night, I went down to help Frau von Witzleben make the lilies for the tree. She and Edel, her eldest daughter, and Lotta, her little daughter, and I worked until nearly eleven o'clock and the lilies were perfectly lovely and so cheap and easy to make. The trees are the prettiest I have ever seen, and you and I must have one like them next year. They had nothing on them but these bunches of white lilies, with gold tinseled streamers, which we also made out of paper, yards of gold tinsel and white candles, but the effect was lovely—so pure and bright. After dinner, we went into Frau von Witzleben's private parlor to see her tree and the presents she and her children had received and, finally, about nine in the evening came the main celebration in the salon of the pension. On a long table were plates of fruit, nuts, clothing and money for the servants, and they all came in and stood around the tree and got their presents and sang 'Silent Night, Holy Night.' After they had gone off beaming, we had punch and delicious cakes to eat and a lot of presents, and one of the guests played and sang, and altogether we had a very pleasant evening."

The letters written on December 31st and January 1st described further activities. "This evening Mother and I went to buy a few cakes and candies for our party tonight—New Year's Eve, which is called *Sylvester Abend* and is a great festival in Germany. All the Christmas trees are lighted again. So the von Witzlebens and several others are coming to celebrate with us and later we are going downstairs to watch the New Year in."

Between Christmas Eve and *Sylvester Abend*, I wedged in another opera—*Aïda*—which my fiancé had written me was one of his favorites and which I made a special point of seeing on that account; and early in the New Year came other pleasant personal experiences. "This morning I went to church with Mother and as I was going out of the door a pretty girl touched me on my arm and asked me if I remembered her. Her face was somehow familiar, but I could not place her and I was obliged to tell her so. So then she asked me if I had not been to Miss Winsor's School and if my first name were not Frances. When I answered yes to both questions, she told me that her name was Sophie Judd and that she had been a senior at Miss Winsor's three years earlier. Of course then I placed her immediately: she is Ruth Farley's cousin, and though she seemed venerable to me the year I lived in Cambridge, I remembered that I admired her with the respect due to one of the big girls. She brought all her family and introduced them to us and begged us to come and see her, which we accordingly did, this afternoon. So we've had a very American day and it's been nice!"[2]

[2] The latest copy of the Winsor Club *Bulletin* carries this notation for the class of 1901: "Sophie Boyd Judd (Mrs. George Paul Cooke), Kauluwai Kottage, Kualapuu, Hawaii, has been teaching herself oil painting, and has sold several pictures, as well as having twenty-two pupils. After having given 300 hours as a teacher of First Aid, and being Chairman of Historic Sites of Molokai, she is now

This chance encounter soon led to a new form of diversion, which proved to be one of the pleasantest in Berlin. "This morning I went skating with Sophie Judd and oh! how I did enjoy it," I wrote two days later. "Just think, I've hardly had on a pair of skates in four years, because of chilblains. I don't know whether they're going to be a real bother again now—they're rather troublesome tonight—but I'm going to try to overcome the handicap they represent, for I never saw such splendid ice."

Neither had I ever seen rinks illumined with garlands of colored bulbs, equipped with booths where hot chocolate, gingerbread, and other pleasant forms of food were available, and even supplied with orchestras to encourage and enliven the execution of fancy figures on the ice. All these attractions, within the next few weeks, were to become familiar to me, and I was duly grateful to Sophie Judd for the first suggestion that I should sample them. The references to them are frequent. "In the afternoon, Boothby Bazely and I went skating—we thought that Lotta and Schulzchen were going, too, but they didn't materialize after all. However—the ice was splendid and I got on much better than I have before. Can you and I skate at Tarleton Pond together? I should think we could go to the lodge and be very comfortable for a day and a night and skate and snowshoe." . . . "In the afternoon Lotta, her brother Wolff, Bazely, Swanfeldt and I went skating," I wrote next. "It was a perfect day and I had a good time, but I still skate so badly that I feel conscience stricken when I go with a number of good skaters. I am afraid I am a burden to them, though they are just as nice as they can be. We got home just in time to dress hurriedly for dinner and the opera, to which Mother, Swanfeldt and I went. It was *Mignon*—so pretty and dainty! Have you heard it? But I still like Wagner best. Just think! I have been to the opera six times and to three splendid concerts since I got here. The Emperor and Empress and all their seven children were at *Mignon* last night and, as our loge was directly opposite the Imperial Box, we could see them splendidly. The Empress is a most attractive woman and one of the boys is decidedly handsome."

Though all the programs of all the operas I heard in Dresden, Munich, and Vienna have been carefully preserved in the famous scrapbook, those of the operas I heard in Berlin have not, through some oversight I find hard to understand. Neither can I understand

---

Chairman of the Free Planting Committee of the Chamber of Commerce." This is certainly a noteworthy list of activities for a lady in her late seventies.

why the letter I have just quoted is the only one which refers to so gala a performance, for many besides that of *Mignon* were attended by the imperial family or at least some portion of it. The Crown Prince's admiration for the beautiful American soprano, Geraldine Farrar, who made her debut in Berlin that winter, was no secret; and whenever and wherever she sang, he was sure to be in evidence. However, even the most incorrigible gossipmongers were unable to smear her name with scandal; her conduct was irreproachable; her face and figure as beautiful as her voice; her triumph a source of pride to every American in Berlin that winter. I once heard a friend say of Lilian Adelaide Neilson that no normal man could see her as Juliet without wishing that he were the lover to whom she lowered her scarf from a balcony. I am sure that everyone who heard and saw Geraldine Farrar in the operatic version of the same role felt the same way. The Crown Prince had plenty of would-be swains sympathizing with him.

Another feature of imperial life that winter, of which I am surprised to find no record, was the daily ride taken by the Crown Prince with his brothers and sister. Promptly at a given hour every morning, the great iron gates of the palace would be thrown open, and out of it would come the six young princes, dressed in splendid uniforms and riding superb horses; less gorgeously dressed and mounted on a smaller horse, but still a figure of beauty and charm, came the one little blonde princess who was the darling not only of her adoring family but of the entire German nation. Though an heir to the throne was a prime requisite to the people, six boys, one after the other, had been more than enough (or so it then seemed!) to assure succession; and when at last a little girl was born, joy knew no bounds. The most popular picture of the period was one which showed the six princes gathered in worshipful attitudes around a beribboned bassinet. The caption of the picture was, "See the treasure that the stork has finally brought us!"

Many years later, I had an opportunity of discussing those gala performances of the opera, those princely morning rides, and that popular picture with the erstwhile Kaiser, then living in exile at Doorn. He and his second wife, Princess Hermine, had become faithful fans of mine; and, after reading *Honor Bright*, they had ordered a complete file of my books sent to the palace; with the order came a letter to my publisher, asking him to transmit to me an invitation to visit them in Doorn the next time I went to Europe. There was then nothing left to suggest a war lord, or even a fallen one; I was greeted at the entrance by a quiet, white-haired old man who made no attempt to hide the withered arm which had been such a cross to him in his days of glory, and who held out for me to receive, from his good hand, a large bunch of lavender sweet peas which he had grown himself. At luncheon, he directed the conversation to the subject of my fictional heroine, Honor Bright, who, he insisted, had married the wrong man; but suddenly he changed the topic and asked me why I had never come to court balls the winter I was in Berlin. "I wasn't going to balls that winter," I answered. "You see, I was engaged to the right man and he was on the other side of the ocean."

That I was not going to balls that winter was very true, but my engagement was only partly responsible for this. Invitations, such as the ex-Kaiser took it for granted that I had received, would have been issued only through the good offices of the American Ambassador, acting as intermediary between the court chamberlain and the privileged guests; and my mother had asked no favors of the Ambassador —who bore the amazing name of Charlemagne Tower!—and none had been extended without the asking. The consul general and his wife and son had endeavored to be courteous, but I had found the son "tedious" when he called and probably had not been at sufficient pains to conceal this; and I went to consular teas under protest, if at all. So, not unnaturally, the Masons did not continue their efforts in my behalf. But it did not occur to me then that I was missing anything because I had glimpsed court life only from afar; and now that two wars, several courts elsewhere, and more than half a century separate me from Berlin, I still have no regrets on that score; at the same time rejoicing that I have such happy memories of my walks in the Tiergarten, my long mornings in the galleries, my longer evenings at the opera, gala or otherwise, the music and lights and hot chocolate at the skating rink, and, above all, the German Christmas as it was then.

Our pleasant contacts with Sophie and her family continued and *haute couture* was now beginning to absorb more and more of my attention. "Most of yesterday was devoted to going around Berlin trying to find a dressmaker who had anything I wanted. I never beheld such frightful clothes in all my life—all covered with bows and bunches, put on without rhyme or reason, tucks and flounces and frills—perfectly hideous. At last, however, I succeeded in finding a very simple model which is to be copied for me in white voile, with a flat waist yoke and a pink belt. I think it will be very pretty. I am also going to have two of my old dresses made over, and one of them is to be really and truly low necked. I am so excited over the prospect of my first low necked clothes!" The enthusiasm did not die down, as there are many subsequent references to it. "This morning I practiced and went to the dressmaker's. My rosebud dress is all made over now and I know you're going to love it—my first really low necked dress! Off the shoulders, with short loose sleeves, yards and yards of pleated pink chiffon and a dear little spray of roses over the breast." The excitement over clothes was further intensified by their connection with photography. "If my photographs sent 'a great deal of cheer to your dark winter night,' as you say, you have no idea how much pleasure two lovely letters from you brought me yesterday. I do feel so happy when you're pleased by anything I do for you that I want to shout for joy and, of course, the photographs were taken especially for you. To answer your questions about them—yes, they were all taken at the same time, and while I agree with you that the big one without a hat is not as pretty as the others, I'm afraid it's the best likeness. It *does* look a little sad, but still. . . . The photographer said, when he took it, that 'the gracious lady' (that's me) 'had the saddest eyes he ever saw,' so I had to cheer up for the other two, which he took immediately afterward. Yes, I think I must have grown thinner, for my clothes are all terribly loose. But it's not unbecoming, and while I can't really hope to 'dazzle' you (nor do I want to, I only want you to love me) I hope you won't find me any *plainer* than when I left home. The dress which you say is 'swell' is only the old blue crepe de chine you didn't like much last winter. It's going to be made over now. I am so glad you like the hat—I love it. The photographer was so taken with it that he gave me an extra sitting."

The letter closes with several questions, quite different in character. "What do you mean by saying you have just missed being put in the position of Acting Governor? You only hint at your disappointment. I am so sorry if anything you really wanted has escaped you." . . . "Whom are you taking out now in the little red sleigh?" . . . "Won't you let me get Gertrude a doll in Paris? You gave me so much money and it would give me so much pleasure to get some little thing for her. I remember my own delight in the toys at the *Nain Bleu* when I was in France before—being a man, you probably do not know that only *German* toys are imported and that the French dolls are the most beautiful in the world. I believe Gertrude is only two years younger than I was when I first saw them."

The questions about the sleigh and the acting governorship remained unanswered, but I received one in the pleased affirmative regarding the doll. I wish I could believe that my offer to get it had been entirely disinterested; but I find my question coupled with an anxious comment: "You spoke in one of your last letters of having had one from Mother. I hope you have answered it, dear. It would be bad policy to offend her now." I cannot help fearing that the suggestion of an olive branch, on my part, was prompted not only by generosity, though this was genuine enough, but by the hope that generosity might come from another direction in return. Be that as it may, the hope was fulfilled. On the eve of my departure from Berlin, I wrote, "Mother got a letter from you today which she says was a very nice one. It pleased her very much. It is only fair to tell you that she has kissed me several times now. I have had my last German and music lessons, both rather sorrowful occasions, for I have enjoyed them very much, though the music more than the German, and we have had a great many callers coming to say good-by. My next letter will come to you from Dresden and two months from today, if all goes well, I'll be on the water, coming back to you as fast as the good ship *Saxonia* can bring me. Will you give me a warm welcome?"

CHAPTER XXVII

Why my mother chose to approach Paris by the roundabout route of Dresden, Prague, Vienna, and Munich, in the dead of winter and at considerable expense, is another of those mysteries which, to this day, has never been solved by me. I should think she would have been thankful enough to exchange the cold and gloom of Berlin for the warmth and sunshine of Italy; but I cannot suspect her of maneuvering to promote another romance at this stage, for we had no acquaintances in any of the places to which we went and, since we were traveling fast—as speed was reckoned in those days—had no time to make any. Therefore, the next few letters give no glimpse of personalities and, for the rest, it was largely the case of "the mixture as before"—picture galleries, operas, palaces, and shopping. Thus I am passing over this part of my travels briefly, pausing only here and there to record the impressions of an eighteen-year-old girl who was something of an eager beaver when it came to extracting all there was to be had out of every fresh experience and who delighted in sharing these impressions with her beloved.

The stop in Dresden, while unremarkable, was very agreeable. The Hotel Bellevue, where we stayed, was directly across from the Theater-platz, the Royal Opera House and the Royal Picture Gallery, so we could walk to both in a matter of minutes; and for a wonder the weather was so pleasant that we could spend a great deal of time out-doors, visiting all parts of the city and many of its charming sur-roundings. We went every night to the opera, beginning with *The Departure*, a one-act opera by D'Albert "which rather interested me because I had heard the composer play in person at a concert, but which was nothing remarkable" and ending up with *Manon* which, I informed my fiancé, "is a fairly modern French opera that I don't think has been given in America yet, though it is creating quite a stir over here. Some of the music is very pretty, but I felt terribly embar-rassed all through it. I suppose that proves I'm something of a prude, but I can't help it! And the final impression was so different from that given by the divine *Lohengrin*, which had stirred my very soul, that I couldn't sleep for thinking of it all night long." It is, perhaps, need-less to say that by the time I saw *Manon* again, I had learned to be less easily shocked and that, in due course, it became one of my favorite operas.

The pleasant but somewhat stereotyped experiences in Dresden were followed by some far less agreeable in Prague, the only place we visited for which I did not find a single good word; but I found plenty to say of Vienna. "The opera Saturday night was *The Ar-mourer*, by Lorking. I had never heard of him or the opera before—had you? But it was just as pretty as it could be and I enjoyed it very much. The opera house, too, is perfectly magnificent, and the people much more attractive and much better dressed than they were in Ger-many. After the opera, we went into the dining room for our usual after-the-theater chocolate, and had a good time watching the gay and handsomely dressed people who had come in for late supper. There was a lovely girl at the table next to us. I think she was engaged, for her only ring was a large solitaire on the fourth finger of her left hand and presently a very good-looking man came in (she was with several older persons) and blushed when he kissed her hand—a perfectly conven-tional thing here. Then he sat down beside her and scarcely ate any-thing, but kept gazing at her as if he would like to pick her up and carry her off to a less public place. She was quite self-contained, but her eyes were very bright and happy, so I don't think the man needed any pity.

"Today we didn't get home until four, after shopping and sightseeing; then we had our dinner—we have been eating at the most unearthly hours—and then I had to dress and read—in German—the text of the opera we were going to see, which began at seven. It was *The White Lady,* by Boïeldieu—another piece and composer that were strange to me. Although very light, it was very pretty and very well given. We had our supper after the opera.

"We lunched at one o'clock today, for as it is a holiday, there was an afternoon performance at the opera—lovely pantomime ballet."

I did not realize it then, but in Vienna, as in Berlin, I was seeing an empire in the final blaze of glory which preceded its annihilation, just as a gorgeous sunset transfigures a sky before the great ball of fire sinks below the horizon and leaves the earth all the darker in contrast to the splendor which came before it. The "magnificence" of the opera in those days was not due entirely to its setting; probably nowhere, before or since, has an audience contributed so greatly to its grandeur. True, the court had never fully recovered from the tragedy of Mayerling; the shadows of the past still flitted across the glowing *mise en scène,* but only as wreaths of mist float across a bright landscape and are dissipated by its radiance; of darker portents there were none. It was a world of waltzes and gaiety and lovemaking; of jeweled tiaras and jeweled orders; of superb dresses and glittering uniforms; of fascinating women and dashing officers; of supreme sophistication and of culture so gilded that it had lost its classicism. I came no closer to it than I had to its less elegant and more ruthless prototype in Berlin; but in both cases it laid a spell on me which has lasted to this day.

And, just as I visualized Berlin afresh, when I visited the ex-Kaiser and the Princess Hermine at Doorn, so did I visualize Vienna afresh when I met the Princess Stephanie at the American Legation, in what was left of that "proud Austrian city," years later. The American Minister, Albert Washburn, and his charming wife were among the most accomplished and delightful diplomatic hosts whose hospitality it has ever been my good fortune to enjoy; and the pale, slim, elderly woman, whose abundant white hair was piled high on her proud little head and whose slender throat was encircled with beautiful pearls, was only one of my many distinguished fellow guests. Her manner was simple and friendly as—in my experience, at least—is that of nearly all those of really great station. I did not catch her name as I was presented to her; and it was only when she had gone on, without haste, to greet someone else that Mrs. Washburn had a chance to whisper to me, "You know, if the fates had decreed otherwise, that lady would have been Empress of Austria-Hungary." I turned to look at the departing figure again and remembered—as one will so often remember items apparently irrelevant—I had heard that she had been pale even when she was young, that her hair had been ash blonde and that this had made her seem colorless to the Crown Prince as he compared it to the brilliant beauty of that vivid brunette Marie Vetsera. Well, Rudolf and Marie were dead now and the old emperor and the empress, too. But this quiet little old lady still survived. And she did not seem colorless any more; her white hair had the glitter of snow.

Imperial Vienna, as I have said, quickly laid its spell on me when I first went there; but it did not enthrall me to the extent of making me want to linger in such splendid surroundings. "We leave tomorrow morning for Munich," I wrote on the 2nd of February, "and I shall be glad to get to Paris and settle down a little, for I am getting most terribly tired. Besides, though I felt we were starting for home when we left Berlin, we will *really* be doing so geographically for the first time tomorrow." Another envelope, bearing the same postmark as the one containing the letter I have just quoted, opens to reveal only a valentine in the form of a pseudo-sonnet. As poetry, it is almost lamentably poor; but as an expression of love and longing it now seems to me rather touching:

"My thoughts are more than ever, dear, with you,
Three thousand miles away across the sea—
And farther still the long way seems to me—
And each day finds them sweeter and more true.
I sometimes think we really scarcely knew
At first how great this deep wide love would be,
That it was life, light, hope, eternity
The world without it—nothing. Few
Places seem dark if only you are there,
If I can feel your hand and see your eyes;
With you, a barren desert would seem fair
Without you, Heaven would not be Paradise.
Knowing that you and your true heart are mine
My life, through you, dear, will be made divine."

Feeling as I did about getting to Paris—though I do not know why I should have ever visualized it as a place for settling down!—Munich was for me hardly more than a way station. However, music, as usual, supplied a welcome diversion. "Last evening we went to *Fidelio*. It would seem as if Beethoven, who wrote only one opera, determined to do himself proud with that one. I enjoyed it beyond words—the music and the story as well. The Second Overture was played before the opera, and the Third—which I hadn't heard before—after it. If only the First had been played between the acts everything would have been perfect."

The elation aroused by the opera was of brief duration and climatic conditions there were certainly not calculated to improve my spirits. "I have managed to contract a most wretched cold somewhere, and really feel rather ill, so I am going to stay in the rest of the day and keep warm and quiet, and let Mother do her sightseeing alone," I wrote shortly after my arrival there. I went to bed as planned and though I slept badly, I felt better the next morning, so "I got up and went with Mother to the new Pinakatek, to see the famous modern pictures of the Munich school. One of them has made a great impression on me—I don't know why it should, but it has. The name of it is 'Sin.' It is a life-size, three-quarter length picture of a girl, with a beautiful dark face, fascinating half-shut eyes—blue-black—and great masses of blue-black hair; and around her—her only covering—is coiled an enormous blue-black snake, its fierce head hanging over her shoulder. Somehow, it just embodies my idea of certain kinds of sin." I have never seen this picture again or any reproduction of it; but the impression it made upon me is just as vivid now as it was then.

"I got thoroughly chilled in the unheated gallery," the letter continues, "and felt so ill I thought I couldn't start for Paris. But Mother decided we had better, so we did, at five in the afternoon, on the so-called Train de Luxe, a very uncomfortable sleeping and dining-car arrangement. Our bunks were right over the wheels and I thought my back would break. We got to Paris at half-past seven in the morning and there was all the bother of having the trunks examined and going to a hotel in a horrible shaky bus. Mother had decided to try a new one and it was a dirty, dingy, impossible sort of place. I was so sick by that time that I had to go to bed, but Mother vowed she wouldn't stay in that hotel overnight, and went to the Bellevue, where we were long ago, to see if there were any rooms. She was successful in her search, so in the afternoon we moved, though I was still so sick that

it was a good deal of an effort to dress and get over here and undress
again. But certainly this is a nice place. We have two pretty sunny bedrooms, facing l'Avenue de l'Opéra, with open fires—such a pleasure
after the big hideous German stoves!—all very clean and bright and
the food is delicious. But none of this made much impression on me
yesterday, for soon after I got back to bed, the medicine that Mother
had been obliged to give me began to work, and I went to sleep and
slept for fifteen hours. When I finally woke at ten this morning and
had some nice chocolate and got properly washed, I felt much better
and was able to appreciate how very comfortable I was. I hope that
tomorrow I am going to feel well enough to start out in search of my
trousseau. I do wish you were going to be with me to help, but I'll
try to remember all your tastes. I know that you don't like ruffles
around my shoulders, or light suits, or bows at the throat, or very
short skirts—is there anything else?"

The hope was fulfilled. "This is going to be a very frivolous letter,
I am afraid, for we have done nothing the last two days but go to
dressmakers and tailors," I wrote next. "Nearly everything is ordered
now, except the wedding dress—Mother and I can't seem to agree on
that—and I actually had my first four fittings this afternoon—they're
used to rushing things through for Americans. I'm sure you will be interested in everything, so I'll give you minute descriptions. I have two
suits. One is a very dark blue, light weight broadcloth. The skirt has
a tight fitting yoke at the top and then wide pleats, so that it flares
out beautifully around my feet—it just clears the ground, for I simply
won't have long walking dresses! The jacket and sleeves are also
pleated and lined with white satin, and then there is a little braided
white broadcloth waistcoat, which doesn't show much. The other suit
is made of rough mixed brown cloth, not unlike that suit of yours I like
so much, with a short unlined skirt and a tight fitting jacket. Then I
have two coats—one to wear in the evening, a dream of white broadcloth, embroidered in white and gold and lined with white satin; the
other, to wear sleigh riding with you in winter, a bright red broadcloth,
lined with red silk and heavily interlined to make it warm, with a great
black fur collar. It's so warm and cosy and will look so pretty in the little red sleigh! Then in the way of dresses, a pink satin, trimmed with
pink chiffon and white lace and pink roses, most attractive—low
necked, of course; a dark blue veiling, very plain, to wear every evening
if necessary, but relieved with a little Persian embroidery and white
lace; and a beautiful high necked dinner dress in three shades of soft

green—about the prettiest thing of all; also a white China silk, with a wide pink girdle. This will be very soft and simple and I can wear it a lot in the summer. Tomorrow we've got to try to get underclothes and blouses, and by the next day the wedding dress will be ordered. Mother would not let me have a black dress made here (she doesn't smile on the project for some unknown reason) but says I may have it made in Boston when I get home."

Gone were the days when my main interests lay in operas and picture galleries. I did go to *Faust*, "but on the whole I was rather disappointed in it." I also went to the Comédie-Française to see *Ruy Blas*, which I dismissed as "a tale of battle, murder and sudden death if there ever was one"; and I wedged in not one but many visits to the Louvre; however, my principal preoccupation was unquestionably my trousseau. "Today we bought most of my underclothes—simple and strong, but plenty of them, and then one or two pretty sets. The wedding set is being made to order and is perfectly lovely. I do hope Mother will consider it proper for me to show it to you when I get home. I've also got twenty pairs of gloves. I am to have two dozen in all, but the other four will be heavy dog skin and must be bought in London." . . . "Yesterday, I succeeded in getting Mother to the Louvre for two hours—the first sightseeing we have done. Of course, it's delicious to be getting such loads of lovely clothes, but if we don't do anything else to change the current of thought, I count up the prices of nightgowns all night long in my sleep, just as I used to conjugate Latin verbs the night before an examination! We walked home—a distance of a mile perhaps—and speedily got into a different atmosphere. Tuesday will be Mardi Gras and the celebrations are already beginning. The streets are crowded with gay happy people, carrying great bags of confetti, which they were throwing about by the handful. Some of them were masked and a few children were in fancy dress. I was quite covered with confetti when I reached the hotel. If you were here, we could go out this evening and have a splendid time mingling with the crowds. I must say there was no rudeness (nothing like what it is in Berlin) or ill nature or vulgarity about anything they were doing." . . . "It being Ash Wednesday, I began the day by going to church, then went and bought hats. The hats are lovely. One is a great big black tulle, with a long graceful feather curling over the top —not a bit of color on it and most becoming. Another is dark blue, trimmed with green (it has birds on it at present and I am begging to have it changed, but do not know whether I shall succeed). Another is brown, with brown ribbons and long quills, very simple and stylish; and still another is red, of no particular kind, but pretty. I may have one more, pink and white, and I may not." . . . "I am dead tired again tonight and don't think you'll be much surprised when I tell you what I've been doing these last two days. Yesterday morning, we went to a place where they have nothing but exquisite blouses, and I was measured for and ordered two—a dark blue silk and a white muslin. Then, finding that we had a little spare time before lunch, we drove right to the other end of the city to Napoleon's tomb and I didn't like it any better than when I was dragged to see it as a small child. After lunch we went to the dressmaker's, where I tried on my blue voile, my white silk and the lining to my pink satin. The blue voile is going to have a little jacket to it, as well as the waist and skirt, so that I can wear separate blouses with it. Everything is getting on well and I think that all the clothes will be exceedingly pretty. Next we went to the tailor's, where I had my last fitting for my two suits and the red coat. They all fit beautifully and each is perfect in its own way—at least Mother and I both think so and I certainly hope you will. Finally we went and had our hair washed and *ondulé* and only got home in time for an eight o'clock dinner."[1] . . . "This afternoon, we went first to the manufactory of Gobelins and watched the making of tapestry, which was awfully interesting, and then to the milliner's— *for my orange blossoms!* Oh, they are the loveliest things! A little crown to wear over the veil, which is *so* becoming and makes me look quite tall and dignified, and a bunch to go at the waist with a long spray to fall down over the skirt. Besides, there are little bunches for the horses' heads, the whip and the coachman. All these beautiful things came home neatly done up in a pretty white box just before dinner and I kissed every one of them. Perhaps you don't think I had delicious little thrills go through me when they were tried on!" . . . "Nearly everything has come home now and everything is very pretty. The pink dress is lovely, both waist and skirt, and fits so nicely—all my new things do. I really believe I haven't grown so terribly much thinner, it's only that my clothes fit better."

My preoccupation with my own purchases was not so intense that

[1] As I have said before, great names meant little to me at that age. I never mentioned the fact that the tailor who made my suits was Amy Linker—a house still as important today as it was then. Neither did I say that the *coiffeur* in question was the great Marcel, for whom the marcel wave was named, and who did more to improve hairdressing than any beauty specialist of modern times until Nestle invented the permanent.

it prevented me from taking an afternoon off to buy the promised doll for my fiancé's little niece, Gertrude. "I went to the *Nain Bleu*, the beautiful toy shop I had enjoyed so much as a child, and had a fascinating time. The shopgirl who waited on me grew as interested as I was and I stayed for over an hour. I bought a beautiful doll, about fifteen inches long, dressed in pink satin, trimmed with pink chiffon and white lace (just like my own best dress) and a big white felt hat with a pink plume. She has pearls around her neck, a little watch and bracelets. Then, that she might be more completely equipped, I got her a little gray coat, lined with white satin, white gloves, an ermine (rabbit) boa and muff, a handkerchief edged with lace and a jump rope; also a nightgown and a little underwaist—an article of clothing which dolls do not usually possess and which I formerly sighed in vain to have for mine. I can't help feeling sure that these things will go to the right spot. We ended up the afternoon by going to Colombin's, a fashionable little restaurant for afternoon tea. I drank just as much tea and ate just as many cakes as I could, in order to stay a long time and watch the people. But since I'm not in a state of perpetual hunger any more, I was finally obliged to stop and come away."

With all our exciting shopping behind us, we were able to spare a day for Fontainebleau, where a decade earlier we had spent so delightful a month. "After lunch, Mother and I went to see Rose, the old servant we had when we were here before. She was *so* glad to see us and we had the nicest little visit with her! When we learned from her that the house where our apartment was, which was the one where Madame de Pompadour's retainers lived, and the one next door, where she lived herself, had all been sold to an American by the name of Jones, it was almost more than I could bear! I always used to think that I should love to go back to Fontainebleau for my honeymoon and have the same little apartment with the beautiful old garden back of it; I loved its little brook and its marble statues and its moss-grown seats and all these I remembered perfectly. I was terribly disappointed to find I could see nothing except the great wall which completely hides those houses and their courtyard and garden; but we walked a little way into the forest, where the drives and rides are so ideal and all the charm of the place came back to me, so I'm still hoping to return again, sometime, with you."

Alas! I have never again penetrated behind that high wall to sit on one of the moss-grown seats among the statues, listening to the trickle of water. But I still long to do so. Perhaps, by some happy miracle, the present owners—whether French or American and whatever their name—will learn of this and permit me to do so. But even if that hope must be forever unfulfilled, the roses of Fontainebleau are among those which bloom imperishably in my December garden.

CHAPTER XXVIII

After a month's thrilling medley of shopping and sightseeing in Paris, it was almost inevitable that our brief stay in London should seem to me somewhat anticlimactic. Not that I failed to appreciate many of its good points. "It does seem so pleasant and comfortable to be safely back in London," I wrote. "And we have had one rather interesting experience. Yesterday, we drove to St. Paul's, expecting to attend the usual half-past ten o'clock service, but when we got there, a little after ten, we found the doors closed and a crowd of people waiting outside. Our genial cabby then informed us that the Centenary Celebration of the British and Foreign Bible Society was to take place and that the King and Queen were to be present. At half-past ten the doors were opened, and Mother and I secured excellent seats, the two next to the middle aisle about halfway down the nave. There we sat, doing nothing, until a little before twelve, when everyone was presented with an order of the service, including a list of the personages who were to figure in the procession. This was very gorgeous, although the King, who is sick, did not come after all, and the clergy were not splendidly dressed, because it is Lent. The procession consisted of several Vergers, the Clergy of St. Paul, the Bishop of London, the Lord Mayor and Sheriffs of London, the Queen, the Prince and Princess of Wales, the Princess Victoria and various ladies in waiting. The music was very beautiful, though we were not quite near enough to hear it to best advantage, and the sermon (of which we heard about ten words) was preached by the Archbishop of Canterbury. This morning, we went out and did a little shopping and this afternoon we have been packing and unpacking and repacking. I am feeling well and in the prime of life, as one of my friends used to say when we were about twelve, and even the nasty London weather and the dullness of the way we have spent most of our time so far are powerless to quell my rapidly rising spirits. It seems impossible that this is the last time I shall write you from Europe, but such is indeed the case. Oh darling, I will be so glad to see you again!"

While my statement that I was now in the prime of life was certainly not true in the most generally accepted use of the term,[1] I was unquestionably in sounder health and higher spirits than I had been in a long while. This was not only because I had benefited by better food and a better climate during the last part of my stay abroad than had been my lot in Berlin, and because I was naturally happy at the prospect of getting home; it was also because I had gained a great deal in the self-assurance which had hitherto been woefully lacking. Susan Sturgis and Dorothea Bigelow were now engaged, as well as Helen Cutler and Elizabeth Sweetser; this made four of my former schoolmates, one of them actually a year younger than I; all had been warmly accepted by the prospective in-laws. From the time I had learned of Helen's precipitate step, I had begun to regard extreme youth as less and less of a disadvantage; now I felt surer than ever that it was not one. I had proved that I knew my own mind and I knew, that even by the strictest standards, there was nothing against my character. I realized that though I should add them both up, I should begin to dwell with increasing cheerfulness on my assets, instead of brooding over the liabilities.

Despite my improvement in health, I knew that I did not have the stable physical vigor that Harry, like most athletes, admired so much and considered such a primary essential. I was subject to bad headaches and worse backaches, I took cold easily and I was periodically prostrated by pain. On the other hand, I had a perfect digestion, perfect eyesight, great recuperative powers, and boundless energy. I was a good swimmer and an excellent horsewoman and I could walk ten miles briskly without fatigue. I had never done much housework, but I was not afraid to try and I was confident that, even in a twenty-five room house, I could cover a good deal of ground. I was aware—little as such matters were then discussed—that Harry wanted very much to have children. I wanted children, too, and I did not doubt for one minute that I would have them.

I was sorry, for Harry's sake, that I was not a beauty and an heiress like my future sister-in-law, Mrs. George Keyes, the former Emily Eaton of Worcester; and I never ceased to be dissatisfied with my hair, but I did have a good figure and a good complexion—the lat-

[1] However, see Webster's Collegiate Dictionary definition!

ter an absolute requisite for any claim to a pleasing appearance in those days—and eyes that attracted attention not only because of their rather unusual color—hazel—but because they were said to be "intelligent," as well as expressive at every passing joy and sorrow.[2] I had beautiful clothes and I knew how to wear them; I was at ease in almost any sort of gathering. I did not think my husband would ever need to be ashamed of either my looks or my bearing; and while I would bring him no fortune, I was going to him far more fully equipped as to trousseau than the average girl, and I believed that, in the course of time, I would have a competence of my own through inheritance. Moreover, though I told this to no one—least of all my fiancé—who regarded my predilection for scribbling with an eye as unfriendly and disparaging as my mother's—I hugged to my heart the hope and belief that someday someone would like my stories and that they might even be a source of modest revenue, which would help pay the butcher, the baker, and the candlestick maker.

I was still bitterly resentful of the fact that I had not been allowed to go to college; but then, not a single woman in the family I was about to enter had received a college education either, and Harry's was the first generation in which the men had been college bred. My background of culture could hardly have been more satisfactory and I had profited by that as well as my own educational opportunities. I had always had free run of my father's, my grandfather's, and my great-grandfather's library; I was as well versed in French and German classic literature as in English and American classic literature and I read Latin for pleasure. I was trilingual; I could even write German script as easily as our own. I was well grounded in both ancient and modern history. The German governess who had been my teacher for three years had been with the Roosevelts before that and had gone afterward to the Vanderbilts; she had been considered adequate in both cases. I had been, for a year, to a good day school in Geneva, where I had done well, and I had been graduated, with honors, from the best private day school in Boston, which was equivalent to saying it was the best anywhere in the United States. I had done several months of postgraduate work in Berlin. Perhaps, under these circumstances, I could afford to dismiss, without too much shame, the fact that I was a poor mathematician and that I had studied no science except physiology. In like

[2] I am inordinately pleased because my twin granddaughters, the youngest of the brood, have hazel eyes.

measure, perhaps I should cease repining over my lack of musical ability.

This required more resolution. I knew that the Keyeses were musical, rather than literary—indeed, Harry's brother George was such a skilled pianist that he might easily have had a professional concert career, if such a vocation had been considered suitable; and his sister Belle was only slightly less accomplished. My own achievements in the musical world were negligible and I was bitterly disappointed because all my faithful practicing in Berlin had borne so little fruit. I had begun by spending at least two hours a day at the piano and had voluntarily increased this amount of time to four; I had never shirked even the most tiresome exercises. "I have learned that scales are the grammar of music," I said in one of my letters. This was a cogent statement, and not merely in its connotation with music, either; it also showed that I realized the supreme importance of grammar in a language—an importance, alas! all too frequently overlooked in the "quickie" methods of teaching a language, which leave the handicapped pupil able to ask, a word at a time, for the necessities of life, but helpless when it comes to carrying on a conversation, because he does not know any verbs. But lacking the little God-given spark which we call talent, and without which no amount of hard work will achieve results, I played very little better after my stay in Berlin than I had at the beginning; and I had to console myself, as best I could, with the fact that I could recognize and appreciate good music, as well as good painting. When it came to the latter, I could tell at sight the school and period to which an artist belonged and usually his individual style and identity; and if I still had only the one parlor trick—the ability to turn off amusing little verses—I already played a reasonably good game of bridge. I danced more than reasonably well and I could hold up my end in almost any conversation.

All this being the case, I felt I should also be able to hold up my head when I faced my future family.

O Mistress mine, where are you roaming?
O, stay and hear! your true love's coming,
   That can sing both high and low:
Trip no further, pretty sweeting,
Journeys end in lovers meeting,
   Every wise man's son doth know.

W. SHAKESPEARE

Part VIII

Journey's End

CHAPTER XXIX

The voyage home must have been uneventful, since I have no recollections of it whatsoever. Of course, no letters were written, for I was to see my fiancé, my family, and my friends as soon as I reached home; but I am sure that if there had been a Mr. Parker or a Mr. Adams or a Mr. Ashley aboard, or the prototype of any one of these, it would not have entirely escaped my memory! However, though there were no evenings spent in moon-gazing and no clandestine visits to the Marconi station, the news that came over the air was printed the same day that the passenger list was distributed, folded into the latter, and that record has still been preserved and still seems to me worthy of note.

WORLD'S LATEST NEWS.

"Transmitted by Messrs. Reuter from London, via Crookhaven Wireless Station, 75 miles west of Fastnet, March 9th.

March 7th.

"Seven Japanese warships yesterday afternoon bombarded Vladivostock for an hour, at five miles range. Russians allege 200 shells fired, majority unexploding, little damage done. Believe Russian squadron left Vladivostock before bombardment, and will there-

fore be unable to return without giving battle, otherwise no important operations since 25th ultimo.

"Russians fortifying both banks of the Yalu River.

"Strong Japanese force occupy Pingyang, Korea.

"Warship 'Cincinnati' has been sent to remove women and children from Pingyang.

"Russian Ambassador at Washington in communication with
Press, complains of the hostility of the American people to Russia.

"French Court of Cessation granted Dreyfus's application for a
revision of trial."

We landed in Boston just before Palm Sunday and went straight
to the Count Rumford house, where, of course, a warm welcome
awaited us, but where the joy of our homecoming was tempered by the
sad and sudden change in my beloved grandmother's physical condition. She had seemed vigorous and merry, despite her advanced age,
when my mother and I left for Europe, and her mind was still as
brilliant as ever; but cancer, the archenemy of all the women on both
sides of my family, had begun its deadly inroads. After some discussion, it was agreed that plans for a large wedding in June should not
be altered—we did not consult my grandmother, for she did not like
to admit that she was not as well as ever, but we knew that would be
her wish; on the other hand, tentative arrangements for the customary
tea, marking the official announcement of an engagement, which in
this case was set for Easter Sunday, were at once abandoned. I grieved
very deeply over the reason for this; my admiration for my grandmother was boundless and my attachment to her very strong; the prospect of life without her darkened my radiant happiness. But I felt no
disappointment whatsoever because the great day—the greatest in my
life so far—was not to be given over largely to preparations for a party
and culminate in several hours of confusion and chatter, repetitious
responses to good wishes, and the tiresome necessity of answering the
same questions over and over again. Instead, I went early in the morning to town and met Harry—frock-coated, silk-hatted, carrying dove-
colored gloves and a gold-headed cane—at the entrance of the Advent
and we went to the glorious Easter service together. He was a respectful, though normally not an enthusiastic churchgoer and he had never
been with me before. I was fairly bursting with pride as I walked up
the aisle with him, and after church he returned to Woburn with me
and spent the rest of the day with me quietly at the Count Rumford

house. It was bright with the flowers that had been sent me in anticipation of the party and we sat in a sunny room and read together the
congratulatory letters which were already beginning to come in. It
seemed to me a much pleasanter way to celebrate than having a tea
would have been.

Most of the letters from my own friends and my mother's expressed
little or no surprise at my engagement; the exception to these were
the notes from Betty Chamberlain and her future mother-in-law.
"Honey, you are a born actress!" Betty wrote. "Naturally, I have wondered and speculated, as everyone who knows you has done, but I
never kept the same opinion for more than a week at a time." Mrs.
Darling expressed herself in somewhat the same way. "I shouldn't have
been surprised at such an announcement last year, but your departure
to Europe gave me other ideas. I am glad to know of Frances' happiness and I congratulate you upon the prospect of having such a fine
man as Mr. Keyes for a member of your family." The two letters that
pleased me most, and that still please me most, now that I have reread them after so many years, came from a former teacher and from
a friend of Harry's.

"My dear Frances"——wrote the former. "At the same time that I
thank you for sending me word of your engagement to Mr. Keyes, I
must express my gratitude to you for not having told me while you
were in school. Rumor told me, of course, but that is quite a different
thing. This whole experience of keeping your secret so long, spending
the winter abroad, etc. must have been a very trying one for you; but
if you have really come out of it in good health, it can't have done you
any harm and I congratulate you heartily that your long waiting is
over.

"Nothing can please me more than the sure fixed happiness of my
girls, and as nothing can be more sure and fixed than marriage, you
can imagine that I am pleased to hear of twelve engagements among
them within a year.

"With the warmest interest in your future, I am

Very affectionately yours,
Mary P. Winsor."

"My dear Miss Wheeler"——wrote the latter. "What I really think
of Harry, I hope sometime to have a chance to tell you in private, for
I should hardly dare put on paper such words of admiration for anybody, although I dare say you would agree they were entirely justified

in this case. But I certainly cannot let this happy turning in his life go by without telling you how keen the pleasure is in hearing of his engagement. The joy in store for him I have a right to estimate; the happiness for you no friend of his can question.

> Sincerely yours,
> John W. Bartol."

On Easter Tuesday, I received my first visit from a member of Harry's family. "Miss Belle was very sweet to me and put me at my ease immediately," I wrote my fiancé. "She seconded your request that I should go and see your mother on Friday and I have promised to. Miss Belle brought me a beautiful gold brooch with three sapphires in it from herself, and two small gold pins, with one sapphire in each, from Charlie. Wasn't it lovely that they hit upon sapphires? I was naturally delighted."

The call on his mother duly took place, and though I was not, on this occasion, wholly at my ease, I had the feeling that she was not, either, and instead of being disconcerted by this was reassured to find that the embarrassment was not all on one side. Moreover, the presentation of the doll did much to relieve the situation. "Gertrude seemed delighted with it," I wrote, "and promptly began to undress it—the highest compliment a little girl can pay, under those circumstances! She and your sister both urged me to stay to lunch and I did wish I could, for I think Gertrude is the *dearest* little thing and enjoy every minute that I am with her. But I had promised to meet Mother and Richard Ware, so I had to say no." I did, however, go to luncheon with my prospective family-in-law on another occasion and also to a large reception which Miss Belle—as I continued to call her—gave in honor of the famous opera singer, Madame Louise Homer. The Keyeses' immense house on Commonwealth Avenue was well adapted to such functions and Miss Belle outdid herself as a hostess—a feat which must have required enormous self-control, as well as great savoir-faire, for at the time her brother Charlie was desperately ill with pneumonia, following a serious operation, and one entire upper story was given over to him and his nurses. My friendly relations with Gertrude, who was nearer my age than anyone else in the family, were soon firmly established. She was having her portrait painted by the famous Hungarian, Gaugengigl, who seldom consented to accept women, much less children, as sitters. The compliment he was paying her was duly impressed on the child and, striving to pay him one in return,

she named her twin goldfish Gaugen and Gigl and proudly told him
she had done so. He did not appreciate the gesture as much as she had
expected; but I thought it was delightful.

The newly established *entente cordiale* was only once threatened
and then not too seriously. The slight strain was over the wedding
date. Mid-June had been the time tentatively agreed upon; this had
been advanced to the eighth, not because of unseemly haste on my
part but for the reason usually considered valid on the part of a bride.
However, in the eyes of my prospective family, this advancement did
not give time for proper preparation and I was a little hurt and a good
deal puzzled by their attitude. My mother and I also had a house in
the country to open—a house where a wedding reception must be
held, a room cleared and set aside for presents, and space somehow
provided for at least eight house guests; moreover, we had to arrange
with the Johnsons, the Chamberlains, and the Darlings to take in the
other out-of-town guests for whom we could not possibly provide ourselves. We, too, had lists to make out, though we had a head start on
those, as we had already been using our address books and deciding
whom we should ask only to the church and the four "at homes" to be
held during August, and whom we should ask to the reception at the
Oxbow as well; if Harry and his family had been equally forehanded—
and I saw no reason why they should not have been—they would not
now be faced with such a monumental task. Furthermore, as I pointed
out, besides working on lists, I had to spend hours at my desk every
day, writing thank-you notes, first for engagement presents and—before I was through with these—for the earliest wedding presents, and
no one else had to do that. And all this was only the beginning as
far as my mother and I were concerned: we had to arrange with a
caterer—Weber—to send the wedding breakfast all the way up from
Boston, with four reluctant waiters to serve it. We still had to buy the
staple linens for everyday use and the corresponding articles of clothing for my trousseau. We had to arrange for the bridesmaids' dresses
and hats, which were to be copied from the pink belted, white China
silk, and the white straw wreathed with pink roses that I had brought
home from Paris. What was more, the wedding dress itself was still to
be made and fitted, for my mother, to my great disappointment, had
reversed her first decision and refused to let me have a white satin
made in Paris, with the same firmness that she had previously vetoed
the black velvet dinner dress of my dreams; instead, the creation of
something more youthful was to be entrusted to a Boston dressmaker

who had gained her confidence—rather tardily, since, for years, she had insisted on having her own clothes made in New York when she did not get them direct from Europe. About what she herself was to wear there had been no question—exquisite black Chantilly lace which her grandmother had worn, over orange satin, at her mother's wedding, and her own mother over moiré antique at her wedding, and which she now proposed to wear over cream-colored grosgrain at my wedding. This was still also to be made. From all this sort of planning, from all this sort of shopping, my bridegroom and his family, like all bridegrooms and their families, were mercifully free. True, the big house at Pine Grove Farm—much larger than the one at the Oxbow—had to be opened; but there was a large and experienced household staff to do this, and there were none of the other side issues with which to contend. I managed to say with a firmness of which I would have been quite incapable a year earlier, and which still surprised me, that if my mother and I could get ready for a wedding the eighth of June, I thought Harry and his family could, too.

Having issued this ultimatum, I did not retreat from it. Serenely I went to the numerous parties given in my honor and carefully observed the manner in which Mrs. Lawrence entertained a group of politicians, recognizing it as a pattern which I might find useful in the future. I went to the annual Vincent Club show, which I did not think quite as good as usual, and to a superb performance of *Carmen* with Calvé in the title role, which I was forced to admit compared more than favorably with anything I had seen in Europe. I spent most of April visiting friends in and around Boston—the Sweetsers in Brookline, the Edmandses in Chestnut Hill, Ruth Farley in Auburndale, Marjorie Lawrence in Medford, Marion Burdett on Bay State Road. This was a pleasant experience in itself and it had the added advantage of affording convenient centers while I had my final fittings, did my final errands, and made my final plans. My discovery that many of my schoolmates, whom I had not been able to include in the bridal cortege, fond as I was of them, nevertheless intended to come to the wedding resulted in an arrangement that I have never seen carried out but once since then and which—at all events, to my somewhat prejudiced eyes—was done much less effectively elsewhere. The choir in the Congregational Church in Newbury is at the left of the platform where the Communion table stands, at the base of the dais provided for the pulpit and three heavily carved and richly upholstered chairs, one for the resident pastor and two for potential visiting clergy or lay lecturers.

This choir would seat at least a dozen persons, and I conceived the idea of having a group of girls, all dressed in white, go in two by two and take their places there, just after the signal had been given for the wedding march, but before the music for it had actually begun. The plan worked out to perfection. All the girls were under twenty, all of them were pretty, all of them carried themselves well, and all seemed happy to take a part, even if secondary, in the ceremony. Mary Tudor, Terry Helburn, Marjorie Lawrence, Bertha Russell, Theoda Bush, Ruth Farley, and Jeannie Darling were all in this group.

In those days, it was quite usual for the bridegroom to choose one of the bridesmaids and the bride one of the ushers. Harry suggested as his choice Mary Kittredge, one of the delightful sisters who had spent several summers with her aunt, Miss Anne Filley, at the latter's home just north of Pine Grove Farm, and of whom he and I had seen a good deal at the time. Mary was now at Smith, in the same class with Marian Edmands, and they, too, had become good friends. The choice was not only a logical one but very pleasing to me. Elizabeth was, of course, to be my maid of honor; the bridesmaids originally chosen, besides Mary Kittredge, were the Edmands sisters, Marion Burdett, Helen Cutler, and my cousin Avis Hill. Avis, however, was at Wellesley, where the powers that were proved less lenient in regard to a leave of absence for a wedding than they were at Smith: she would have to forfeit a whole year if she took two days off to come to Newbury at this time. Regretfully, she withdrew. I was fond of Avis, but my heart had long been set on having Betty Chamberlain for one of my bridesmaids. My mother had insisted that it was impossible to consider more than six for lack of house room; we could not send one or two elsewhere to stay and have the rest with us; that would smack of favoritism. At the same time, I was not willing to give up any of my Boston friends and we seemed to have reached an impasse. Now Providence—in the form of the Wellesley authorities!—had taken charge of the situation. Avis's half-finished dress was sent to Newbury; Mrs. Chamberlain, who was a skilled needlewoman, adjusted it to Betty's slimmer figure and the deed was done.

With ushers, I was not so fortunate. I had begun by asking Foster Kellogg and he had begun by accepting, provisionally; then he found he would have to be at Red Top with the Harvard crew on June 8th. Next I invited Richard Ware, who accepted unconditionally, only to find, as tardily as Avis had discovered that she would have to be at college, that he would have to be in court. At that point I gave up and left Harry to settle the question of ushers without help from me. His elder brother, George, was to be his best man, his younger brother, Charlie, now happily recovered, the head usher. The others were two Canadian cousins, George and Will Butters; an American cousin, Wilder Pierce; Dr. John W. Bartol of Boston, and Arthur P. Butler, the headmaster of the Morristown School.

I went home in May and was touched and pleased with the reception given me by the members of the Keyes family who lived in Newbury. "Mrs. Thomas Keyes has called twice—we were out the first time, so she came again," I wrote proudly. I happened to meet Miss Harriet Keyes in the street before she had time to call and she stopped me, kissed me fondly, and said, "Now you are my little cousin"; the next day she sent me a beautiful old silver ladle, which had belonged to her grandmother. Like everyone else in Newbury, I had always felt an immense respect for Mr. and Mrs. Thomas Keyes and Miss Harriet Keyes; they were all outstanding citizens and pillars of the church; but I had never felt very close to them. As I have said before, they were not included in the cousin parties of the Johnsons, the Bayleys, and the Chamberlains. Now I was very grateful that they wanted to claim kinship with me.

My trousseau and my plans were complete when I reached the Ox-bow, but there was still a great deal to do before the wedding day. We had two good maids, but they were new, both to Newbury and to us, and it was not as if we could have had Ina or Sadie at the helm. My mother good-naturedly mounted to one of the attic chambers and gave up her large front room on the second story for the presents which, by now, were arriving thick and fast. ("I certainly am getting a little desperate over silver baskets. One came yesterday afternoon from Mr. and Mrs. Thomas Keyes and two more this morning, so we now have no less than *ten* silver baskets and dishes. What on earth we shall do with them all, I am sure I don't know. I also hope I will not get any more jewelry, as I have more than I know what to do with. But we have had other nice things: three awfully pretty pieces of pottery and a beautiful card case and a dozen pretty bread and butter plates, which are certainly welcome, considering that we have practically no china; also a lovely upstairs clock." Before we got through, I had twenty silver dishes in all, a good deal more jewelry, and a total count of more than three hundred wedding presents.) The other large front second-story bedroom was assigned to the Edmandses and Marion Burdett. Elizabeth and I had twin beds in my room and

Helen a cot in the erstwhile nursery back of it, now dignified by the name of study. The ground floor bedroom had been set aside for Mrs. Sweetser and my mother's friend Mrs. Catterall of Chicago, who were to arrive only on the eve of the wedding; so until then it was available for any stray guests who might come along, and of these there were plenty. Mary Kittredge could, of course, stay with her aunt, and Betty Chamberlain at home, so we did not have to provide places for them to sleep; but I am sure that had it been necessary we would have managed somehow.

I had agreed to see Mrs. Haviland, the organist of the church, who had formerly been my music teacher, about the selections for the wedding; also Mr. Prentiss, the resident pastor of the Congregational Church in Newbury, and Mr. Flanders, the rector of the nearest Episcopal Church—St. Luke's in Woodsville—about the marriage service. I wanted this performed by an Episcopal clergyman and Mr. Prentiss had been most courteous and co-operative. Mr. Flanders, I am sorry to say, had been less so. Rather grudgingly he had consented to allowing Mr. Prentiss to begin the service, provided he would wear a robe, which, as it happened, Mr. Prentiss was in the habit of doing anyway; but on no account could he be permitted to proceed further than the introductory passage to the ceremony which begins, "Dearly beloved, we are gathered together in the sight of God and this congregation." Harry, who was becoming increasingly nervous as the eighth of June grew nearer and who had no patience with denominational differences, was much annoyed at what seemed to him "splitting hairs"; but in the end I succeeded in calming Mr. Flanders and everything was amicably arranged.

By the sixth of June, families and friends had assembled in full force; Pine Grove Farm and the Oxbow were both bulging—not to mention the other houses which had kindly been put at our disposal—bulky wedding presents were arriving by every train, and telegrams about the wedding breakfast, the bridesmaids' bouquets, and other items which seemed to us of supreme importance were fluttering in every few minutes. As nearly all my bridesmaids were in the house anyway, no special party was planned for them; but Harry had his ushers' dinner at Pine Grove Farm and, like the majority of such occasions, it proved so festive that the celebrants lost track of time. The two clergymen, my mother, my maid of honor, my six bridesmaids, and myself had all foregathered in the church at eight o'clock, the appointed time for the rehearsal on the seventh, and there was still no sign of anyone from across the river. My mother, like Harry, had become more and more nervous and now, half in jest and half in earnest, she began to tell tales of brides who had been deserted on the eve of marriage. These were all more or less legendary, but she soon hit upon something nearer home: the old covered toll bridge, spanning the Connecticut, was known to be in a very rickety condition; no doubt it had finally collapsed, just as Harry and his ushers were driving over it!

Elizabeth, with her usual good sense, was the one who laughed at these tales and surmises and prophesied that the missing gentlemen would not only turn up soon but that they would be in fine fettle—which, of course, proved to be the case. As soon as the rehearsal was over, she hurried me home to bed; and the next day it was she who arrayed me in my bridal finery and draped the veil under my crown of orange blossoms, with half of the tulle in front so that it would fall over my face. In those days, it was more customary than it is now for a bride to have her veil arranged in this way as she went to the altar; then, at the conclusion of the ceremony, the front part was folded back. Personally, I have always felt that this manner of marking the last moments of her maidenhood was beautifully symbolic; and certainly it was extremely becoming—which was not the least of its merits!

I had elected to carry the prayer book, bound in white leather, from which the marriage service was to be read, instead of the traditional bouquet. Since then, several persons have told me there was something nunlike, rather than bridal, in my appearance; I was shrouded so completely in a mist of tulle that my draperies of lace and chiffon were obscured by it, and the slim white book in my hands completed the illusion. Others have variously described the effect as "fairylike" and "ethereal." However I looked, I felt very much like a bride and there was certainly nothing mystical or magical about the looks of my attendants. Elizabeth, who was all in pink—pink chiffon dress, pink chiffon hat—carried pink roses; the bridesmaids, in pink and white, pink sweet peas. Since my brother had steadfastly refused to come to the wedding, my mother had decided to give me away herself, and she and I rode together to the church in a black brougham which she considered the height of elegance, but which was certainly as depressing looking a vehicle as I have ever beheld. In the course of our ride to the church, which took about fifteen minutes, she rather tardily bethought herself of all the good advice that anxious mothers usually give to timorous brides and tried her best to have a "little talk" with me. There was not enough time for it.

In its account of the wedding, one of the Boston papers described the church as "a bower of beauty"; and I do not feel this was an exaggeration, though none of its loveliness was due to the ministrations of a professional florist. Devoted and accomplished friends had arranged a screen in which they mingled boughs of fir, newly tipped with verdure, and fresh green branches from young maple trees; this screen covered the rear of the dais. In the foreground and encircling the choir, roses were solidly massed. Since, of course, there are no *prie-dieus* in a Congregational Church, cushions had been covered with two of the superb white crepe shawls, lavishly embroidered, which the beautiful Delia Maria's second husband had brought her from the Orient. The heavy silk fringes swept the floor on either side; there was actually something regal about this improvised kneeling bench.

I had stipulated beforehand that I should not start up the aisle until I saw my bridegroom with his best man and the two clergymen stationed at the other end of it; and it was agreed that they would leave the pastor's robing room as soon as they saw the signal—to begin the wedding march—which the head usher would give the organist and for which they would be watching from their place of seclusion. Faithful to their promise they emerged from their place of hiding at the given sign. The organist had of course caught it, too; but she was very proud of the piece she was playing and she decided to go on to the end of it, instead of bringing it to a close with a few well-chosen chords. Meanwhile, my unfortunate bridegroom, blushing more and more deeply by the moment, stood and faced the congregation, and the small vestibule was in a state of turmoil. It had been hard enough to crowd fifteen persons into this when they were more or less composed; now that Charlie kept leaping up and down and exclaiming, "My God! Why doesn't that woman start playing the march?" our composure was at an end. Of course, that was what we were all wondering and we all became restless. Moreover, I was stricken with the thought of poor Harry's discomfiture, for which I was responsible.

At last, however, the selection—"The Song of the Evening Star" from *Tannhäuser*—came to an end and the welcome strains of Mendelssohn's march came through the door of the vestibule. These were thrown open to release us and we started up the aisle. I am told that I gave all the responses in the service very distinctly, though I do not remember that part with much clarity. However, I do remember the feeling of the new ring—a very slender band of gold—as it was slipped into place and the lifting of the tulle which had veiled my face. For a description of my expression, as I went down the aisle, I am indebted to Alma, for many years my mother-in-law's incomparable cook, who with all the other faithful retainers of the Keyes family attended the ceremony. "That young girl has got the best man on earth," Alma declared, "and she looks as if she knew it!"

Just how my bridegroom looked, I do not know. Mentally I was dwelling, with eager anticipation, on the first words he would say to me now that at last we were man and wife. But he did not speak at all until we were in the funereal-looking brougham or even immediately thereafter; he was engaged in reefing in yards and yards of tulle so that he could close the door. There seemed to be no end to the veiling in which I was encased; we were both more or less tangled up in it. When at last he succeeded in freeing himself and in shutting the door, he leaned back with a long drawn-out sigh of relief.

"Thank God, that's over!" was all he said.

The white paneled parlor at the Oxbow was as lavishly decorated as the church. We took our places before the long mirror and one of Weber's waiters came forward, bowing.

"Would Mrs. Keyes like a glass of punch?" he inquired respectfully.

"She hasn't come yet," I answered. "We left the church before she did. But she'll be here any minute now. I think she probably would like some."

Harry laughed. He had entirely recovered from his stage fright and his annoyance and at long last was looking radiant.

"The man is talking to you, honey," he said.

The morning had been bright and fair but abnormally hot—extreme heat is rare in Vermont, even in June. Now the sky was suddenly dark and there was a rumble of thunder, followed by flashes of lightning; then came a veritable downpour of rain. The guests who had not left the church promptly were deluged and arrived dripping; again there was temporary confusion, for though we had tried to limit the number of guests to the reception, we had not been very successful. When they could fan out on the piazzas and lawn there was no overcrowding; but as long as they had to stay indoors, there was a good deal of congestion. As many as possible were lured upstairs to look at the presents; but they were hungry by this time and the breakfast was inviting; so were the little square white boxes, initialed in gold, which contained the wedding cake. Every feminine guest wanted to secure one of these, so that she could take it home and put it under her pillow. If she did this, whatever pleasant dream she had that night was supposed to come true. . . .

The thunder began to rumble more distantly, the flashes of lightning came farther and farther apart, the patter of rain ceased and with it the congestion in the parlor, the library, and the dining room. Sounds of merriment began to float in from out of doors, above the music of the orchestra. The time came when Harry and I could leave our places in front of the mirror and steal upstairs to my study, where we ate our wedding breakfast, with Elizabeth standing guard outside. Harry had surprised me by telling me about the merciless horseplay which had taken place when his cousin Kitty Cobb had married Charlie Colby; somehow, it did not seem in harmony with the traditionally decorous behavior of the family I had now entered. At all events, I was determined that nothing of the sort should happen to us. The clothes into which Harry was to change were hidden in a locked closet on the third floor; and when I had given him the key and he had left us, Elizabeth unlocked the closet of my study where mine were hidden. I shed my chiffon, lace, and orange blossoms for the tweed suit I had bought so proudly in Paris and met Harry at the head of the stairs. As I had no bouquet to throw, we were not delayed by clamor over that as we ran down and out of the front door to the waiting runabout. The confetti with which we were showered fell gently over us, the rice pelted a little harder. But it was a swift and happy farewell.

A groom had been standing by the runabout, holding the reins, but Harry took them from him and there was no one with us when we drove away. We were going no farther than the little camp on the quiet lake, where we had already spent so many happy days together. Now there were to be three happy weeks. I had been offered a wedding trip and had declined it in favor of the camp, knowing that such a decision would be pleasing to the man I was going to marry. And it had been made with no hidden regrets on my part, but with contentment and thanksgiving.

I was glad to feel that at last I had reached my journey's end.

Epilogue

It is very quiet in the paneled parlor. The tree and the candles are lighted, the crèche is in the fireplace, there are wreaths at all the windows, and cards and presents are scattered about in every available space, for Christmas has come again. But though there is no one here but myself, as I sit writing these last lines, I do not feel lonely, for the room does not seem empty. It is thronged with all the other people who have spent Christmas here, in the century and a half since the house was built; with the many happy couples who have celebrated their weddings here, as I did; with the merrymakers who have danced the Virginia reel at the cousin parties; with the beloved dead who lay here at peace before they went to their last rest in the cemetery, where, as children, my playmates and I used to go on Sunday afternoons, nor feel this was a sad thing to do. There is nothing sad about the paneled parlor, either. It is a lovely room. In it, I am filled with a sense of contentment and fulfillment greater, if possible, than when I laughed and danced here as a girl, almost as great as when I stood here as a bride.

Probably I should feel differently if there had been no choice, if I had been obliged to spend Christmas Day alone. But all my sons and their wives urged me to come to them for the holidays; and though I customarily enjoy such visits, this year I had a great yearning to stay in my own house. Besides, as I told my family, I knew my old friends would not forget that I was there and I was right. I have been to dinner with the Darlings and by-and-by I am going to supper with the Cobbs. This restful solitude only marks an interval between two festive gatherings.

At the Darlings' everyone wanted to talk about the new book. "Did you put in about the cave and the time the rock fell on your back?" Richard asked, as he carved the golden brown turkey.

"Yes."

"And about the time you went through the fence on the Flexible Flyer?" he continued, as he scooped out savory dressing with a big spoon.

"Yes."

"And about the time Richard came up behind you on our porch

and cut off one of your curls?" Lucia inquired, slicing cranberry jelly.

"No. I thought that might sound as if he were rough and, of course, he wasn't really."

"Your mother was very indignant; she called on my mother and complained," Lucia continued.

"I haven't forgotten. But I thought it didn't sound very well in a book and there were so many nice things I could say."

Richard laughed. "There's no reason why you shouldn't tell that story—now. You never knew the whole of it. I cut that curl for Alvah. He wanted a lock of your hair and he never could manage to get one. So I told him I'd get it for him. I didn't mind being blamed for acting rough. I thought it was in a good cause. But then I minded a lot because Alvah's father found the curl and threw it in the fire. That hurt. You had pretty curls in those days, Frances. Why don't you write that story the way it really was?"

"All right, I will, now you've told me the whole of it. I'll be happy to write it."

So now it is written and with gladness. But I am glad, too, that this is not a day when I need to write much. No one else has reminded me of something I had left out and I have not thought of anything myself. So I can take the afternoon off and sit quietly in my paneled parlor until it is time to go to the Homestead, where the parlor is so much more famous than mine, and rightly so, because of the courting corner and the marriage arch that Isaac Bayley built: not because he realized he was creating a beautiful architectural design, but because he was safeguarding his daughters.

Every now and then, I pick up one of the gifts on the table in front of me and look at it again. My family and friends are always very generous; I have received a good many Christmas presents. Among them are cups and saucers and plates to supplement the set of Imperial Rose Canton china, the nucleus of which I inherited, and to which I have been gradually adding. Now at last I have enough for the kind of old-fashioned tea party which is the only kind I really enjoy—a tea party patterned on those in England about which I have been writing. Tomorrow I will call up some of my old friends and we will have such a tea party; and at least half of the guests will be the same that came to this paneled parlor as I first remember it.

I have been given a new picture of the granddaughter who is also my namesake and who is now seventeen years old. She has "dates" instead of callers and encounters opposition (from her elders) when it comes to "going steady," for which there was no exact equivalent in my time, though I believe "an understanding" was the nearest approach to it. (Our elders generally opposed that, too.) She will have to work things out for herself, just as we did, and I hope and believe she will be equally successful.

I think she is very pretty. I will put her picture on the piano, between the one of me, taken in the full regalia of feathers, brocade, and train, which I wore when I was presented at the Court of St. James; and the one of Merry Hebert, the dear young friend who lives in Louisiana and who honored me by wearing my wedding dress when she was married. She is wearing that dress in the picture—a soft white dress which was a foam of lace and chiffon; my mother said I was too young for the formal white satin dress I wanted. Never mind. Now that I see it as it looks with Merry wearing it, I realize that it is lovely, that it was lovely when I wore it. The picture of my namesake will look charming when I have it in its proper place. But I will not bother to move it tonight. It is so pleasant to have the parlor quiet that I have no inclination to stir around. Tomorrow will do just as well. For the moment, I will leave it beside the bottle of my favorite perfume and the new embroidered guest towels and the big glass punch bowl I needed so much. Perhaps I had better have an eggnog party later in the week, after I have recovered from the tea party.

I am glad that so many of the presents I have received have taken the form of flowers. Here, in a Vermont village, we do not often give each other flowers at Christmastime; we do that in the spring and summer and autumn. We send each other mayflowers and lilies of the valley and iris; pansies and sweet peas and phlox; larkspur and zinnias and dahlias. But my friends who live in large cities and in the Deep South give me roses at Christmastime—red roses mostly, as being especially suitable for the season; but always some yellow ones, too, because, after all, those are my favorites and my friends know this. They were my mother's favorites, too. She often told me how she loved to see them, coming into bloom on either side of the garden path, as she walked slowly up and down, on my father's arm, during the weeks before I was born. The yellow roses were an essential part of the Virginia spring.

I am very conscious of my mother in this room. That is not strange, since my earliest memory centers around her marriage to my stepfather, which took place here, and from that time on, she continued to animate it until the day of her death. Indeed, after that. One of the cousins who came in to see her here at the very last said, wonderingly, "She has charm, even in her coffin." It was true. And it is her charm, her vitality, her inextinguishable zest for life that I feel more strongly in this room than any of her other qualities. She adored my sons and made a practice of giving them annual birthday parties. One year, when she was approaching ninety, and had been very ill with pneumonia during January, we felt we should say nothing about the next such party, which would normally have been held in March. She was aggrieved; we had hard work in convincing her that our scheme had not been due to dissatisfaction with previous festivities under her auspices. When at last she was reassured, she said, "Very well. We will make the usual arrangements for the twenty-second, except that this time I should like to have you plan for fourteen, instead of twelve. I should prefer not to play bridge, because of all the new conventions that were adopted during my illness; so I want you to make up three tables without me and provide me with an attractive young man with whom I can converse while the rest of you are playing." This was done and "the attractive young man" afterward reported that he had had the time of his life! He had found my mother witty, gay, and lovely to look at; he further remarked that she was "exquisitely dressed." This did not surprise me. A year and a half later, when she died, there were forty-eight dresses, all of the latest style and finest fabrics, hanging in her closet.

So the yellow roses that add such splendor to the Christmas scene are those that remind me most joyfully of my mother. But my friends have sent me pink roses, too, and I am glad of that, because there is something so eternally fresh and youthful about those. It was pink roses, almost as a matter of course, that Elizabeth carried when she was my maid of honor. How beautiful she was that day—and always! There is not a single marring note in my memory of her.

Now I think of it, it was in this room that the long box from Galvin's, containing American Beauty roses with still longer stems, was handed me on my fifteenth birthday. They were the first intimation that I was being courted, that I must learn how to accept a grown-up present and act like a grown-up girl. Was that really nearly sixty years ago, that prelude to a marriage which was "sure and fixed," as my old teacher took it for granted marriage should be? I took it for granted, too.

Perhaps I ought to put fresh water in the vases containing all these varicolored roses. But if I disturb them, the petals of some that are in full bloom may begin to fall, and I should like to keep them all, the way they are, as long as possible. Besides, of course, they have thorns which would prick my fingers; I would rather keep my hands folded calmly in my lap when I am not using them to write. As long as I merely look at the roses, I am not conscious of the thorns, only of the fragrance and the beauty. Someone else can rearrange them tomorrow. Tonight I will simply sit here in the stillness and enjoy them.

It is so wonderful to have roses in December.

The Oxbow
Newbury, Vermont
Christmas, 1959

Author's Note

For once, I have written a book without a foreword, which I hope will please reviewers, who do not care much for my forewords. On the other hand, I hope its absence will not disappoint the many readers who have been kind enough to say they do like them; because the whole book is simply a foreword to another, carrying on from where I have left off now, provided that this much has given pleasure.

However, in the absence of a foreword, I must at least briefly express my gratitude to the friends who have authenticated my recollections and complemented these by recollections and stories of their own, which they have permitted me to use.

I believe it will surprise no reader to learn that I feel the friends in Newbury who have helped in these ways should be mentioned first. I am greatly indebted to Mary and Harold Hale, Mrs. Harry Wells (nee Lucia Darling), Jeannie and Richard Darling, Mrs. Ervin Johnson (nee Laura Chamberlain), Haines Johnson, and Richard and Frederic Cobb for such assistance. There are, of course, many others who could and would have helped, among them Norman Cobb, Frederic Cobb's father, if this book had been written a few years earlier. Now alas! I cannot reach them.

For the early history of the Sewing Circle, I am indebted to Miss Marian Homans and Mrs. Charles Lewis Slattery. For the early history of the Fragment Society and for early recollections of Miss Winsor's School—now the Winsor School—as it was before my time, I am indebted to my friend, Mrs. Henry Endicott (nee Katharine Sears) of Boston; Miss Mary Cunningham, Miss Hilda Williams, Mrs. John Swift (nee Nanny Winsor), Mrs. Geoffrey Lewis (nee Louise Lincoln), Mrs. Arthur Crosby (nee Barbara Niles), and Mrs. Russell Mott (nee Helen Cutler), who all attended Winsor at the same time that I did, have contributed their share of reminiscences; and, besides those of our school days, Mrs. Russell Mott has been able to recall some amusing details of my wedding, at which she also was one of my bridesmaids. Mrs. Guy Rogers (nee Mary Kittredge), who was also a bridesmaid, added to these details.

My lifelong friends, the Misses Marian and Grace Edmands of Chestnut Hill, have supplied me with photographs, as well as memoirs; the same is true of Mrs. C. Moorfield Storey (nee Susan Sweetser) of Boston; Miss Margaret Lothrop of The Wayside, Concord, Massachusetts; Miss Eleanor Deming of New City, New York, formerly of "Nipnet"; and Mr. John Wyllie of the University of Virginia. Mrs. Harold Hale who, being younger than her husband and her sister-in-law, came upon the Newbury scene after our childhood and, therefore, could not enter fully into the discussions of early days; nevertheless, she was extremely helpful in the matter of old photographs, which she was able to supply from an excellent collection.

My cousins Mary Wheeler and Edith Robertson have been helpful with general information, and it was through the good offices of my cousin Helen Cooper that I secured the photograph of our grandfather, Gilbert Melancthon Wheeler, with which I was heretofore unacquainted.

Miss Gertrude Baker, the Reverend Gordon Poteat, and Mr. C. Moorfield Storey have all helped me to interpret the Boston scene as it was in my childhood and youth. Miss Ruth French has been equally helpful in regard to the Milford scene, and Mrs. Cabell Smith in regard to the Virginia scene.

My secretaries, Geraldine Bullock and Veronica Hornblower, have also contributed, not only in the ways that might logically be expected but by the often caustic and occasionally complimentary comments which they have made as we went along. The caustic comments have been responsible for some revision and some deletion; the complimentary ones have encouraged me to persevere with what has often seemed endless work.

I am grateful to all these persons and also to my mother and aunt for keeping so many old letters and to my husband for doing the same and teaching me to keep a scrapbook.

F. P. K.

Index

Adams, J. Donald, 209
Adams, Mr., 265, 267–68, 274–76, 286, 309
Alcott family, 83–84
Aldrich, Thomas Bailey, 35
Alexandria, Va., 21
Alger, Russell, 136
Alvah, 130–31, 167–68, 173, 181, 187, 190, 323
American Revolution, 23, 40, 56, 65, 83
American Revolution, Children of, 85
American Revolution, Daughters of, 60, 74, 77, 133, 135
Ashlawn, 11
Ashley, Mr., 266, 309
Atkinson, Fanny, 147
Author's mother, 12–13, 15, 19–21, 24–30, 35–36, 38, 40–41, 43, 46, 49–50, 53, 57, 59–62, 70–71, 73–81, 83, 85, 87–92, 95–96, 98–101, 103–13, 117–23, 125–26, 131, 133–36, 138, 140, 147–53, 160–71, 181–87, 189–92, 197, 201, 207–8, 211–15, 220, 223–26, 232–43, 245, 248–49, 252, 256–58, 260–66, 268–71, 274–80, 282–83, 285–89, 291, 293, 297–302, 304, 310, 312–19, 323–25, 328

Back Bay, 35, 72, 177, 233
Baker, Ezra Henry, 76–78, 121, 244
Baker, Mrs. Ezra Henry. See Gertrude Keyes
Baker, Gertrude, 119, 121, 207–8, 222, 244, 263, 292, 301, 312, 328
Baltimore, Md., 12, 18–19, 22, 154
Barbara, 15, 36, 71
Barbour, Charlotte Berger, 121–22
Bartol, Dr. John W., 312, 316
Bates, Rev. S. L., 28–29
Bayley, Ellen, 55, 57, 142, 161
Bayley, Frank, 160
Bayley, Henry, 57, 67, 125, 161
Bayley, Isaac, 56, 60, 323
Bayley, Jacob, 56, 60, 65–67
Bazely, Boothby, 286–87, 289

Beacon Hill, 72, 178, 185, 233
Beacon Street, 30, 35, 47–48, 51, 70–73, 76, 84, 87, 90–91, 148, 152, 158, 177, 196, 225, 227–29
Belgium, 98, 100
Benton, Josiah H., 73–74
Benton, Mrs. Josiah H., 73–76
Berlin, 18, 27, 186, 232, 273, 275–78, 280–82, 289–91, 293, 295–96, 299, 303–5
Bigelow, Dorothea, 155, 303
Bonn, 18, 26, 107
Bonn, University of, 19, 102
Boston, Mass., 12, 15, 24, 28, 30–31, 36, 43, 46–47, 54, 59, 63, 70, 72–75, 77, 79, 83, 96–97, 99, 105, 117–19, 130, 147–50, 152, 155–56, 160–61, 163, 165, 167–70, 172, 177, 181, 185–86, 193, 202, 208–9, 212, 216, 225, 229, 234–35, 240, 245, 258, 260, 265, 273, 275, 299, 304, 310, 313–15, 319, 328
Boston University, 17
Bowditch, 24–25
Bowdoin College, 11, 15, 19
Brace, Gerald Warner, 16
Brock, Frank, 203
Bronx, 21
Brookline, 71, 148, 159, 165, 185, 190, 247, 286, 314
Brooks, Phillips, 53
Browne and Nichols, 161, 175, 190
Brunswick, Me., 11
Brussels, 276, 278
Bullard, Maude Sanderson, 61, 202, 264
Burdett, Everett W., 70–71, 73, 220
Burdett, Mrs. Everett W., 70, 74, 160, 220
Burdett, Marion, 70–72, 118, 150, 160, 179, 184–85, 201, 217–22, 226, 236, 248, 250–51, 255–57, 314–17
Burdett, Paul, 160, 218–19, 251
Burke, Billie, 175
Bush, Dr. Foster, 237, 245
Bush, Theoda, 156, 237, 248, 315

California, 214–15
Cambridge, Mass., 19, 54, 135, 161–63, 170–71, 174–75, 185, 190–91, 207, 288
Canada, 23, 65–66
Carleton, Dudley (I), 66
Carleton, Dudley, 173, 190, 192
Carleton, Guy, 173, 187, 190, 192–93
Carleton, Sir Guy, 23, 66
Carroll, 91–92, 96, 101, 112
Carroll, Miss Bertha, 50–51, 70–72, 76, 97, 110
Carter, Charles, 37
Carter, Morris, 37, 265
Carter, Royal, 37–38
Castle, Mrs. William R. *See* Margaret Farlow
Chamberlain, Betty, 202–4, 242, 249, 311, 315, 317
Chamberlain, Mrs. Edgar, 202–3, 315
Chamberlain, Ezra, 57
Chamberlain, Helen, 57
Chamberlain, Laura, 161, 203, 210–11, 213, 327
Chamberlain, Lizzie, 57
Chamberlain, Remembrance, 57, 203
Chamonix, 102, 105
Champagne, 90–91
Chavonnes, Lake, 105
Chesières, 97, 100, 102, 106, 110
Chester, 267–68, 278
Clark, Isabella, 155, 157–58, 163, 178
Cobb, Agnes, 57, 59, 128, 161
Cobb, Frederic, 60, 327
Cobb, Katherine, 55, 139, 142, 161
Cobb, Norman, 55, 58, 142, 161
Cobb, Richard, 55, 57, 127–28, 142, 161, 327
Colby, Francis, 209, 211
Colorado, 119, 214
Commonwealth Avenue, 31, 70–71, 148–49, 177, 312
Concord, Mass., 83, 328
Congregational Church, 22, 59, 314, 317, 319
Connecticut River, 31, 60, 65, 67, 73, 206, 318
Connecticut Valley, 56, 65, 99, 208
Cook, Eleanor, 171–72
Cook, Katherine, 171, 173, 187, 228
Cook, Mrs., 171, 173, 179–80, 190, 193, 196, 226
Cook, Will, 171, 173, 181, 183, 187, 191–92

Cooper, Lady Diana, 86
Cooper, Sir Duff, 253
Cooper, Helen, 15, 328
Count Rumford House, 18, 37, 43–44, 48, 89–90, 119, 163, 185, 310
Craig, Mrs., 57, 135
Craig, Robert, 57
Crosby, Mrs. Arthur. *See* Barbara Niles
Crown Prince of Germany, 282, 290
Cunningham, Mary (Polly), 155, 174, 179, 192, 227–28, 247, 284, 327
Cutler, Helen, 156, 179, 184, 192, 208, 216, 220, 235, 255, 284–86, 303, 315–16, 327

Dan, 15, 25, 62, 118, 126–27, 133, 150
Danforth, Frank, 149
Danforth, Ina, 149, 192, 248, 316
Dardelle, Mlle., 103, 110
Darling, Mrs. C. Francis, 54, 311
Darling, Jeannie, 54, 56, 67, 139–41, 212, 249, 315, 327
Darling, Lucia, 57, 67, 323, 327
Darling, Maida, 56, 67, 139
Darling, Richard, 57, 67, 128–31, 139–40, 202–3, 322–23, 327
Dartmouth, 21, 40
Deming, Eleanor, 328
Deming, Harold, 87, 117, 217, 236
Deming, Horace, 29, 85–87, 90, 280
Deming, Mrs. Horace, 85, 87, 269
Denver, Colo., 73, 108, 119, 121, 215
Detur Prize, 17
Dillingham, Hon. W. P., 124, 242
Dimick, Mrs. C. W., 135, 161, 184
Dimick, Muriel, 135, 184
Dodd, Helen, 202
Dodd, Walter, 202
Doe, Richard, 54, 128–29
Doe, Mrs. Richard, 55, 129–30
Dow, Moses, 31
Dresden, 289, 293–94

Edmands, Grace, 70–72, 78, 118, 150, 160, 165, 187, 215, 246, 315–17, 327
Edmands, I. P. T., 71
Edmands, Mrs. I. P. T., 72, 246
Edmands, Marian, 70–72, 78, 118, 133, 150, 160, 165, 173, 187, 192, 215, 217, 232, 235, 245–46, 315–17, 327
Ellsworth, Col. E. E., 21–22

Endicott, Mrs. Henry. *See* Katharine Sears

England, 18, 85, 100, 109, 273, 276, 323

Europe, 31, 39, 63, 69, 90, 95, 97–99, 103–5, 118–19, 141, 162, 229, 233–34, 240, 242, 252, 256–57, 260, 263, 265, 268, 276, 290, 303, 310–11, 314

Farley, Ruth, 227, 248, 288, 314–15
Farlow, Margaret, 148, 156
Filley, Anne, 203, 315, 317
Filley Farm, 203–4
Fisher, Mary, 73
Flanders, Rev., 317
Fontainebleau, 100–2, 105, 108, 111–12, 301–2
Fragment Society, 74, 235, 237
France, 64, 95, 100, 265, 276, 292
Francestown, N. H., 40
French, Ruth, 44, 90, 328

Garland, Dr., 182, 237
Gay, Dr., 78–79
Gay, Elizabeth Kent, 117, 141
Geneva, 39, 83, 90, 96–97, 100–3, 107, 109–13, 117, 125, 127, 304
Germany, 19, 98, 100, 265–66, 273, 276, 285, 288, 294
Gildersleeve, B. L., 18, 20
Glessner, Alice, 54
Glessner, Frances, 54
Glessner, George 53–54
Gloucester Street, 35, 50–51, 71, 90, 165
Goodwin, Frances, 174–76, 193
Gordon, Dr. A. J., 72
Gordon, Dr. George, 50–51, 72, 74
Gordon, Harriet Hale, 72
Gordon, Theodora, 72
Greely, Washington A., 57
Greely, Mrs. Washington A., 135
Griswold, Miss, 182, 187
Gunther, John, 127

Hale, Harold, 57, 327–28
Hale, Mrs. Harold, 328
Hale, Mary, 57, 83, 139, 327–28
Hale, Virginia, 101, 103, 107
Hamilton, N. Y., 21
Harris, Mrs. William J., 137
Harrison, Benjamin, 78, 135
Harrison, Mrs. Benjamin, 78

Harrison, Dr. James F., 13
Hart, Mr., 224, 240, 252, 265
Harvard Annex, 15, 19
Harvard University, 14, 16–19, 25, 30–31, 43, 51, 54, 81, 87, 108, 117, 168, 171–72, 179, 192, 225, 229, 256, 271, 315
Haskell, Miss, 50
Haverhill, N. H., 31, 65, 119, 203–5, 208, 211, 213, 216, 243
Haviland, Mrs., 317
Havre, Le, 95, 100, 112
Hawthorne family, 84
Heath, Mrs. Bigelow. *See* Dorothea Bigelow
Helburn, Theresa, 176–77, 227–28, 245, 315
Hermine, Princess, 206, 290, 295
Hill, Avis Wheeler, 37, 43, 105, 118, 122, 217, 235, 315
Hill, Frances Wheeler, 17, 37, 43, 48, 95–96, 105, 111, 118, 122, 126, 191, 260, 264, 328
Hill, Gertrude, 121–22
Hill, Isabel, 108, 121, 215
Hill, Nathaniel, 72–73, 108, 120–21
Hill, Mrs. Nathaniel, 72, 120–21
Hill, William, 37, 42, 264
Holland, 31, 98, 100, 263
Homans, Marian, 327
Home for Little Wanderers, 74
Homestead, The, 55, 60, 65, 128, 150, 160–61, 323
Howe, Fannie, 155

Idaho Springs, Colo., 119–22, 214
Italy, 100–1, 103, 206, 265, 276, 293

Jacques, Hattie, 156
Jarvis, Dr. DeForest Clinton, 132
John, 173, 184, 187, 189
Johns Hopkins, 18
Johnson, Abigail Carleton, 23, 66
Johnson, Ann, 55–56
Johnson, Anna Cummings, 23, 62–64, 67
Johnson, Betsy, 56, 60
Johnson, David, 22–24, 55, 63, 118, 304
Johnson, Mrs. David, 22–23, 232
Johnson, Delia Maria, 22–24, 29, 38–42, 63, 75, 87, 111, 277, 314, 319

Johnson, Edward Carleton, 21–22, 24, 39, 63, 304

Johnson, Ervin, 160, 167–68, 180, 191, 203, 210–11, 213

Johnson, Mrs. Ervin. *See* Laura Chamberlain

Johnson, Geoffrey, 33

Johnson, Haines, 54, 56, 67–68, 76, 126, 128–29, 142, 150, 160, 203, 327

Johnson, Louise, 56, 67, 76–78, 89, 135, 160, 203, 249

Johnson, Maria, 55

Johnson, Mary, 55, 67, 142

Johnson, Sidney, 55, 67

Johnson, Thomas, 55

Johnson, Col. Thomas, 23, 55–56, 60–61, 65–67, 162

Jones, Charlotte, 36, 43, 46, 50, 70

Jordan, Dorothy, 72, 177–78, 200

Jordan, Robert, 72, 220

Judd, Sophie, 156, 227, 288–89, 291

Kaiser, the ex-, 206, 289–91, 295

Kaweah, 25, 126–27, 150, 170, 204, 207, 222

Kellogg, Foster, 219–22, 226–27, 237–38, 251, 256, 280, 315

Keyes, Belle, 57, 59, 76–77, 119, 122, 207–8, 222, 224, 244, 263, 305, 312

Keyes, Charles Walter, 31, 76, 239, 243, 263, 312, 316, 319

Keyes, Frances Parkinson, II, 323–24

Keyes, Francis, 98, 214, 322, 325

Keyes, Freeman, 31

Keyes, George, 76, 239, 243, 263, 305, 316

Keyes, Mrs. George, 303

Keyes, Gertrude, 59, 76–78, 119, 167, 263

Keyes, Harriet, 59, 61, 316

Keyes, Henry, 24, 31, 59–60, 76–77, 262

Keyes, Mrs. Henry, 31, 59–61, 76, 119, 122, 207–8, 222, 224, 244, 262–64, 312, 320

Keyes, Henry W. (Harry), 30–32, 59, 61–62, 76, 82, 124, 127, 166–70, 181, 185–87, 191, 193, 204–8, 210–11, 213, 216–20, 222–27, 231–32, 234–36, 238–45, 249–50, 252, 256–64, 267–69, 271–72, 274, 276, 278–79, 282–89, 292–94, 298–305, 309–21, 328

Keyes, Henry W., jr., 43, 82, 98, 214, 322, 225

Keyes, Horace, 31

Keyes, John Parkinson, 98–99, 154–55, 322, 325

Keyes, Sarah, 77

Keyes, Thomas, 59, 61, 316

Keyes, Mrs. Thomas, 316

Kinsman, Rebecca, 174, 177, 182, 186–87, 196, 230, 234

Kittredge, Mary, 203, 315, 317, 327

Labarthe, Mlles., 97

Labarthe, Pension, 101, 103, 113

Lawrence, Marjorie, 155, 314–15

Leo XIII, Pope, 103–4

Lewis, Ada Cook, 86

Lewis, Mrs. Geoffrey. *See* Louise Lincoln

Lincoln, Louise, 155–56, 228, 327

Lodge, Henry Cabot, 25, 29

London, 27, 99, 207, 271–78, 299, 302

Lothrop, Margaret, 83–85, 328

Lothrop, Margaret Sidney, 83–85

Louisiana, 48, 69, 324

Lyon, Mary, 41

McCabe, Capt. William Gordon, 15

MacFarlane, Mr., 264–65

McKinley, William, 136, 174

McKinley, Mrs. William, 136

McKissock, Helen, 156

Madison Avenue, 21, 39

Madrid, 83, 99

Maine, 11, 167, 169

Malvern, 268–69

Manila, 99, 127, 206

Marion, Mass., 208–9, 217, 219, 221, 248, 250, 258

Marlborough Street, 30, 35, 37, 43, 49, 52, 148, 225, 235

Miles, General, 136–37

Milford, N. H., 43, 45–46, 48, 73, 90, 328

Moller, Kenneth, 220, 286–87

Monroe Hill, 11, 20

Montebello House, 23–24, 29

Montgomery, Roselle Mercier, 115

Monticello, 11

Moody, Minnie Hite, 145

Moore, Rev. Humphrey, 45

Moore, Mrs. Humphrey, 45
Moosilauke, 81–82
Mott, Russell, 284–85
Mott, Mrs. Russell. See Helen Cutler
Munich, 289, 293, 296–97
Munthe, Axel, 164
Myrtle, Minnie, 63

Nain Bleu, 96, 99, 292, 301
Nashua, N. H., 40–41, 243
Nason, Olive, 155, 157, 160–61, 165
Newbury House, 23–24, 29
Newbury, Vt., 11, 21–24, 26, 29–31,
46–47, 53–54, 56–57, 59–63, 65,
68–69, 73–74, 76, 81, 83, 87, 90,
103, 108, 110, 113, 118–19, 122–24,
127, 129–30, 133, 135, 142–44, 147,
149–50, 155, 160–63, 165–66, 168,
170, 181, 202, 205–8, 210–13, 215,
242, 246, 248, 252, 258, 277, 314–
17, 326–28
New England, 19, 37, 108, 115, 203,
210, 227, 248
New Hampshire, 14, 40–41, 45, 54, 65,
74, 125, 203, 205, 242–43, 252
New Old South Church, 50, 72, 74, 76
New Orleans, La., 12, 85
New York City, 12, 19, 21, 24, 27, 39,
63, 65, 75, 85, 87, 89, 95, 109, 111–
12, 117, 122, 154, 177–78, 314
New York Times, 63
Niles, Barbara, 156, 327
"Nipnet," 85–86, 117, 119, 328
Noble and Greenough's, 17, 148–49,
161
Nolton, Don, 219–20
Nord, Café du, 101, 107
North Haverhill, N. H., 73, 205, 236
North Woburn, Mass., 14, 17–18, 25,
37, 43, 46, 48, 91, 97, 118, 122, 126,
260, 310

Olmstead, Gladys, 72, 76, 184
Orr's Island, Me., 165, 167–68
Oxbow, The, 23, 26, 54, 56–57, 62,
65–66, 105, 130, 133, 140, 147, 191,
196, 198, 208, 210, 213, 222–25,
248, 261, 272, 313–14, 316–17, 320,
327
Oxford, 109, 269, 272

Packard, Vance, 59, 148
Packer, Joy, 58

Page, Dr., 12, 16, 20
Paris, 39, 63, 96–97, 100, 111–13, 270,
278, 293, 296–97, 302, 313, 321
Parker, Mr., 266–67, 309
Parker Scholarship, 19
Parkinson, Henry, 40
Patsy, Aunt, 12
Phillips Exeter, 25
Pillsbury, Albert E., 14, 25, 28–30, 35,
43, 46–47, 49, 70–71, 73, 75, 80–81,
87–91, 150, 225, 324
Pillsbury, Elizabeth Dinsmoor, 43–44,
46, 90
Pillsbury, Elizabeth Dinsmoor, II, 46–
47, 88
Pillsbury, Josiah, 43–44, 90
Pillsbury, Louise. See Author's mother
Pine Grove Farm, 31, 54, 59–61, 119,
133, 203–5, 207–8, 222, 224, 232,
243–44, 250, 262–63, 314–15, 317
Pompadour, Mme. de, 100–1, 301
Poteat, Rev. Gordon, 328
Prague, 293–94
Prentiss, Rev., 317
Preston, 12, 36, 48–49
Princeton, 16, 40

Quebec, 23, 66
Quezon, Manuel, 127

Radcliffe, 15, 171, 173
Rainsford, Christina, 263
Rainsford, Kerr, 173, 181, 187, 190
Raymond, Henry, 63
Reed, Katherine, 156, 168
Reed, Margaret, 155, 165, 168, 193–94
Revere, Paul, 45, 65
Rhallys, Dr. G., 270–71, 274–76, 282
Rich, Adrienne Cecile, 199
Richardson, Judge, 74
Riensberg, Mlle., 109, 111–12, 118,
123, 129, 147, 151
Robertson, Edith, 328
Robinson, Gertrude, 10
Rogers, Mrs. Guy. See Mary Kittredge
Rognvaldo, St., 269–70, 280
Rome, 19, 39, 101–4
Roosevelt, Franklin D., 109
Roosevelt, Mrs. Franklin D., 109, 206
Roosevelt, Mrs. Theodore, jr., 104, 134
Ross, Ishbel, 64
Rothschild, Alfred, 276, 282
Russell, Bär, 27, 29, 186, 277–80, 286

Russell, Bertha, 227, 233, 247–48, 315
Russell, Mrs., 27, 29, 186, 277–80

Sadie, 248, 250, 316
Sanderson, Mabel, 30, 202
Sanderson, Maude. See Maude Sanderson Bullard
Saratoga Springs, N. Y., 23, 63
Saxonia, 252, 263–64, 293
Schulzchen, 280, 289
Sears, Katharine, 148, 327
Sedgwick, Ellery, 104
Shreve, Carmelita, 72, 118, 150, 177, 235–36
Shreve, Wilhemina, 72, 118, 150, 177, 235–36
Sihler, Ernest G., 18
Slattery, Mrs. Charles Lewis, 327
Smith, Adon, 21–23
Smith, Mrs. Adon, 21–23, 314
Smith, Mrs. Cabell, 328
South Woodstock, Ct., 85, 117
Souvenir, 102, 110, 125
Spain, 97, 100, 233
Spring Hotel, 23–24, 29, 83
Stark, John, 40
Stephanie, Princess, 295–96
Stone, Edward, 218–19, 221–22
Stone, Harry, 221
Storey, C. Moorfield, 328
Storey, Mrs. C. Moorfield. See Susan Sweetser
Sturgis, Susan, 155, 187, 303
Sweetser, Elizabeth, 155–60, 163, 165, 178–79, 184, 187, 189–90, 192, 194–95, 208–9, 220, 227–28, 232, 235, 237, 246–48, 255–56, 284, 286–87, 303, 315–16, 318, 321, 325
Sweetser, Frank E., jr., 187–89, 209–10, 222, 227, 280, 284
Sweetser, Mrs. Frank, 159, 190, 209, 317
Sweetser, Homer, 159, 209
Sweetser, Jack, 159
Sweetser, Susan, 159, 328
Swift, Mrs. John B. See Nanny Winsor
Switzerland, 39, 98, 100–1, 105, 111, 273

Taggart, Charles Ross, 212
Taggart, Mrs. Charles Ross, 212
Tarleton, Lake, 208, 289, 321
Thorpe, Louise Hall, 84

Tudor, Delia, 228
Tudor, Elsa, 228
Tudor, Mary, 227–29, 233, 245, 247–48, 315
Tudor, William, 29, 229, 233

Underhill, James, I, 12, 21, 88
Underhill, James, 12, 15, 19, 25, 27–30, 50–54, 58, 81–82, 87–88, 90, 96, 98, 106, 108, 119–21, 125, 214–15, 224–25, 318
Underhill, Louise Johnson. See Author's mother
Underhill, Lucy Stoller, 214

Vail, Theodore, 30
Vail, Mrs. Theodore. See Mabel Sanderson
Vanderbilt, Gladys, 110
Vatican, 19, 103
Vendome, Hotel, 149–50, 160, 238
Vermont, 12, 24, 63, 65–66, 117, 124, 131–32, 141–42, 147, 153, 166, 206, 262, 267, 320, 324
Vienna, 289, 293–96
Violet, 91–92, 96, 101, 112
Virginia, 12, 20–21, 56, 75, 99, 324, 328
Virginia, University of, 11, 13, 15, 20, 24–25, 30, 48, 75, 137

Ward, May Williams, 93
Ware, Darwin E., 117
Ware, Mrs. Darwin E., 30, 88, 118, 181–82, 216, 225–26, 235–36, 238
Ware, Richard, 30, 117–19, 225–26, 236, 265, 312, 315
Warner, Mrs., 217–18, 220–21, 251, 256–57
Warren Academy, 17
Warren, Haskell, 101, 103, 107, 113
Warren, Mrs. Haskell, 101, 113
Washburn, Albert, 295
Washburn, Mrs. Albert, 295–96
Washington, D. C., 22, 57–58, 68, 77–78, 85, 89, 99, 124, 133, 135, 137–38, 155, 161, 242, 310
Washington, George, 65–67, 138
Washington, Mount, 82, 106
Wayside, The, 83–85, 328
Weeks, Allen, 218–21, 238, 251, 256
Wells, Frederick P., 60
Wells, Mrs. Harry. See Lucia Darling

Wheeler, Caroline, 14, 17, 119
Wheeler, Edward, 14, 17, 40
Wheeler, Elizabeth, 17
Wheeler, Frances Parkinson, 11, 13–14, 17, 25, 37–38, 40–45, 48, 51, 87, 89–90, 105, 118, 162, 169, 185–87, 217, 310
Wheeler, Gilbert Melancthon, 17, 37, 41, 45, 328
Wheeler, John Henry, 11–21, 24–26, 28, 30–31, 40, 43, 46, 87–88, 101–2, 107, 125, 137, 150, 166, 229, 250, 262, 280, 304, 324
Wheeler, Gen. Joseph, 136–37
Wheeler, Mrs. Joseph E., 328
Wheeler, Louise Underhill. See Author's mother

White House, 57, 77–78, 135–37, 206
White Mountains, 31, 81, 99
Whitmarch, Dr. and Mrs., 269
Wilder, Thornton, 147
Williams, Hilda, 155–56, 247, 327
Winsor, Mary, 148–49, 154, 174, 178, 187, 193, 197–98, 212, 227–28, 246–48, 311, 325
Winsor, Nanny, 155, 327
Winsor School, 147, 149–50, 155–56, 159–60, 165, 170, 174, 177–78, 186, 193–94, 212, 216, 227, 288, 327
Witzleben, Edel von, 280, 287
Witzleben, Frau von, 280–81, 287–88
Witzleben, Lotta von, 287, 289
Wyllie, John, 328